Sino-Soviet Diplomatic Relations, 1917-1926

Sino-Soviet Diplomatic Relations, 1917-1926

SOW-THENG LEONG

THE UNIVERSITY PRESS OF HAWAII
AND THE RESEARCH CORPORATION
OF THE UNIVERSITY OF HAWAII
Honolulu

Simultaneously published by Australian National University Press
Manufactured in the United States of America

Cover design by Russ Fujita

Library of Congress Cataloging in Publication Data

Leong, Sow-Theng.
  Sino-Soviet diplomatic relations, 1917-1926.

  Bibliography: p.
  Includes index.
  1. China—Foreign relations—Russia. 2. Russia—Foreign relations—China. I. Title.
DS740.5.R8L36   327.47'051   76-4960
ISBN 0-8248-0401-5

Contents

Maps

Preface

For more than a decade the open antagonism between the People's Republic of China and the Soviet Union has exerted a powerful impact on global politics, and seems certain to continue as an imponderable factor in the foreseeable future. A sound historical perspective is vital to the understanding of their current troubled relations, not least because the rift has an important historical component, a deep feeling of historical grievances held by the Chinese over past injustices. The present volume delves into one individual phase of the tortuous and relatively unstudied course of Sino-Soviet relations. It relates to the first decade or so after the October Revolution of 1917 in Russia, also the decade repeatedly referred to in recent Sino-Soviet polemics.

The selection of 1926 as the ending date should be explained. As with no other phase of Sino-Soviet diplomacy the historian is fortunate to be able to consult the complete official records of at least one side. The principal source materials used in this study are the papers of the Chinese Ministry of Foreign Affairs. The Nationalist Government took these papers to Taipei when it withdrew from the mainland and has, to date, opened them as far as 1926. The year may also be taken as the closing date of the first phase of Sino-Soviet diplomacy when Soviet Russia achieved all her diplomatic objectives in China.

Melbourne, 1974

S-T.L.

Acknowledgments

I should like to take this opportunity to thank many persons who have encouraged and assisted my work over the years. I am profoundly grateful to two teachers at Harvard University, Professors John K. Fairbank and Benjamin I. Schwartz, who guided my studies in modern Chinese history and supervised the doctoral dissertation from which the idea of the present book originated. I also owe special debts to Professors C. Martin Wilbur, Akira Iriye, and Andrew Nathan for their patient reading and incisive criticism of an earlier version of the manuscript.

In Japan, where part of the research was carried out, I benefited enormously from many kindnesses and advice of Professors Banno Masataka, Chō Kiyoko, Etō Shinkichi, Hosoya Chihiro, and Ichiko Chūzō. I wish to express my deep gratitude to them.

The writing of this book was accomplished mainly at the Department of Far Eastern History of the Australian National University where I was Research Fellow. I am most grateful to Professor Wang Gungwu and other colleagues for intellectual stimulation.

Many other friends and colleagues have been good enough to read parts or all of the manuscript. I appreciate especially the criticism and advice provided by Arthur Huck,

Con Kiriloff, Frederick Teiwes, and Colin Mackerras. Mr. Peter Daniell kindly provided the maps.

This book is dedicated to my wife Victoria and my daughter Tania.

Abbreviations

BGD	British Government Documents
CER	Chinese Eastern Railway
COKH	*Chung-O kuan-hsi shih-liao*
CP	*Ch'u-ping Hsi-pei-li-ya*
CTTL	*Chung-tung t'ieh-lu*
IPCS	*I-pan chiao-she*
OCP	*O cheng-pien yü i-pan chiao-she*
TCTY	*T'ing-chih O shih-ling tai-yü*
TPPF	*Tung-pei pien-fang*
WCST	*O tui-hua wai-chiao shih-t'an*
WMK	*Wai Meng-ku*
DVP	*Dokumenty vneshnei politiki SSSR*
FRUS	*Papers Relating to the Foreign Relations of the United States*
JMA	Japanese Military Archives
USDS	United States, Department of State, Decimal Files
WCP	Wai-chiao Pu (Chinese Foreign Ministry)
WCPA	Wai-chiao Pu Archives

Introduction

The first decade of the existence of Soviet Russia coincided with a major phase of the Chinese Revolution. In that massive political and social upheaval Soviet Russia played a role of signal importance. China of this period is alternately referred to as Warlord China because of the political dominance of semi-independent warlords all over the country, or as Young China because of the prominent role of China's youthful intelligentsia as national and social revolutionaries. Political and ideological cleavages resulted in the phenomenon that Soviet Russia meant very different things to different Chinese. The Chinese public by and large saw Russia as a state reborn, sincerely championing China's nationalist aspirations. To the Chinese Communist Party, brought into existence with Soviet assistance, Russia was the fountainhead of social revolution. To the Nationalist Kuomintang, Russia was an ally in the struggle against imperialism and a source of aid in its drive for power. Even some of the Chinese warlords either actually effected or intended a strategic alliance with Russia in the domestic contest for supremacy.

Soviet Russia's revolutionary role in China in this period has been as thoroughly investigated as the sources allow, as has the impact of Bolshevik organizational innovations on China's political and institutional change been frequently noted. But Soviet Russia played still another role, one which the Nationalists belatedly in late 1920s and the Communists only recently in an open way recognized, but which had been perfectly clear to the official government of China at the time. The official Chinese in Peking saw Russia without her ideological visage. To them, Russia was a foreign power returning to China after the temporary distraction of revolution and civil war to reassert Imperial Russia's position. Russia was aggressively reclaiming Imperial Russian interests and influence, practising not selfless diplomacy but hard-headed power politics. As such, she was to be resisted along with all other imperialist powers. For their peculiar image of Russia the official Chinese had concrete reasons: the detachment of Outer Mongolia from the Chinese Republic as a Soviet satellite and the reestablishment of Russian political and economic dominance in north Manchuria.

Russia's latter role, the policies and actions that went with it, and their interactions with those of the Chinese government constitute an area which has been particularly neglected by scholars hitherto.[1] The neglect has been due partly to the greater interest in the rise of the Chinese Communist Party and in the revolutionary events of 1925-7, and partly to the nonavailability of materials. As a result, much ignorance and misconception still prevail over the first and critically important phase of interstate relations.

Thus, much of the literature dealing with Far Eastern international relations stresses Soviet revolutionary diplomacy as distinct from the old diplomacy of imperialism. Soviet diplomacy is seen as devoid of self-interest, guided by the principle of revolutionary internationalism. However, the earliest decade of Bolshevik diplomacy witnessed successes in preserving Russian power in the postwar Far East. One influential study argues that Soviet diplomacy began with 'a new, revolutionary diplomacy of self-denial' but shifted within a year or two to 'a traditional, nationalistic diplomacy of self-interest'.[2] Closer scrutiny of the evidence, however, indicates that the Bolshevik statesmen were preoccupied from the outset with the problem of national security, and their policies and actions in a pragmatic, evolutionary way were responses to a concrete external threat in the Far East. Again, in discussing the interactions between the Soviet and Chinese governments, the existing literature underscores China's ineptness whereas, in fact, the Chinese carried out a very valiant attempt to roll back Russia's interests and rights in China. Indeed, underlying the Sino-Soviet diplomatic process was an intense, protracted contest between two official nationalisms. And, viewed in the broader context of Far Eastern international relations, the bipartite contest was, in reality, a tripartite one, with Japan occupying the central position in the policies of Russia and China towards each other.

During World War I, Japan emerged as the dominant power in the Far East, with ambitions in both Siberia and China. The October Revolution destroyed the prewar Russo-Japanese balance of power in northeast Asia when Japan embarked on the Siberian Intervention and, in addition to her already influential position in China, sought to inherit the Tsarist possessions in China. But in the 1920s, she was put on the defensive by a combination of external and internal pressures. This both facilitated the return of Russian power to the Pacific as well as sharpened the clash of nationalistic will between the Soviet and Chinese governments.

Soviet Russia, weakened by revolution and civil war, reacted to the Far Eastern situation in the early years with a two-pronged policy. On one hand, she sought to avoid a direct confrontation with Japan at all cost. This policy of appeasement with Japan was to become a permanent feature of Soviet Far Eastern policy up to World War II. Our preoccupation with the Great Revolution of 1924-7 in China, in which anti-British slogans loomed large because Britain was predominant in the parts of south and central China where the events took place, has obscured the centrality of Japan in Soviet policy. On the other hand, Soviet Russia sought to counter the Japanese threat indirectly through China. She did so by being conciliatory to the Chinese government at first and by appealing to Chinese nationalism, but more typically by acquiring a zone of defense in China's borderlands. This in effect meant the return of Russian power to north Manchuria and Outer Mongolia. When Soviet policy is linked to the regional context, it is possible to see how the continuity of the Far Eastern environment determined the apparent continuity between Soviet and Imperial Russian policies towards China. The official Soviet policy towards China therefore should be seen as an integral part of an overall policy towards the Far East.

It is well known that since the October Revolution the Bolshevik regime was, at one and the same time, the guardian of Soviet state interests and the promoter of world revolution. Accordingly its foreign policy was designed equally to preserve the Soviet state and to encourage revolution abroad. For world revolution, however, the Bolshevik leadership scanned primarily the European horizon. The October Revolution was viewed by its makers as no more than the spark that would set off the proletarian socialist revolution in Europe, for only that could rescue Russian socialism from the hostile forces surrounding it. The Far East clearly occupied second place in that concern. There the pursuit of national security took precedence from the outset. Russia's departure from the war and the October Revolution gave rise to the double dangers of foreign intervention and counterrevolution. The first weeks of the October Revolution saw the Bolsheviks desperately attempting to gain control of the Chinese Eastern Railway and the heavily Russian-populated railway zone. In the first few months, motivated by the desire to forestall the same dangers, they tried to implant their influence in Outer Mongolia where, as in north Manchuria, the authority of the officials of the old regime still prevailed.

This initial preoccupation with national security acquired a consistency of its own, evolving with increasing momentum in subsequent years. Revolution was not forgotten but because of the distance, size, and complexities of Chinese society, it was years before a proper analysis could be made, the prospects and direction of the revolution appraised, and organized activity set in motion. By the time the revolutionary front began full operation, the pursuit of security goals was already well in advance as the dominant trend of Soviet policy.

As this study is not concerned with the revolutionary front, it has not been felt necessary to delve into the knotty question of the relationship between Soviet ideology and national interests. Whiting has pointed out that the two fronts sometimes worked separately and at cross-purposes, sometimes remained distinct but parallel.[3] Where Russian interests and Communist interests proved incompatible, Russian interests became paramount.[4] The clearest case in point is the armed intervention in Outer Mongolia. Whereas the revolutionary strategy called for an alliance with Chinese nationalism, the pursuit of national interest ran the risk of alienating it. But, in the case of China, perhaps too much emphasis has been laid on the distinction between revolutionary and security goals as opposite, separate categories. The pursuit of revolution and the pursuit of national interest should perhaps be seen as mutually reinforcing policies, complementary means of defending the national interests.

While the relationship between ideology and national interests will always remain uncertain, the impact of ideology is evident in the peculiar style of Soviet diplomacy. Just as ideology transformed the goals of Soviet external policy into a mixture of the old and the new, the means employed combined the traditional with the most unconventional. Familiar means of the old diplomacy, such as intimidation, intrigue, and invasion, were used in the new spirit that in dealings with governments of a different class, any means, including conscious deceit, were warranted so long as the ends were secured. The Sino-Soviet Treaty of 1924 bears the hallmark of this diplomatic style: promises were made which were never meant to be fulfilled; and principles were agreed upon but were ignored in practice.

The other main interest of this narrative concerns the response of the Chinese government in Peking to the October Revolution and to the policies and actions of the new regime in Russia. Viewing the pattern of interactions through Peking's eyes brings to light much that is unknown and unexpected. Studying Peking's performance in detail affords a rare glimpse of the obscure workings of foreign policymaking in the context of warlordism. Such a study poses fundamental questions to several widely accepted assumptions about the incompetence of the Peking government in foreign relations, the puppet-like relationship of the government to the warlords, and the link between warlords and imperialists.

Warlord China, as the term implies, was a country of

widespread political fragmentation and endemic chaos. Throughout the period, presidents, cabinets, and parliaments changed and civil wars came and went in monotonous succession. The government in Peking claimed sole, if doubtful, legitimacy at home while functioning as the only official government abroad. The internal disunity vastly limited the power of the government, for the warlords were able to safeguard their own interests against the dictates of Peking. Still, it would be mistaken to suppose that each successive administration was little more than a puppet controlled from backstage by the particular faction or factions of militarists which happened to be ascendant at the time. For while all the warlord factions sought control of the official apparatus of government in order to give their power legitimacy, their influence on the government, indirect after 1918, varied more from cabinet to cabinet than most people realize. Just how the various administrations came to enjoy some very real powers remains to be explored, as do the tortuous workings of warlord politics.[5]

In the conduct of foreign relations, the situation is more easily understood. There was never any dispute on whether China should have a single government, only who should control it. The Peking government at this time owed its official status virtually to the recognition of the foreign powers. This provided the government with a degree of immunity in foreign relations from the interference of the warlords, for the latter understood full well that foreign recognition was predicated upon acceptable diplomatic relations. Consequently, the Wai-chiao Pu (Ministry of Foreign Affairs) was a far more viable policymaking organ, it had more power and independence and greater continuity than any other department of government. It was staffed at home and abroad by personnel specially selected for their expertise. By virtue of their training and the nature of their work, the foreign affairs experts were nationalistically motivated men, dedicated to the advancement of China's international standing.

Thus, in regard to Russia, the Wai-chiao Pu was quick to capitalize on Russia's initial weakness by embarking on a program of recovering sovereign rights. It did so in an atmosphere of acute suspense: China had to beat Japan to the Tsarist rights and interests and succeed before Russia had recovered sufficiently to reclaim them. This effort of rights recovery has gone unnoticed just as the substantial achievements have been ignored.

Because of the foreign omnipresence, it is easily assumed that Peking was denied independence in dealings with Russia. The notion that the Wai-chiao Pu resorted to dilatory tactics in deference to foreign pressure was first actively fostered by Soviet envoys and subsequently crept into the writings of Western analysts. However, the evidence points clearly to the contrary. Instead of a sell-out, the Wai-chiao Pu's decisions were of a pragmatic nature. Thus, it was a positive policy to join the war against the Central Powers so that China might profit from the postwar negotiations on the basis of whatever goodwill she could get from the Powers as an ally. From this policy logically flowed China's participation in the Siberian Intervention. Despite disappointment, Peking continued to act in concert with the former Allies with regard to Russia in order to use their countervailing influence against Japan. By the time this necessity ceased to exist, Peking was already confronted with a resurgent Russia, rigidly insisting upon the reinstatement of Imperial Russia's rights and interests. There followed a protracted diplomatic duel between one determined to reestablish its power in China's borderlands and the other nationalistically opposed to it. This narrative traces how China, in the brief interval between the fall and rise of Soviet power, maximized her gains; and how, with the return of stability to Russia, the situation was restabilized with a few of China's gains made permanent but no exclusion of Russian power from the northern borderlands.

Sino-Soviet
Diplomatic Relations,
1917-1926

1

North Manchuria
on the Eve of the Russian Revolution

Relations between China and Russia for a quarter of a century up to the Russian Revolution of 1917 were inextricably linked to Japan. In this triangle China was the prostrate victim of her neighbors' territorial aggrandizement. Manchuria, a land rich in natural resources, was the most logical place for the imperial expansion of Russia and Japan to meet. Here they collided explosively but subsequently achieved a balance by dividing Manchuria into two mutually exclusive spheres. These were later extended into Inner and Outer Mongolia.

Between Russia and Japan, the balance of power generally favored Japan. Russia's century-long rivalry with Britain, in Europe and Asia, made possible the Anglo-Japanese Alliance of 1902, which was not dissolved until the Washington Conference of 1922. The Alliance emboldened Japan to a test of strength with Russia in the war of 1904–5, in which Russia's military inferiority was exposed. But Russia's vulnerability was due less to the alliance of her two powerful traditional enemies than to long-term internal factors. She had expanded more rapidly than her internal resources warranted, with the result that the growth of her territory had outstripped the means available for its administration and defense. Japan's rapid industrialization and the consequent rise of her military power accentuated the unhappy contrast.

China's weakness, Japan's superior strength, and Russia's over-expansion and perennial preoccupation with defense—these constituted the essential ingredients of the international relations of northeast Asia before and after the Russian Revolution in 1917.

The triangular relationship to 1917 went through three phases. After successfully acquiring the Amur and Maritime Provinces from the Manchu empire in the middle of the nineteenth century, Russia suffered from difficulties of food supply and transportation and sparseness of population. For several decades after the 1860s, her policy in this region was passive, but in the 1890s she resumed vigorous expansion by constructing the Trans-Siberian Railway. This expansion eastwards ran head-on with the opposite drive of Japan.

The first phase began in 1895 with Russia's attempt to dispossess Japan of some of her gains in the war with China of 1894-5. Regarding Manchuria and Korea as her primary defense zone in the Far East, Russia brought German and French pressure to bear on Japan to restore the Liaotung Peninsula leasehold to China. She got French and Russian banks to lend 100,000,000 gold roubles (about US $76,890,000) at a low interest rate to help China pay off the Japanese. And for her services she demanded and received handsome rewards. She offered a secret treaty of alliance against Japan, which China accepted, and obtained a concession to route the Trans-Siberian Railway 1,520 km across north Manchuria to Vladivostok.

In 1898, during the scramble for concessions by the European powers in China, Russia took for herself what she had forced Japan to give up—the Liaotung leasehold. She also extorted the right to build a north-south railway linking the ice-free port of Dairen and the Port Arthur naval base at the tip of the peninsula to the east-west line. Thus originated the Chinese Eastern Railway, a T-shaped instrument which threatened to draw all of Manchuria unto itself and to Russia.

Japan's patience wore even thinner when Russia declined to recognize her paramount interest in Korea in exchange for her recognition of Russia's paramount interest in Manchuria. Then, in 1900, Russia introduced regular troops into Manchuria, purportedly in order to protect her railway against the Boxers, and subsequently refused to withdraw them.

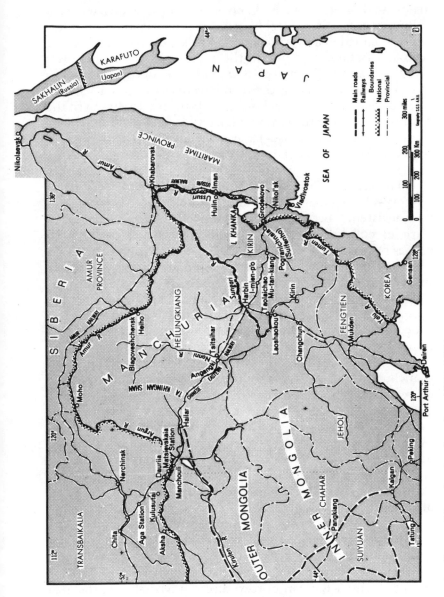

1 Russo–Manchurian border, 1917–1924

In 1904, bolstered by her alliance with Britain, Japan struck with a vengeance. Each side fielded a quarter of a million men and there were enormous casualties on both sides. The war ended in a pyrrhic victory for Japan and was to carve deep and lasting imprints on the minds of the two peoples. The Portsmouth Treaty of 1905 closed the decade of intense rivalry. Included among the terms were cession by Russia to Japan of the Liaotung leasehold and 800 of the 1,040 km of the southern branch of the Chinese Eastern Railway. China, helpless spectator of the Russo–Japanese collision on her territory, acquiesced in the settlement by a treaty with Japan in the same year.[1]

The second phase lasted until 1915, the year of Japan's Twenty-One Demands on China, and was a decade of peaceful coexistence between Russia and Japan, reinforced by a spirit of collaboration. Collaboration was desired by both parties because each would have been in a position to consolidate and further develop its sizable interests in its respective sphere without fear of the other or outside parties. The Sino–Japanese agreement, whereby China acknowledged the Portsmouth Treaty, already provided the ground for fruitful cooperation. Whereas the Russian-owned Chinese Eastern Railway was governed by a specific contract, the southern section belonging to Japan, which came to be called the South Manchurian Railway, was to be operated in conformity with the original Sino–Russian contract so far as circumstances permitted. Moreover, Japan would withdraw her troops, renamed railway guards, if Russia agreed to do likewise, or 'when China shall have become herself capable of affording full protection to the lives and property of foreigners'. Russo–Japanese interests were thus mutually reinforcing, and each party could ignore the Chinese completely, secure in the belief of support from the other.

The new spirit of cooperation manifested itself during the decade in a series of conventions between Russia and Japan, defining their mutual interests and pledging mutual respect and defense. The 1907 Convention drew a horizontal line from the Russo–Korean border through Manchuria: the area north, comprising north Manchuria, was to be Russia's sphere of special interests, and the area south, comprising Korea and south Manchuria, was to be Japan's. The spheres were mutually exclusive. Each was free to carry on economic activity within its own sphere, but political activity was also envisaged even though the convention acknowledged China's independence and territorial integrity.

The 1910 Convention concerned only Manchuria, and the two powers served public notice to third parties that they would together sustain and defend their spheres of exclusive interests by whatever means necessary. Each recognized the other's right freely to take all measures to defend and further develop those interests; each might indulge in political activity, and the earlier reference to China's independence and territorial integrity was dropped. The Convention of 1912 prolonged the demarcation line through Mongolia, so that the eastern portion of Inner Mongolia fell within Japan's sphere, and Outer Mongolia as well as the rest of Inner Mongolia fell into Russia's.[2]

Aside from Mongolia, it was to be expected that Russia's activity in north Manchuria would be bound not by her treaties with China, but by the three conventions with Japan. The second phase therefore witnessed Russia's energetic, almost frantic, effort at strengthening her grip on north Manchuria to offset losses in the south and improve her position vis-à-vis Japan. This was the period of Russia's colonization of north Manchuria. Besides a wide range of economic activity, the Chinese Eastern Railway Company undertook the civil administration of the railway territory, the formation of a Russian police force to maintain law and order, the development of a system of courts of justice, and the maintenance of an occupation army disguised as railway guards.

The outbreak of World War I closed the second phase of Russo-Japanese relations, and inaugurated the third, marked in 1915 by Japan's far-reaching demands on China, known as the Twenty-One Demands, which envisaged China's subordination to Japan's will. Russia's preoccupation with the war in the west drained her strength and vastly weakened her position in north Manchuria. As the other Western powers were also distracted, Japan was free to pursue her course of continental expansion. She expressed her freedom of action in the Twenty-One Demands on China. The leases of Dairen

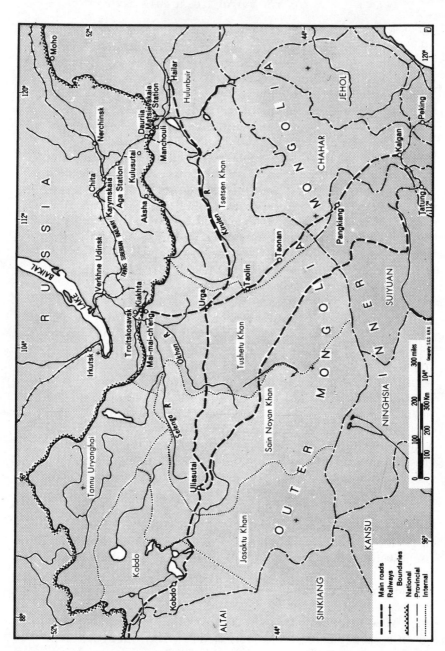

2 Russo–Mongolian border, 1917–1924

and Port Arthur were extended to ninety-nine years, and China's right to redeem the South Manchurian Railway after the period specified in the Sino-Russian contract was cancelled. In addition, Japanese subjects gained the right to lease land for industrial or agricultural activity in Manchuria, to live freely among the Chinese wherever they chose, and to exploit specified mining areas. Russia was naturally most envious of such Japanese gains. Through her representative in Peking, she demanded comparable concessions but was in no position to exert the same kind of pressure as Japan.[3]

Russia's vulnerability in north Manchuria rebounded to Japan's advantage, but Japan acted with restraint. She was alive to the danger of contributing to a separate peace between Russia and Germany, with the possible consequences of the defeat of her British ally and of a victorious and vengeful Germany returning to the east in league with Russia against herself. In July, 1916, she signed a fourth convention with Russia. Among the provisions was a definite defensive alliance against 'any third power' hostile to both countries and seeking political domination over China. The convention removed Russia's fear of a German–Japanese rapprochement and, more immediately, satisfied her need for munitions from Japan. For Japan, it forestalled a Russo–German rapprochement and helped preclude a challenge from any third power, such as the United States, to her dominant position in China. Moreover, as payment for an immediate supply of munitions, she was to receive a section of the southern branch of the Chinese Eastern Railway. However, the October Revolution erupted before the transfer could take place.[4]

The Bolshevik seizure of power on November 7, 1917, and the events that immediately followed, had a fundamental impact on Russo–Japanese relations. Aversion to Bolshevik extremism and the Bolshevik policies of separate peace with Germany and dishonoring of Imperial Russia's international obligations, produced in Japan a hostility so profound as to spell disaster for Russia's northern Manchurian possessions and eastern Siberia as well.

But Japan was not the only claimant to Imperial Russia's legacy in north Manchuria. China, too, in an effort that surprised everyone, bestirred herself to the opportunity presented by the recession of Russian power of reasserting her sovereign rights.

By 1917, after two decades of feverish exertions, Russia had succeeded in turning the Chinese Eastern Railway and the territory contiguous to it into a colonial domain, much as Japan had done in south Manchuria and Germany in Shantung.[5]

The precise legal status of the Chinese Eastern Railway was hotly disputed between the Chinese and the Russians after the Bolshevik Revolution. The Chinese insisted it was a joint enterprise, to be jointly owned and controlled by China and Russia, whereas the Russians maintained it was a Russian state property and insisted on operating it like one. In fact, it was neither. The Treaty of Alliance between China and Russia, signed on June 3, 1896, in which China gave the railway concession, specified that the construction and exploitation of the railway was to be accorded to the Russo-Chinese Bank. The Russo-Chinese Bank, formed in December 1895 by Russian and French banks and subsequently renamed Russo-Asiatic Bank, was designed by Russia as an agency to promote commercial, industrial, and railway projects in China. A contract was signed between the Chinese government and the bank. The bank in turn transmitted the concession to the Chinese Eastern Railway Company, chartered by the Russian government on December 16, 1896, so that the management of the railway bore the character of a private commercial enterprise.[6]

In practice, however, this was a fiction which disguised the fact that the Russian government was the *de facto* possessor and controller of the railway. The company's initial capital of 5,000,000 roubles was supplied to the Russo-Chinese Bank by the Russian treasury. The remaining resources were raised by the issue of bonds which were subscribed by the Russian government. By 1917 the Russian treasury was in possession of bonds worth between 350,000,000 (about $269,115,000) and 425,000,000 roubles (about $326,783,000). It had also loaned the company enormous sums to meet its deficits. The Russian government coupled ownership with tight control. The railway operated under the ultimate authority of the finance minister, through the intermediary of the Russo-Chinese Bank, its sole shareholder. The finance minister confirmed the election of the chairman of the board of directors, the selection of the chief engineer of construction, the general manager, and other executive officers.

China's interest in the enterprise was from the beginning quite small and kept so by the Russian government. According to the contract, the Chinese government was to contribute 5,000,000 taels (about $3,000,000) to the Russo-Chinese Bank and participate in its profits and losses. The company, in return for the concession, was to pay the Chinese government a similar amount from the date of business operations. No money ever changed hands, so that China's share amounted to no more than 5,000,000 taels, which was about 1 per cent of the total outlay of the Russian state treasury.[7] China's sovereign interests could have been safeguarded only by the right to appoint the president of the company. This official's duty was vaguely defined as seeing to the scrupulous fulfilment by the bank and the company of their obligations to the Chinese government, without any say as to the company's internal management. Worse still, after the first president (Hsü Ching-ch'eng) was executed in 1900 for his anti-Boxer memorials, Russia, at first alone and later with Japan's help, was able to block any other appointment for the next seventeen years.

According to the contract, China had the right to redeem the railway at cost after thirty-six years from the date the railway opened (i.e. July 1, 1903), and take possession free of charge after eighty years. But the capital outlay of the enterprise, which was designed as much for political as for economic purposes, was so enormous that financial considerations alone would have made it extremely difficult for China to exercise her right in the shorter term.

The railway contract also entitled the company to acquire Chinese government land free of charge and private land by lease or purchase. By 1907 the company had expropriated a total of 1300 km² for the railway. The size of the expropriations varied from 1 km² to as many as 20 km² at each point on the railway lines, depending on its economic and strategic significance. Some of them eventually developed into sizable communities, and together they constituted what was called the Chinese Eastern Railway Zone. In 1917 there were as many as 200,000 Russian residents in the area, soon to be joined by large numbers of refugees of revolution and civil war in Russia.[8]

Motivated by defense needs, the Russians were naturally not disposed to be bound by their undertaking not to infringe China's sovereign rights. The railway simply became an instrument of Russian colonization. By 1900 Russian regular troops were occupying the area, and the railway company was beginning to think in terms of instruments of Russian law enforcement and civil administration.

The Russian troops, called railway guards, formed the backbone of Russian power in Manchuria. The right of guarding the railway was usurped, because the contract clearly specified that the right and responsibility of assuring the safety of the railway and of the persons in its service belonged to the Chinese government. The railway guards began in 1897 as a body of several thousand civilians under the command of a military officer, but in 1900 they were transformed into regular army units, which Russia had sent ostensibly to protect the railway against the Boxers. To anticipate Chinese protests, they were renamed the trans-Amur district guard, as part of the All-Russian system of frontier guards, distinct from the Russian army. The strength of the guard was fixed at 25,000 men, but when the war with Japan broke out in 1904 the number increased ten times in order to match the Japanese army in Manchuria. The Treaty of Portsmouth fixed the numerical strength of the railway guards at 15 men per kilometer, and the trans-Amur district guard decreased accordingly to about 21,000 (comparable to the Japanese Kwantung army of 16,600), and remained at that figure until the outbreak of World War I. These railway guards were paid for by the railway company, and their commander was immediately subordinate to the chief officer of the Chinese Eastern Railway Administration.[9]

As large numbers of Russians and Chinese congregated in communities in the railway zone, the company was faced with the pressing problem of maintaining law and order. Before the railway was opened for traffic in 1903, the railway guards had carried on the additional duty of a police force, but thereafter a system of police, drawn from the guards, was organized and directed by the department of police within the C.E.R. Administration. Up to 1917, the police force consisted of military men.[10]

Another important aspect of law enforcement obviously was the administration of justice. There was nothing in the railway contract specifically on litigations, beyond the broad principle that 'criminal cases, lawsuits, etc., upon the territory of the railway must be settled by the local authorities in accordance with the stipulations of the treaties'. This simply meant that Russians were entitled to extraterritoriality and came under consular jurisdiction. However, no Russian consulates existed in the railway zone until China opened Harbin and other centers in 1907 as places of international residence and trade; and the Russians themselves, jealous of their preserve, preferred Manchuria to remain closed.

Initially, justice for Russians was entrusted by the Russian government to the chief engineer in charge of railway construction, who in turn delegated the authority to the commander of the railway guards. After 1901, when this was no longer practical, Russians living west of Harbin came under the jurisdiction of the Chita court, those east of Harbin under that of the Vladivostok court, and those along the southern branch subject to the Port Arthur court within the Liaotung leasehold. But from the outset, the courts in Chita and Vladivostok quietly dispatched special officials to deal with litigations on the spot. After the Russo-Japanese War, the pretense was dropped when the Port Arthur court was moved to Harbin and renamed frontier court, and it assumed jurisdiction over the entire Russian population in the railway zone. In time, a complete system of courts was organized, which, notwithstanding China's protests, lasted until 1920.

For mixed cases involving Russians and Chinese, the C.E.R. Administration used a system of joint tribunals, although the law applied was that of the defendant's nationality. Between 1899 and 1902, evidently quite oblivious to Chinese sovereign rights, the Chinese local governments of the three Manchurian provinces entered into agreements with the Russian chief engineer for each province to set up an office in Harbin, called bureau of railway foreign affairs (T'ieh-lu chiao-she chü), with branches elsewhere to handle jurisdiction over Chinese nationals in the railway zone. The effect of these agreements was that a member of the Chinese bureau and a representative of the C.E.R. Administration jointly examined and investigated cases involving Chinese nationals, whether or not in the railway's service. This procedure was extended to purely Chinese cases as well.[11]

While all Chinese nationals in the railway zone found themselves subject to the railway's jurisdiction, the Russian residents who were unconnected with the railway successfully resisted it. Before the opening of consulates, the Russian foreign ministry simply designated a special officer to examine such cases jointly with the Chinese intendant. Thus, two alternative procedures for Sino-Russian cases were applied, depending on whether the Russians involved were connected with the railway or not.[12]

The organization of the railway communities into municipalities under the direction of the C.E.R. Administration took place largely after the Russo-Japanese War and the 1905 Revolution in Russia. Responding to the clamor of the local Russian residents, the Russian government decided in 1906 to introduce a system of local self-government, modelled on the self-governing bodies (*zemstva*), which were much in vogue in Russia at the time. Wherever feasible in the railway zone, there was to be set up a municipal government, comprising an assembly and an executive council, with the power to levy taxes and the responsibility for various public services, including public works, sanitation, and education. Election to the assembly was open to all nationalities but restricted by property qualifications. The municipal council was to consist of five persons, three from the assembly, one from the consular corps, and one appointed by the C.E.R. Administration. The decisions of both the assembly and the council were subject to the approval of the department of civil administration within the C.E.R. Administration. Harbin took the lead in 1907, and was soon emulated by other communities, amidst China's strenuous protests and foreign disapproval.[13]

Protracted altercations resulted in a Sino-Russian preliminary agreement in 1909, in which Russia reaffirmed her recognition of China's territorial sovereignty over the railway zone. It was agreed that China should share supervision of the municipalities with the C.E.R. Administration, with the details to be worked out later.[14] Distracted by domestic problems, the Chinese soon lapsed back in to their passivity, and the situation of municipal government reverted to what it had been before. The foreign powers resisted the arrangement much longer, but in 1914–17 all except the United States finally accepted the state of things by entering into appropriate agreements with Russia.[15]

Thus, by 1917, the Chinese Eastern Railway had become the very significant economic and political nucleus of a rapidly developing colonial domain of Russia. This dramatic advance of Russian interests was largely the handiwork of the Tsarist local representative, General Dmitri L. Horvath (Khorvat), who headed the C.E.R. Administration without interruption from 1902. The best measures of General Horvath's talents are the multiple roles he played: chief executive officer of the Chinese Eastern Railway and the Ussuri Railway (which also came under the C.E.R. Administration), commander of the Russian forces, civil administrator of the railway zone, and diplomat protecting the Russian colony from the Chinese and the Japanese.

An aristocrat by birth and military engineer by training, Horvath brought to his post unusual administrative ability and incomparable experience in railway matters, having served earlier on the Trans-Caspian and the Ussuri. He enjoyed a status equal to that of governor-general of the Russian Far East; he ruled the railway zone like an autocrat, respected and feared but never challenged.[16]

But the elaborate structure of Russian interests in Manchuria which he had helped to build began to shake and crumble under the combined impact of the war and the revolution. First to go was the main prop, the trans-Amur district guard, which was mobilized for the German front in 1915. In its place was organized a body of 8,000 men of the older reservist classes. This drastic reduction of Russian forces by two-thirds could not fail to have a strong impact on the colonial order in the railway zone. The revolutionary upheaval which followed shook the foundations of Horvath's regime, and exposed Russia's possessions to the eager gaze of the Japanese and the Chinese.

2

The Harbin Soviet

Harbin in 1917 was a bustling international city. It was the junction of the three sections of the Chinese Eastern Railway, and the seat of the C.E.R. Administration. It had a total population of 90,000, half being Chinese, a third Russian, and the rest Japanese and other nationalities. Harbin was the most populous of the railway communities and a rapidly growing industrial centre.

The Russian population in Harbin divided neatly into three strata. At the top was a handful of high-salaried railway, government, and military officials, aristocratic by birth and monarchist in outlook. In the middle were the railway staff, merchants, and professional people, and at the bottom the masses of railway workmen, guards, and laborers of various industrial enterprises.

News of Tsar Nicholas II's abdication and the rise of the Provisional Government was generally well received by the middle and lower classes of Manchurian Russians. Indeed, the middle class immediately organized a body called the Executive Committee as a counterpart to the Provisional Government in Petrograd. The railway staff organized themselves into the Union of Railway Employees, and the lower classes the Soviet of Workers' Deputies and Soviet of Soldiers' Deputies. As the colonial domain in north Manchuria was an extension of the Russian empire, a strategic corridor to eastern Siberia, the revolutionary upheaval in Russia had its inevitable reverberations here.

The pattern of Russian political struggles in the railway zone from March to November went through three phases. At first, the Executive Committee, supported by the Soviets (in which the preponderant moderate socialists were disposed, as in Russia, to cooperate with the bourgeoisie), sought to reverse the existing power structure, by superimposing its authority over the C.E.R. Administration. Shortly thereafter, in a turnabout, it trimmed its pretensions, and limited itself to demanding a share of Horvath's power. It also pressed for reforms to eliminate some of the oppressive features of Horvath's regime, including the secret police, arbitrary arrests, and deportation. It wanted to remove the head of the department of civil administration, the chief of police, and several leading railway administrators, and to appoint others in their places. A situation of 'dual power' arose, in which the Executive Committee and the C.E.R. Administration separately wielded power in the railway zone. The third phase began considerably later in June when the two soviets fused as the Soviet of Workers' and Soldiers' Deputies. Following Lenin's April slogan, 'all power to the Soviet', the Bolsheviks tried to capture control of the Harbin Soviet and to gain power in the railway zone. In the end, they were isolated and driven out by the combined forces of the moderate socialists, the Executive Committee, and the C.E.R. Administration, with the help of Chinese troops.[1]

The restraining hand on the Executive Committee during the second phase was the minister for finance of the Provisional Government. He enjoined the Executive Committee against attempting to apply the political changes in Russia to the railway zone *in toto*. The administrative authority there, he said, should be based on the rights which China had given the C.E.R. Administration, and those rights carried obligations to China and other powers as well. He had accordingly instructed the C.E.R. Administration to carry on with local administration in accordance with the existing treaties, and he expressed the hope that the Executive Committee would help preserve peace and order while the C.E.R. Administration undertook various reforms. He warned that disturbances of the peace and interference with the railway administration might give rise to international complications, which would adversely affect the interests of Mother Russia as well as the railway enterprise itself.[2]

The Russians in Manchuria were of course fully aware of the peculiar international status of the C.E.R. Zone and they readily saw the good sense of the minister's injunction. Whatever interests Russia possessed were derived from the agreements with China and, as in the case of municipal affairs, with other foreign powers as well. The enjoyment of these rights carried certain obligations which Horvath had heretofore discharged to the satisfaction of all Russians concerned. To the Manchurian Russians Horvath stood for Russian interests that had been acquired over decades at the cost of lives and great fortunes. Except perhaps for the most radical, they could rally to the political symbolism of national interests. Without exception, all of them shared a lively distrust and animosity towards the Japanese, as did Russians in the entire Russian Far East. Given Russia's momentary weakness, adherence to existing treaties seemed to be the only means of avoiding provocation of Japanese encroachments. These were the reasons why the majority rallied behind Horvath as the savior of Russian national interests. When the Bolshevik chairman of the Soviet, Ensign M. Riutin, moved on July 19 to discontinue recognition of the Executive Committee and remove Horvath, his proposal was overwhelmingly voted down.[3]

On the other hand, the Manchurian Russians were not prepared to allow Horvath's regime to continue unreformed. For the first time since 1902, Horvath's vast local powers were challenged. First to erode was his authority over the railway guards, where discipline broke down as class struggle cleaved a chasm between officers and rank and file. The railway troops in Harbin at the time consisted of three infantry units of 2,800 men (558th, 559th, and 618th Militia), plus other smaller technical units. Bolshevik influence was especially strong in the 559th and 618th Militia, where the Bolsheviks had at least 600 active supporters and many more sympathizers.[4]

Another development, one that caused deep concern to the diplomatic community, was the breakdown of the police system with the consequent increase of crime and lawlessness. Policemen ignored their officers, while the Executive Committee and the department of civil administration of the C.E.R. Administration competed for authority over the police. With the Bolshevik coup in Petrograd, the situation in Harbin deteriorated still further.[5]

Details of the events in north Manchuria following the Bolshevik seizure of power in Petrograd are already available elsewhere, and need only be summarized here.[6] On November 7, emulating their comrades at home, the Bolshevik faction in the Harbin Soviet called an emergency meeting and tabled a motion to oust Horvath. As before, it failed to secure the necessary majority. The alternative resolution which was passed called for power to be given to the popular majority and concerted opposition against counterrevolution, lest the monopoly of power by one segment cause international complications for Russia and adversely affect the interests of Russian residents of the C.E.R. Zone. It was resolved to form a provisional revolutionary committee to maintain law and order, and to provide a proper police force. The committee was to be constituted by representatives of various organizations which were clamoring for a voice in the administration of the railway zone and it was to co-opt two members to the C.E.R. Administration to watch its operations in the public interest. The Executive Committee recognized the Soviet resolution on November 8 and sent two members to the provisional revolutionary committee. The moderates in the Soviet had prevailed once again over the radicals, continuing their cooperation with the bourgeois Executive Committee.

For Horvath, however, the revolution had 'deepened' considerably. His administration was now subject to the provisional revolutionary committee's supervision, and he and several close collaborators were in danger of arrest by the Bolshevik faction. But Horvath was a man of considerable political skill, and he knew he could depend on the threat of foreign intervention as his trump card. His hand was greatly strengthened on being told on November 10 by the British and the American consuls that they recognized him as the head of the local administration, the protector of their nationals' interests, and that his removal would result in foreign intervention.[7] The local Bolsheviks were caught in a dilemma. In the words of one Soviet historian, 'They had no clear idea as to what tactic to follow in view of the special conditions of the C.E.R. zone which lay in foreign territory'.[8] They deferred further action and waited for instructions from the Council of People's Commissars in Petrograd.

The consular corps in Harbin meanwhile had grown greatly concerned over the dramatic increase in crime due to the absence of police authority. On November 21, the corps met to consider measures to be taken. The British consul suggested forming a committee, with Horvath included, which would discuss improvement of the Russian police and direct its activities. The French consul did not think it possible to improve the Russian police and recommended a dispatch of Chinese and Japanese troops to Harbin instead. Consul Satō, who had been urging his government to dispatch troops, went along with the French idea, but he observed it would be easier to entrust the whole matter to Japanese police alone. In the end, the meeting returned to the British proposal as worthy of a try. Horvath was given two weeks to show improvement of the Russian police, failing which the consuls would propose to their respective home governments the dispatch of an international police force. The decision was communicated to Horvath and widely publicized.[9]

At a joint meeting of the Executive Committee, the Soviet, and various other groups, Horvath warned they were sitting on top of a volcano, pleaded that multiple voice over police matters should cease, and asked that he be given sole command. The Soviet delegation refused. Eventually, a compromise was reached whereby the railway's department of civil administration would exercise police authority under the supervision of the C.E.R. Administration, the Executive Committee, and the Soviet. The compromise soon proved unworkable because of conflicting interpretations: to the Soviet, unified police authority did not mean that they should cease their revolutionary activity; to Horvath it meant just that.[10]

The long-awaited order of the Council of People's

Commissars finally reached the Harbin Bolsheviks on December 4. It instructed them to 'take power in the name of the
proletariat and the government'. Here is a perfect example of
the dualistic foreign policy of the Soviet government that
came into being from the first moment of the victory of the
revolution. The Bolshevik leadership was concerned equally
to spread revolution abroad and to secure the defense of the
new Soviet state. The taking of power in the railway zone was
both ideologically sound and politically imperative. With a
population, of 200,000 Russians, predominantly anti-
Bolshevik, the Chinese Eastern Railway area adjoined the least
defensible part of the Soviet state. It could conceivably become a hotbed of counterrevolution and launching pad for
foreign, especially Japanese, intervention. The first impulse of
the Bolshevik leaders,·therefore, was to gain control of the
railway and its territory.

The directive from the Council of People's Commissars
caused a panic in Harbin as rumors of an imminent Bolshevik
uprising circulated. On the same night, the consular corps
unanimously resolved not to recognize the authority of the
Soviet. They cabled their respective governments for troops.
Horvath also took the precaution of inviting 500 Chinese
soldiers into the city. The next day, well aware that only
Horvath could prevent foreign intervention, the Bolshevik
leader Riutin offered Horvath a bargain: the Bolsheviks would
desist from causing any disturbance if Horvath would accept
Soviet supervision. Horvath consented, confident that he
would be able to bring the radicals under control with the help
of moderate Russians and the foreign powers. As he had
expected, the consular corps notified him on the same day that
it absolutely would not recognize Bolshevik authority which,
it maintained, represented no recognized government; nor
would it accept Soviet supervision over his administration.[11]

In Peking, on the same day, the Harbin crisis brought the
Allied ministers together to consider suitable measures that
would transcend their conflicting national interests. An international patrol constituted by Americans or anybody else was
unacceptable to Japan, which wanted no other foreign influence in Manchuria. The only alternative was to ask China to
send troops. This was proposed by the Russian minister,

Prince Kudashev, who now found it advantageous and necessary to insist that China was the sovereign power of the territory concerned and therefore responsible for law and order there. His argument, of course, camouflaged an ulterior motive: Chinese were preferable to Japanese because anything taken away by China could more easily be recovered later. There was unanimity on the Russian minister's proposal, and it was formally communicated to the Chinese government.[12]

On December 8, the Bolshevik leaders decided to cable the Council of People's Commissars in Petrograd for advice:

Telegram regarding transfer of power received by the Soviet. Its execution has met with great obstacles despite our having the majority in the Soviet. The consuls declare they do not recognize Soviet authority, the removal of Horvath as commissar of the old government will result in the introduction of foreign troops. Our attempt to make Horvath our commissar also rejected by them. . . . The railway administration has organized its own militia, which undoubtedly will be sent against the Soviet. Mensheviks, Socialist Revolutionaries, and the Union of Railway Employees have organized a Committee of Public Organizations for struggle against the Soviet. We intend to disperse the municipal council. The struggle is coming, which may end in a bloody clash. What should we do with Horvath and about seizing power? We dare not take decisive action without your advice. The international situation is better known to you. We await your immediate reply.[13]

As the days passed, the Soviet leaders grew desperate. Finally, on December 12, one day before a reply was received, they decided there was no alternative but to take the plunge. The much rumored Sino–Japanese intervention would have to be faced. Should it materialize, they would simply make a hasty exit and leave the rest to the central government. Accordingly, on that day, the Soviet organ *Golos Truda* announced that the Soviet had assumed power over the C.E.R. Administration, the Executive Committee, and the municipal governments.

The Petrograd telegram, when it arrived, only repeated the directive contained in the December 4 telegram. It ordered the Soviet to replace Horvath and all uncooperative Russian officials in north Manchuria. The Soviet was now ready to use force to achieve its ends, but waiting in the wings were the Chinese, equally ready to intervene.[14]

The local Chinese officialdom in Manchuria consisted of the three provincial governments of Fengtien, Kirin, and Heilungkiang. By 1917 Chang Tso-lin, the military governor of Fengtien, had come a long way towards achieving supremacy over the three provinces and he was beginning to assert an influence on national politics. The possession of a base with incomparable resources and strategic defensibility combined with a superior degree of opportunism to make him one of the most successful militarists in the warlord era.

With his base of support well within Japan's sphere of interests, Chang's connections with the Japanese were inevitably long and close, but it would be rash to conclude that he was a Japanese puppet. Chang's relationship with Japan, according to one Japanese biographer, was never an easy one. On the one hand, he was inescapably dependent on Japan by virtue of her influence in south Manchuria but, on the other, he was not insensitive to being cast as a traitor by a nationalistic public.[15] His position was remarkably similar to that of another alleged Japanese puppet, Tuan Ch'i-jui, leader of the Anhui (later, Anfu) clique. Like Tuan, one may assume that he carefully weighed each push from Japan in terms of the determination of the Japanese policymakers and his own political prosperity before making an appropriate response. Unlike Tuan, Chang was able, in the interest of self-preservation, to keep as many options open as possible, and an effective means was to invite mutually competing foreign influences into Manchuria to forestall monopoly by anyone.

Born of poor peasant background in Hai-ch'eng, Fengtien, in 1876, the illiterate Chang enlisted in the imperial cavalry for two years before taking to the hills as a bandit leader for the next seven. Shortly before the Russo-Japanese War he rejoined the official military system as a battalion commander over some 200 ex-bandit followers. Assisting Japan in the war against Russia, which the Japanese never forgot, Chang rose in 1911 to become the commander of the Mukden city garrison. Then, for supporting Yüan Shih-k'ai for the presidency, he was awarded command of the 27th

Division in 1912 while his rival and another ex-bandit, Feng Te-lin, took command of the 28th. In 1915 he failed in a bid for the military governorship of Fengtien when Yüan appointed a trusted lieutenant, Tuan Chih-kuei, to the post instead. But Yüan's fall in 1916 enabled Chang (with Japanese field officers' cooperation) to force Tuan out and take the post for himself.[16]

Chang's next move, in summer 1917, was to support Tuan Ch'i-jui, leader of the ascendant military clique in north China, in the struggle against the monarchists, and he thereby ensured that the remaining two Manchurian provinces would come under his sway. Before the monarchist coup Chang's rival, Feng Te-lin, had been nominated to the vacancy of military governor of Heilungkiang; Feng then forfeited the appointment by having supported the monarchists. With Tuan Ch'i-jui's consent, Chang was able to put in that post a fellow provincial, Pao Kuei-ch'ing.[17]

Pao had trained at the Tientsin military academy and risen through the ranks under Tuan Ch'i-jui's patronage. With a keen eye for local talent needed for an expanding domain, Chang evidently saw that Pao was a man of unusual ability. Pao was chief of the Peking military academy at the time when he was installed as military governor of Heilungkiang. Before the year 1917 ended, Chang had transferred ten battalions of his Fengtien troops to Pao and, as he was wont to do, consolidated the relationship by giving a daughter's hand to one of Pao's sons.[18]

The only remaining obstacle to ·Chang's ambition for Manchurian unification was the military governor of Kirin, General Meng En-yuan. Like Pao and Chang, Meng had risen from lowly origin to become commander of the border defense of Kirin in 1908, and military governor of the province in 1914. In the events of the summer of 1917, Meng was a supporter of the monarchists, and was subsequently ordered by Tuan Ch'i-jui to relinquish his post to one of Tuan's own generals. Meng and his followers defied the order and declared independence in October. This crisis made Chang the final arbiter. He obviously stood to gain by having Meng removed, but Meng, a loner amidst the constellations of military cliques, was distinctly preferable to a nominee of Tuan. Working behind the scenes, therefore, Chang made known to Tuan his desire for Meng to remain in his post, whereupon Tuan issued the face-saving announcement of extending Meng's incumbency by two months. That was the beginning of November, when the Harbin crisis erupted, and it fell upon Meng to handle the situation.[19]

For Meng, the Harbin crisis was an opportunity to improve his precarious political position before Chang moved to oust him. Chang's vulnerable point was his dependence on Japan. To resist him, Meng employed the weapon of anti-Japanism, a very popular cause in Kirin, as elsewhere in China. He cast himself as a nationalist, concerned with recovering China's lost sovereign rights and preventing them from falling into Japanese hands.

The request of the Allied ministers to the Peking government for a dispatch of troops to quell the Harbin disturbances was an opportunity beyond all Chinese dreams to reassert Chinese sovereignty in the Russian colonial domain in north Manchuria. It was an opportunity to be hastily seized, as the Russian and American ministers underlined to the Chinese government, lest Japan beat China to it. On the same day of the Allied ministers' request, the Chinese cabinet approved a dispatch of troops by General Meng of Kirin, and urged Generals Chang and Pao to assist him if necessary. On December 13, two presidential aides, Ho Tsung-lien and Chang Tsung-ch'ang, left for Harbin to direct operations on the spot. Their instruction was: 'support Horvath to the end, suppress the Bolsheviks by force if need be, and, if circumstances permit, assume responsibility for guarding the railway'.[20]

At this point, Japanese sources disclose some interesting feelers made by Chang Tso-lin to Japanese officials. At several conversations, Chang asked to be informed of Japan's attitude towards Russia's defection from the war, and more specifically towards the Harbin situation. He pledged full cooperation if Japan should decide to intervene in north Manchuria. He would positively unite the three Manchurian provinces behind that policy, he said, regardless of what Peking's attitude might be. Indeed, he would be pleased to see Japan occupy the eastern section of the railway, which traversed General Meng's province, while he himself would take over the western section in Heilungkiang.[21]

But the Japanese government at this time was not ready to intervene, vigorous pleas by its local agents notwithstanding. The events in north Manchuria had broken too soon; the army general staff had only just begun elaborating plans for an armed expedition to the Amur basin. The Chinese dispatch of troops had to be tolerated for the time being.[22] Japan's probable intervention, and Chang Tso-lin's propensity to collaborate with her, predetermined the degree of success that China was to have in reasserting her sovereign rights in north Manchuria.

On December 15, the two presidential aides conferred with General Meng and arrived at a four-point program of action: to deploy troops along the railway so as to protect the C.E.R. Administration, appoint a Chinese president to the C.E.R. board of directors, suppress any attempt by the Bolsheviks to exercise power, and proscribe political activity by Russian nationals in the C.E.R. Zone. Thus, while defending the Horvath regime, the plan allowed for the reassertion of Chinese sovereign rights through the Chinese president of the board of directors, backed by Chinese troops.[23]

The First, Third, and Fourth Kirin Mixed Brigades, totalling some twenty battalions, immediately took up position in the vicinity of Harbin. The Third was assigned to the city, the First and the Fourth to the eastern section of the railway. Three battalions of Heilungkiang troops were also on hand. In all, some 4,000 troops were mobilizied to deal with the situation.[24]

The conflict between General Horvath and the Bolsheviks had meanwhile sharpened. On Petrograd's renewed instructions of December 13, the Bolsheviks threatened Horvath with violence unless he relinquished his post. On December 16 Horvath retaliated by disbanding 600 Bolshevized troops. The Bolsheviks countermanded Horvath's order the next day, and declared Horvath and several other key administrators of the railway dismissed. On December 19, when the Bolsheviks shut down the Executive Committee by force, Chinese troops entered the city. Horvath was told to disarm and deport the 559th and 618th Militia, along with the Soviet leaders, within three days. Faced with a real intervention, the

Soviet abruptly rescinded its dismissal of Horvath on December 21 and asked, instead, that he get the Chinese to
withdraw. Confident now that the radicals would eventually
comply, Horvath appealed to the Chinese for a little more
time. Then, on December 24, suspecting that Japanese troops
disguised as civilians were pouring into Harbin, the Chinese
issued the Soviet an ultimatum to clear out within twenty-four
hours. On Christmas Day, despairing of their cause, the
Soviet leaders quietly fled the scene. Prodded by the diehards,
the pro-Bolshevik troops wavered between laying down their
arms and resisting, at which point, Horvath signalled for the
Chinese. In the early hours of December 26, the Harbin Soviet
was surrounded and disarmed.[25]

The immediate result of Chinese intervention was to
restore the railway and its zone to its pre-March status. The
political struggle ended on Chinese insistence. General Horvath survived the revolution and continued as head of the
C.E.R. Administration. The department of civil administration also revived. But the powers of the C.E.R. Administration were never to be restored, as the Chinese hastened with
reasserting sovereign rights.

The first step was to appoint a Chinese president to watch
after China's interests. As the Kirin troops moved into Harbin, the central government and Manchurian leaders began
consultations for a suitable candidate. As was to be expected,
Chang Tso-lin was careful not to allow an injection of the
center's influence into what he regarded as his satrapy. He
chose the mild-mannered civil governor of Kirin, Kuo
Tsung-hsi, not only because Kuo and Meng were mutually
antagonistic but Kuo was not likely to upset his relationship
with the Japanese.[26]

In these circumstances, China had two options in dealing
with the railway. One was to take over management temporarily until order returned to Russia. This appealed to General Meng and others who believed it would keep the railway
and the zone out of the Russian civil war and enable China to
regain her sovereign rights. But Kuo chose to be more moderate, justifying his position on the grounds that the Japanese

would resent any act that might have an implication for their South Manchurian Railway. Instead of taking over management of the railway, he proposed to stick closely to the contract, which meant dealing with the Russo-Asiatic Bank, an organization now led by anti-Bolshevik Russians.[27]

Kuo's policy affected the effort of rights recovery as well. During the two weeks following the collapse of the Harbin Soviet, about 7,200 Russian railway troops were disbanded by Horvath, who was contemplating the organization of a civilian guard. All that remained was a small unit of 700 men, stationed in Harbin, and another wholly new unit of 800 led by the Transbaikal Cossack, Ataman Grigorii Semenov, who entered the Manchouli-Hailar area late in December. In place of the Russians, Chinese troops took over the guarding of the railway. Those of General Meng patrolled the eastern and southern sections, and those of General Pao, the western section. General Meng proposed that even the two small Russian units be asked to disband, but Kuo resisted.

Similarly, Kuo insisted that the existing regulations governing the municipalities be observed, and not unilaterally revised by China, because of the large numbers of Japanese residents involved. He was content with China sharing supervision with the C.E.R. Administration at the council level. The police system, too, was jointly controlled, and Chinese and Russian police were detailed to duties alongside each other in the railway communities. The judicial system was changed even less. The 'frontier' courts continued to deal with purely Russian cases, mixed cases continued to be heard at 'mixed attendance'. The only change was that purely Chinese cases were placed under Chinese local courts. The first phase of China's rights recovery in the C.E.R. Zone turned out to be a piecemeal affair.[28]

The Manchurian situation after the expulsion of the local Bolsheviks understandably caused anxiety to the Soviet government in Petrograd. In the wake of China's armed suppression of the Harbin Soviet, counterrevolution reared its head. Horvath and Semenov, aided by a number of the Allied Powers, were busy organizing anti-Bolshevik detachments. Japanese intervention was in the air. Something had to be done to deny the White Guards their Manchurian sanctuary and check Japanese hostility. The Bolshevik leaders apparently realized that counteracting counterrevolution and foreign intervention hinged largely upon winning China to the Soviet side. What the local Bolsheviks had failed to achieve by direct action, the Soviet government now tried to obtain by diplomacy.

As an Ally, China's policy was to act in concert with the Allied governments towards the Bolsheviks. In the early days of the Soviet regime, this meant withholding official recognition while maintaining unofficial intercourse, until the status of the new government was determined by the Constituent Assembly. Such a policy made possible some informal contacts between China and the Soviet government in Petrograd.

On January 18, 1918, Polivanov, a deputy commissar of the Narkomindel (People's Commissariat of Foreign Affairs), informed the Chinese legation that the Soviet government did not recognize Prince Kudashev's diplomatic mission in Peking and General Horvath as head of the C.E.R. Administration. He asked that a joint Sino-Soviet committee be formed to solve the Chinese Eastern Railway question.[29] The next day, A.N. Voznesensky, chief of the eastern department of the Narkomindel, told the legation that he had been appointed Soviet representative to China, and asked to be allowed to proceed to Peking. If China accepted him, he said, the Soviet government would renounce extraterritoriality and return the concession territories in Hankow and Tientsin.

The legation secretary, Li Shih-chung, advised Voznesensky that China was acting in concert with the Allies. Before official recognition, all contacts had to be strictly informal. The Chinese government was prepared to explain in a public statement that it had acted in Harbin in accordance with the 1896 Contract by discharging its responsibility for the security of the railway and its personnel. The expulsion of the local Bolsheviks was not intended as a hostile act against the Soviet government.[30] Beyond this, everything would have to depend on what policy the Allies decided to adopt towards the Soviet republic.

That, in brief, constituted China's initial policy towards the new regime in Russia. China had entered the war on the

Allied side in August 1917, and the Bolshevik Revolution was an Allied problem because the new rulers were suing for a separate peace with the enemy. It was, in any case, suicidal for China to take an independent attitude towards a regime which had antagonized practically all the Great Powers by dishonouring the international obligations contracted by the previous government.

Voznesensky nevertheless pressed for a discussion of the Chinese Eastern Railway. The subject had been deliberated at a special inter-ministerial conference, chaired by the commissar for finance, where it was decided that until the conclusion of a new Sino–Soviet treaty, the 1896 Contract between the Chinese government and the Russo–Asiatic Bank should remain in force. Soviet legal control of the railway was to be secured through nationalizing the Russo–Asiatic Bank. Voznesensky was instructed to secure a reorganization of the railway administration by negotiation with the Chinese.[31]

Voznesensky's proposals were that the railway be managed by a Sino–Soviet committee; Chinese and Russian troops be evacuated and a Sino–Russian civilian guard organized under the command of commissars of both governments; and the municipal administration be reorganized on a democratic basis and placed under a council of equal numbers of representatives of Russian and Chinese workers. The Soviet government also wanted Horvath arrested for anti-Soviet activities.

Voznesensky said he realized China's difficulty in entertaining these proposals before official recognition, but if China ignored the niceties of international law, 'the Soviet government will go to whatever extent possible to satisfy China's interests'. The problem of official recognition, however, was an insurmountable obstacle. Before recognition, Li replied, an official joint committee was not possible; and an unofficial committee was meaningless. Horvath was in Chinese territory and therefore not subject to arrest by the Soviet government. Regarding other proposals, Li maintained that the railway was legally only a business enterprise; whatever political rights it had previously exercised had been usurped. Voznesensky went away without achieving any results.[32]

On the evening of January 24, Li Shih-chung returned the call and had another conversation with Voznesensky and his superior, Polivanov. The five-hour conversation covered practically all topics of mutual concern—the Chinese Eastern question, Outer Mongolia, and Soviet policy towards China and Japan. Some of Polivanov's remarks must have profoundly perturbed the Chinese secretary.

Li reiterated that the railway was purely a business enterprise, and declared China was neutral in the Russian civil war. Polivanov retorted quite rightly that the railway was political in the sense that the Horvath administration was conducting anti-Soviet activity. Moreover, China's neutrality was belied by the fact that Semenov's detachments were raiding Soviet territory from his Manchurian sanctuary. He asked what China could gain from protecting Horvath. The new government was offering to abolish extraterritoriality and return the concession territories, if only China would respond. The Soviet government was asking China to redeem the railway immediately. If this was beyond China's means, then the only alternative was joint management.

As for Outer Mongolia, Polivanov disclosed that in 1915 when Russia entered into an agreement with China for guaranteeing Mongolian autonomy, she was secretly working to absorb the territory. The Soviet government, on the other hand, was prepared to annul the Kiakhta Convention of 1915, and make Outer Mongolia a fully independent state or return it to China. Asked his personal preference, Polivanov said Outer Mongolia was culturally too primitive and politically too despotic to become a viable independent state; he preferred a period of Chinese tutelage.

If Polivanov's views on Outer Mongolia pleased the Chinese secretary, those on Soviet policy towards Japan did not. According to Polivanov, Soviet policy in the Far East could be stated in two principles: first, the Soviet government wished to see China become independent, politically and economically; secondly, it was ready to open eastern Siberia to Japanese exploitation and had in fact so proposed to the Japanese embassy. Visibly worried, Li hastened to point out that the two principles might be contradictory. Japan was by now practically the master of China. How would the Soviet government achieve its first objective if Japanese influence were to expand into eastern Siberia as well? 'True', Polivànov rejoined, 'but the situation has left us with no other alternative. But this is only temporary; we will try to get the Japanese masses to overthrow their monarchy'. He believed that the mounting hostility between Japan and the United States would end in a war, and what the European war had done for the Bolsheviks, the American–Japanese war would do for the Japanese masses:[33]

Soviet policy towards Japan, as Polivanov revealed, was one of temporary appeasement. It was ominous for China because Russia and Japan had cooperated against China's interests in the past, and the two neighbors might do so again. This fear of Soviet–Japanese rapprochement was to become a basic part of Chinese official thinking in the years ahead.

In fact, just when the Narkomindel was seeking negotiations with the Chinese legation, it was proposing to the Japanese ambassador a review of Russo–Japanese treaties. Polivanov had been nominated as envoy to proceed to Tokyo for talks. The proposals were renewed by Karakhan in the spring of 1918, and again by Voznesensky in May, but the Japanese were not forthcoming.[34]

Before the Chinese mission withdrew from Petrograd at the end of February, Voznesensky persisted with representations for changes in the Chinese Eastern Railway. He also put pressure on the railway board of directors in Petrograd by demanding that the company submit to the new government, disband its troops in the railway zone, revise the municipal regulations, and recall Horvath. He threatened the board with imprisonment if it refused. However, Voznesensky was told that the railway was a purely commercial enterprise, built within Chinese territory, and governed by a contract with the Chinese government. It was therefore outside the jurisdiction of the Soviet government. In any case, China's consent was necessary for the changes to be carried out. On February 4, Voznesensky called on the Chinese secretary once again, put forward the same proposals as he had done on January 19, and got the same reply.[35]

The railway and its zone eluded Soviet hands until 1924. All attempts by the Soviet government to gain control and to forestall counterrevolution and foreign intervention had failed, whether by direct action or diplomacy with the Chinese, or by pressure upon the Russo-Asiatic Bank and the railway's board of directors. The president of the bank, A.I. Putilov, fled to Paris, reopened the bank's headquarters there under French protection, and then appeared in Peking where in April 1918 he organized a new board of directors. The last, in reality, was the nucleus of a new non-communist Russian government.[36]

The February 4 conversation was the last of any significance between the Narkomindel and the Chinese legation. Contrary to Soviet claims, the talks were not serious negotiations from the Chinese point of view. They represented nothing more than informal discussions. Serious proposals were of course put forward by the Narkomindel, which was anxious to win Chinese support, but there never was any question of China's seriously entertaining them due to her need to act in concert with the Allies.[37]

Much is revealed in the above three conversations to discredit the general view that Soviet policy in China began with revolutionary self-denial. Two additional pieces of evidence shed light on the question. One is a set of instructions issued by the Narkomindel on February 22, 1918, to departments of external affairs organized within various local soviets in eastern Siberia. The instructions were intended to guide the local soviets on policy towards China and Japan, and they illustrate the mixture of revolutionary idealism and hard-headed realism that characterized that policy. Local Bolsheviks were told to publicize the Soviet desire for completely new relations with the eastern peoples, and to exhort them to look to socialist Russia as their 'salvation from the dangers of seizure, violence, and lawlessness of the Japanese–European capitalists and oppressors'.

The Peking government was portrayed as reactionary, and Canton, which was the base of Sun Yat-sen's constitution protection movement, as progressive. Local Bolsheviks were warned that the Japanese government was definitely bent on aggression. They were instructed to 'vigilantly watch' every move of the Japanese, but cautioned against provoking them. Finally, a special guideline was laid down for the Chinese Eastern Railway:

> It should be remembered that the treaty of 1896, which is recognized by us and against which China has not protested to this time, remains in force; hence, China retains sovereign right on the territory in which the railroad lies, and is obligated to protect it without interfering in the internal affairs of the railroad and in our self-government.[38]

In this document are three fundamental elements of Soviet policy: the desire to avoid Japanese intervention, Soviet sympathy for the south China government, and recognition of the 1896 Contract as being still valid. The Soviet government evidently did not think its nationalization of the railway or its insistence on self-government for the Russian residents in the railway area contradicted in any way its avowed recognition of Manchuria as Chinese sovereign territory.

The second document outlining Soviet policies towards China and Japan is the speech of the Commissar for Foreign Affairs Georgii Chicherin to the Fifth Soviet Congress on July 4, 1918. Reporting the steps he had taken since the October Revolution to achieve normal relations with China and Japan, Chicherin said, with regard to China, the government had repudiated all the Russo–Japanese secret treaties, had renounced the conquests of the Tsarist government in Manchuria, and had restored to China her sovereign rights in the railway zone. Moreover, the government had proposed that 'if part of the money invested in the construction of this railroad by the Russian people were repaid by China', she might redeem it immediately. He then outlined other offers: to recall all military consular guards, and to renounce extraterritoriality and the Boxer indemnity, provided the money was spent on mass education.

Chicherin reported a division in Japan between the 'reactionary militarists' bent on armed intervention in Siberia and the moderate liberals who 'wish to receive from us certain concessions peacefully'. He declared that the Soviet government was ready to permit 'peaceful exploitation of the natural resources in Siberia' and 'broad participation in our industrial and commercial life' by Japanese citizens. Furthermore, 'we are ready, if China is agreeable . . . to sell to Japan the southern branch of the Chinese Eastern Railway, and also make this branch and others easier for the export of Japanese products and commodities to Russia'.[39]

The generous offers made to Japan by the Soviet government evidently were a desperate attempt to stave off the armed thrust into Siberia that Japan was preparing. Those made to China were not as generous as usually believed. North Manchuria was Russia's first line of defense against Japan, and in the struggle for survival revolutionary principles gave way to expediency.

3

China and the Siberian Intervention

The Inter-Allied Intervention in Siberia grew out of the October Revolution which, in turn, was born of the European war. These momentous events revolutionized the prewar power structure of the Far East. The war raised Japan to the dominant position in China previously enjoyed by Great Britain; the revolution destroyed the balance between Japan and Russia established by the Russo-Japanese War and the conventions of 1906-16; and intervention signified Japan's drive to inherit Imperial Russia's political and economic interests in China and to expand into eastern Siberia as well.[1]

Given Japan's predominance, China's Russian policy not surprisingly became absorbed into Japan's Russian policy. This is shown in the negotiation for the pact called the Sino-Japanese Secret Military Convention for Joint Defence, which Japan needed to achieve her objective *vis-à-vis* Russia. The pact has hitherto been viewed by historians as the natural result of the Peking government being controlled by the Anfu clique of miltitarists which was closely affiliated with Japan. But a closer examination of the way in which it was negotiated and subsequently implemented discloses a far more complex picture. China's Russian policy, which led to her involvement in the Russian civil war, is found not to have originated with the Anfu clique alone, but in combination with the Chihli clique with which it shared power. Also the Wai-chiao Pu is found to have influenced the Anfu clique towards a more rational policy, although in the end its views were disregarded by the tough-minded militarists. Finally, the Anfu clique appears to have displayed considerably more recalcitrance towards their Japanese supporters than is generally conceded.

In 1917 the Terauchi Cabinet of the Chōshū military clique was in control of government in Japan. In October of the previous year, it had succeeded the Ōkuma Cabinet which, among other things, had presented China with the Twenty-One Demands and deeply alienated the Chinese. The Terauchi Cabinet was satisfied with Japan's relations with Russia, and decided to concentrate its energies on China. There it sought Japan's political and economic hegemony in anticipation of postwar competition from the Western powers. Employing more moderate means than those of its predecessor, it sought to eradicate Chinese hostility and initiate a new era of cooperation. Concretely, by means of military and financial support, it tried to build a broad political, economic, and military coalition with the ascendant Anfu clique in Peking, led by Tuan Ch'i-jui.

But Russia's defection from the war led the Terauchi Cabinet to revise its priorities drastically. As early as November 1917 it adopted two new policies. One was to commence preparations to send troops to the Amur basin. The Siberian Planning Committee was set up by the Army General Staff and it began work in the same month. The other was to obtain an agreement for joint defense from the Peking government, so that Japanese troops could move freely through Chinese territory to ensure the success of the Siberian venture. A few weeks later, the Terauchi Cabinet adopted a further policy of giving financial and armed assistance to 'moderate elements' among prominent Russians to enable them to organize a friendly anti-Soviet buffer state in Siberia. These so-called 'moderate elements' were soon found in the persons of the Transbaikal Cossack leader, Ataman Semenov, the Ussuri Cossack leader, Ivan Kalmykov, and the chief executive of the Chinese Eastern Railway, General Horvath.[2]

The Chinese government began receiving informal feelers from Japanese army agents for a joint defense pact in mid-November. Politics in Peking at the time reflected the

continuing crisis of political institutions and leadership that
had resulted from the collapse of the Confucian monarchy.
The Tuan Ch'i-jui coterie which Japan had singled out for
support was one among clusters of loosely associated military
leaders who, as the collective heirs of Yüan Shih-k'ai, dominated a dozen provinces in northern and central China. Personal rivalries and conflicting aims were beginning to produce
two major cliques, one centering around Tuan Ch'i-jui, the
premier, and the other around Feng Kuo-chang, the president.
The two cliques, respectively known as Anfu and Chihli,
together shared power in Peking, united externally against the
southern provinces which had rebelled against the north, but
divided internally in a struggle for dominance.

Japanese support for Tuan Ch'i-jui had begun early in the
summer of 1917 when Peking was plunged into political tur-
bulence over the question of whether China should declare
war against Germany. The Kuomintang's opposition produced a deadlock in the parliament, which opportunity was
seized by the monarchists to attempt a restoration. After the
coup was suppressed by Tuan in July, a reorganized parliament was reconvened without the Kuomintang parliamen-
tarians, who promptly organized a 'rump' parliament in Canton, and rallied the half dozen or so southern provinces to
challenge the north's legitimacy. In the north, Tuan Ch'i-jui
became premier with Japanese assistance while Feng Kuo-
chang became president, and the Tuan Cabinet declared war in
August. The Tuan Cabinet justified the declaration of war,
which had general Allied support, by the benefits that would
accrue to China, such as the enhancement of her international
standing and rewards at the peace settlement. But Tuan also
had selfish motives, such as desire for extra war powers and
the right to contract foreign loans.

Discord between the president and the premier increased
with the Tuan clique's ascendancy, and was further fueled by
disagreements over policies towards the south. Premier Tuan
advocated armed unification, President Feng peaceful conciliation. The premier had his way in the autumn when the north
engaged the south in Hunan and Szechwan, but the fighting
ended rather inconclusively. Late in November, following the
failure of his policy, Premier Tuan found it necessary to step

down. The balance of cabinet strength was modified somewhat in the Chihli clique's favor, but the Tuan clique remained powerfully represented by Communications Minister Ts'ao Ju-lin and War Minister Tuan Chih-kuei. Although in temporary retirement, Tuan Ch'i-jui assumed charge of the War Participation Bureau in December, which had the responsibility of discharging China's obligations as participant of the European war. By March 1918, with Japanese support, Tuan Ch'i-jui was to be back as premier.

In their attitudes towards Japan, there were subtle differences between the Anfu and Chihli cliques. Generally, of course, Japan's dominant position in China was so keenly felt that Chinese politicians of all shades had to come to terms with it. The Anfu clique was more positive towards Sino-Japanese cooperation, partly because it had been singled out by Japan for special favor, and partly perhaps because it genuinely believed that Japan had indeed revised her policy towards China. The Chihli clique, on the other hand, was negative if only because Japanese aid was responsible for its rival's strength, but its resistance to Japan's pressure never developed into outright defiance. In short, one seems to have cooperated in good faith, the other out of necessity.

This difference in attitude was narrowed further by one other factor. Although Japan considered Tuan to be her protégé, she was not to find him a mere puppet, pliant to her every wish. Tuan could not remain oblivious to his unpopularity with the Chinese public on account of his Japanese orientation, nor to the denunciations by his political enemies for selling out the nation's interests. Desiring Japan's continuing support and yet sensitive to his domestic image, he was to behave in a typically opportunistic fashion.

It was during Tuan's temporary retirement from the premiership that Japanese army agents began sounding out the Chinese leadership in Peking on a joint defense pact. The most active among the Japanese agents were Major General Banzai Rihachirō and Lt General Aoki Nobuzumi, who were employed as advisers in the office of the president, and Major General Saitō, the military attaché. They found the Chihli clique president and premier too timid to refuse, but disinclined to do anything. On the other hand, Banzai learned in a conversation that Tuan Ch'i-jui would welcome a military partnership, provided he had the money to prepare the necessary forces. The army agents discovered that the president and the premier were the stumbling block to Japan's plans, and recommended to their superiors that Tuan be supported back to power. A sum of ¥20,000,000 was immediately sent to Tuan, as head of the War Participation Bureau, to pave the way for his comeback.[3]

On February 19, after much pressure from his Japanese advisers, President Feng finally accepted joint defense in principle, but insisted on the proviso that cooperation be kept outside Chinese territory. As a precaution, he also instructed the foreign minister quietly to alert other Allied governments.[4]

Foreign Minister Lu Cheng-hsiang was to play a key role during the negotiations. Trained in foreign learning at the Kiangnan arsenal language school and the T'ung-wen kuan, he had joined the Chinese diplomatic service in 1892. His talents had attracted the attention of President Yuan Shih-k'ai in 1912, who appointed him foreign minister of the new republic. A man of deep sensibilities and frail health, he commanded a measure of respect among Yuan's tough-minded heirs because of his expertise and nonpartisanship.[5]

On February 21, Foreign Minister Lu placed before the cabinet a motion concerning joint defense with Japan. He acknowledged that a threat from Russia did exist, referring, among other things, to rumors of German-Austrian prisoners of war in Siberia being rearmed under a Soviet-German understanding to strike in the east. With hindsight, but only with hindsight, the so-called 'threat' can be seen to be purely imaginary. The Chinese government did not labor under any greater misinformation or misapprehension than any other foreign government at the time. The frontiers being under threat, the foreign minister urged that military preparations begin early and on a scale which would have to be considerably greater than if troops engaged in the south could be transferred to reinforce the border garrisons. Besides the threat from Russia, he was also apprehensive of Japan's aggressive intent. 'Unless we make preparations now', he warned his colleagues, 'when armed intervention in Siberia becomes a reality, it is feared that the nimble-footed Japanese will force us to open our territory to the passage of their troops. In that eventuality, north Manchuria will become another Shantung'. The best strategy, he said, was for China to check the Siberian threat with her own troops, so that there would not be any room for the Japanese. But,

> if they should compel us to cooperate on the pretext of protecting their interests, we will not be able to resist. The only alternative will then be to consult the Allies in order to bring about an inter-Allied intervention, so that Japan can be checked. . . . An inter-Allied effort will be far more in our interest than a unilateral intervention by Japan.[6]

Here lies the central premise in the thinking of the foreign minister: unless intervention was an inter-Allied effort, China would have little to choose between a Soviet-German strike and unbridled Japanese aggression.

Since the end of 1917, Britain and France had been agitating for a military mission to Siberia in order to reconstitute the eastern front against Germany. As a start, they had proposed to occupy Vladivostok so as to protect the enormous war stores there as well as the Trans-Siberian (including the Chinese Eastern) Railway system. Unable to undertake the task themselves, they had looked to the United States and Japan. In reply, Japan had asked that the undertaking be left to her alone if and when it proved to be necessary. While assuring the Allied governments that she would not act without full understanding with them first, she also reserved freedom of unilateral action if her vital interests should be threatened. Britain saw the undesirable implications of Japan's position and, together with France, approached Washington with the idea of requesting Japan to intervene as a mandatory for the Allies. There the proposal was stalemated for more than six months. The American government was doubtful that Japan would move her troops beyond Irkutsk, several thousand miles away from the war front; it also feared that intervention might produce the reverse effect of causing the Russians to play into German hands. As stated by Secretary of State Lansing on February 13, the American position was that any intervention should be an inter-Allied effort. The Chinese Eastern Railway should be guarded and protected by the military forces of China.[7]

When Foreign Minister Lu saw the American minister on February 23, he was told the content of Lansing's statement. In Washington, when the Chinese minister, Wellington Koo, discussed Japan's proposal for joint defense with the third assistant secretary, Breckinridge Long, he was advised that China should do nothing to jeopardize her own territorial sovereignty. The Chinese government should make it clear to Tokyo that, in the event of an intervention, China would guard and protect the Chinese Eastern Railway with her own troops. Long saw no reason why the Japanese troops should go through north Manchuria, since it was far easier for them to enter Russian territory at Vladivostok. As far as joint action outside Chinese territory was concerned, Long felt the proposal was premature, since it would be more than enough to guard the war stores at Vladivostok, and the Amur and Ussuri Railways.[8]

The American view would have encouraged Foreign Minister Lu considerably were it not for the fact that intervention was still a hypothetical question for Washington. The Americans had given free advice but not of a kind that China could accept. Unlike the United States, China bordered on Russia for thousands of miles and the Chinese garrisons could not withstand the Soviet-German tide for a moment. If the situation in Russia should deteriorate further, the Japanese army probably would have no qualms about moving into and through Chinese territory. The Chinese government yielded to Japanese pressure.

On February 23, Chinese Minister Chang Tsung-hsiang in Tokyo informed the Japanese Foreign Minister Motono that China was prepared to discuss conditional cooperation. Motono rejected the condition outright, offended by China's mistrust of Japan's motives. He declared that Japan's motive was purely to check the eastward spread of Russo-German power.[9] The cabinet mulled over Chang's telegram inconclusively on February 26. Meanwhile, sensing difficulty in Peking, the Vice Chief of Army General Staff, Tanaka Gi'ichi, tried to allay Chinese suspicions. He told Minister Chang that assurance would be given of the prompt withdrawal of Japanese troops from Chinese territory when the situation no longer required their presence. He offered a choice between two procedures for the conclusion of an agreement. One was for the diplomatic authorities to sign an agreement first and the military authorities to work out detailed arrangements later. The other was that the military authorities should decide upon the arrangements first, and the diplomatic authorities conclude an agreement at an opportune moment later. The difference between the two was that the second procedure envisaged a less formal and binding agreement. Disarmingly, Tanaka expressed preference for the second.[10]

At this point, even those less enthusiastic about Sino-Japanese cooperation began to see some virtue in a written agreement which would circumscribe Japanese activity on Chinese territory. Such an agreement might specify the duration of joint defense and Japan's respect for Chinese territorial sovereignty and pledge to evacuate Japanese troops at the end of hostilities. It might lay down the terms under which the Chinese Eastern Railway could be used without prejudice to existing interests. Tanaka's assurance of troop withdrawal and offer of alternative forms of agreement further encouraged the thought that it was harmless to have a contingency plan which need never be activated unless absolutely necessary. All these assumptions and calculations were to surface in the course of the long and hard bargaining with Japan.[11]

On March 2, the cabinet went over a number of crucial points such as the definition of the target of the pact, the need to prepare the Manchurian officials and public for cooperation with Japan, the handling of the Chinese Eastern Railway, and the prevention of a repetition of Japanese behaviour in Shantung. It strongly recommended that Minister Chang be instructed 'to mince no words' in bringing these matters to Japan's attention and ask for proof of Japan's new friendly disposition by an amicable settlement of the Shantung question and pending cases in Manchuria. The cabinet opted for Tanaka's second procedure and, in a telegram to Minister Chang, it explained why. Firstly, a less public and binding agreement would avoid giving rise to suspicions of other powers or violent censure by opponents of the central government. Secondly, the procedure would retain for China the freedom to decide when the agreement should be activated. Unlike Japan, China needed to avoid offending Russia as much as possible. The propinquity of China and Russia required that 'China will not use military force unless absolutely necessary'. In acceding to Japan's request for joint defense, the Chinese government was merely taking practical precautions and it signified nothing more.[12] The next step, then, was for the military authorities of both governments to proceed to detailed discussions.

On March 8, the Japanese foreign minister, apparently competing with the army for policymaking on China, unexpectedly injected a new element when he asked for a diplomatic exchange of notes first, so that the exchange would form the basis of the military talks. Tanaka subsequently backed Motono's demand, and the Chinese proceeded to negotiate the exchange of notes under the alternating pressure of Motono's rigidity and Tanaka's sweet reasonableness.

When Motono saw Minister Chang on March 8, he already had a ready draft, which reads as follows:

> On account of the German influence extending into the territories of the Far East and menacing the peace and order of the general situation, the Government of China and the Government of Japan, for the purpose of coping with the situation, have to consider the necessary measures in common.
>
> In accordance with the foregoing the means and regulations of cooperation of the Army and Navy of the two countries for carrying out what may be decided upon by mutual agreement between the two governments shall be arranged by the authorities of both countries concerned, who shall from time to time consult with each other carefully and sincerely upon all questions of mutual interest.[13]

On March 11, Minister Chang was instructed to tell Tokyo that the Chinese government was prepared to exchange notes but only under certain conditions: Motono should confirm that Tanaka's second procedure was still contemplated, and the notes should state explicitly that cooperation would be valid only for the duration of the European war.[14] On March 13, Motono confirmed that the second procedure was still contemplated, but he refused to include the period of validity in the notes. He said it did not accord with 'the original idea of permanent friendship', and proposed that the matter be left to the military authorities to determine.[15]

The next few days must have been agonizing to Foreign Minister Lu and his colleagues. Motono did not relax the pressure. On March 15, he called Chang in again to say that the situation in Siberia was growing more critical. He believed the Bolshevik troops at Irkutsk to be commanded by a German chief of staff. The negotiations brooked no delay. China should shed its suspicions about Japan's motives, and he hinted at a lack of sincerity on China's part. He also warned that the talks be kept absolutely secret. 'If any complications should arise it would only offend the friendly sentiment of Japan'. Reporting to Peking, Chang, too, added his pressure. He reported that some Japanese circles were advocating that Japan should act alone without China's cooperation. If this should happen, Russo-German-Japanese conflicts would break out immediately on Chinese territory and then China would find it impossible to drive the belligerents out and it would be too late to obtain an alliance with Japan.[16]

Finally, on March 17, a vexed foreign minister cabled his reply, explaining to Chang why the government was taking time to study Motono's proposal. The cabinet had previously opted for Tanaka's second procedure in order to avoid concluding a formal agreement, but Motono's insistence on an exchange of notes had altered its original meaning. The government had in mind only temporary joint defense. The slightest slip might turn it into a permanent alliance. He wished Chang to insist that Japan should reaffirm that the second procedure proposed by Tanaka was still contemplated, agree to make the notes public, and to embody Tanaka's promise of withdrawal, and Motono's agreement to have the military authorities determine the period of validity in a separate exchange of letters.

To Motono's draft, he proposed a number of changes. Whereas Motono envisaged Sino-Japanese cooperation as indefinite, and something which concerned the two countries exclusively, Lu desired it to be understood that Sino-Japanese cooperation meant no more than the two countries 'doing their share in the Allied cause for the prosecution of the present war'. In short, China's military cooperation with Japan constituted her participation in the war as a member of the Allied camp, and it was to be limited to the current war.[17]

By March 19, Motono evidently had come to appreciate fully the degree of resistance in Peking. In order not to jeopardize the final goal, he acceded to all of Lu's changes, except secrecy. The exchange of notes took place on March 25.[18] Two days before that, the notes mysteriously leaked in the Chinese press, with the hint that China had acted under duress. The military delegates of the two countries proceeded to negotiate the detailed arrangements, amidst stormy popular protests.[19]

The Japanese delegation, led by Major General Saitō, had arrived in Peking on March 19, with drafts of military and naval agreements. They had been preceded by one day by Premier Terauchi's personal agent and advocate of Sino-Japanese cooperation, Nishihara Kamezō, whose machinations resulted in Tuan Ch'i-jui's resumption of the premiership on March 23.[20]

The composition of the Chinese delegation was finalized at the end of the month. It consisted of Field Marshal Chin Yün-p'eng, chief of staff in Tuan Ch'i-jui's War Participation Bureau, as chief delegate, four military officers, and one representative from each of the Manchurian leaders. The composition of the delegation reflected the interests of the two north China cliques, in addition to those of Manchuria. Field Marshal Chin personified the spirit of the delegation. A loyal associate of Tuan, Chin maintained generally good relations with the Chihli faction. He did not belong to the mainstream of Tuan's clique with its powerful and abrasive spokesman Hsü Shu-cheng.

Apart from Chin, the figure who played the most vital role in shaping the military and naval agreements was Foreign Minister Lu Cheng-hsiang. An old hand at such negotiations, the foreign minister was to press for precision of language and rescued his colleagues from pitfalls. There was a consensus that the agreements were important enough for all segments of the government to be consulted at each stage of the negotiations.

As noted, Japan's principal objective was to occupy the Amur basin as far as Lake Baikal to meet the Soviet-German threat. Essential to this objective was that China's war participation army should be organzed on the basis of a partnership with Japan. The partnership should entitle the Japanese army free movement in Chinese territory, especially on the Chinese side of the Amur basin, whence the thrust into Transbaikalia would be staged. Such an arrangement, the Japanese believed, would enable them to justify unilateral action to the other Allied powers and thereby enhance their freedom of action.

The draft brought over by the Japanese delegation embodied the basic principle of joint defense that the forces of the two countries would cooperate in their *separate* special areas, not in combination with the other. The dividing line was drawn vertically through central Mongolia so that the Japanese army would operate 'mainly in the area from northern Manchuria, eastern Mongolia, and the Russian Far East [i.e. the Maritime Province] to eastern Siberia'. The Chinese army, on its part, would operate 'mainly in the area from central Mongolia to eastern Siberia, and part of it will defend the western Mongolian and Sinkiang area'. In essence, if China agreed to the draft, northern Manchuria and the eastern half of Mongolia would be occupied by Japanese troops.[21]

So deep was Chinese distrust in Peking that Major General Saitō had to drop the principle of territorial division lest the whole draft be rejected outright. Even then, the revised draft was so sweeping that Field Marshal Chin was not permitted to open formal negotiations until it had been examined and annotated by each ministry, and the annotations collated, finalized and approved by the cabinet.[22]

Over the next two weeks, the two delegations informally reviewed one draft after another. Finally, in mid–April, something like a final draft emerged on which negotiations could begin. In place of the principle of territorial division, the draft stated that the military areas should be decided by the military authorities in accordance with the military strength of each country. The Japanese agreed to respect Chinese territorial sovereignty. Concerning the Chinese Eastern Railway, Japan agreed as follows: 'When military transportation necessitates the use of the Chinese Eastern Railway, the provisions in the original treaty regarding the management and protection of the said railway shall be respected'.[23]

Despite a number of Japanese concessions, the two parties still stood widely apart on the duration of the pact, the definition of the enemy, and secrecy, which had been encountered during the negotiations on the text of the notes.

Another difference was over the procedure for activating the pact. The distinction between Tanaka's two alternatives had been blurred by the exchange of notes, and now the Japanese delegation insisted that the military agreement should go into immediate effect, upon being signed. The Chinese insisted on adding the clause: 'The time for commencing actual military operations shall be decided by the highest military organs of the two countries'. By this the Chinese hoped to postpone activation until it became absolutely necessary according to their own assessment of the situation.[24]

This was where the matter stood up to May 14. According to one scholar, the Tuan cabinet was brought round by Tanaka's threat, made to Minister Chang on May 3, to stop supplying loans or arms unless the agreement was signed.[25] In fact, the gap was closed by Japan's caving in to Chinese demands, all except secrecy, and the military agreement was signed on May 16.

Negotiations over the naval agreement lagged a few days behind the military agreement. The Japanese wanted the use of inland waterways as well as the open sea, meaning the Amur River system, and the right to make surveys and soundings of Chinese territorial waters. Again, the Chinese were immovable and eventually had their way. The naval agreement was signed on May 19.[26]

The Japanese insistence upon secrecy went up in smoke when these agreements, like the notes, leaked in the press.

As it stood at the end of May, the pact with Japan was, from China's point of view, little more than a contingency plan which need never be implemented until the contingency for which it was intended should arise.

By June, the Japanese Army General Staff had completed planning for the Siberian expedition. It was proposed to occupy various strategic points in Russian territory east of Lake Baikal and along the Chinese Eastern Railway in preparation for operations against Russia and Germany. The plan called for two forces, totalling seven divisions made up of 150,000 men. One force was to be directed at the Maritime Province, the other at Transbaikalia. The first, consisting of two divisions, was to occupy Vladivostok, Nikol'sk–Ussuriisk, and Khabarovsk, and would then extend operations along the Amur Railway and the Amur River. The second force of five divisions (in conjunction with about 10,000 Chinese troops) was to advance along the Chinese Eastern Railway to Manchouli, thence to Chita, and as far west as the lake to secure that area. Part of the second force was to secure the Chinese Eastern Railway as its line of communications. A third force was envisaged for central Mongolia whence, in cooperation with Chinese troops, it would proceed to Transbaikalia.[27]

Although the army's planning was complete, the Terauchi Cabinet was not ready to move until certain other conditions were fulfilled. Opposed to the army were the political party civilians led by Hara Kei, who were strong in the diet, and whose views the Chōshū leaders, even with their predominant power, could not afford to ignore. Deeply suspicious of the army's intentions, the anti-interventionists rejected intervention until Japan's security was threatened to a dangerous degree and until the necessary understanding with the West, especially the United States, was obtained.

The Chōshū leaders were therefore more moderate than certain extremists who would disregard all opposition to achieve their objectives. Sensitive to liberal opinion and desirous of good relations with the West, the Terauchi Cabinet held back.[28]

This was one factor in China's favor. Another was the hopeful development on the Sino-Russian border where, despite White Guard provocations, the Red Guards displayed a conciliatory attitude towards the Chinese. Thus, when the Semenovites were pushed back against the Chinese border by the Bolsheviks in June, and the Japanese appeared to be on the point of intervening, Foreign Minister Lu Cheng-hsiang instructed Minister Koo to inform the American government secretly: 'The present Siberian situation does not call for Japan's dispatch of troops. . . . The Japanese are trying to create a situation and agitate for intervention simply from ulterior motives. The Chinese government does not feel the time has come for joint defense or to begin preparations for it'.[29]

However, by the time Koo communicated with the State Department, the American decision to intervene had been made. For months, the American government had resisted the appeal from Britain, France, and others but its resistance weakened in June and early in July gave way to a new course. The British and the French launched another appeal on July 2, this time in the name of the Supreme War Council. They asked for American participation in an effort to send 100,000 men to Siberia, principally Japanese and under Japanese command. To their two previously enunciated objectives of firming Russian resistance to the Germans and weakening Germany by a reconstituted eastern front, they tagged a third—of bringing assistance to the Czechoslovak forces—and this appealed to President Wilson.[30]

The Czechoslovaks then lived in subjection within the Austro-Hungarian empire and formed part of the Austrian army in the war. Large numbers of them had deserted and defected to Russia where in 1914 they formed the Czech Corps, intending to fight on the Allied side so as to achieve independence at the peace conference. Their position in Russia was made untenable by the Soviet peace with Germany and, on French request, the Bolsheviks gave them permission to proceed across Siberia to depart for Europe via Vladivostok. In March 1918 the armed Czechs set out in a long column along the Trans-Siberian Railway. However, in May, following some obscure incidents, after the vanguard had reached Vladivostok, the Soviet government ordered the Czechs to be disarmed and detained. The vanguard of 15,000 promptly revolted, deposing the Bolsheviks in Vladivostok and preparing to rescue their compatriots stranded in the west. The Czechs then became inextricably involved in the Russian civil war.

The formula reached by Wilson amounted to an American–Japanese undertaking to furnish arms and munitions to the Czechs, and to land Japanese and American marines at Vladivostok who would guard the lines of communications of the Czechs as they sought to join up with their compatriots west of Irkutsk. The decision was based largely on the mistaken belief that the Czechs were beleaguered not by the Bolsheviks but by Austro-German armed prisoners. The purpose of the undertaking was to see the Czechs safely out of Russia, without infringing upon Russia's political and territorial sovereignty or interfering in Russia's internal affairs. The proposed intervention was limited both as to its purpose and its scope. It was to be confined to Vladivostok and each side was to contribute about 7,000 men.[31]

Plainly, it was not the kind of intervention desired by the British and the French who were, moreover, outraged at not being invited to participate. They reacted by sending one battalion each and sought to influence the venture to suit their purpose. Nor did the American proposal bear any resemblance to the long-developing plans of the Japanese interventionists. In contrast to the American plan, the Japanese one envisaged an all-out intervention in the Amur basin, not a limited expedition confined to the Vladivostok area. The Japanese plan called for seven divisions, not 7,000 men, or the 12,000 which Washington later conceded. The American objective was to render assistance to the Czechs while the Japanese army sought political and economic hegemony in the Amur basin. The Japanese interventionists noted the divergence in the scope and the purpose of the two plans but decided to accept the American invitation and expand it to suit their purposes.

For months, Japanese intervention had been restrained by the reservations of the non-interventionists. The American invitation broke the deadlock. After an agonizing adjustment of views between the Chōshū leaders and the liberal forces, the Japanese government replied: it welcomed the proposal to join in rescuing the Czechs and would send one division (normally about 12,000 men) to Vladivostok, but it reserved the right to send more. The reply also hinted that in view of Japan's 'special position' it might be necessary in future to operate beyond Vladivostok.

Premier Terauchi had assured Hara that the second expedition would consist of one division only and its purpose would be limited to protecting the Trans-Siberian Railway; no reinforcements would be sent without prior consultation. Shortly after that, however, the Chōshū leaders lost controlling influence in Japanese politics; the civilians took over the reins of government whereas the military extremists took over the Siberian expedition.[32]

The American decision to intervene was a mixed blessing for China. Indirectly, it triggered the Sino-Japanese military pact and Japanese occupation of north Manchuria. The American military involvement in the Asian continent, on the other hand, did mean the fulfilment of China's original hope that the intervention would be a joint venture of multiple powers which might have a moderating effect on the Japanese. Additionally, it had the effect of reducing China's isolated vulnerability to Japanese pressure, and thus of modifying the behavior of the entire Chinese political leadership.

On July 20, the Tuan Cabinet decided to participate in the Vladivostok venture with a token force of 1,000 to 2,000 troops. This was conceived as China fulfilling her obligations as a cobelligerent and, at the same time, as rendering protection to the Chinese community at Vladivostok. The expedition being primarily an American-Japanese undertaking, the Wai-chiao Pu proceeded to seek an invitation from the two powers.[33] Japanese Minister Hayashi counselled that China's participation was unnecessary since Chinese troops would be better used in the area where the German threat was real. He felt that China should act in concert with Japan in view of the Sino-Japanese pact. His statements were promptly leaked to the press and vociferously criticized. On July 24, an angry Hayashi officially informed the Wai-chiao Pu that the matter was up to the Chinese government to decide, and expressed irritation over Chinese inconsistency in wanting intervention in Vladivostok on the one hand, and acting in an unfriendly manner towards the Semenovites on the other. Simultaneously, Foreign Minister Gotō told American Ambassador Morris that the Chinese request to participate 'should as a matter of policy receive favorable consideration'.[34]

For different reasons, the United States' initial reaction to China's request was also lukewarm. On July 20, Acting

Foreign Minister Ch'en Lu and a personal representative of Premier Tuan approached the American Chargé MacMurray with the question of China's participation, but MacMurray's reply was noncommittal. In Washington, Minister Koo again and again assured the State Department that his government had every wish to cooperate with the American government and follow any policy it might outline, but could get no satisfactory reply. The reason for Washington's attitude was simple. Japan had proved to be unwilling to accept the frame of reference with regard to the Vladivostok intervention, and had spoken openly of the need to occupy the Trans-Siberian Railway as far as Karymskaia. Chinese participation could only compound the problem of restraining the Japanese in view of the Sino-Japanese pact, and result in Japanese occupation of the Chinese Eastern Railway.[35]

Finally, on July 29, Acting Secretary of State Polk instructed Ambassador Morris in Tokyo to state to Foreign Minister Gotō that in view of the Chinese wish to participate and Japan's favorable consideration of such participation, it was

> most logical and proper that some Chinese military activity should be exerted in controlling that part of the Trans-Siberian Railway within Manchuria without interference from any of the governments participating in the Siberian enterprise. As that is Chinese soil and as the Chinese Government desires to take a part in the undertaking it is felt that she should be allowed to play this specific part and that a small contingent of Chinese troops be in addition added to the international force at Vladivostok.

The American move was well thought out for, if accepted, it would have precluded the stationing of Japanese troops along the Chinese Eastern Railway as well as undercut Japan's second expedition to Transbaikalia. Gotō told Morris he did not think the Chinese would prove effective in helping the Czechs but he and his colleagues wished to act in full accord with American views. Morris reported to Washington his impression was that the Japanese government would agree to use only Chinese troops in Manchuria. He had failed to see the evasive nature of Gotō's reply.[36]

Japan could still circumvent the American proposal by

means of the Sino-Japanese pact. She therefore pressed the Tuan Cabinet to associate itself with a Japanese intervention, separate from the Vladivostok venture. The distinction between the two was that one was directed at Transbaikalia for the purpose of common Sino-Japanese national defense, and the other, an inter-Allied undertaking directed at Vladivostok, was for the purpose of rescuing the Czechs. The approach of the Tuan Cabinet to the choice of either course was typically opportunistic in that it decided to continue cooperation with Japan, reap the benefits, but get America's countervailing influence to check her. To understand why the Tuan Ch'i-jui clique gave in to the activation of the pact, one need only note what it had at stake. At this time, negotiations were underway which resulted in a contract, signed on July 31, for a supply of arms worth about ¥25,000,000; an agreement, signed on August 2, for a loan of ¥30,000,000 for gold mining and forestry in Heilungkiang and Kirin; a loan for Sino-Japanese joint defense of ¥20,000,000, another loan for four railways in south Manchuria and eastern Inner Mongolia, yet another for two extensions of the Shantung railway—all of which were signed on September 28. On this last date, too, the cabinet carried out the notorious exchange of notes, in which it 'gladly' agreed to Japan's terms concerning the Shantung question, apparently as one of the conditions for the foregoing loans.[37] Opportunism resulted in China's participation in the American-proposed Vladivostok intervention and acquiescence in Japan's unilateral expedition without actual participation in it.

On July 26, clearly acting in accordance with the terms of the pact, Major General Saitō wrote to War Minister Tuan Chih-kuei, on behalf of the Japanese Army General Staff, that the Japanese government had accepted the American invitation to join in the Siberian intervention but expected to send another force soon for the purpose of joint Sino-Japanese defense. The latter expedition being in accord with the Sino-Japanese pact, he asked that the two military commands agree to devise plans and send troops jointly when the opportune moment arose. The size of the Chinese contingent, wrote Saitō, was immaterial. The next day, War Minister Tuan sent a laconic reply: 'The Chinese supreme command expresses agreement to the proposal of the Japanese supreme command'.[38] The next step then was for the two sides to work out the detailed arrangements as Saitō's letter requested, but the Chinese did nothing.

On August 8, Minister Hayashi spoke to Premier Tuan about the 'dangerous' situation at Manchouli—whither the Red Guards had pursued the Semenovites—and asked if he would consent to a joint dispatch of troops. Tuan replied that, since there was a defensive alliance, he would of course agree 'whenever the situation calls for it'.[39]

Again, nothing happened. Then, on August 11, Minister Hayashi called a Wai-chiao Pu functionary to the legation and asked him to apprise the premier of Japan's decision to move troops from south Manchuria on August 13. Premier Tuan immediately replied that the decision was too sudden, and asked for a few days' delay in order that the local authorities could be forewarned and the necessary preparations carried out. The Japanese postponed the dispatch until August 15. On that day, the Seventh Division of 12,000 of the Kwantung Army at Liaoyang started moving north. In no time Japanese troops occupied the Harbin-Manchouli section, forcing out the Chinese guards, taking over their barracks, and mounting guard at key installations along the railway. The uninformed Kirin and Heilungkiang officials were taken by complete surprise, and showered the center with angry reports and protests.[40]

Later, pleading to the Americans as the wronged party, the Chinese claimed that they had never received an official notification of Japan's dispatch of troops. However, both Major General Saitō and Minister Hayashi had done just that. In fact, Saitō had written to War Minister Tuan Chih-kuei again on August 12 to say the Kwantung governor generalcy would send to Manchouli one infantry brigade of its Seventh Division to render protection to Japanese residents there and prepare for future military operations, and another infantry brigade to join up with Chinese troops in guarding vital technical installations of the Harbin-Changchun and Harbin-Manchouli sections of the railway.

Saitō's letter had perturbed War Minister Tuan because the proposal plainly went beyond the military agreement.

Notwithstanding the pledge to respect China's territorial sovereignty, the Japanese forces were rendering protection to Japanese residents, and notwithstanding the clause that the existing agreements on the Chinese Eastern Railway would be respected the Japanese were taking over the guarding of the railway. In his reply of August 14, Tuan expressed agreement to the dispatch of troops but took exception to the above two aspects.[41] But, as in her dealings with Washington, Japan began moving troops while both sides were still in the midst of discussions. The differences were ironed out at two meetings on August 19 and 23 between Saitō and the Chinese War Ministry. In the end, it was agreed that Japanese troops should not take up guard duties for the railway, or assume the right to render protection to Japanese nationals. The Chinese accepted the *fait accompli* of Japanese troops having entered north Manchuria but maintained that as far as they were concerned, they did not think that the time had come to commence joint defense, and would not take part in the Japanese expedition.[42]

Meanwhile, the issue came to a head between Tokyo and Washington. In order to neutralize American opposition, Foreign Minister Gotō had told Ambassador Morris that his government was concerned about the recent defeat of the Semenovites and the invasion of Chinese territory by the Bolsheviks organized by German prisoners. 'After consulting with the Chinese Government', his government had decided to send a Japanese force to Manchouli, since a part of that city was being bombarded by the enemy forces and the Chinese troops quartered there were very weak and even having friendly intercourse with them. 'The movement of Japanese troops within Chinese territory was effected only with the consent and agreement of China. . . . Consequently, it is entirely different in nature from the present joint intervention in Vladivostok . . . and the only nations that have interests involved are Japan and China'.[43] The Japanese ambassador in Washington also informed the State Department that the dispatch of troops was 'actuated solely by the spirit of harmonious cooperation between Japan and China', that the Japanese government would 'scrupulously respect the sovereignty of China as well as the rights and interests of the local population'.[44]

From the Chinese, the State Department received diametrically opposite reports. They denied that the Bolsheviks had made any military encroachments on Chinese territory or bombarded Manchouli. They declared China had not been consulted by Japan under the terms of the military convention.[45] Secretary of State Lansing then confronted the Japanese ambassador with Koo's statements. The Japanese ambassador assured him that Japan had gained Peking's consent.[46]

Angry and embarrassed, the Japanese demanded that Koo be instructed to correct himself. In a subsequent telegram to Koo, the Wai-chiao Pu explained rather incoherently the source of the controversy. The gist of it was that China had decided to accept the Japanese dispatch as a *fait accompli*, give *post facto* recognition to the activation of the pact in the hope that it would have the effect of circumscribing Japanese activity within Chinese territory.[47]

On August 27, believing that north Manchuria would survive the crisis, Premier Tuan instructed the local officials to quieten down, and to promote cordial and harmonious relations with the Japanese troops.[48]

Thus, the Chinese associated themselves with the inter-Allied intervention by sending 1,600 combat men. These entered the Maritime Province at the end of August and were to remain in the Nikol'sk-Ussuriisk and Khabarovsk area until the spring of 1920, as China's token participation in the Allied cause.[49] In the growing American-Japanese tensions which colored the whole Siberian Intervention, they stood conveniently in between.

The development in north Manchuria added to the numerous distressing problems which confronted the American government in the wake of its decision to intervene. Throughout the fall and winter months, the Americans groped for an effective remedy. Two approaches were attempted. One was to quarter American troops in Harbin or some similar place on the Chinese Eastern Railway instead of Vladivostok. When the Tuan Cabinet was asked to give its consent, its official reply was that since the railway was being used by all Allied forces for a purpose in which the Chinese government was also associated, it had no objection. Unofficially, the Wai-chiao Pu said that the Chinese government 'not only consented but heartily welcomed the presence of American troops in the railway zone, although it feared that any expression of that sort might be resented by Japan'. The obstacle turned out to be a practical one of accommodating the troops, as all the barracks and troop accommodation east of Irkutsk had been occupied by the Japanese.[50]

The other approach, less direct in restraining Japan but in the end more effective, was a proposal to put the entire Trans-Siberian Railway, including the Chinese Eastern, under the control of the Russian Railway Corps. The Corps, which was a group of American railway experts led by John F. Stevens, had been organized in June 1917 at the request of the Kerensky government to help Russia reorganize and operate the chaotic Trans-Siberian system. Some of the men were employed at Harbin as railway instructors by Horvath, who was trying to keep a distance between himself and the Japanese. Washington justified its proposal by the fact that the Corps was maintained from funds previously set aside by the Kerensky government and the railway experts were solely motivated by service to the Russian people.

When the plan was placed before the Peking government, War Minister Tuan Chih-kuei's views prevailed. He argued that the Chinese Eastern Railway, being a Sino-Russian joint enterprise, should not be put in the same category as the rest of the Trans-Siberian system. Moreover, China could not very well accede to the American proposal after it had insisted to Japan that the existing agreement governing its operation and protection should be respected. Only recently he had rejected Saitō's proposal for joint protection by the two countries' forces. As a result, although Foreign Minister Lu had appeared very favorably impressed by the American proposal and promised to urge it upon the cabinet, no reply was ever given.[51]

Meanwhile, the American proposal was modified in the course of consultations with the British and French, and long altercations with Japan. The resulting agreement, signed on January 9, 1919, put general supervision of the railways in the zone of military operations under an inter-Allied Commission. Under that Commission were instituted two inter-

Allied committees. One, called the Technical Board and consisting of railway experts of the nations having military forces in Siberia, was to administer technical and economic management of all railways in the military zone. The other, called Military Transportation Board, was to coordinate military transportation under the instruction of the proper military authorities. The former, based in Harbin, was presided over by Stevens; the latter, based in Vladivostok, was headed by a Japanese. It was also agreed that each power should control different sections of the railways, and that the commission should function until the withdrawal of all Allied forces, at which time the railways were to revert to their rightful owner.[52]

The Chinese Eastern Railway was then fitted into the scheme by an invitation to China to join the commission. But the Chinese government agreed to participate only on its own terms: the railway, being in Chinese territory, should be managed by China herself and the Chinese Eastern Railway should be guarded by Chinese troops. Further American appeals for international control of the railway, as the only safeguard against seizure by Japan, were of no avail.[53]

The Inter-Allied Technical Board was instituted on March 9, 1919, and during the next three crucial years served as a watchdog against Japanese seizure of the Chinese Eastern Railway.

4

Official Nationalism:
Amur River Navigation

The present and following three chapters are devoted to discussing the transformation of Imperial Russia's possessions in
China wrought by China in the wake of the fall of Russian
power. For two decades Chinese officialdom and public had
been harboring lively feelings of resentment, particularly towards Russia and Japan. Unlike other imperialist powers,
Russia and Japan held territorial ambitions and, in the face of a
rising Chinese nationalism, had been prepared to use force to
achieve their ends. Against these two powers the official policy of balancing them against each other had proved to be
particularly disastrous; their capacity to cooperate to China's
disadvantage came to be firmly fixed in official thinking.
Chinese anti-imperialist sentiment specifically towards Russia
developed early and intensified at each successive outburst.
The anti-Russian feeling engendered by the Ili crisis in 1879-81
was one of the earliest manifestations of Chinese nationalism.
It erupted again at the time of the Russian occupation of
Manchuria in 1902-3 and again at the announcement of the
Russo-Mongolian Treaty of 1912.

Russia's distraction with revolution and civil war was an
opportunity too good to miss. The Chinese government
seized it eagerly, anxious because Japan too aspired to the
Russian possessions, and with a particularly sweet vengeance.

The assault against Russia's rights and interests was clearly nationalistic in motivation, carried out by the government in the name of the recovery of sovereign rights. It was directed against Russia's monopoly of navigation of the Amur River system, her protectorship of Outer Mongolia, her quasi-colonial domain in north Manchuria, and her extraterritorial privilege and concession territories. The changes were carried out as part of a broad strategy in future negotiations with Russia. The Chinese expected the new regime in Russia to seek official recognition by China, at which time they intended to trade *de jure* recognition for Russian acceptance of the *faits accomplis*.

That the official government of Warlord China was capable of what may be called official nationalism in its foreign policies is seldom appreciated. There are several explanations for this. The period was not particularly distinguished in the recovery of sovereign rights; marked gains came later, largely the work of the Kuomintang. Peking seemed like a nominal capital while real power resided in the hands of the warlords. The warlords who were big enough to dominate and thereby limit the power of the government were for the most part ambitious, self-interested men. They were motivated primarily by the short-term consideration of self-preservation in a highly competitive situation and were generally impervious to such abstract ideals as national interests. To a certain extent, this image of the warlord-government relationship is true; the warlords more often than not impeded rather than supported nationalistic endeavors by others, especially when their local interests were at stake. The government's success in rights recovery varied from case to case and one of the determining factors was the degree of cooperation it could get when needed from any of the warlords.

But it would be wrong to suppose that the government was totally powerless or incompetent in conducting foreign relations. Indeed, when it came to foreign affairs, the warlords displayed considerable self-restraint. The contending warlords sought control of the official apparatus of government for the advantages it could bring, particularly the legitimacy conferred upon their power by virtue of the Peking government's being recognized by the foreign powers as

China's legal government. The desire to retain foreign recognition for the government proved strong enough to deter them from excessive interference in the operations of the Wai-chiao Pu so that it would be able to conduct relations to the satisfaction of the foreign powers. Moreover, they seemed to realize that foreign affairs, being too complicated, were best left to the experts.

Two important consequences flowed from this unique position of the Wai-chiao Pu. It was one of the few government departments left with any substantive national functions. The foreign ministers and their subordinates were permitted to function to the best of their ability as nearly independent experts of foreign relations. Hence, in the words of one scholar, they were 'the most successful civilian leaders in China, who, through their adroit exploiting of the international balance of power and current world sympathies, were able to achieve results completely out of proportion to the power of China'.[1]

The other consequence was that some of the best talents were attracted to fill various positions within the Wai-chiao Pu and abroad. For instance, the four main figures, Lu Cheng-hsiang, Ch'en Lu, Yen Hui-ch'ing, and Ku Wei-chün (Wellington V.K. Koo), who were successively foreign ministers from 1917 to 1924, were outstanding civilian leaders.[2] Lu had been a foreign affairs expert of proven ability since 1892, having served as foreign minister from the founding of the Chinese Republic. Ch'en, Yen, and Koo had all been trained as experts of legal studies abroad and had had long diplomatic experience before leading the Wai-chiao Pu. Although personal connection with warlord cliques cannot be ruled out altogether in one or two cases, it appears to have been secondary to their expertise as the criterion of their appointment. Indeed, it may be because they were non-partisan, in addition to being foreign affairs experts, that they were repeatedly called upon to officiate as premier before a suitable candidate, conforming to a new power situation, could be agreed upon. These men, along with the representatives abroad, were the bearers of nationalism within the establishment. More than anyone else, they were keenly aware of China's weakness as a nation among nations, simply from the day-to-day running of the foreign ministry, or from being representatives posted overseas. They were the natural advocates of rights recovery.

The nature of their work and the enormity of the task of restoring full sovereignty to China produced an outlook in the official nationalists which put a distance between them and the leaders of popular nationalism. The popular nationalists were impatient to revolutionize the existing order overnight by a mighty effort of human will. The official nationalists had no alternative but to accept the concerted insistence of the foreign powers that the relinquishment of special privileges and interests be carried out within the framework of orderly, scheduled change. Thus, tariff autonomy was predicated upon fiscal reforms, and the abolition of extraterritoriality upon judicial reforms. This was to put the government in a dilemma: internal disunity and instability made reforms painfully slow and impractical, while the popular nationalists passed from impatience to acts of violence, which in turn made the foreign powers even more reluctant to review their treaties.

Where the opportunity existed, as in the case of attacking Russian interests and rights, the official nationalists were able to demonstrate what they were capable of. Although their effort was never given any public approbation, it is important to examine each area of rights recovery in turn in order to show that in the Sino-Soviet Treaty of 1924 China received nothing that the official nationalists had not securely recovered during the brief interval of the fall and rise of Russian power in China.

The Amur River system began assuming a peculiar importance only at the beginning of the twentieth century as access waterways to the immensely rich Manchurian heartlands and the Russian side of the river basin. Up to 1917 Imperial Russia had treated the river system, except for the Sungari tributary which flowed entirely within Chinese territory, as her national waters. Her three shipping agencies—the Chinese Eastern Railway shipping department, the Amur Railway shipping department, and the Amur commercial shipping company—monopolized commercial shipping on the river system. By 1917 these had built up a fleet of

262 steamships and 300 lighters, as an important auxiliary to rail transport. Chinese vessels were to be found only in the Sungari, where they numbered no more than 10 per cent of the vessels sailing on that river.[3]

The antecedents of the navigation question can be traced to the Aigun Treaty of 1858 and the Peking Convention of 1860, both extracted by Russia while China was at war with Britain and France. The Aigun Treaty made the Amur River the boundary between Russia and China and restricted navigation of the common river to the subjects of both nations. But two years later, China ceded the land east of the Ussuri to Russia and thereby transformed the Lower Amur into a Russian waterway. Until the turn of the century, China assumed that her right of navigation of the Lower Amur was guaranteed by the Aigun Treaty. Russia on her part did not formally insist on her advantage since the Sungari was analogous to the Lower Amur. Hence, in the St Petersburg Treaty of 1881, the right of the subjects of both countries to navigate and trade on the Amur, the Ussuri, and the Sungari was reaffirmed. But the treaty also stipulated that navigation be regulated by a detailed agreement to be worked out later. Owing to Russia's deliberate design and China's lack of interest in shipping, this was never carried out. Consequently, Russia undertook the administration of the river system, installing navigational facilities on the Chinese side of the river without even consulting the Ch'ing government.[4]

Navigation became an issue for the first time in 1908 when Russia used the absence of a regulating instrument as an excuse to refuse permission for Chinese merchant ships to sail on the Amur. She asked China to pay half the cost of the facilities, but the amount was set to discourage Chinese navigation altogether. She also demanded that Chinese vessels allowed on the Amur follow Russian regulations, which China rejected as tantamount to recognition of the river as Russia's national waterway. When the question was raised again in 1915 after China's capitulation to Japan's various demands the Russian attitude was even more rigid. The Russian minister refused to discuss navigation or any other question unless Russia received concessions in north Manchuria commensurate with those given to Japan in the south. Two weeks before the Bolshevik seizure of power, Prince Kudashev still insisted on these terms.[5]

The October Revolution had the effect of undermining Russian domination of the river system by the civil war that ensued in the Amur basin. The Chinese were quick to seize the opportunity of gaining control of the river, being anxious also to forestall the entry of Japan's influence. With official encouragement, the Chinese business community in Manchuria began to show an interest in shipping. When the sailing season opened in spring 1918, therefore, the situation on the Amur was completely different from before. Blagoveshchensk, Khabarovsk, and Harbin, the three wintering ports for Russian vessels, were under Bolshevik, White Guard, and Chinese control, respectively. The Bolshevik's attempt to seize the vessels forced their owners to flee to Harbin and offer them for sale. Half a dozen Chinese shipping companies mushroomed overnight. The largest, the Wu-t'ung, eventually acquired about 40 per cent of all Russian ships in the Amur.[6]

Official backing was obviously crucial if the opportunity of recovering the right of navigation was to be translated into reality. In May 1918, on the initiative of General Pao Kuei-ch'ing of Heilungkiang, the Peking government decided to make financial loans available to Chinese merchant groups interested in forming shipping companies and purchasing Russian vessels, to resume negotiations with the Russian minister for a regulating instrument, and to institute a river defense force of gunboats and patrol launches.[7]

The Wai-chiao Pu found Prince Kudashev as rigid as before. While prepared to lift the wartime ban on sale of vessels in order to prevent them from falling into Japanese hands, he adamantly refused to permit Chinese vessels on the Amur, declaring he no longer possessed the authority to discuss the question. The Bolsheviks in Blagoveshchensk who controlled the middle and upper courses of the river, on the other hand, were anxious to conciliate the Chinese. Motivated by their struggle against the White Guards and the desire for shipments of supplies from Manchuria, they gladly entered into an agreement in May 1918 with the Wai-chiao Pu commissioner at Heiho, Chang Shou-tseng. The agreement permitted Chinese vessels on the Amur, exempt from Russian inspection though subject to Russian regulations in Russian ports. In the same month, the first Chinese ship, the *Ch'ing Lan* of the Heilungkiang postal bureau, steamed out of the Sungari and proceeded upstream to Heiho. It was followed by other vessels, plying the middle and upper courses until the river froze again in late November.[8]

When the Amur reopened for navigation in May 1919, the situation was again different. The Bolsheviks had gone underground. The Allied intervention in Siberia was in progress. The area east of Lake Baikal was under the authority of General Horvath at Vladivostok as supreme plenipotentiary of Kolchak's All-Siberian Government at Omsk. Chinese vessels were still free to sail on the Amur but faced a new threat from the Japanese. The Japanese had seized and armed several Russian vessels and were sailing them under their own flag, ignoring Horvath's demand for them to be handed over.[9]

To counter the threat, the Peking government redoubled its effort of organizing a river defense force. In July, 1919, the cruiser *Chiang Heng*, accompanied by the three gunboats, *Li Yüan*, *Li Chieh*, and *Li Ch'uan*, all fitted with new cannons, steamed north to Vladivostok as the first stop in the journey to the Amur and the Sungari. The enterprise was directed by Wang Ts'ung-wen as head of the newly organized Kirin-Heilungkiang river defense bureau (Chi-Hei chiang-fang ts'ou-pei ch'u).[10]

Simultaneously, the Wai-chiao Pu renewed its pressure on the Omsk government and its representatives in Peking and Vladivostok for an agreement guaranteeing the right of Chinese vessels to use the Lower Amur. The Russians, standing on solid legal grounds, argued that neither the existing treaties nor international practice entitled Chinese warships to navigate in Russian national waters. They also confided their fear that acceding to China's wishes might make it difficult to resist a similar demand from Japan which also wanted free navigation of the Amur. No amount of Chinese pressure therefore could change the Russian attitude.[11]

The naval minister, Liu Kuan-hsiung, meanwhile grew impatient and ordered the river defense force to proceed north forthwith. As it was merely passing through, he said, he saw no reason why any difficulty should arise. General Pao, too, was insistent that China seize the rare opportunity of recovering the right of navigation. Since the government had raised the question, it could not back down without losing face and admitting it did not possess the right.[12]

On August 20, amidst Russian threats of violence, the four vessels sailed north, tailed by four Japanese torpedoboats, apparently intent on following the Chinese into the Amur. After four days, they anchored at an island in the Tartar Strait, still 200 km from the mouth of the Amur, short of provisions and too small to withstand the high autumn winds and isolated from relief. There they waited while Chinese officials elsewhere pleaded with the Russians for the vessels to be allowed to take shelter at Nikolaevsk. Kolchak's government finally assented on September 17, on humanitarian grounds, but warned the Chinese against proceeding further beyond Nikolaevsk.[13]

But the Chinese were intent on pressing on to the ultimate objective. The military attaché at Omsk, Major General Chang Ssu-lin, advised Peking that the river defense force should continue its journey since Kolchak's authority was quite ineffective in the Far East. The Wai-chiao Pu was unsure but exhausted by long and fruitless arguments with Russian officials. Wang Ts'ung-wen was in favor of pushing on and Naval Minister Liu Kuan-hsiung left the matter to his discretion. The final decision to proceed into the Amur was made by the commanders of the four vessels. Leaving the battered *Li Ch'uan* behind, the rest set out on October 18, expecting to reach Khabarovsk in a week. On the night of October 25, they were fired upon by one of Kalmykov's Ussuri Cossack units and were forced back to Nikolaevsk.[14]

While the drama of the river defense force unfolded, another vessel, the *Nan Hsiang* of the Wu-t'ung Company, tried to sail on the Lower Amur from upstream. Protracted altercations finally led Kolchak to make an exception because the ship was carrying food supplies to Nikolaevsk. In late September, the *Nan Hsiang* made its historic journey downstream but on its way back it was waylaid by scores of Russians in civilian clothes and fired upon. The ship made it back to Khabarovsk but the battle for the right of navigation of the Lower Amur had ended ingloriously.[15]

The position of the Omsk government on Chinese navigation of the Lower Amur was that war vessels were barred totally, but commercial shipping would be permitted provided a suitable agreement was signed. The Wai-chiao Pu was reconciled to the reality of international law, although the more extreme view that Chinese war vessels had the right of way on the Lower Amur was held by many in the government. The Russians were ready to enter into a conference on navigation in July 1919 and then procrastinated because of the controversy over the Chinese river defense force. The conference was overtaken by political changes in Siberia early in February 1920 when the socialists drove out the White Guards and set up a local government in Blagoveshchensk and Vladivostok. In March, the commissar for navigation in the Blagoveshchensk government offered to negotiate on commercial shipping, but the Wai-chiao Pu felt constrained to let the opportunity pass in view of the international agitation over the Karakhan Manifesto.[16]

The prospects of China's river defense were not improved by the political changes in Siberia. The Vladivostok government consented in March 1920 to the passage of the four vessels to their destination, but on humanitarian grounds only. It made clear that neither the existing treaties nor international law gave Chinese war vessels the right of way and that its consent was not to be used as a precedent.[17] In the same month, a massacre of Japanese residents by Bolshevik partisans occurred in Nikolaevsk and the Japanese retaliated by seizing control of the Lower Amur. The four ill-starred vessels were detained for allegedly abetting the Bolsheviks until late in the sailing season when they were permitted to proceed upstream.[18]

Thus, up to 1920, Chinese naval vessels were allowed into the Amur but once. Commercial shipping continued without prospering for lack of a firm basis. The middle and upper courses of the Amur, common to both countries, were still accessible on the strength of the provisional agreement of May 1918 with the Blagoveshchensk Bolsheviks. But, without a permanent agreement, there was always the danger that one spring the Russians might block Chinese vessels on the Sungari from entering the Amur. This was precisely what happened in 1923 and the problem of navigation was added to the numerous issues for Sino-Soviet diplmacy.

5

China's Recovery of Outer Mongolia

Next to Manchuria, Outer Mongolia was the most important area of Sino-Russian relations. The boundary between the two empires fixed by the Treaty of Nerchinsk (1689) cut through Mongol lands, separating the Transbaikal Buryats from their cultural cousins the Khalkhas. Until the beginning of the twentieth century, Russian contact with Outer Mongolia was largely commercial. The Kiakhta Treaty (1727) funneled trade through the border town Mai-mai-ch'eng, and new treaties in the nineteenth century opened up more trading centers. Since Imperial Russia was fully occupied in central and northeast Asia, her political interest in Outer Mongolia developed comparatively late.

But there was another reason for the delay. In Outer Mongolia Russia was not only dealing with China but with the Mongols as well. As she was already experiencing difficulties with the nationalistic Buryats within her own borders, she was concerned that intruding herself into Outer Mongolia might fuel the very flame of Pan-Mongolism which she was seeking to contain.

Ironically, it was China's measures taken in response to the spread of Russian power north of her borderlands that precipitated the favorable circumstances for a forward Russian policy in Outer Mongolia. Until the end of the nineteenth century, the Manchu government's main concern was to preserve Outer Mongolia as a buffer without disturbing its internal feudal order. The Manchu court conferred on the Mongol nobility titles and seals of office, allotted retainers and gifts in return for tribute; and it was represented by the military governors at Uliasutai and Kobdo, and the imperial agent at Urga.[1]

This policy of benevolent non-interference was reversed at the turn of the century when the Manchu government carried out a vigorous program of Sinicization. It promoted colonization, introduced Chinese administration, garrisoned troops, and expanded trade and agriculture. This in turn produced a response among the Mongols of Inner and Outer Mongolia similar to that of the Buryats to Russification. Nationalism was particularly strong in Inner Mongolia, the first area to be absorbed into the Chinese provincial administrations.

In Outer Mongolia, resentment against Sinicization and indebtedness to Chinese traders led many to espouse separatism as an escape. The religious primate at Urga, the Jebtsun-damba Khutukhtu, became the unifying symbol of resistance against the Chinese. And the lamas and princes decided as early as July 1911 to turn to Russia for aid and protection for the political independence that they intended to establish. Although Russia immediately supplied some arms, she was not enthusiastic about Outer Mongolian independence for reasons of her own. The scheme was fraught with international complications and ran contrary to Russia's desire to keep the region as her special preserve. Besides, the independence of the Mongols was liable to encourage Buryat separatism.

In November 1911, when China was preoccupied with the republican revolution, the Outer Mongolian lamas and princes nevertheless declared independence, and enthroned the Jebtsun-damba as the Bogdo-gegen or king. They were joined by Inner Mongolian dissidents and those of Hulunbuir. The Manchu imperial agent fled from his post as did the military governor of Uliasutai together with his garrison. The garrison at Kobdo resisted briefly but it too withdrew into Sinkiang after a ceasefire mediated by the Russians. The Manchu authorities in Hulunbuir were similarly expelled. Only the Inner Mongolian malcontents were eventually suppressed by the Chinese. The opportunity was thrust upon Russia to implant her influence at little cost to herself when Outer Mongolia sought her protectorship.

Russia promptly seized the opportunity, firstly, by sorting out Mongol lands into more precise spheres of influence with Japan. The Russo-Japanese Convention of 1912 marked out eastern Inner Mongolia as Japan's sphere, and all the rest as Russia's. Next, she signed the Russo-Mongolian Treaty of November 3, 1912, whereby she defined the extent of her assistance and what she expected in return. She pledged to assist Outer Mongolia to maintain its autonomous, not independent, regime, its right to have a national army, and 'to admit neither the presence of Chinese troops in its territory nor the colonization of its land by the Chinese'. In a special protocol, Russian subjects gained the right to reside and move freely in Outer Mongolia, to engage in industrial, commercial and other business, to import and export without duties every kind of product of the soil and industry of Russia, Outer Mongolia, China, and other countries. They could lease or own land for cultivation and business purposes.

Applying the techniques of political penetration that had proved successful in Manchuria, the Russians obtained allotments of land, called 'factories'. These were located at the seats of Russian consulates or centers of Russian trade and residence, and came under the exclusive control of the consuls or heads of business enterprises. A system of joint jurisdiction similar to the one in the Chinese Eastern Railway Zone was applied to Russians, Mongols, and Chinese.[2] Later, Russia received from Outer Mongolia a pledge to consult her on railroad construction and accept her assistance, and a concession to build a telegraph line between Monda and Uliasutai.[3]

The Russo-Mongolian Treaty of 1912 was followed by the Sino-Russian Treaty of November 5, 1913, and the tripartite Kiakhta Convention of June 7, 1915.[4] Under these agreements, Russia recognized China's suzerainty in Outer Mongolia, and China recognized the autonomy of Outer Mongolia. Russia and China agreed not to garrison troops in Outer Mongolia, intervene in its internal administration, or colonize its land. All matters of a political and territorial nature were to be decided by all three parties concerned.

The Khalkhas not only failed to achieve an independent state embracing all Mongol speaking areas, but had to be satisfied with a reduced territory. Autonomous Mongolia comprised only the regions previously under the jurisdiction of the Manchu imperial agent at Urga and the military governors of Uliasutai and Kobdo, that is, 'the limits of the banners of the four aimaks of Khalkha and of the district of Kobdo'. Excluded were Hulunbuir, Inner Mongolia, the Altai district, Tannu Uryanghai, and of course Buryat Mongolia.

Russia, the honest broker, came into possession of a protectorate politically and economically amenable to her influence. She next proceeded to control Pan-Mongolism and detach portions of Mongol land of particular interest to herself. Hulunbuir was organized by arrangement with China into a special district, a kind of Sino–Russian condominium.[5] The Altai district was occupied by Russian troops in February 1914.[6] Tannu Uryanghai was declared a protectorate of Russia in the same year, and completely barred to Chinese commerce.[7]

The party that lost most was clearly China. Everything she retained was of a purely ceremonial nature. The Chinese president conferred on the Jebtsun-damba his title. Chinese suzerainty was represented by a tu-hu shih (high commissioner) at Urga, who occupied the first place of honor on all ceremonial or official occasions. He was entitled to a military escort of 200, and each of his assistants at Uliasutai, Kobdo and Mai-mai-ch'eng allowed fifty each. (The Russian consul was allowed 150, and each vice consul fifty.) Chinese subjects were put in an inferior position since, unlike Russian, they were required to pay taxes on trade in Outer Mongolia.

Before Russia could consolidate her position in Outer Mongolia, however, she became preoccupied with the war in Europe, and then with her internal upheaval. The Chinese almost immediately reestablished their economic dominance. The autonomous government at Urga could not be made viable overnight. Its financial problem was not overcome by Russian loans, and its military weakness not altered by Russian advice. Politically, a self-reliant viable Mongolian regime required the Khalkhas to make the transition from feudalism to some form of centralized state. This was impeded by the conflict of interests between the secular nobility and the lama hierarchy, which intensified as the lamas pushed harder for centralism.

At first, despite disappointment of the hopes for an independent Pan-Mongolist state, the larger part of the ruling stratum seemed reconciled to a smaller autonomous entity. Supporters of autonomy included the Jebtsun-damba, his influential wife, three of the four *aimak* khans (Sain Noyan, Tushetu, and Tsetsen), and much of the religious hierarchy and the secular nobility. These faced only a sprinkling of opponents, such as the Jasaktu Khan, certain high religious figures, and some lay nobility, who were less anti-Chinese and more anti-Russian. The alliance of the religious and secular hierarchies produced a fairly effective central government at Urga for a time. Under the Jebtsun-damba, a council of ministers of six portfolios functioned like a European-type cabinet. Effective leadership was provided by the Sain Noyan Khan, a staunch advocate of autonomy, who had risen to the top after liquidating his rivals the Jasaktu Khan and the Tushetu Khan in 1915. The *khoshun* (sub-*aimak*) princes, of whom there were slightly over 100, were given a voice on important matters by the institution of a *khuraldan* (congress). The Jebtsun-damba retained supreme control by the power of sanctioning the decisions of both the council of ministers and the *khuraldan*.

The October Revolution in Russia had the immediate impact of depriving Autonomous Mongolia of Russian protection. The ruling alliance of secular and religious hierarchies began to shift, and the supporters of autonomy dwindled to the lamaist hierarchy, plus a few lay aristocrats holding powerful positions in the Urga government. The majority of the secular nobility, on the other hand, had become increasingly disgruntled by lamaist encroachments of their traditional prerogatives. They began 'looking inwards' to China, ready to sacrifice autonomy as a means of overthrowing lama power. This polarization between the secular 'black' clique and the ecclesiastical 'yellow' clique was to culminate in an open struggle for power in the summer of 1919.

With the waning of Russian power, the Outer Mongolian vacuum began to attract many competing external influences. The Bolsheviks sought a foothold there as part of their civil war strategy; the Chinese endeavored to recover lost rights; the Japanese worked for an 'Asian' Mongolia barred against Western influence; and the White Guards sought control of the region by riding on the crest of Pan-Mongolism.

First of the external pressures came from the Bolsheviks who, before the Siberian Intervention, tried to gain control of Outer Mongolia in order to forestall a flank attack by anti-Soviet elements. In February 1918 they were voted into power at Kiakhta by the municipal council, and Russians with property hastily moved across the border to Mai-mai-ch'eng for protection.

In Peking, the situation in Outer Mongolia was not immediately seen as an opportunity of reasserting lost rights. Rather, the prevailing mood was fear of a Soviet-German thrust. The situation called for a dispatch of Chinese troops which automatically put the Kiakhta Convention in abeyance. Although Russian power was gone and the Urga government was vulnerable, the Chinese government nevertheless felt it wise to have full consultations with the Urga leadership first. Hence, on February 14, 1918, the Wai-chiao Pu instructed the tu-hu shih at Urga to discover whether the autonomous government had any concrete plans to meet the threat from the north, and whether it was willing to accept more Chinese troops on Peking's assurance of their prompt withdrawal at the end of the crisis. Ch'en I found the Mongol leaders distinctly cool to the proposal. They preferred to rely on their own troops for the time being, and Ch'en I advised the Wai-chiao Pu that Mongol distrust of China was strong and it would be unwise to insist.[8]

In the next few months, the situation in the northern border area became more critical. Early in April, a detachment of 300 Red Guards occupied Kiakhta and began making demands on Urga. They wanted the diplomatic representatives of the old regime expelled and their own accepted. They also asked for the arms of the Russian community in Mai-mai-ch'eng to be handed over. The council of ministers at Urga was deadlocked over whether to treat with the Bolsheviks or not. In the end, with Ch'en I's quiet prompting, the Jebtsun-damba decided against it.

The Mongols possessed at the time a Russian-trained army of about 4,000, quartered in the four *aimaks*. According to Ch'en I, no more than 500 of them were suitably equipped for combat. Still, Urga would not ask for more Chinese troops. When Ch'en I renewed his suggestion in mid-April, he was told the matter was for the Russians to decide. Both the Russian minister in Peking and the consul at Urga were alarmed by the Bolshevik threat, but they were loath to allow the slightest modification of the Kiakhta Convention.[9]

It was not until May when the Russian civil war began spilling over the Mongolian border that the Russian minister Prince Kudashev and Consul Orlov became resigned to an increase of Chinese troops and the Urga government accepted the Chinese offer. Even so, Urga was only prepared to accept one battalion for the time being, on Ch'en I's guarantee of good conduct and subsequent withdrawal of the troops. As part of the bargain, Peking also made a loan to Urga.[10] Typically, the dispatch of troops by Peking became bogged down over whose troops were to be sent. The military governor of Chahar was willing to put two battalions at a point far away from the critical border area, to be used as reserves only. Eventually, the military governor of Suiyuan made available a cavalry unit of 500. When this unit, commanded by Kao Tsai-t'ien, reached Urga in mid-September, the Allied intervention had driven the Bolsheviks underground, Kiakhta had been occupied by Semenov's troops, and Tannu Uryanghai by those of the Omsk government. The Russian minister was not without reason when he questioned the necessity of the dispatch.[11]

Urga's acceptance of the Chinese cavalry battalion was the thin edge of a wedge with which Peking could pry Outer Mongolia open to Chinese influence. The circumstances were propitious: the Russians were preoccupied with civil war and foreign intervention, and more and more Mongol leaders were 'looking inward' to China. Yet it was not till the beginning of 1919 that the Peking government began seizing the opportunity. The delay was due to political changes in the capital, which had a bearing on Outer Mongolia in that the Anfu militarist General Hsü Shu-cheng was thwarted in his ambitions and subsequently wrecked the Mongolian policy of his political opponents in the government.

As Tuan Ch'i-jui's righthand man, Hsü had supplied the organizational energy (and Japan the money) to bring Tuan back to the premiership in March 1918. Over the next six months, he worked to oust the Chihli clique of President Feng whose term of office expired in October. To gain the presidency for Tuan and an important position for himself, he organized the Anfu Club, manipulated the summer elections, and succeeded in packing the parliament with Anfu supporters. But frustrations were in store for him. Tuan's personal unpopularity made it impossible for him to assume the presidency, and a political nonenity, Hsü Shih-ch'ang, was eventually nominated. Tuan's policy of armed unification of the country was dealt a serious blow by the popular clamor for peace and foreign exhortation that the north and the south settle their differences at a conference. Finally, the Terauchi Cabinet in Japan, which had been the Anfu clique's foreign support, was succeeded in October by the Hara Cabinet of the liberal party with the new China policy of favoring no particular Chinese clique and working with the Western powers in bringing an end to the Chinese civil war. When the new cabinet in Peking appeared in January 1919, Tuan had gone into semi-retirement and the post of premier became purely honorific, and Hsü's longtime rival, Field Marshal Chin Yün-p'eng, took the War Ministry which Hsü had wanted for himself, and was to become concurrent premier later in the year.

Until now, the Wai-chiao Pu, with the assistance of the tu-hu shih at Urga, had been largely responsible for policymaking on Outer Mongolia. The Wai-chiao Pu was temporarily headed by Deputy Foreign Minister Ch'en Lu. Ch'en Lu had been one of the negotiators of the Kiakhta Convention of 1915, and moreover he had served as the first tu-hu shih from 1915 to 1917 when Ch'en I succeeded him. Both the acting foreign minister and the tu-hu shih were therefore experts of Mongolian affairs. They favored a conciliatory policy rather than precipitous action as a means of bringing the Mongols back to the Chinese fold, in the belief that it was only a matter of time before the Mongols voluntarily renounced Russian protection.

As the first step, Ch'en Lu recommended to the cabinet that the Urga government be asked to consider a new agreement in place of the Kiakhta Convention, which would be included among China's terms for recognition of the future Russian government. The new agreement should transfer to China various economic privileges granted to Russia by Autonomous Mongolia, give China the right to garrison troops and the power of investiture. On January 5, 1919, Ch'en I was instructed to put the proposal to the Urga government.[12]

The Chinese initiative coincided with the appearance of a new menace to Outer Mongolia—Japan's desire to bring about an 'Asian' Mongolia. Since the conclusion of the Sino-Japanese joint defense pact in May 1918, a number of Japanese army agents had gone to the area for military reconnaisance. Ch'en I and his subordinates, suspecting that the central government lacked the will to resist the Japanese, strongly urged that the defense of the area be assumed by China alone. The Mongols, too, saw the presence of the Japanese agents as the harbinger of Japanese domination.[13]

Before his new instruction from Peking, Ch'en I had on several occasions exchanged views with the Mongol minister for foreign affairs, Tsereng-dorji, on the future of the Sino-Mongolian relationship. Tsereng-dorji, a Khalkha commoner risen to be a leading career civil servant in the autonomous government, was half-Chinese and half-Mongol, and a man of uncommon energy and ability. Ch'en I found him well-disposed and unusually open.[14] Tsereng-dorji had intimated that the autonomous regime would not outlast the blind and aging Jebtsun-damba. The main proponents of independence were dead and the Urga government lacked men of ability to maintain its current course. He felt that the independence movement had been a mistake for which Mongols and Chinese were equally to blame, and he regretted especially the Russian intervention. He said he was prepared to leave Outer Mongolia's foreign relations in the hands of Peking, concerned as he was about Japan's wish to inherit the economic rights and privileges previously granted to Russia. When

Ch'en I broached the subject of a new Sino-Mongolian agreement, therefore, Tsereng-dorji reacted quite favorably. He said most of the princes were disposed to return to Chinese rule although none had the courage to advocate this openly.[15]

After speaking with Tsereng-dorji, Ch'en I heard nothing for about a month. The premier, Sain Noyan Khan, was away on leave, and became seriously ill when he returned to Urga. Then, on February 14, Ch'en I was asked to present a concrete proposal.[16]

The substance of Peking's Mongolian policy in the early months of 1919 was derived largely from Ch'en I's memorandum of February 21. The cabinet's instruction to Ch'en I on January 5 had called for an actual recovery of political and economic rights, not a nominal cancellation of autonomy, but Ch'en I did not believe these goals were feasible in the existing circumstances in Outer Mongolia. He argued that the Kiakhta Convention had been harmful not so much in giving autonomy to Outer Mongolia as in limiting China's sovereignty. The Mongols had grown accustomed to self-government; cancelling their autonomy would embroil China in their factional politics. He suggested that Mongolian autonomy be left well alone, confident that the Mongols would eventually return to the Chinese fold of their own accord, and that the autonomous regime would not survive the Jebtsundamba.

Concerning Peking's desire for the economic rights alienated to Russia, Ch'en I reported that the Urga government was unwilling to transfer them to anyone else. He pointed out that Chinese economic interests had not really suffered in any way despite the Russo-Mongolian agreements. However, he recommended that Urga be required to consult Peking on further economic concessions to foreigners, as a means of preventing another outside power from monopolizing those rights. This would have the effect of rendering the Russo-Mongolian agreements inoperative and checking the Japanese as well.[17]

The acting foreign minister gave his full support to Ch'en I's recommendations and persuaded the cabinet to limit its objectives to substituting Chinese for Russian influence for the present. But before concrete talks between Ch'en I and

Tsereng-dorji could begin, a fresh crisis—the Pan-Mongolist Movement—preempted the Mongolian scene. The negotiations did not start until late in the summer, in the wholly new circumstances brought about by that movement and the internal power struggle of the lamas and princes at Urga.

The moving spirit behind the Pan-Mongolist Movement of 1919 was Ataman Semenov, who had occupied Transbaikalia with Japanese support from the start of the Siberian Intervention. Early in 1919, Semenov found his position becoming increasingly insecure. His insubordination to Kolchak's government at Omsk and his disruptive activity were causing the Allied Powers to put pressure on the Japanese to discontinue their support for him. Pan-Mongolism seemed to promise him an alternative territorial base. He undoubtedly expected the Japanese to provide financial and military assistance but, contrary to the general view that the movement was actually engineered by Japan, it received little aid from the Japanese and failed for that reason. The episode is important in that Outer Mongolia's need for more Chinese troops to counter the Pan-Mongolists led directly to General Hsü Shu-cheng's playing a big role in Outer Mongolia.

Quiet deliberations among Semenov and his co-conspirators began as early as November 1918, and culminated in a series of organizational conferences at Dauria and Chita in February-March 1919. Prominent among the self-appointed delegates were Sampilon Dashi, a Buryat nationalist from Transbaikalia;[18] Fu-hsiang, the grandson of the Hulunbuir leader and the only conspirator with any degree of semi-official backing;[19] and Fusengga of Jehol, an associate of Babojab's abortive attempts in 1912 and 1915 for Manchu-Mongol independence, who now commanded a 2,000-man detachment at Dauria as part of Semenov's forces.[20] The movement was nominally led by one Jolai-bogdo of Inner Mongolia.[21] As the Khalkhas were the only group of Mongols under the least foreign subjection and the Jebtsun-damba an invaluable symbol to rally Mongol unity, the Pan-Mongolists regarded Outer Mongolia's participation as essential. This became the movement's biggest obstacle because Urga looked upon it as a vehicle of Japanese expansion into Outer Mongolia.

The Dauria conference began on January 10 with the first order of business the nomination of a delegation to the Paris peace conference to seek foreign support and recognition. But since the representatives from Outer Mongolia and elsewhere failed to arrive, the nomination had to be postponed. On January 14, Sampilon cabled the Urga government that the international situation was favorable for Mongol self-determination and urged that representatives be sent to the next conference. This was probably the first of a series of similar cables ignored by Urga.[22]

The crucial Pan-Mongolist conference was held at Chita from February 25 to March 6. Among those present were Jolai-bogdo, Sampilon, Fu-hsiang, Fusengga, and Semenov. Urga's representatives were again conspicuously absent. The conference nevertheless resolved to ask Jolai-bogdo to lead a provisional government, and produced an eleven-point declaration. A 'Great Mongol State' was immediately proclaimed, constituted by Transbaikalia, Hulunbuir, Inner and Outer Mongolia, and those areas populated by the Oirat Mongols. The conference decided that the constitution of the Pan-Mongol state be determined by a constituent assembly made up of delegates from the various parts, and meanwhile nominated a provisional cabinet. The provisional government, located at Hailar, was empowered to ask the Tibetans and the Manchus to join the new state, to raise an army, and to employ foreign advisers. It was decided to form a five-man delegation to the Paris peace conference to publicize Mongol aims and seek international support.[23]

The main problem of the Pan-Mongolists was to obtain Urga's cooperation. Urga was asked to accept the portfolio for interior and to nominate a representative to the Paris delegation.[24] Wholly convinced that this was a Japanese-Semenov plot, Urga reacted by asking the Omsk and Peking authorities to suppress the movement. At the same time, it sent about 2,000 troops to the eastern border because of rumors that Semenov intended to force Outer Mongolia into cooperating with his scheme.[25]

Receiving no reply to successive telegrams, the Pan-Mongolists sent groups of emissaries to Urga, but Urga remained unmoved. Finally, in mid-June, the last of the delegations led by Fu-hsiang and the Buryat Tsedypov delivered an implied ultimatum, hinting that force would be used to secure Urga's participation.[26] Pragmatic and realistic as the Urga leadership was, it readily saw the dangers in Pan-Mongolism. It meant secession from China and encouraging the Buryats to secede from Russia. Moreover, the Pan-Mongol state was likely to be dominated by the more advanced Buryats. Urga therefore resolved to resist to the end. To play for time, it asked the Pan-Mongolists to wait for the decision of the *khuraldan*, scheduled for the latter part of July.[27]

The Urga leadership was faced with two equally repugnant alternatives. Its army was not capable of resisting the Pan-Mongolists. On the other hand, it feared for its autonomy if more Chinese troops were sent for. Tsereng-dorji called on Ch'en I repeatedly to sound out Peking's intentions, and Ch'en I did his best to assure him that Peking's only concern was to remove the restrictions on Chinese sovereignty imposed by Russia. He said Mongolian autonomy would not be modified and Chinese troops would be kept under strict discipline. On June 27, with the Jebtsun-damba's approval, the council of ministers finally decided to ask for more Chinese troops. Russian Consul Orlov made a similar request to Ch'en I, frightened by the possible consequences of Pan-Mongolism.[28]

The Peking government meanwhile had been no less perturbed by Semenov's Pan-Mongolist intrigues. The problem was essentially a military one, and so it turned to the War Participation Army of Tuan Ch'i-jui. By now, with General Hsü Shu-cheng as the chief of staff, Tuan had expanded the army to a total of three divisions and four mixed brigades. These had been freshly trained, equipped, and financed by the Japanese. When the Pan-Mongolist Movement became a serious threat, the Anfu militarists were faced with a problem that concerned the very survival of the War Participation Army. Under foreign pressure, the north-south peace conference had finally opened in Shanghai in February 1919 and then become deadlocked over the south's demand for the disbandment of the War Participation Army. The south had the sympathies of the Great Powers, which did not wish to see the War Participation Army used for the Chinese civil war. For Tuan and Hsü, the Mongolian crisis was an excellent way to avert the threat to the very backbone of their power. They simply rechristened the army, assigning it a nominally different function. The three divisions were renamed Border Defence Army (Pien-fang chün) which on paper was designed to protect China's borders against Bolshevik encroachments. The remaining four mixed brigades were called the Northwestern Frontier Defence Army (Hsi-pei pien-fang chün) and given the responsibility of handling the situation in Outer Mongolia.[29]

Once given the Mongolian assignment, General Hsü Shu-cheng could scarcely fail to see that the power vacuum in Outer Mongolia was an opportunity for the Anfu clique to acquire additional territory. In April, he placed before the cabinet a broad and assertive program to raise the cultural and material standards of Inner as well as Outer Mongolia. It called for the institution of a Commissioner for the Northwestern Frontier (Hsi-pei ts'ou-pien shih) with vast local powers, the development of railway and motor car transport, the expansion of agriculture and herding, mining and commerce. The general proposed that the government as a start float $50,000,000 worth of bonds for his program, using the border enterprises as the collateral.[30]

The program inevitably stepped on a host of existing interests of others, especially those of the military governors of the three Inner Mongolian special districts and, more importantly, of Chang Tso-lin of Manchuria, who wanted Outer and Inner Mongolia for his own sphere. It also foreshadowed General Hsü's usurpation of policymaking on Outer Mongolia. Acting Foreign Minister Ch'en Lu was perturbed by Hsü's transparent ambitions and foresaw Urga's violent reactions to what amounted to 'Great Han' chauvinism coming from a notoriously heavy-handed Chinese militarist. Courageously he warned of grave dangers of tampering with Mongolian autonomy. He said it would be contrary to the world current of national self-determination and would mean a violation of the Kiakhta Convention. For some time now, the Mongols had been drawing nearer to China, their refusal to be involved in the Pan-Mongolist Movement being eloquent proof of it. Antagonizing the Mongols now might invite another foreign intervention, he warned, and years of achievement would be dissipated in a day.[31]

Despite Ch'en Lu's reservations, the cabinet nevertheless adopted Hsü's program in June when Semenov's pressure on Urga mounted. Hsü was named Commissioner for the Northwestern Frontier and Commander-in-Chief of the Northwestern Frontier Defence Army. Of the four mixed brigades, one commanded by Brigadier General Ch'u Ch'i-hsiang immediately entered Outer Mongolia. This addition of 2,500 men brought the strength of Chinese troops in the summer of 1919 to slightly over 3,000.[32]

The *khuraldan* of the Mongol princes which met on August 4 unanimously rejected the Pan-Mongolist plan as the Jebtsun-damba and the council of ministers wished that it should. On August 19, bolstered by the newly arrived brigade of Chinese troops, the Urga government gave its final answer to the Pan-Mongolist emissaries.[33]

The force threatened by Semenov and his associates never materialized. The movement in fact petered out very rapidly. Semenov had learned as early as April that Japanese aid would not be forthcoming, and thereafter he tried to extricate himself, risking violent reactions from such men as Fusengga of Inner Mongolia and Fu-hsiang of Hulunbuir.

Japan's involvement in the movement was suspected at the time by the Mongol and Chinese officialdom and foreign official circles, and it has become the accepted view of historians.[34] However, recent evidence makes this view no longer acceptable. Initially, with or without the knowledge of the Army General Staff, secret Japanese agents and field officers probably did encourage Semenov's scheme, but were quickly stopped by higher quarters. The army had been supporting Semenov as the spearhead of a separatist eastern Siberian buffer state and this had resulted in Semenov's insubordination to the Omsk government and Allied censure. The Hara Cabinet, unlike the army, was anxious to conciliate and act in harmony with the Allied Powers and therefore favored a Siberian policy which envisaged a revived Russian government under Kolchak. After protracted discussions, the Hara Cabinet was able to persuade the army in May 1919 to unite behind a decision to restrain Semenov. After May 25, all arms and economic assistance to Semenov were channeled through Kolchak. Though unable to get the army to abandon Semenov altogether, the Hara Cabinet nevertheless did secure its agreement to make Semenov behave more responsibly.[35]

In these circumstances, it would have been too compromising for the army if Semenov associated himself with the Pan-Mongolist Movement. According to the British military attaché in Peking, the Japanese at this time warned him against further connection with the movement.[36] This is corroborated by a report of the Japanese consul at Chita who had been instructed by the Japanese foreign minister to ascertain the truth of the army's involvement in Semenov's Pan-Mongolist Movement. 'Recently, Japan's attitude on this question having become clear', wrote the consul, 'our military authorities in the field have warned Semenov that he should wash his hands of the movement. As a result, the prospects of the movement have become quite hopeless, and Semenov himself is in a predicament. . . . There is no reason to believe that our army officers are in anyway connected with the movement now'.[37]

Semenov's predicament was how to pacify Fusengga, Fu-hsiang and others who had become thoroughly disillusioned by his false claims and promises. The first sign of trouble appeared late in July when Fusengga defied Semenov's order that he hand over his arms and lead his men back to Inner Mongolia. The Hulunbuir leader intervened on Fugengga's behalf, wanting the Inner Mongols to remain in Hulunbuir. In September, violence erupted at Dauria when Fusengga tried unsuccessfully to wrest arms from Semenov's troops for a descent upon Urga, and perished in the skirmish.[38]

Japan's dissociation from the Pan-Mongolist Movement did not of course mean that she was not interested in Outer Mongolia. A former Russian sphere like north Manchuria, Outer Mongolia was a vacuum that she naturally endeavored to fill, as part of the general policy of establishing her hegemony over China. Indeed, the Hara Cabinet decided in January 1919 as a matter of policy 'to attempt to remove the Russian enterprises resulting from an imperialist policy, and to prevent the establishment of additional ones'.[39] The Japanese army agents in Urga made clear to the Mongols Japan's desire to exclude Western influence from Outer Mongolia, and they pressed in vain for diplomatic representation and a variety of economic concessions. To the Chinese officials there, they expressed the desire for railways to be built by 'Asian capital', and for Japanese advisors to be attached to the Urga government.[40] None of these efforts seems to have produced any result.

The presence of the *khoshun* princes in Urga in connection with the *khuraldan* provided the setting for a power play between the secular and religious élites that had long been simmering. The princes' grievances were numerous. Economically, they had been losing their subjects because these, unlike the subjects of the ecclesiastical order, were liable for military service, corvée, and menial tasks in the government offices, and many had been allowed to change their status. Moreover, the Shabi yamen (the office in charge of the affairs of the ecclesiastical subjects) was arbitrarily appropriating a portion of the revenue of the autonomous government for costly construction projects, and the result was heavier levies on the princes. But far more serious among the princes' grievances was lama interference with the customary law of hereditary succession and encroachments on other traditional prerogatives. With the wish to unseat the ecclesiastical élite and a lingering mistrust for the Chinese, the princely clique secretly approached Ch'en I with a proposal for a conditional renunciation of autonomy.

Keeping the lamas in the dark, the four leagues each quietly nominated a representative from the high officials in the autonomous government to negotiate with Ch'en I. Justice Minister Nawangnarin represented his own Tsetsen League, Vice Minister for Interior Puntsuk-tsereng the Tushetu League, and War Minister Jamyang-dorji the Sain Noyan League. The Jasaktu League nominated Jalakanja Khutukhtu of the Jebtsun-damba's entourage who shared the princes' outlook. These in turn deputed Foreign Minister Tsereng-dorji to negotiate on their behalf.

The proposal Tsereng-dorji conveyed to Ch'en I on August 13 was the surrender of autonomy on the following principles: Outer Mongolia was to be placed under two senior officers of equal rank, one Chinese designated by the Chinese president and one Mongol nominated from among the princes; the existing five ministries were to be reorganized under the two senior officers and staffed by Chinese and Mongols; the princes were to organize local self-governing bodies under the senior officers' supervision to decide matters affecting the banners; the Peking government was to have the right to operate economic enterprises without infringing upon Mongol title rights to the land; it was to pacify the ecclesiastical élite with subsidies and other favors; and it was to have charge of Outer Mongolia's future relations with Russia.[41]

The proposal clearly exceeded what Ch'en I had hoped for earlier in the year. Abandoning his previous scruples against getting involved in Mongol factional politics, he hastily commended it to the central government. Acting Foreign Minister Ch'en Lu and his colleagues were likewise jubilant and proceeded to respond with all haste. To anticipate objections from Russia or any other quarter, Ch'en I had advised that the Mongols be asked to petition voluntarily for the cancellation of their autonomy before the start of negotiation. This was moved by Ch'en Lu and adopted by the cabinet on August 21.[42] When informed of Peking's wishes, the princes countered with the proposal that the signature of the conditions and the presentation of the petition be carried out simultaneously. Ch'en I and Tsereng-dorji then sat down for a series of secret sessions. At the end of a month, they produced a cumbrous document of more than fifty articles, with a few outstanding vital points yet to be finalized. In that form, the princes placed the document before the council of ministers for action.

The council was then headed by the 73-year-old Minister for Interior, Dalama Badma-dorji, who had been concurrent premier since the Sain Noyan Khan's death. He and other lamas on the council put up a strenuous fight, but they were outvoted. Badma-dorji conceded defeat tactically and forwarded the document to the Jebtsun-damba. His hope was that the powerful camarilla of high lamas around the Jebtsun-damba would be able to exercise an influence against the proposal.[43]

But, according to Ch'en I, the Jebtsun-damba himself had been warming towards China for some time. He was not opposed to giving up autonomy in principle, but wished to add another dozen or more articles to safeguard the interests of the ecclesiastical élite. A storm of controversy broke over his amendment of one article which the princes had put in to rectify lama encroachments upon their traditional prerogatives. Ch'en I now found himself embroiled in a fierce power struggle between the yellow and the black cliques. Against the secular aristocrats stood the ecclesiastical élite which adamantly refused to surrender the autonomy on which its power depended. Ch'en I did his best to pacify the princes with assurances that their interests would be looked after by the central government, and on October 1 sent the draft, which now contained sixty-three articles in all, to Peking. On his advice, the Chin Yün-p'eng Cabinet accepted them with minimal amendments on October 28, and sent the document back to Urga for signature.[44]

Meanwhile, two new factors had arisen to alter the situation at Urga radically. One was that during the month of October, the lama clique made a series of skillful maneuvers. Under Dalama Badma-dorji's leadership, a powerful opposition was taking shape, numbering among its members the Jebtsun-damba's wife, the Shangtsadba or head of the Shabi yaman, and Vice Minister for Interior Puntsuk-tsereng, who had switched sides on certain promises from Badma-dorji. Under their influence, the Jebtsun-damba began to have second thoughts. To play for more time needed to consolidate the opposition, the lama clique decided to convene a *khuraldan* to consider the whole question. Since the *khoshun* princes had already departed after the August conference, it was some time before they could be assembled again.[45]

At the same time, the lama clique decided to engage in a bit of grand diplomacy. One group of lamas left for Peking on October 20, bearing a message from the Jebtsun-damba to President Hsü Shih-ch'ang. The Jebtsun-damba respectfully expressed uneasiness over 'Ch'en I's sudden proposal for the abolition of autonomy' which, if carried out, would put the blame on Urga for tearing up the Kiakhta Convention. This was especially undesirable since his government only recently had rejected Pan-Mongolism in preference for the *status quo*. The matter was too important to be decided by the autonomous government and required deliberation by the *khoshun* princes as a whole.[46] One week later, another group left for Peking with another letter from the Jebtsun-damba. Couched in notably less cordial language, it informed President Hsü that not all the *khoshun* princes had arrived but those already at Urga were opposed to giving up autonomy. It accused Ch'en I of forcing the proposal upon the Mongols and asked that he be recalled. In conclusion, it said the autonomous government wished to continue to abide by the Kiakhta Convention and retain its autonomy.[47] Ch'en I subsequently learned that, apart from petitioning the Chinese government, this delegation also delivered a letter to the American minister in Peking, asking him to establish diplomatic representation at Urga, so that American influence could be used to check both China and Japan.[48]

Not only had the Chin Yün-p'eng Cabinet and Ch'en I failed to take fully into account the dangers of getting involved in Mongol factionalism, but they had also committed the serious error of not consulting the Commissioner for the Northwestern Frontier, General Hsü Shu-cheng. They had kept the general in the dark even though his terms of appointment made him the most senior official in Outer Mongolia. There had been a clear divergence of views between General Hsü and the cabinet over Outer Mongolia and various other issues. The cabinet, already tired of his refractory nature and incessant meddling in the affairs of government, naturally excluded him from its deliberations.

The Mongolian question arose at a time when General Hsü's personal political fortunes were particularly low. He had been disappointed in capital politics. A chill was creeping into his relationship with Tuan Ch'i-jui, who deplored his harrassment of the government.[49] The Anfu clique was being virulently attacked by the nationalistic public for having sold out the country to Japan. In this frustrated mood, on October 29 he charged into the brittle situation in Urga. Outer Mongolia momentarily provided scope for his ambitions. Here was an opportunity to add more territory to the possessions of the Anfu clique, but more immediately it was a chance for fence-mending. By reincorporating Outer Mongolia into the Chinese Republic, he would be able to show he was not impervious to the nation's aspirations. He expected to emerge covered with glory and winning the grudging praise of Peking. Little did he realize how destructive his actions would be.

Shortly before he left Peking, the cabinet had informed Ch'en I that General Hsü was going to Urga purely in a military capacity, to inspect the garrison troops. Ch'en was instructed to continue to take charge of the negotiations with the Urga leadership. The general took this delineation of authority as a personal affront and, in an outburst of righteous indignation, declared war on those who were undermining the legality of the Chinese Republic.[50] Pushing Ch'en I aside and enjoining Peking to maintain strict secrecy of his activities, he promptly assumed direction of the negotiations.

He found the draft of sixty-three conditions which Ch'en I had negotiated to be radically opposed to his own ideas. The fewer and simpler the conditions, he argued, the less opportunity there would be for future disputes, and the quicker would China's recovery of sovereign rights be. Whereas he wanted an assertive program for cultural and material progress, the conditions amounted to refeudalization; and whereas he wanted direct and concrete control of Outer Mongolia for China, the conditions amounted to a nominal cancellation of autonomy. Worse, the conditions made no provisions whatsoever for his office and his powers.[51]

In Peking, Premier Chin took personal offense at General Hsü's insolence. He told his colleagues the conditions had been worked out between Ch'en I and the Mongols, and these had already been approved by the cabinet. Any change now would amount to bad faith. He was ready to call off the entire undertaking rather than allow General Hsü to undermine his cabinet's prestige. On November 12, the cabinet cabled General Hsü to halt his high-handed interference, but he would not be stopped.[52]

The *khuraldan* assembled on November 13. With the exception of a dozen or so princes of the Tushetu League under the influence of the vice minister of interior, all the princes voted in favor of abandoning autonomy. The lama clique still would not admit defeat, however. On the night of November 14, to cut the Gordian knot, General Hsü called on Badmadorji, accompanied by his staff officers. He placed before the Dalama a draft of eight articles, and gave him, the Jebtsun-damba and others twenty-four hours to sign. Otherwise, he would arrest and send them all to Peking for punishment. This had the immediate effect of galvanizing the two erstwhile warring factions into a solid bloc of opposition, but they had nothing to resist General Hsü with. The next day, through Ch'en I's intercession, it was agreed that the Mongols should present the petition first with the assurance that the conditions would be renegotiated later.

Accordingly, on November 17, the Mongols presented their petition to General Hsü as representative of President Hsü. On November 22, the president in a public proclamation acknowledged the petition, noting the 'sincerity' of the Jebtsun-damba, the lamas, and the princes in their desire to return to the Chinese republic, and commending them for their 'love of the nation' and their 'full understanding of the significance of the family republic of five races'.[53]

Early in the next year, a delegation of twelve Mongol princes and four lamas visited Peking to salvage some of their rights and dignity. As far as one can tell, the terms were dictated by General Hsü rather than negotiated. They were limited to an adjudication of differences between lama and princely interests under the formula that the princes recovered their right of hereditary rank and agreed in return to support the lamas with fixed subsidies.[54] The offices of the autonomous government were absorbed into the Bureau of the Commissioner for the Northwestern Frontier which soon developed into a sprawling structure of eight departments, dealing with general administration, finance, commerce, post, agriculture and husbandry, forestry and mines, religion and education, and defense.[55]

By the beginning of 1920, therefore, China had come a long way toward reasserting her sovereignty over Outer Mongolia. This was true of all Mongol lands formerly within the Chinese empire. The Altai district, occupied by Russian troops up to the October Revolution, was incorporated into Sinkiang by a decision of the Chinese government on June 1, 1919.[56] Tannu Uryanghai, the scene of recurrent Red-White skirmishes, was occupied by Chinese troops in June 1919 and brought under the control of the tu-hu shih at Urga.[57] Hulunbuir renounced its special status and formally returned to the Chinese republic in Janurary 1920.[58]

But the Chinese success was ephemeral. General Hsü's personal control of Outer Mongolia did not last beyond the summer of 1920 when the Anfu clique was·crushed by its rivals. The residue of the Mongols' profound ill-will long survived him and had an important place in the succession of events that launched Outer Mongolia into the Soviet orbit in 1921.

6

Decolonization of North Manchuria

Throughout 1920 China's major effort at reasserting rights in the former Tsarist sphere in north Manchuria was conducted, unlike in Outer Mongolia, under somewhat closer coordination between central and local authorities and consequently produced more permanent results.

Profound chaos had prevailed in the Chinese Eastern Railway area since the start of the Siberian intervention. The region had become a busy thoroughfare for armed forces of numerous nationalities, a sanctuary for Russian refugees, and a pivot of international rivalry. Under the management of Russian monarchists, the railway had run into great financial and physical strains. It was operated by Russian and Chinese workmen with wages behindhand, prone to clandestine radical agitation and strikes. A greater menace was posed by the Japanese troops, who justified their presence along the line through appeal to the Sino-Japanese military pact and persistently tried to gain control of the railway. The chaotic situation was mitigated to some extent only by the Inter-Allied Commission (at Vladivostok) through its Technical Board at Harbin; under the American John F. Stevens, the board endeavored to ensure smooth operation and discourage extraneous interference.

As noted earlier, the Chinese had come a long way since the October Revolution in asserting their position. Manchurian troops had gone far towards recovering the right of patrol in the aftermath of the Harbin Soviet, which right had been further strengthened by the inter-Allied agreement of January 1919 which placed the security of the railway under Chinese responsibility. The designation of Kuo Tsung-hsi as president of the railway's board of directors had enabled the Chinese to begin removing Russian encroachments upon Chinese sovereign rights.

The opportunity for the Chinese to take over temporary management of the railway had arisen since early in 1918 but, despairing at the lack of human and financial resources and wary of Japanese reactions, President Kuo had favored instead the more moderate policy of adhering to the railway contract ·and statutes. This meant in effect recognizing the reorganized board of directors as the railway's executive body with General Horvath, the vice president and managing director, exercising sole authority while Kuo, the president, watched over China's interests.

Pertinent to the process of decolonization were the dramatic changes in the Manchurian power structure in the summer of 1919. Chang Tso-lin had received the appointment of inspector general over all three Manchurian provinces in 1918 for his services to the Anfu clique; he had allowed General Meng En-yüan and his forces to remain in control of Kirin province until the summer of 1919 when, in the showdown, General Meng's forces were overpowered and removed. The success crowned Chang's drive over two decades and put him in absolute command over all of Manchuria and a part of Inner Mongolia, capable of separatism at will or of making a bid for national supremacy.[1] In an astute move, Chang put his 27th Division commander, General Sun Lieh-ch'en, in the place of General Pao Kuei-ch'ing as military governor of Heilungkiang, and transferred the unusually able General Pao to Kirin with triple posts: military governor of Kirin, president of the Chinese Eastern Railway Company, and commander-in-chief of the Chinese railway guards. China's far-reaching recovery of rights in north Manchuria may be attributed largely to General Pao.

The year 1920 opened with a rapid succession of events which heralded dangers as well as opportunities for China in north-Manchuria. On January 5 Kolchak's government disintegrated completely; on the 9th, the Americans announced their decision to withdraw, followed by other Western powers; on the 13th, the Japanese government reinforced the Siberian expeditionary army with another half division, avowedly determined to protect their Manchurian and Korean interests; and on the 31st, a coalition of Russian revolutionaries established a provisional government at Vladivostok for the Maritime Province.

Kolchak's fall immediately produced a two-way struggle between Semenov and Horvath. On January 10 Semenov declared himself legitimate successor to Kolchak, claiming jurisdiction over all Russians, including those residing in the Chinese Eastern Railway Zone. Not disposed to recognize 'an upstart with a Napoleonic complex' as Horvath considered the Cossack leader, Horvath issued his own proclamation on January 14 to the effect that, pending the formation of the official Russian government, he would function as head of the Russian administration in the railway area. Once again, the region seemed destined to be the scene of another Russian power struggle.[2]

The confusion resulting from the failure of the Allied intervention in Siberia in turn set off frantic preparations in as many directions as there were parties with high stakes in north Manchuria: Chinese leaders in Peking and Manchuria, Russians, monarchist and radical, the Western powers and the Japanese.

For the Chinese, the disengagement of the Western powers from Siberia signalled the loss of the latter's countervailing influence to Japanese militarism. Of special concern was the fate of the Chinese Eastern Railway in particular and north Manchuria as a whole, whether the region would be submerged under Japanese militarism or the Bolshevik tide. There was, first, the immediate problem of how to prevent the Semenov-Horvath contest from erupting within Chinese territory, and, secondly, the longer-range one of reasserting sovereign rights in order to ward off extraneous influences. These difficult tasks fell upon General Pao Kuei-ch'ing. General Pao himself, as we have seen in his handling of the Russian civil war on the western Manchurian border, was a man of great vigor and decisive action. He was more assertive than his predecessor Kuo Tsung-hsi, and he enjoyed a fuller degree of the confidence of Inspector General Chang Tso-lin. Led by General Pao, the Chinese were able, step by step in the course of the year, to transform the railway into an enterprise more truly Sino-Russian in character and the railway area into a region where Chinese sovereignty once more prevailed.

First, between Semenov and Horvath, a host of considerations suggested to General Pao and others that the latter should be given Chinese support whilst the Semenovites should be kept out of Chinese territory by reinforced frontier and railway guards. Horvath was preferable partly because he was less closely identified with the Japanese and partly because he was more amenable to Chinese purposes. The once haughty defender of Tsarist interests was now looking to the Chinese for help. Although he still directed the railway administration and possessed a sizable force of railway detachments and police, his strength was nevertheless rapidly eroding from internal fissions: between railway administrators loyal to him and workmen who wanted him removed, between commanding officers of the guard detachments and the police force who willingly obeyed his orders and the rank and file who, like the railway workmen, were showing insubordination.

Apart from the Semenovites, another equally disturbing development for Horvath and the Chinese was the renewed radical politicization among a large segment of the middle and lower classes of Russians following the failure of the counter-revolution in Siberia. On January 27, radical organizational activity produced in Harbin the United Conference (Ob'edinennaia Konferentsia), an amalgam of some thirty Russian social organizations, whose object was to agitate against Japanese militarism. When the Vladivostok government appeared, the conference openly declared allegiance to it, and demanded of Horvath that he relinquish all authority in favor of that government.[3]

As before, disunity among the Russians presented an opportunity for the Chinese to step in. After promising Horvath support against the Semenovites, General Pao then countered Horvath's proclamation of January 14 with one of his own on January 29. In it, he declared that Horvath's assumption of administrative authority constituted an impairment of China's sovereignty, that Horvath was merely a railway executive without any political authority whatsoever, that the Chinese government alone as the sovereign power would assume responsibility for the peace and order in the railway area.[4] Then turning to the radicals, he announced a ban on mass meetings and demonstrations by the United Conference, again giving public notice to the effect that Chinese territory was not to be used for Russian political purposes. With the central government's approval, General Pao also asked the Siberian high commissioner, Li Chia-ao, to contact the leaders of the Vladivostok government secretly with a view to inducing them to restrain the radicals.[5]

The unsettling combination of events at the beginning of 1920 also turned the minds of the Chinese leaders in Manchuria and Peking towards devising means to meet the various dangers to which north Manchuria together with the railway was exposed. As in the early months of 1918, the Chinese once again had two options: the radical one of appropriating the railway temporarily until the end of the Russian political disorganization, or the more moderate one of retaining some semblance of its status as governed by the railway contract, but with a greatly enlarged Chinese role in its management. The central government favored temporary appropriation and the Manchurian leaders the more moderate approach.

The proposal for appropriating the railway was first raised by the minister for communications, Tseng Yü-chün, at a cabinet meeting towards the end of January. He justified it as the best means of stemming the Red tide. It was supported by Acting Foreign Minister Ch'en Lu, which indicates that the Wai-chiao Pu was prepared to handle the diplomatic side of things. In the end, the cabinet as a whole was ready to authorize General Pao to use force to compel Horvath's compliance.[6] The Manchurian leaders, on the other hand, chose to be cautious for a variety of reasons. Firstly, an abrupt move to appropriate the railway in which the French had invested enormous sums and to which other powers had made loans during the intervention was liable to rouse foreign opposition. Although the central government was prepared to handle any international complications, the move might so alienate the Western powers as to deprive Manchuria of their countervailing influence against Japan. Secondly, the available human and financial resources in Manchuria fell short of the task. Both the ministries of finance and communications promised maximum effort at solving these problems but, from the Manchurian point of view, those two portfolios were strongholds of the politically aligned Anfu and Communications cliques, whose intrusion into the Fengtien clique's domain was to be avoided at all cost. Finally, fear of Japan's unfavorable response ranked high among the Manchurian leaders' worries, for any radical modification to the Chinese Eastern Railway management inevitably impinged upon the South Manchurian Railway. Guided by these considerations, the Manchurian leadership made sure that whatever measure they took conformed generally to the terms of the railway contract which gave the railway its legal basis. Much of the Tsarist incubus could be swept away, they believed, by an exact interpretation of the provisions in the contract.[7]

After a week's personal study of the situation at Harbin early in February, General Pao drew up a two-pronged plan for action. First, he would insist upon joint management by a reorganized board of directors with equal Sino-Russian representation. According to the company's statutes, the enterprise was managed by a board of nine directors, plus a president appointed by the Chinese government. In the 1918 reorganization, one more Chinese (Yen Shih-ch'ing) had been admitted to the board. By 1920, the board had three Russian vacancies and General Pao proposed to coopt three more Chinese to the board so that representation would be equalized to five each. He would further insist that the board be located at Harbin to ensure a Chinese majority at all times.[8]

General Pao's interpretation of the Chinese Eastern Railway as a Sino-Russian joint enterprise (ho-pan) accorded better with the Ch'ing government's original intent than with the actual wording of the contract. But, reflecting the public nationalistic mood of his time, he evidently felt justified in departing from a contract which the Russians themselves had consistently ignored. The fact that the railway lay within Chinese territory alone, if not the government's investment of 5,000,000 Kuping taels, justified a degree of control by China.

The other half of General Pao's plan was to insist upon a clear distinction between *business* rights, which the company rightfully possessed, and *political* rights which it had wrongly usurped. In the latter category fell the railway guards, the police force, the C.E.R. Administration's supervision of the municipalities, and the damaging system of jurisdiction. By means of this two-pronged attack, the railway would be returned to its original character, a business enterprise completely dissociated from politics, jointly managed by the two countries and obliged to respect Chinese sovereignty.[9]

While the Chinese formulated their plans, the Russians themselves, including General Horvath, Prince Kudashev, and leaders of the Russo-Asiatic Bank, had been engaged in intensive discussions, ever since the collapse of Kolchak's Omsk government seemed imminent, as to what to do with Russia's Manchurian possessions. Prince Kudashev was a strong advocate for placing the railway under French protection, whereas Horvath was reluctant, at first, to permit his own life-work to pass into another's control. However, by the beginning of 1920, he seemed resigned to the idea.

As Kudashev saw it, the railway was a fully ripened fruit, for which there were many scramblers. He saw dangers from the Bolsheviks who were able, even without Chinese official recognition, to exert an influence on the Chinese in regard to Russian individuals and institutions in China. Japan's desire for the railway also had long been transparent. Moreover, the Chinese, the French, and others were in the race as well.

From the consultations among the Russian monarchists, there emerged a set of three principles designed to safeguard the possessions for the future Russia. The first was to see that the line went to the weakest of the aspirants so that Russia could get it back later more easily; secondly, to insist that the transfer was strictly temporary, pending the return to normalcy in Russia; and, thirdly, to stress that the railway was a commercial enterprise of a private company, so that its seizure by Tsarist creditors could be avoided. In concrete terms, the railway was to be handed over to the Chinese government, to be managed in trust for Russia, and the company itself was to be placed under the authority of the Russo-Asiatic Bank with semi-official French protection.

The strategy of these self-appointed guardians of Russian interests combined realism with a touch of wishful thinking. They believed that the Japanese would be deterred from any rash action by the combined opposition of China, the United States, and France, the last being Russia's biggest creditor. The French and the Americans would act in solidarity since there was something in the plan for each: the French should derive satisfaction from some control over the railway through the Russo-Asiatic Bank; and the Americans should have nothing against the scheme since it might enable them to recover some of their wartime loans to France. The Chinese, too, should be delighted by the formula whereby the company would be placed under the authority of the Russo-Asiatic Bank, recognized as its sole shareholder, and under the surveillance and actual management of the Chinese government until such time as Russia was ready to take it back.[10]

Ironically, the threat to Russian interests did not come from the strongest but from what the Russians believed to be the weakest aspirants—the Chinese. They were to find that the Chinese would not be content with the role of mere safekeeping but would seize the opportunity to insist upon a fundamental transformation of the enterprise. A basic contradiction in the monarchists' scheme was, on the one hand, to insist upon the railway's being a private business enterprise and, on the other, to expect the Chinese to be content to leave the C.E.R. Administration with all its colonial powers.

Taking Horvath by storm, General Pao laid out his demands on February 13 for the main office of the company to be set up in Harbin and a new board of directors constituted on the basis of equal representation. He intimated that he had authorization to use force. Confronted with Pao's determination and shaken by his own loss of control over a worsening situation, Horvath eventually gave in.[11]

But, on the next day, General Pao returned with new demands concerning the railway guards and the police force. After the disbandment of the Trans-Amur district guard early in 1918, Horvath had ignored the Chinese warning that he should recruit no more than 500 civilians to guard the railway. By the beginning of 1920, he had steadily built up detachments of military guards (*okhrannaia strazha*) numbering about 3,000 men, which patrolled the railway in five groups. In addition, about 1,000 men of his fatherland-protection corps were stationed at Harbin, most appropriately called the White Guards. The military police force had similarly been disbanded after the Harbin Soviet and a militia of about 400 had taken its place.[12]

When General Pao demanded the abolition of both the military guards and the police force, Horvath stubbornly refused, referring him to the railway contract and the Portsmouth Treaty. After protracted arguments and some concession on Pao's part, it was agreed that the company could maintain a railway guard (*zheleznodorozhnaia strazha*) of 3,000 men; these were to be civilians, not to be organized in military formations and without the character of combat units. Their duties were strictly limited to guarding cashboxes at railway stations, watching warehouses and the like, while patrol was to be the exclusive responsibility of the Chinese guards, which then numbered about 3,500 men. No agreement was reached on the police question since Pao himself was somewhat pessimistic about a Chinese police force being equal to the very difficult task of keeping law and order in the large, predominantly Russian, communities along the railway.[13]

Thus, by February 19, General Pao had obtained Horvath's consent to reorganize the board of directors and the railway detachments. But then Horvath took to delaying tactics. Within less than a month, he was thrown out of Harbin and General Pao was able to realize his objectives, thanks to an upheaval brought about by the United Conference.

With restlessness among the Russian railway workmen mounting, the United Conference had been gathering numbers and momentum, intensifying the agitation for the expulsion of Horvath and other counterrevolutionary forces from the railway area. On March 12, it served Horvath an ultimatum: relinquish authority to the Vladivostok government within 24 hours or else face a general political strike. When the ultimatum expired on the next day without Horvath's compliance, the railway workmen walked off their jobs, and Harbin city closed down with red flags flying everywhere. The Russian civil war now raged within Chinese territory, while the ubiquitous Japanese hovered in the wings. Horvath was rendered helpless as class struggle created an internal cleavage within both his guard detachments and the police force.

General Pao promptly seized the opportunity of announcing his intention to prosecute any individual or group found engaging in political activity in the railway area. Chinese guards were ordered out to round up the leaders of the United Conference. Simultaneously, he asked High Commissioner Li Chiao-ao to renew his representation to the Vladivostok government, promising to deal severely with Horvath if the provisional government would restrain the United Conference. Between Reds and Whites, he found it expedient to lean towards the Reds. 'By eradicating the Whites', Pao wired the central government, 'we will give proof to the Reds of our friendly disposition towards them'.[14]

Turning to Horvath, in a public note of March 15, General Pao demanded that the railway executive divest himself immediately of all political authority. In a last bid to save the situation, Horvath apparently proceeded to hold secret talks with Semenov which were immediately uncovered by Chinese intelligence. On March 16, General Pao struck. Two more regiments were brought up to Harbin to reinforce the five regiments already alerted on the line. Chinese guards then surrounded the headquarters of the guard detachments, the fatherland-protection corps, and the police force. Horvath was put under protective surveillance and compelled to instruct his men to lay down their arms. On the next day, the United Conference also ended the strike on orders from Vladivostok.[15]

Over the next month, General Pao pressed on with his plans for rights recovery. First he had to get rid of Horvath whose presence at Harbin had engendered the crisis. The problem was complicated by two factors: first, the Japanese had sought, at the Inter-Allied Technical Board, to block Horvath's removal. Under Allied agreement, the managing director of any line under the board's control had to be a Russian. The board upheld the Japanese protest, which meant that after Horvath's removal, another Russian had to be found to replace him. The other problem was that after seventeen years as head of the C.E.R. Administration, Horvath had built up a loyal following, especially in the top and middle tiers on whom the smooth running of the railway depended. These might refuse to cooperate if Horvath was unceremoniously ousted. In the end, General Pao came up with the time-honoured policy of *chi-mi* ('bringing barbarians under control through concessions'). The president of the Chinese republic was to honor Horvath with a personal invitation to visit Peking and the ministry of communications was to retain him as high adviser. The idea was for the central government to shower him with honors, treat with him ceremoniously, but keep him in Peking under close surveillance.[16] On March 31, Horvath submitted a request for leave, apparently believing that the situation could only be salvaged by his personal diplomacy in Peking.

With Horvath out of the way, General Pao was free to pursue his plans. The board of directors which he had just set up at Harbin comprised himself as president, Yen Shih-ch'ing (who had joined the board in April 1918), and three new members, Wang Ching-ch'un (Dr C.C. Wang), Chinese representative on the Inter-Allied Technical Board, the Harbin Taoyin Tung Shih-en, and Ho Shou-jen. On the Russian side, there was only Pimenov. The latter was promptly elected in Horvath's place as managing director and vice president.[17] The board then formally approved General Pao's motion that the Chinese Eastern Railway henceforth was to be a purely commercial enterprise, and that all departments and agencies of a political and judicial nature were to be abolished at the earliest opportunity.[18]

The extent to which Chinese control had entered the railway administration can be seen from the additional powers assumed by the president. In the past, he had had no direct role in the management, his functions being limited to seeing that the company discharge its obligations to the Chinese government in accordance with the contract. The Russian vice president had been the railway's highest executive, chairing the board meetings and signing all official documents. After General Pao's reorganization, the president functioned with the powers of the vice president. The railway was now firmly in Chinese hands.[19]

The next step was for the Chinese government to formalize its *de facto* acquisition of provisional control of the railway with the Russo-Asiatic Bank. The legality of such a move was questioned by the foreign powers whose view was that the railway concession having been negotiated originally by the Russian government and built by Russian state funds, only that government had the right to sign away control of the enterprise. However, the Chinese in 1920 plainly resented the excessive advantage that the Tsarist government had taken of the Ch'ing government in the mid-1890s. Even the Ch'ing government in those days, fully aware that the enterprise would be practically owned and operated by the Tsarist government, had insisted that the concession should take a private form, whereby the Ch'ing government entrusted the construction of the railway to a private body, then known as the Russo-Chinese Bank. The contract was signed between the government and the bank. Here was the legality on which the Chinese now stood when they claimed that the railway was only a private, commercial enterprise and proceeded to strip it of its other attributes. On this basis, too, they felt justified in negotiating a supplementary agreement with the bank.

Anxious to regain some control of the enterprise, the Russo-Asiatic Bank asked the Chinese government in May for the shareholders' meeting to be convened in Peking. The Ministry of Communications seized the opportunity to lay down several preconditions. The bank was asked to issue the Chinese government with the proper certificates for its contribution of 5,000,000 taels, which had never been received; and to enter the 5,000,000 taels which the Chinese government was to have received (but never did) from the bank upon completion of the line as additional Chinese capital, plus an amount of accrued interest equivalent to the principal itself. The bank was to agree to China's appointment of the president and four directors to a board of ten, and to accept all the changes in the administration as brought about by General Pao. Most importantly, the bank was to undertake that the railway company would henceforth confine itself to purely business operations and abolish all agencies of a political nature.[20]

The negotiations between the Chinese government and the bank were strung out over several months, punctuated by the outbreak of the Anfu-Chihli War and the consequent change of cabinet in the summer. The slow progress was due also to the fact that both sides had to research into past, entangled records to substantiate each other's claims.

By the time the new minister for communications, Yeh Kung-ch'o, was ready to take up the Chinese Eastern Railway question in August, it had grown considerably more critical as a result of the continuing presence of Japanese troops and the new talk of internationalization of the railway by the Anglo-American powers. Carrying over the policies of General Pao and former Communications Minister Tseng, Yeh was determined to bring to a conclusion the twin policy of transforming the railway into a private commercial enterprise under equal joint management and separating out political from business rights. Forthrightly, he declared that while China had no wish to impair Russia's rightful interest, neither had China any intention of forgoing its own sovereign rights. He wanted negotiations with the Russo-Asiatic Bank to be concluded forthwith.[21]

Meanwhile, the negotiators had considered several successive drafts but had made no progress owing to General Horvath's intransigence. However, talk of internationalization among the Western powers did bring him around to the Supplement to the Agreement for the Construction and Exploitation of the Chinese Eastern Railway, signed on October 2. The preamble listed the considerations whereby the Chinese government felt justified in its decision to assume, temporarily, 'the supreme administration of the railway', pending an agreement with a subsequently recognized Russian government. Included among them were China's partnership in the enterprise, the company's debts to the Chinese government, the complete disorganization in Russia, and considerations of sovereignty.

Under the agreement, the company bound itself to pay the Chinese government in bonds of the railway, guaranteed by a mortgage on all its property, the sum of 5,000,000 Kuping taels (plus 6 per cent compound interest up to 1920 and 5 per cent thereafter) which ought to have been paid to the Chinese government beginning from the day of the opening of traffic (Art. 1). The Chinese government received the right to appoint, besides the president of the company, four members of Chinese nationality to a board of ten. In cases of even ballot, the president would have the casting vote, in addition to his consulting vote (Art. 2). But the quorum required was seven, and no decision was binding unless approved by at least seven members (Art. 3). It was agreed that the offices on the railway would be equitably distributed among Chinese and Russians; moreover, in line with General Pao's earlier proposal, Chinese assistants were to be attached to the Russian chiefs of departments (Art. 5). Finally and most important of all, the separation of political and business rights was formalized as follows: 'The rights and obligations of the Company will henceforward, and in every respect, be of commercial nature; all political action .and attribution is absolutely forbidden to the Company. The Chinese government reserves for itself the right to prescribe restrictive measures of every kind to this effect at any moment'.[22]

The signing of the supplementary agreement was followed by the shareholders' meeting in Peking to elect five Russians to the board. To avoid offense to the Russian radicals, the Chinese overruled the nomination of General Horvath and other Russians of notoriety. The resulting board consisted of Engineers V.D. Lachinov, I.I. Desnitsky, S.I. Danilevsky, K.B. Richter, and V.V. Pushkarev. General Horvath was retired with the honorary sinecure of high adviser to the company. The Chinese representation remained unchanged.[23]

This new arrangement—which governed the Chinese Eastern Railway over the next four years until the Sino-Soviet Treaty of May 31, 1924—climaxed the Chinese effort at recovering sovereign rights in north Manchuria since the collapse of the Tsarist government. During the period of trusteeship, the Chinese government would endeavor to whittle the C.E.R. colonial administration down to a business corporation, and thus build up a strong bargaining position in future negotiations with a new Russian regime. It remained to be seen, at these negotiations, whether Chinese nationalism could triumph over Soviet national interests.

Once having reduced the railway to a commercial enterprise, the Chinese began the long and difficult process of reclaiming a variety of sovereign rights once usurped by the

C.E.R. Administration. They were to find that the act of denying the Russians these rights seemed effortless compared to giving substance to sovereignty. The burden of implementing the rights now recovered—controlling, operating, and financing the railway, maintaining a body of railway guards capable of providing protection against the Japanese, the Semenovites, and hunghutzu banditry, keeping up a police force capable of maintaining law and order over a predominantly foreign population, and meting out justice to Russian nationals who had never been subject to Chinese law—was essentially a problem of men and money, which neither the Pèking government nor the Manchurian authorities could adequately provide.

In the running of the railway itself, the Chinese seem to have discharged their trusteeship fairly tolerably. This was due partly to the recruitment of B.V. Ostroumov, a man with unrivalled railway experience, by the Russo-Asiatic Bank as the managing director in February 1921. Assisted by Dr C.C. Wang, one of China's best railway experts, as deputy managing director, Ostroumov carried out drastic improvements in the various departments, reduced expenses and retrenched personnel, and from 1922 succeeded in putting the railway in a sound financial position.[24]

The implementation of various recovered rights proved to be a great deal more difficult. The C.E.R. Administration had hitherto functioned like a government with control over an army, a string of municipalities, a police force, and a system of law courts, not to say schools, hospitals, parks, etc. Because of the large foreign component in the population, and the kind of institutions that had sprung up over the years, the railway area had to be treated as a special category even though now under Chinese sovereignty. Accordingly, it was reconstituted in December by the central government as the Special Manchurian Region (Tung-sheng t'e-pieh-ch'ü). But it was not until two years later, with the appointment of General Chu Ch'ing-lan as administrator of the region under Inspector General Chang Tso-lin, that authority was unified and Chinese sovereign rights given greater substance.

The crisis in March 1920 saw the permanent end of Russian troops in the Chinese Eastern Railway area. The patrolling function was exercised by a total of five Chinese regiments drawn from all three Manchurian provinces and paid for by the respective treasuries. Apart from being inadequate in numbers for the task involved, the Chinese guards were also poor in quality. Ill-treatment of Russians, interference in traffic, appropriation of goods and effects off the trains and from the stations, smuggling of opium, etc. were frequent complaints. Part of the problem was the personal nature of the Chinese army in the warlord period. As commander-in-chief of the railway guards, General Pao in fact did not exercise unified command as the troops from each province had their separate command. His orders were not carried out by the Fengtien troops of Inspector General Chang or the Heilungkiang troops of General Sun Lieh-ch'en unless he went round to the latter leaders. As one Wai-chiao Pu functionary dispatched there to investigate the situation remarked, the problem was insoluble unless Inspector General Chang, the senior man, was given charge of guarding the railway.[25]

The problem of maintaining civil order in the large foreign communities proved to be difficult to surmount, as shown by the fact that several hundred Russian police were kept on. Along with these, Chinese police drawn from the three Manchurian provinces, too small in numbers and poor in quality, maintained law and order in Harbin and other settlements along the line. On December 10, the central government publicized the Principles for the police organization in the Special Manchurian Region (Tung-sheng t'e-pieh-ch'ü ching-ch'a pien-chih ta-kang). Police headquarters was to be located in Harbin, with branches in Changchun, Manchouli, and Suifenho. Harbin Taoyin Tung Shih-en was named chief police officer.

The problem of police was inherently an insoluble one in view of the very nature of the communities to which they were assigned, for even the most efficient police staff could not be expected to deal satisfactorily with a population with whom they had no language in common. The best solution in the view of many at the time was to organize a municipal police, under the control of the municipal councils in the settlements, but that would be tantamount, in the Chinese view, to turning the clock back.[26]

If the railway guards and the police force, given time, were capable of being improved in quality and numbers by Chinese effort, the obstacles to a complete recovery of the right of municipal administration could not be overcome by the Chinese alone. The municipalities had existed for a dozen years under the supervision of the department of civil administration of the C.E.R. Administration, and all the foreign powers with nationals residing in them (except the United States) had accepted the order of things by treaty with the Russian government. Without a unanimous agreement of all these powers to renounce the special status of their nationals, what the Chinese could recover was perforce minimal.

Previously, Kuo Tsung-hsi's moderate representation to both the C.E.R. Administration and the Harbin municipal council that China be represented on the council in accordance with the 1909 Preliminary Agreement, had produced no result. It was only after General Pao's energetic push that the council finally, after protracted arguments, admitted Tung Shih-en as Chinese representative in August. Armed with the Supplementary Agreement, the Chinese then pressed for the abolition of the department of civil administration. On February 5, 1921, the Bureau for Municipal Affairs of the Special Manchurian Region (Tung-sheng t'e-pieh-ch'ü shih-cheng kuan-li chü) was organized in Harbin with Tung Shih-en as chief, which took over the functions of the department of civil administration. The latter went out of existence on May 5. The Chinese role in municipal administration, however, was still restricted to general supervision only. The municipalities continued to abide by the regulations and by-laws laid down for them by the C.E.R. Administration since 1907.[27]

The new cabinet organized after the Anfu-Chihli War also made a determined attack on the extraterritorial privilege of the Russians. We shall deal with this in the next chapter and confine ourselves here to the changes effected by the Chinese government to the system of justice prevailing in the railway area.

As noted before, a complex judicial machinery had evolved, governing purely Russian, Sino-Russian, and purely Chinese cases; the handling of the last derogated most severely from Chinese sovereignty. For purely Russian cases, the Russians had built up a system of 'frontier' courts, with a tribunal and a court of appeal in Harbin and a half dozen justices of peace in other settlements. This had arisen out of an arbitrary interpretation of Art. 5 of the railway contract whereby the Russians had converted land leased for business purposes to a territorial enclave under Russian jurisdiction. Sino–Russian cases were handled by mixed attendance involving a Chinese official and the Russian consul or an official of the C.E.R. Administration, depending on whether the Russian was involved with the railway or not; the law applied depended on the nationality of the defendant. The Russians also claimed an interest in purely Chinese cases arising within the railway area and treated them as mixed cases. Up to 1920, all that the Chinese had recovered under Kuo Tsung-hsi's leadership was to have the purely Chinese cases handled by local Chinese courts exclusively.

The Chinese clamor for the recovery of the right of jurisdiction in the railway area, therefore, pertained to the abolition of the frontier courts and of mixed attendance concerning Sino–Russian cases where the defendant was Chinese. But, by the time the Chinese government took decisive action towards this goal in September 1920, it had also resolved to suspend recognition of the Russian diplomatic and consular officials with the concomitant effect of suspending Russian consular jurisdiction. Following the presidential proclamation of September 23 discontinuing relations with Russian diplomats, the frontier courts were forcibly sealed off on October 1. Russian cases pending were transferred to the Chinese court at Harbin, 600 or more cases in all. For some time, anarchy reigned at the Harbin judiciary which possessed no judges versed in Russian and other foreign laws, competent interpreters, or finance. In place of the frontier courts, the Chinese government proposed to set up new Chinese law courts of different degrees—a high court and a lower court in Harbin and several local courts in other settlements—modelled on the frontier courts both in organization and location. Former Russian judges were to be employed as advisers and interpreters recruited. These measures were embodied in three official pronouncements on October 31, 1920: regulations for the organization of law courts in the Special Manchurian Region

(Tung-sheng t'e-pieh-ch'ü fa-yüan pien-chih t'iao-li), regulations for the appointment of special judges (T'e-chung ssu-fa kuan hsüan-jen chang-ch'eng), and regulations for the appointment of foreign advisers (Wai-kuo tzu-i-teng jen-mien chang-ch'eng).

With the C.E.R. Administration denied further judicial authority and the Russian diplomatic and consular officials dispossessed of official status, all cases in the railway area came under Chinese courts although, for a time, Russian law continued to be applied to Russian subjects.[28]

Thus in 1920 the Chinese assumed 'supreme administration' of the Chinese Eastern Railway provisionally, pending an agreement in the future with a Russian government recognized by the Chinese government. In Chapter 1, it has been shown that the railway subsisted on the unprecise legal basis of a private enterprise in name but a state property of the Tsarist government in fact. The supplementary agreement signed on October 2 reflects this ambiguity. The Chinese assumed trusteeship only implicitly on behalf of Russia and it was their hope that this instrument of Tsarist aggression in China would become wholly Chinese-owned by agreement with the future Russian government. As in the case of Amur River navigation, however, the recovery of sovereign rights lost through the railway concession proved to be short-lived owing to Soviet Russia's reclaiming Tsarist interests.

When the time came to negotiate with the Soviet government, the Chinese would have reason to regret, too, that they had not taken over supreme administration in greater substance. In the spring of 1920, General Pao's moderate approach of acting within the framework of the original contract seemed less hazardous than the central government's view that the railway should be taken over outright. Inhibited by fears of unfavorable Japanese reaction, lack of human and material resources at Manchuria's disposal, and other foreign interests, General Pao, no doubt at Chang Tso-lin's behest, chose only to transform the railway into a joint enterprise of equal partnership between China and the Russo-Asiatic Bank. As set out in the supplementary contract, equal representation obtained in the 10-man board of directors, but no decisions were binding unless approved by at least seven. Moreover, the manager was a Russian. It was on this basis that the Soviet government consented to enter into an agreement four years later.

At the time, the Manchurian leaders had reason to be satisfied not only because the changed status of the railway contrasted so favorably with the old, but also because of the decolonization of the railway zone which the Soviet government was to be forced to accept as a *fait accompli*. The supplementary agreement formally reduced the Chinese Eastern Railway to a business enterprise, completely dissociated from politics. One by one, the various governmental functions previously performed by the C.E.R. Administration were taken over by the Chinese, the net result being the reassertion of Chinese sovereignty in an area that for nearly two decades had been Russia's semicolony.

The Chinese Eastern Railway, however, was too vital an institution to be purely an affair between the Chinese government and the Russo–Asiatic Bank. It was a question to which were tied a whole bundle of political, military, and financial interests of a host of foreign powers which had participated in the Siberian intervention. First of such foreign interests was Japanese; Japan had ambitions to fill the North Manchurian vacuum and, at the very least, had a claim to the Changchun-Laoshaokou section as payment for wartime supplies to Russia. The Americans, with British and French support, were determined to contain Japanese expansionism and prevent Japanese absorption of the important railway. The French of course shared a keen interest in the enterprise if for no other reason than the fact that the construction of the railway had been financed by French loans.

This play of foreign interests paralleled the Chinese endeavor to effect changes to the railway and matured into a proposal for international finance and control. This stemmed from the Western powers' belief that the Chinese were simply incapable of controlling, operating, or financing the railway themselves, without eventually handing it over to the Japanese. Moreover, they looked askance at the Chinese reassertion of sovereign rights in the railway area, especially with regard to the abrogation of Russian extraterritorial privilege. China's whole effort concerning the railway and its territory ran into difficulties from foreign interests.

Interestingly enough, it was the British who first broached to the Americans and the French a plan of joint action by the Western powers as a foil to Japanese ambitions, and the Americans assumed the lead later. The British initiative may be traced to the British Minister in Peking, Sir John Jordan, who on February 8 expressed his concern to Foreign Secretary Lord Curzon over the fact that Japan seemed to be hoping to profit by the existing chaos on the railway, and might succeed in establishing her hold on the line.

So long as her troops remain in Transbaikal, her right to safeguard her line of communication is difficult to dispute. Even if she decides to withdraw from Siberia she may still fall back on the Sino-Japanese Military Convention and the plea of excluding Bolshevism from South Manchuria and Korea. Japanese control of the Chinese Eastern Railway would mean the introduction of preferential rates and the other means of peaceful penetration to which we are accustomed in South Manchuria. Apart from its strategic value, the line is bound to remain an important link in an international highway whatever the future of Siberia may be, and it would seem unwise to acquiesce in its domination by any one Power to the exclusion of other foreign interests.

As one countermeasure, Jordan felt that the Inter-Allied Technical Board at Harbin should remain in existence despite the Western Allies' military withdrawal as 'a valuable check against any overt act of aggression against the line'. He inquired of the British foreign secretary whether a solution might be found in some form of international control.[29]

Before the end of the month, the British Foreign Office had worked out a set of proposals for American and French consideration: (a) the control of the railway to continue under the Inter-Allied Agreement of 1919, 'on the premise of recognizing the primary interest of Russia, the secondary interest of China, and the moral obligation of Allied trusteeship'; (b) Chinese and Japanese troops to protect the line jointly; and (c) an international consortium to finance the operation of the railway.[30]

The British initiative took on greater urgency in the course of the next few months when the danger of a Japanese outright seizure reached a new height following the massacre of some 600 Japanese at Nikolaevsk in March by Red partisans. In a massive counteroffensive, the Japanese military abruptly seized several stations on the Harbin–Manchouli section and, in the process, manhandled, arrested, and even shot numerous Russian workmen who had gone on strike. For months, the fate of the railway hung in the balance. The Chinese government pinned its hopes on the Allies' keeping the Inter-Allied Technical Board in existence and on getting the international consortium or just the American group to finance the railway as means of offsetting the Japanese.[31]

In June, Washington and Paris finally united behind the British plan and the three powers then *en bloc* presented it to Tokyo. The Japanese government consented to the first and second proposals, but rejected the third, insisting, as they always had, upon their 'special position' *vis-à-vis* Manchuria and Mongolia, that their national defense and economic existence required those areas to be reserved for Japan's 'exclusive' activities.[32]

Undampened by Japan's offhanded rejection, the British and Americans continued mutual consultations and evolved a plan to couple international finance with international control as a solution to the Chinese Eastern problem. This time, it was rejected out of hand by the Peking government in September. The previous cabinet had sought British and American finance as a means of thwarting Japan's designs but evidently had not expected international control as a concomitant. Communications Minister Yeh Kung-cho found the notion of international control repugnant because of the impairment of Chinese sovereignty as well as the alteration to the Sino-Russian character of the railway that it entailed. He did not rule out the possibility of contracting foreign loans in future but believed that, in such an eventuality, it should be on the principle of equal opportunity, that is, involving all interested powers in a creditor relationship so that none would dominate.[33]

The Western powers were taken by complete surprise by the Supplementary Agreement which was announced only after negotiations had been concluded under strict secrecy. American Minister Charles R. Crane expressed dismay and concern for what he termed as 'an unmistakably hostile attitude' on China's part towards Russian interests.[34] At the back of his moral outrage was of course also the anxiety that whatever China took back from Russia might eventually end up in Japan's hands. For the time being, the matter was permitted to rest by the Western powers who could still count on the Inter-Allied Technical Board to check the Japanese. The Chinese themselves were not ungrateful for the protection of a watchdog. Later, at the Washington Conference, the Chinese Eastern Railway question would again be discussed, the plan for international trusteeship again raised and again rejected by the Chinese.

7

Extraterritoriality and Concession Territories

The Russian diplomatic and consular officials of the Tsarist government would have lost their official status after the Bolshevik assumption of power, had it not been for a combination of unusual circumstances. The Bolshevik regime so alienated the Allied Powers by its conduct that the latter withheld official recognition and continued to treat with the envoys of the previous government for quite some time. China was no exception.

In China, however, neither Prince Kudashev nor his fellow diplomatic and consular officers were ordinary foreign servicemen carrying on normal transactions. They were the guardians of Russia's wide-ranging treaty rights and interests. The maintenance of the extraterritorial privilege for Russian nationals and the administration of the concession territories in Tientsin and Hankow, for instance, depended on the presence of these officials. With powerful friends in the Japanese and French who shared their anti-Bolshevik sentiments, these survivors from the Tsarist and Provisional governments enjoyed Chinese official recognition until as late as September 1920; they were always ready to raise vigorous protests against any encroachment of Russian interests but represented no government and were incapable of transacting any business where Chinese interests were involved.

Even more distressing to the Chinese was the fact that the Russian legation and consulates in China (and, indeed, the entire Russian diplomatic establishment in the Far East) were financially maintained by the Boxer Indemnity payment. Prince Kudashev had participated in the Allied decision of November 30, 1917 permitting China to suspend the Boxer Indemnity payments for five years, as a form of Allied assistance to China's war participation. However, the Russian minister, who had been receiving the lion's share, consented only to suspending receipt of £30,000 of £80,000 per month, the balance of £50,000 being deposited, as heretofore, with the custodian, the Russo-Asiatic Bank. Anxiety over the possibility that the money was being used to finance counter-revolution, thereby offending the Soviet government, caused the Chinese government to suspend payment in January 1918, but the decision was soon reversed after Kudashev's prompt protest, which was supported by the British, Japanese, French, and Belgian ministers. Another Chinese proposal in May 1918 to deposit the money in Chinese banks to be held in trust for the future Russian government was blocked by Kudashev, with the Japanese and French ministers' backing. It was not until August 1, 1920 that Peking felt strong enough to end payment altogether.[1]

As early as February 26, 1920, the cabinet had adopted the recommendations of Lenox Simpson, adviser to President Hsü Shih-ch'ang, that the Russian diplomats be repudiated and the indemnity payments suspended, but nothing came of it.[2] After the Anfu-Chihli War, the new cabinet under former Premier Chin Yün-p'eng felt relieved of previous constraints. The Wai-chiao Pu returned to normalcy with the appointment of the veteran diplomat Yen Hui-ch'ing (Dr W.W. Yen) as foreign minister. Reviewing China's Russian policy, the new foreign minister immediately initiated two interrelated policy changes. One was to treat with the Yurin Mission of the Far Eastern Republic which the previous cabinet had kept at arm's length at Kiakhta since June, the other to discontinue relations with the old Russian diplomats. The new policy of 'drawing close to the new faction [i.e., Russian radicals] and away from the old [i.e., Russian conservative forces]' stemmed from a growing conviction in Peking that the Bolsheviks were destined to be legitimate rulers of Russia. Dissociation with the old diplomats and acceptance of the Yurin Mission were intended by Foreign Minister Yen as a sign of China's friendly disposition towards the new regime.[3]

Peking's desire to befriend the new rulers was only one motive behind its decision to suspend relations with the old diplomats. Another was the desire to abrogate Russian extraterritorial privileges and recover the concession territories, which would follow automatically from the breach of relations. Both these objectives were to encounter hot censure from the Great Powers, however. In its attitude towards the new regime, Peking had no real alternative to acting in concert with these powers; the new initiative was, in fact, based on this old premise and was new only in actively testing the limits of endurance of these powers. On the other hand, in its anxiety to recover rights, the Chinese endeavored to override foreign opposition and scale down as little as possible, emboldened by previous experience and encouraged by the knowledge—from the Karakhan Manifesto—that the new Russian rulers were not opposed.

We shall confine ourselves here to the discontinuation of relations with Russian diplomats and the resulting struggle to recover extraterritoriality and the concession territories, and leave relations with the new Russian regime to our next chapter. A survey of other powers' treatment of the Russian diplomats, conducted by the Wai-chiao Pu in August, showed no uniformity of practice. These officials no longer enjoyed any status in London, Paris, or Rome. Only in Washington and Tokyo were Russian diplomats found to be still active.[4] With this false sense of freedom of action, the foreign minister turned to the Committee for the Study of Russian Treaties (O-yüeh yen-chiu hui), set up within the Wai-chiao Pu, to prepare revisions of treaties with Russia, and to discuss how to proceed with breaking relations with Prince Kudashev and his fellow officers. On August 24, the committee took up Lenox Simpson's suggestion simply to notify them of Peking's intentions but quickly discarded it as likely to provoke foreign opposition. Out of the discussions emerged the strong consensus that the Russian legation and consulates should be allowed to go out of existence in a natural way.[5]

The subject was discussed again on August 30, this time among the Wai-chiao Pu councillors and department heads. Once again, the dominant mood was one of caution. An open break was felt to be too risky in view of what Japan might do in north Manchuria as a response. Some middle course between continued recognition and a complete official break was deemed desirable. In the words of Councillor Chang Tsu-shen, who chaired the meeting, 'We need a *de facto* discontinuation of relations without giving the impression that anything has changed'. The break should not be too obvious as it would be publicly linked with the presence of the Yurin Mission in Peking. A pretext was needed to get the idea across to Prince Kudashev that the Chinese government could no longer meaningfully transact any further business with him. The deliberators hit upon the Kalmykov case.

This concerned the Ussuri Cossack, Ivan Kalmykov, who at the beginning of the year had fled across the eastern Manchurian border from his Red pursuers. To placate the Reds, who charged him with the crime of absconding with Russian state gold, General Pao Kuei-ch'ing arrested Kalmykov and kept him under guard in Kirin city. One day in July, on one of his visits to the Russian consulate, he disappeared and was discovered several weeks later hiding on the consulate premises. The complicity of the Kirin consul was the perfect excuse for the Chinese government to freeze relations with Kudashev altogether.[6]

On September 2, Foreign Minister Yen sought cabinet action on a long draft resolution he had prepared. The statement raised the problem posed by the Russian diplomats, but emphasized the need for caution. 'Since we are committed to acting in concert with the Allied governments, we must approach the problem cautiously to avoid their opposition'. As the first step, he proposed to send a statement to Kudashev concerning the Kalmykov case, implying that such abuse of China's goodwill had made it impossible for the Wai-chiao Pu to transact any further business with him or his fellow officers.

The Chinese government should then wait and, if no obstacles appeared, it should formally notify him of a suspension of relations. But it should be made absolutely clear that China's action was prompted by the fact that 'they can no longer discharge their duties satisfactorily and are causing us difficulties'. There was no change in 'our neutrality towards the Russian civil war, in our common stand with the Allies, or in our desire for friendly relations between the two peoples'. This way, foreign opposition, especially that of Japan, could be avoided. The proposal further allowed room for certain functions of the consulates, particularly those pertaining to commerce, to be retained, depending on local circumstances. On the important question of Russian extraterritoriality, the memorandum laconically reads: 'We naturally cannot permit that to continue'. The matter was entrusted to the ministry of justice.[7]

Cabinet approval was immediately forthcoming. Meanwhile, Foreign Minister Yen had wired his statement to Inspector General Chang Tso-lin for his blessing. In his reply of September 3, Chang raised no objection but thought that the moderate approach of not abolishing the consulates entirely was a good idea. He was worried mainly about how Horvath and Semenov would react. Fully alive to the fact that the survival of Manchuria depended on balanced antagonism between competing foreign influences, he stated: 'Ever since these two men lost power, they have been leaning towards Japan. The Japanese have gone all out to befriend them, wishing to use them on the Chinese Eastern Railway for their own designs'. Chang enjoined the foreign minister to act in a way which would prevent such dangers.[8]

The planning stage over, the Wai-chiao Pu moved into action. Prince Kudashev was first denied the privilege of coded communication on the grounds of the Kalmykov affair. At a subsequent meeting with the foreign minister, he was asked to resign his position voluntarily, but the prince refused, stating that his recognition did not depend upon his own desire but upon the Chinese government.[9]

On September 23, by a presidential mandate, the Chinese government suspended recognition of the Russian minister and consuls. The relevant document reads in part:

China, while now ceasing to recognize the Russian Minister and Consuls, nevertheless preserves, with regard to Russian citizens, the same friendly feelings as before. Therefore efficient measures towards the safeguarding of the persons and property of peaceful Russian citizens residing in China must be taken just as before. As for the civil war which is taking place in Russia, China will, as hitherto, observe neutrality and allow herself to be directed by the attitudes of the Powers of the Entente.

The mandate concludes with the statement that Chinese authorities had been instucted 'to devise adequate measures with regard to questions concerning Russian concessions, the leased territory of the Chinese Eastern Railway and the Russian citizens residing in China'.[10]

The presidential mandate came as an unpleasant jolt not only to the Russians but to the rest of China's jurisdictionally immune alien population. It promised 'efficient' and 'adequate' measures without specifying how the Chinese government intended to handle Russian extraterritoriality and concession territories. The official statement designed to allay foreign fears and communicated through diplomatic channels was equally vague on these points. It outlined China's intention (a) to protect Russian life and property as before; (b) to maintain neutrality towards the Russian civil conflict and to act in common with other powers towards Russia; (c) to place Russian affairs temporarily in the hands of commissioners of foreign affairs; (d) to distinguish between the effects of a breach of diplomatic relations (in which case, existing treaties remained valid) and the results which follow a declaration of war; and (e) to maintain the *status quo* as much as possible in all things pertaining to the Russians.[11] Nothing was said of extraterritoriality and concessions. If the act of discontinuing recognition of the Russian diplomats constituted only a breach of diplomatic relations, it followed that Russian nationals would continue to enjoy treaty rights. Yet, the Chinese government plainly intended to use the occasion to abrogate Russian extraterritoriality and concessions. Its vague external posture was a measure of caution; it had to feel its way and see how far it could go.

To a discerning observer at the time, however, China's

assault on Russian extraterritoriality and concessions could be seen as part of a momentum which had begun at the turn of the century. Since the post-Boxer decade the Chinese had been trying to reform the judicial system with a view to abolishing the extraterritorial privilege, the solid buttress for foreign rights and interests in China. Upon entering the war, the Chinese government had taken over German concessions with dispatch and placed enemy subjects under Chinese jurisdiction. At the end of the war, other foreign groups, such as the Poles, the Czechoslovaks, and the Yugoslavs, joined the ranks of Germans and Austro-Hungarians as non-treaty nationals subject to Chinese law. Finally, at the Peace Conference, the Chinese presented, among several *desiderata*, the eventual abolition of extraterritoriality and synchronous foreign rights and privileges in China, although they were not given a hearing. The abrogation of German and Austro-Hungarian extraterritorial right, as one scholar has put it, was 'the first real breach in the dike of foreign rights in China, and formed a precedent for Chinese attempts to abolish unilaterally the special privileges of other Powers during the decade which followed'.[12]

When the Committee for the Study of Russian Treaties sat on August 24 to discuss how to go about severing relations with the Russian diplomats, it also reviewed a memorandum drawn up by the Political Affairs Department of the Wai-chiao Pu on the handling of jurisdiction of Russian citizens. Intended as a *modus vivendi* until the normalization of relations with Russia, the memorandum treated Russians as non-treaty nationals like Germans and Austro-Hungarians, all subject to ordinary Chinese law courts. Special courts for Russians were specifically ruled out for fear that they might evolve into some form of mixed courts.

The memorandum set out a number of specific guidelines. In areas under China's complete jurisdiction, Russian criminal cases affecting the local peace and order should be heard in Chinese courts; other cases not related to the local peace and order or involving other foreign nationals should be taken up or rejected at the court's discretion. Sino-Russian criminal cases were to be heard in Chinese courts. Civil suits among Russians should be accepted or rejected at the court's discretion while those between Russians and other foreigners, initiated by the latter, should be handled by the Chinese court. Where Russian residents were numerous, the judges for civil and criminal cases as well as the public prosecutors should be proficient in Russian or have the assistance of competent interpreters. At the end of the memorandum, the Wai-chiao Pu's Political Affairs Department recommended that these procedures should not be made public in order to avoid foreign opposition. Instead, they should be communicated quietly to local commissioners of foreign affairs and the judiciary.

The Committee for the Study of Russian Treaties, however, approached these proposals with great diffidence. While firm in the view that Russian consular jurisdiction should be discontinued since the Russian consuls were dispensing justice with no sanctions behind them, the committee was also conscious that Russian treaty rights were still in effect. It felt overwhelmed, moreover, by the enormity of the task of abrogating Russian extraterritoriality. Large-scale preparations by the Chinese courts were obviously needed to exercise jurisdiction over such large numbers of Russians. In the end, the committee decided to recommend to the foreign minister that the ministry of justice should be asked to work out appropriate measures, and the commissioners of foreign affairs should be instructed by the Wai-chiao Pu to take the place of the Russian consuls in the matter of jurisdiction over Russian nationals. The committee added that cases not involving Chinese subjects should be ignored for the time being.[13] On that basis, Foreign Minister Yen Hui-ch'ing proceeded to abrogate Russian extraterritoriality and to confront the storm of foreign opposition that the step produced.

Foreign officials had been subject to a series of rude shocks from the Chinese government over the preceding twelve months, first the unilateral dismantling of the Kiakhta Convention governing Outer Mongolia, then the tearing up of the contract governing the Chinese Eastern Railway, and now the presidential mandate and all that it implied. They were left with the distinct impression that the Chinese government seemed perversely bent on infringing Russian treaty rights and interests and putting itself outside international law.

The latest act concerning Russian extraterritoriality and concessions was the most alarming of all, and the cumulative dissatisfaction with Chinese conduct exploded with vehemence. As one English observer commented at the time: 'The suspension of the recognition of the official Russian representation in China, for all practical purposes, if not in theory, brought under Chinese jurisdiction the majority of all foreigners in this country . . . a decisive development in the status of all foreigners in China'.[14]

Within two weeks of the presidential mandate, Foreign Minister Yen, under pressure from the American and British ministers, conceded two points: first, that the measures taken were purely provisional and subject to the agreement of the future officially recognized Russian government, and, second, in cases where other foreign subjects brought suits against Russians in Chinese courts, Russian laws would be applied insofar as they were not in conflict with Chinese.[15]

On October 11, the Diplomatic Body asked the Wai-chiao Pu for a written guarantee on the first point, and further suggested a *modus vivendi* to be elaborated between itself and the Wai-chiao Pu for the administration of Russian interests. In his reply (October 22), Foreign Minister Yen confirmed that the measures were of a temporary nature. However, he rejected the suggestion of a *modus vivendi*, implying strongly that other powers had no legally valid interest in the disposition of Russian affairs in China. He was prepared to make two minor exceptions only. First, in civil and criminal cases involving Russians as defendants and other foreign treaty nationals as plaintiffs, 'the Chinese court may apply Russian laws, but only those which do not conflict with Chinese laws'. Secondly, in the disposition of the concessions where other foreign interests were involved, 'the Chinese Government will take over the management of all administrative affairs within their limits, temporarily without introducing any changes'. He added, however, 'the Chinese Government may make improvements' where circumstances made them necessary.[16]

On October 30, 'Rules for the administration of Russian citizens residing in China' were promulgated. Russian citizens were allowed to continue to take up residence and pursue their professions as before, and to receive protection of their persons and property. 'They are, however, bound to obey Chinese laws and regulations, both in force at present and those which will be promulgated in good time in future'. Deportation was reserved for special cases, and a passport was required for travel in the interior.[17] Thus, Russians were reduced to non-treaty nationals, subject to Chinese law. It was found later that in criminal cases, the Chinese applied the Provisional Criminal Code, with the exception of capital punishment.[18]

The suspension of recognition of the Russian diplomatic representation was followed by Chinese attempts to take over the consular premises. Some Russian consuls gave in, others resisted, so that in the end, some were taken over by the Chinese while others went into the custody of the diplomatic body. The consulate inside the Shanghai International Settlement carried on its functions for a time with the diplomatic body's recognition and beyond reach of Chinese authority. Later, through protracted mediation by the diplomatic body, Foreign Minister Yen permitted a chancery of Russian affairs to be organized, presided over and controlled by the Chinese commissioner of foreign affairs but administered like a consulate by the ex-consul as the commissioner's deputy. The ex-consul sat in the Shanghai Mixed Court as an assessor for Russian lawsuits involving Chinese or other foreign nationals.[19]

In Peking, the Russian legation lay within the Legation Quarters, also beyond reach of Chinese jurisdiction owing to the Boxer Protocol, and it was taken over by the diplomatic body.

The Hankow Concession was originally part of the French Concession acquired in 1885. It was signed over to Russia in 1896 by the French with Chinese consent.[20] The Tientsin Concession, on the other hand, was acquired by Russia during the Allied expedition to relieve the Boxer siege of Peking. Both concessions had an identical set of rules and regulations of administration. Each was run by a municipal council (kung-pu chü) with an executive body, called board of directors (tung-shih hui), at the top. The Russian consul chaired the board, had supervisory powers and the right of executive orders. The council administered the municipality and its police force. Members of the board, other than the chairman, were elected from residents of the concession, regardless of nationality but heavily weighted in favor of property ownership in the concession.[21] No Chinese sat on either the Tientsin or the Hankow board, a point of great concern to the Chinese. At each place the Wai–chiao Pu had a special commissioner of foreign affairs (T'e–p'ai yüan) through whom relations between the concession and the Chinese government were conducted.

The original intention of the Chinese government may be gauged from a set of guidelines proposed on September 23 by the Ministry of the Interior for taking over administration of the concessions. A special superintendent was to be appointed jointly by the ministries of foreign affairs and interior who, together with the special commissioner, would exercise the functions formerly discharged by the Russian consul. The appointee was to enjoy supervisory powers over the police and municipal government, including a veto on council decisions; the special commissioner was to be in charge of foreign affairs.

> Existing rules and regulations governing the municipal administration and the police are to remain in effect temporarily. However, where they conflict with Chinese laws and regulations and where special circumstances make it necessary, they can be stopped or revised. Chinese laws and regulations are to be applied in the concessions depending on the circumstances.[22]

In Tientsin, Special Commissioner Huang Jung–liang and his colleague carried out their instructions with energy and dispatch. On September 25, police authority was taken over and the Chinese flag raised over the municipal council. The chief of police was asked to resign and offered an advisory post, while his 100 or more Russian police force changed over to Chinese uniform and were placed under the Chinese bureau of police of Tientsin. Several scores of armed Chinese military police then entered the concession and mounted guard—an event without precedent. The Russian consul wound up his business on October 4, whereupon the two Chinese officials took over his duties.[23]

The forceful action of the Chinese produced a deluge of protests from various foreign quarters. The Italians made vigorous representations, reliving the Boxer nightmare as their concession, adjacent to the Russian concession, was now exposed to Chinese on all sides. The American minister took Foreign Minister Yen to task for various changes introduced in the Russian concession despite the latter's previous assurances. The municipal council demanded that the police force should remain under its control, and continue to wear the old uniform; and the Russian flag should continue to fly. The Chinese maintained that they could not discharge the responsibility of keeping the peace and order without authority over the police, and offered to lower the Chinese flag if the other side would not insist on raising the Russian flag. Growing foreign pressure eventually forced the Chinese to yield ground. The ex-chief of police was employed as assistant to the special commissioner with charge of all police matters, and the ex-consul as the special commissioner's deputy, being given direction of all Russian affairs.[24]

In the Hankow Concession, Special Commissioner Wu Chung-hsien was a fainthearted individual but he faced greater obstacles than his counterpart in Tientsin. The Russian consul and the municipal council were determined to resist to the end, and they were supported by the French who threatened to land marines to take back the concession, to order the Annamite police force employed in the Russian concession to disobey Chinese orders, and to advise the French residents to withhold taxes. Eventually, the Chinese succeeded only in taking over the duties of the Russian consul. A chancery of Russian affairs was organized with the ex-consul appointed as Special Commissioner Wu's deputy, in charge of all matters concerning Russians. Control of the police force remained under the municipal council until the concession formally reverted to China by the Sino-Soviet treaty in 1924.[25]

In the foregoing four chapters, we have traced Chinese efforts to recover rights once lost to Tsarist Russia in four different areas. The Chinese undertook these efforts while Russia was helplessly torn within in the hope that, when the time came for normalizing relations again, the new state of affairs could be presented to the new Russian rulers as *faits accomplis*. In each area, the effort was hampered by certain obstacles which resulted in a mixed and varied record. It is worthwhile singling out the major obstacle in each case for its significance in Sino-Soviet diplomacy.

In the effort to recover the right of navigation of the Amur River, the Chinese encountered in the Medvedev socialist government at Vladivostok an intransigent attitude which closely resembled that of the old and foreshadowed that of the later Soviet rulers on almost all Sino-Soviet diplomatic issues. Like its predecessors, the Medvedev government rejected the Chinese demand for the right of navigation largely to avoid setting a precedent that it knew the Japanese would endeavor to claim. This underlines the continuity of the Far Eastern international environment from Tsarist to Soviet times, more specifically, the continuing need for a Russo-Japanese balance. The desire for security from the Japanese menace motivated Soviet as much as Tsarist behavior towards China.

The recovery of Outer Mongolia made a promising start but the means employed by General Hsü Shu-cheng jeopardized the very ends that he and others had set out to gain. The episode highlights the political fragmentation of the time, the capacity of militarists to act independently of the formal government in Peking, sacrificing long-term national goals for short-term personal ends.

The effort to 'decolonize' the Chinese Eastern Railway was spearheaded under the effective leadership of General Pao Kuei-ch'ing with maximum central and local cooperation. The end results were nevertheless mixed, owing to the lack of human and material resources at the disposal of the Chinese.

Finally, the abrogation of Russian extraterritoriality and recovery of the two Russian concessions encountered the concerted opposition of the entire diplomatic body. The result was a great deal of variation in the procedure and the laws applied in jurisdiction for Russian nationals, depending on the nature of the suits and their locality. In both the Tientsin and Hankow Concessions, the Chinese succeeded merely in taking the place of the Russian consul without significant changes to their organization or administration. As will be brought out in a subsequent chapter, another important consequence of foreign intervention was that, owing to the difficulties encountered in implementing one part of his policy, Foreign Minister Yen recoiled altogether from the other initiative of entering into relations with the Yurin Mission. The episode highlights the limited freedom of action that China enjoyed in its diplomacy with the new Russian regime at the early stage.

All these factors—Soviet preoccupation with Japan, the insubordination of Chinese militarists to the formal Peking government, a dearth of human and material resources, and the attitude of the former Allies—in varying combinations complicated each stage of Sino-Soviet diplomacy.

8

The Karakhan Manifestoes

The first Karakhan Manifesto of July 25, 1919—famous for being the most basic document of Soviety policy towards China in our period and for the controversy to which it gave rise—was formulated at the time of Soviet Russia's most complete isolation from the outside world. White Guard forces abetted by foreign interventionist powers surrounded it on all sides, threatening the very existence of the regime. Especially critical was the danger from the east where the Allied Intervention had turned into an effort at supporting Kolchak's anti-Bolshevik cause while Japan, the principal enemy and main imperialist power in eastern Asia, endeavored to carve out eastern Siberia as new territory for herself. Consciousness of isolation and weakness caused Soviet foreign policy to take on its most outspokenly revolutionary complexion.[1]

In the summer of 1919, an upsurge of Chinese nationalism expressed in hostile demonstrations against the Versailles Treaty led the Soviet government to launch a new initiative towards China. Although aimed at the Versailles Powers collectively for the unequal and oppressive policies they had traditionally pursued in China, the new initiative took special account of the pointed anti-Japanese animus evident in Chinese nationalism. In the best style of foreign policy by revolutionary proclamation, the Karakhan Manifesto offered, as *quid pro quo* for immediate official relations, terms of extraordinary generosity: (a) unconditional return of the Chinese Eastern Railway, (b) renunciation of the Boxer Indemnity, (c) rendition of concession territories, and (d) abrogation of extraterritoriality.

When the text of the manifesto appeared in the Soviet press on August 26, however, the unconditional transfer of the railway was omitted. But the text communicated to the Chinese in March 1920 included that offer, which Soviet envoys later strenuously disavowed in heated dispute with the Chinese. Allen S. Whiting has established beyond question that the unconditional return of the railway was in the original, by reference to the text appended to Vilensky's official publication of that year, *Kitai i Sovetskaia Rosiia*.[2] It has been assumed that the text published in the Soviet press represented a rethinking of policy positions and that the one subsequently handed to the Chinese was the wrong one. In 1958 the Soviet historian, M.S. Kapitsa, in a study based on Soviet archives, endeavored to end the controversy by the assertion that, at the time that the Karakhan Manifesto was formulated, 'There was in fact a rough draft in which there was a paragraph which read that the Soviet government transferred to China, without compensation of any kind, the Chinese Eastern Railway, all coal, timber, gold and other concessions seized by the Tsarist government, etc.' However, Kapitsa continues, this version 'was not submitted to the government for approval'. Vilensky published it 'by mistake' and the Chinese subsequently received this erroneous text.[3]

The textual controversy might have ended on that note were it not for the fact that an examination of Chinese official documents leaves no doubt that the Chinese received the *intended* text. It will be shown presently that the Chinese were handed several copies of the same text from separate sources, all including the clause but probably all originating from Vilensky. When Vilensky personally communicated the text to the Chinese consul at Vladivostok on March 31, 1920 he explicitly pledged its authenticity.

Without further Soviet documentation it is probably idle to speculate on the mystery, but a hypothesis may nevertheless be attempted here. The existence of alternative versions of the document plainly reflects divided opinions in Soviet circles over perceptions of Soviet interests and Chinese political realities which existed at the outset. The division may be identified loosely as between realists and idealists, and the difference pertains solely to the question of the Chinese Eastern Railway. Until the drafting of the Karakhan Manifesto, it may be recalled, the offer of all the terms in that document, except the unconditional transfer of the railway, had previously been made to the Chinese in talks at Petrograd in January 1918, and renewed in Chicherin's public declaration in July the same year. The previous Soviet position on the railway was to recognize the 1896 Contract as being still in force and, on that basis, to offer the Chinese the alternative of immediate redemption or joint management. Without the renunciation of the railway, therefore, the Karakhan Manifesto contains nothing new.

The evidence suggests that from the latter half of 1918 the belief about China's revolutionary potential increasingly gained ground among certain Soviet leaders, whom we shall call the idealists. Viewing events in China from an obfuscating distance and being engrossed in their own revolutionary undertaking, these men could hardly make such observations without gross distortion. For example, the August 1918 siege of southern Fukien by the troops of General Ch'en Chiungming, an associate of Sun Yat-sen, was seen by some in Moscow as the beginning of a Soviet revolution in south China. Referring to that event, Liu Shao-chou, President of the 50,000 strong Union of Chinese Workers in Russia, a man to whom Soviet leaders occasionally turned for information about China, told an audience of Chinese workers at Petrograd that 'in South China a revolution is gaining strength, and there exists the desire to establish soviet power and follow Bolshevism'.[4] The same event prompted Commissar of Nationalities Joseph Stalin to observe that 'soviets of deputies' were being organized in China.[5]

The May Fourth Incident was of course liable to the most rosy interpretation. For instance, Voznesensky, Chief of the Eastern Department of the Narkomindel, saw in the widely reported protests 'a rising tide of Bolshevism'.[6] Indeed, in some quarters, these were even hailed as 'an armed insurrection of the Chinese Communists'![7]

Vilensky is probably the most important key to the mysteries of the Karakhan Manifesto. Soviet historians have asserted that he did indeed participate in the drafting of the document; indeed, he may well have been its principal author. By his utterances, he was certainly of the idealist disposition. In an article dated August 13, he wrote that in China, especially in the south, 'a revolutionary struggle has been going on for many years, growing over into a revolutionary class struggle'.[8] In his pamphlet, too, he argued for a generous policy towards China, particularly in regard to those *desiderata* which China had demanded but failed to obtain from her Allies at the Paris Peace Conference, a conference from which Soviet Russia, viewed as a rebel and hostile faction, had been excluded. A list of the Chinese *desiderata* appears in the pamphlet and comparing this with the manifesto, it becomes apparent at once that the manifesto simply incorporated those demands that applied to Russia. Among them were the transfer of the Chinese Eastern Railway to China and the revision of unequal treaties. Referring to these two items, Vilensky wrote:

> Soviet Russia can resolve these questions with a light heart in China's favor and thereby secure China's alliance for herself. The creation of Soviet Russia's alliance with revolutionary China is one of our foremost tasks, for the attainment of which we should apply all the energy and resources at our disposal.[9]

Thus, there were the idealists who saw an exaggerated significance in the May Fourth protests and who advocated a departure from the previous policy. Specifically, these insisted that the Chinese Eastern Railway be turned over to China 'without compensation of any kind', a dramatic renunciation of the most concrete symbol of Tsarist aggression. To these observers, such a gesture would help propel Chinese social revolution along desirable lines and secure a Sino–Soviet alliance against Japanese imperialism on the Asian continent. If things were what they were imagined to be, then an alliance with 'revolutionary China' was worth any price.

Against these idealists were those who saw things in China more realistically, who preferred a more cautious handling of the strategically and economically valuable railroad.

These realists were therefore in favor of adhering to the policy decided upon in the early days of the Soviet regime, namely, the Soviet government should renounce the Boxer Indemnity, extraterritoriality, return the concession territories, but not the Chinese Eastern Railway, which should be subject to negotiations with the aim of retaining title to it or, alternatively, of obtaining adequate compensation for relinquishing it.

To speculate further, the conflicting assessments of the Chinese situation requiring different policies need not necessarily be viewed as hardened positions taken by separate groups of policymakers. Indeed, the two positions may only have been different states of mind shared by most, if not all the policymakers at the time.

In any case, the evidence points to what seems to have been the ultimate decision reached by the Narkomindel: that of adopting both positions and of maneuvering between them with flexibility. If the Chinese government should indeed succumb to Soviet offers, then the gains—Chinese *de jure* recognition of the Soviet regime, assertion of independence from the imperialist powers, and alliance with the Soviets against Japan—would be worth the price. On the other hand, if the gamble was lost, then the Narkomindel could fall back on the more realistic position. Whatever embarrassments might arise from the failure of the first course could be handled later. This would explain why Vilensky was authorized to approach the Chinese with the text he personally favoured. It is inconceivable that he should have made the mistake of disseminating the wrong one, unmindful of the debate that had occurred in higher quarters, all the more so since he did pledge its authenticity when specifically asked by the Chinese to do so.

Before the Narkomindel was in a position to make direct contacts with the Chinese, it was apparently decided to release the less dramatic version to the press. One can only guess what the motives were, but it may be significant that in view of Japan's undisguised desire for the railway and its being in the actual possession of the White Guards, the Soviet government would have been most unwise independently to renounce its interest in it.

Aside from the press release of August 26, 1919, the

Narkomindel took no immediate step to transmit the document to China.[10] This can easily be explained by the fact that until late in the year Bolshevik strength was still blocked by Kolchak's forces in western Siberia.

This account of the Karakhan manifesto differs in two essential respects from that of Whiting. He deduces that a favorable change in the civil war in Siberia between the dates of the two versions of the manifesto encouraged the Soviet government to rethink the importance of the Chinese Eastern Railway and hence modify its position on giving it back to China without compensation of any kind.[11] He attaches great importance to this change of mind in Moscow as marking 'the shift in Soviet policy from a new, revolutionary diplomacy of self-denial to a traditional, nationalistic diplomacy of self-interest'.[12]

Given Moscow's immediate publication of the later version of the manifesto and the fresh evidence, presented more fully below, that the more generous version had been communicated to Peking in good faith, not by mistake, I have hypothesized that the two versions reflected real policy alternatives. As we shall see, the shift in fact began in June 1920, after the self-denying policy had been tested and failed to have the desired effect in China.

The other, more fundamental difference is that Whiting assumes that, until the impact of victories in the Russian civil war brought a new nationalistic emphasis into Soviet foreign policy, the Soviet regime took a revolutionary, self-denying stand towards China, whereas a principal thesis of this book is that Soviet diplomacy in China was self-interested from the beginning, and remarkably consistent throughout the decade. The self-denying policy is more properly seen as an abberration; the subsequent shift was no more than a reversal to an earlier position.

In the early months of 1920, the prospects of the Soviet republic improved in some ways, but deteriorated in others. The Red Army was able to sweep its way to Lake Baikal and put the Kolchak forces to rout. Local partisan forces seized the opportunity and overturned the White administration at Vladivostok on January 31, Blagoveshchensk on February 6, and

Verkhne Udinsk on March 9. The Western interventionist powers were disengaging from Siberia and lifting the economic blockade. However, the Japanese expeditionary force of 40,000 seemed determined to stay, and to crush by force any attempt to sovietize any part of eastern Siberia. On the western front, a new danger arose from an imminent armed conflict with Poland, which absorbed the resources and dictated the policies of the Soviet state. Vilensky summed up the situation well when he wrote:

> In 1920 Soviet Russia had many weak spots in her outlying regions . . . but the weakest spot was the Far East. Here, she had inherited the legacy of the imperialist policy of Tsarist Russia which, in a feverish century-long race to the shores of the Pacific, had managed to seize huge territories it did not know how to absorb . . . As a result, an enormous territory was acquired, [equivalent to] more than half of Europe, with a population of only one and a half to two million souls. Furthermore, Tsarist policy built the Chinese Eastern Railway which became the headquarters of Russian influence in Manchuria. Here Soviet Russia was forced to confront this heritage at a moment when she was losing blood in a severe struggle in the West. It was the eve of the Polish War. Soviet Russia could not spare a single Red Army man, not one locomotive or wagon beyond Lake Baikal.[13]

From this desperate situation flowed the important policy decision of seeking appeasement and accommodation with Japan. It meant the establishment of a buffer state over the whole of eastern Siberia. The Red Army was not permitted to proceed beyond Irkutsk. Next, the local partisan forces had to be restrained. One gets a sense of the Bolshevik despair by reading, for example, Trotsky's letter of February 18, 1920 to Ivan N. Smirnov, the Chairman of the Siberian Revolutionary Committee at Irkutsk:

> The clash of our regular troops with the Japanese will give rise to rabid chauvinistic agitation in Japan and give preponderance to those advocating the sending of more occupation troops. It is necessary to hasten the creation of a buffer so that military operations and diplomatic negotiations in the area east of Lake Baikal go under the banner of the buffer. Beware of the snare of the Japanese interventionists![14]

Lenin backed Trotsky up in a letter to him the next day:

I fully share your advice to Smirnov. It is necessary to revile the opponents of the buffer state with all speed . . . threaten them with party trial and demand that everybody in Siberia carry out the slogan: 'Not another step further to the east, strain every nerve to hasten the movement of troops and locomotives to western Russia'. We will prove to be knaves if we allow ourselves to be carried away by foolish movement into the depths of Siberia, and at a time when Denikin [the White general in southern Russia] is reviving, and the Poles are striking. It is treason![15]

One immediate result of this policy was the phenomenon of an elected self-governing body (*zemstvo*) assuming administration in each of the Maritime, Amur, and Transbaikal provinces. These were compromise governments in both the international and the political sense. Internationally, all three existed as separate entities from the Soviet Republic. Politically, with the exception of Amur, they were coalitions of Bolsheviks and non-Bolsheviks. Amur Province, unlike the others, was relatively free from Japanese occupation, and there the *zemstvo* body almost immediately gave way to an openly Bolshevik government led by Trelisser. At Vladivostok, a compromise government headed by the Rightwing Socialist Revolutionary, A.S. Medvedev, functioned for the Maritime Province. At Verkhne Udinsk, a coalition group called the 'Political Center' led by the Bolshevik, A.M. Krasnoshchekov, ruled the western part of Transbaikal Province only, since the eastern part was in the hands of Semenov's government at Chita.[16]

The next step was to unite the three provinces into a centralized buffer state under the guise of a bourgeois democracy, as an instrument to negotiate the Japanese forces out of Russian territory. The formation of the Far Eastern Republic ran into numerous difficulties, however. First, rivalry inevitably developed among the three governments over such questions as the location of the political center and the extent of each other's territorial jurisdiction. Secondly, ignoring Moscow's warning, a partisan detachment led by one Triapitsyn clashed with the Japanese at Nikolaevsk in March, slaughtering some 600 Japanese settlers, including the Japanese consul. The Japanese were given an added excuse to stay, they launched a massive retaliatory offensive, and landed troops on North Sakhalia as well. The incident also served as a catalyst for the buffer. Transbaikalia spearheaded it by proclaiming the Far Eastern Republic on April 6, expecting the rest to join, but it was not until December that unity materialized. The whole buffer idea was underlined by Lenin's observation at the Eighth Soviet Congress in December: 'We should do everything to try not only to postpone a war with Japan but to avoid it if possible, because it is beyond our strength'.[17]

The above forms the essential background for understanding the Soviet diplomatic initiative towards Japan and China in the spring of 1920. A special delegation consisting of Vilensky, Y.D. Yanson, and a certain Rudoi, arrived at Irkutsk on February 14 and immediately set out to contact Japanese and Chinese officials.[18] To the Japanese military command at Vladivostok, Vilensky conveyed a proposal for peace, couched in courteous language, in which the Soviet government 'fully recognizes the special economic and commercial interests of Japan in the Russian Far East, interests surpassing in several respects those of other countries'.[19]

Appeasement of Japan was paralleled by other moves to check it and enhance the Soviet position. One was to address Washington with a note expressing Russia's desire to start peace negotiations and holding out wide perspectives for American trade in Siberia.[20] Another—the one which exclusively concerns us here—was to convey the Karakhan Manifesto to the Chinese.

On March 2, Yanson sent the document to the Chinese consulate in Irkutsk with an accompanying note in which he requested that it be transmitted to Peking, and proposed an immediate opening of negotiations. Yanson's communication was not, for some reason, relayed to the Wai-chiao Pu immediately and so did not reach Peking until April 9 when Consul Wei Po brought it back in person.[21] Receiving no reply, Yanson decided to wire the document to Peking himself on March 26.[22] A few days before this, another Soviet official by the name of I.G. Kushnarev, identified in one source as an emissary of the Central Committee of the Russian Communist Party, contacted Major General Chang Ssu-lin at Harbin and handed him a copy of the document.[23] Then on March 31, Vilensky, too, handed a copy of it to the Chinese consul-general at Vladivostok, Shao Heng-chün.[24]

Meantime, the Chinese public also learned about the Karakhan Manifesto from the newspapers. Vilensky had released it at Vladivostok to the *Krasnoe Znamiia*, an organ of the Far Eastern Bureau (Dal'buro) of the RCP, on March 19. From there it was picked up by the Chinese press as early as March 25.[25] All these texts without exception were identical and included the unconditional transfer of the Chinese Eastern Railway.

Before considering Peking's response to the Soviet diplomatic feeler, the evolution of its policy position *vis-à-vis* Soviet Russia should be noted. From December 1919 through the first two or three months of 1920, Peking's position evolved so far that it constituted a new policy, but this did not occur independently of the major powers. It may be recalled that after a phase of about nine months of what may theoretically be called neutrality and non-interference in the Russian turmoil, Peking's policy took a new turn in the latter part of 1918 before Tuan Ch'i-jui's premiership ended. First, anxious as before to act in concert with the Western Allies, Peking associated itself with the originally American intervention project in the Maritime Province by sending a token detachment there. Secondly, with its eyes on war participation loans from Japan, the Anfu clique yielded, no doubt against the wishes of many (especially the Wai-chiao Pu) to Japan's desire to activate the military pact which would add a gloss of legitimacy to her expedition to Transbaikalia. The actual unfolding of the intervention to a large extent obviated the strain of having to choose to follow either one or the other of the antagonistic powers, Japan or the United States. The Chinese conveniently placed themselves in the middle but did not hesitate to use American influence to check the Japanese occupying north Manchuria. Thus, the *leitmotif* of following the Allied Powers as a whole in order not to be too closely tied to Japanese purposes—evident in the earlier phase—was submerged by association with Japan's project, even if limited to the activation of the pact.

Thus, until the end of 1919, China was, like all the other participants, in fact interfering in the Russian civil war.[26] In the course of time, the *leitmotif* just mentioned once again began to assert itself in circumstances difficult to explain. The political reorganization of October 1918 which installed Hsü Shih-ch'ang as President might have been a significant factor, since Hsü welcomed American influence as a counterwieght to Japan. Another was the rise of the Hara Cabinet in Tokyo with its policy of harmony with the West. Finally, the May Fourth protests, even if they did not deter the Japanese on whatever level to exert an influence on China's Russian policy, served to buffer Chinese leaders against Japanese demands.

Whatever the reasons for Peking's new-found sense of freedom from earlier restraints, a notable reappraisal of the Russian policy began in December 1919, looking forward to resumption of the neutral stand towards the Russian civil war and *de facto* intercourse with Bolshevik Russia.[27] The change resulted from a number of stimuli which appeared from the last months of 1919 and the early months of 1920: the downfall of Kolchak, Britain's move towards talks with Bolshevik Russia concerning prisoners of war and commerce, the Western Allies' announced intention to disengage from intervention, the lifting of the economic blockade, and the determination of the Japanese army to remain in Siberia.

The first initiative of policy rethinking in the record came from President Hsü Shih-ch'ang, who displayed an unusual interest in the Russian question. Indeed, throughout his tenure, he played an active role in formulating Peking's Russian policy, assisted by a number of foreign advisers who kept constant tap on shifting international opinions on the Soviets and proffered recommendations. Thus, early in December, Lenox Simpson called his attention to Britain's adoption of a new policy towards the Bolsheviks and the fact that Kolchak's government was being forced to flee to Irkutsk. On December 10, President Hsü wrote to the cabinet:

> When Irkutsk falls, we will be having a common frontier with Bolshevik Russia. The Wai-chiao Pu should carefully study the Bolshevik Party and its leaders so that we will be ready to deal with them in the future. The area east of Lake Baikal, which the Japanese are endeavoring to absorb, borders on ours. If it is true

that the European powers are adopting a policy of non-interference, when Soviet power spreads to the Baikal region, it seems harmless for us to enter into contact and come to an agreement with it. Such an agreement should bind both parties against mutual aggression, thereby ensuring our border security . . . Moreover, it will have the effect of countering Japanese aggression, a matter which requires our closest attention now.[28]

The cabinet reviewed the president's statement on December 15 and decided that China should follow the tendencies of the Great Powers. The Wai-chiao Pu was accordingly instructed to ascertain through its ministers in foreign capitals what those tendencies were.[29]

The Wai-chiao Pu's survey only confirmed the changing attitudes of several major powers toward the Soviet regime. The early months of 1920 were a time of anxiety for the Chinese government. The Allied decision to withdraw from Siberia left it with a deep sense of international isolation and vulnerability to Japanese aggression, accentuated by Japan's declared intention to remain in Siberia, and by the Soviet government's appeasement policy towards Japan. Early in March, the Chinese government formally adopted a Wai-chiao Pu motion for *de facto* intercourse and, before the end of spring, the Chinese detachment in the Maritime Province was pulled back behind the Manchurian border.[30]

It was at this time that the Karakhan Manifesto reached Peking. The foregoing paragraphs on the change in Peking's attitude and the underlying motivation make its response to the Soviet initiative understandable. It cannot be overemphasized that the new policy was conceived on the premise of acting in concert with the Allied Powers as a whole, the need for which had become more acute than ever from the early months of 1920. Peking could not afford to take an independent stance or proceed to exchange *de jure* recognition for the generous offers of the Soviet government, simply because it had to keep in step with the Western Allies, remain in their good graces, if only to avail itself of their restraining influence on Japan. The Soviet initiative was therefore doomed to failure even though undertaken on the ground of common hostility to Japan.

The Wai-chiao Pu learned about the Soviet offer on

March 24 from Consul Shao's March 22 cable which summarized the Karakhan Manifesto as reported in the *Krasnoe Znamiia*. The cable was introduced at the cabinet meeting of March 26 where it was decided that Shao should 'find out whether the declaration is authentic and enter upon unofficial contact as opportunity arises'. No action was taken pending Shao's further report.[31]

The Wai-chiao Pu instructed Shao accordingly, and simultaneously alerted the Chinese legation in Copenhagen where the Soviet representative, Maxim Litvinov, was reportedly carrying on talks with the representatives of other governments. The question of the authenticity of the declaration was settled at a meeting between Shao and Vilensky on March 31. Handing Shao a copy of the document for transmission to Peking, Vilensky stated:

> In view of the geographical proximity of China and Russia, the similarity of their situation and their external problems, the Soviet government regards it a primary objective to seek a close relationship with China with the view that the two countries should stand together as allies. For this purpose, we are willing to return to China all those rights that were seized by the Tsarist government, including the Chinese Eastern Railway. As an expression of sincerity, we are willing to revise all the unequal treaties. All that we ask from China is a word of response, and exchange of views, and that China enter into negotiations on these matters.

Vilensky went on to observe that one of the things that exercised the Soviet government most was the congregation of White Russians in the Chinese Eastern Railway Zone, such as Horvath, Semenov, and other civil and military officials of the former regime. The removal of these persons by the Chinese government, Vilensky emphasized, would be the basis for the Karakhan Manifesto, any exchange of views, or any agreement on general principles. Asked if he could guarantee all the items in the document, Vilensky gave the assurance that the offers had been made by his government with sincerity.[32]

The question of authenticity being settled, the Wai-chiao Pu brought forward, on the instruction of the premier, a concrete statement of views for cabinet discussion on April 3. The Wai-chiao Pu's reactions highlight the dubious value of foreign policy by revolutionary proclamation designed simultaneously to secure diplomatic recognition and generate Chinese revolutionary fervor. Acting Foreign Minister Ch'en Lu was disturbed by both the format and the content. The Karakhan Manifesto was clearly 'not an official document' in the usual sense since it was addressed not only to Peking, but also to the rival Canton government and the Chinese people in general. Moreover, its publication while being communicated rendered Soviet motives suspect.

In terms of content, the unconditional transfer of the railway was welcome but all the other offers were problematic from the Chinese point of view. The Chinese government could not cease Boxer Indemnity payment to the Russian Legation without foreign opposition. The renunciation of extraterritoriality and the concessions was 'just' but 'of no value' since Soviet power was not for the time being extended over Russian nationals in Chinese territory. Moreover, the foreign minister took offense at what appeared to be Soviet intention to incite the Chinese people against their own government and the Allied Powers.[33]

At the April 3 cabinet meeting, the foreign minister's reservations were taken into careful consideration while the cabinet deliberated on the problem of response. Ch'en Lu could not have failed to report, too, on the unfavourable representations he had received from Japanese Minister Obata, French Minister Boppé, and Russian Minister Kudashev.[34]

The outcome of the discussion was that two decisions were taken. One was that the Soviet proposals being 'linked to China's relations with other countries', the Chinese government 'cannot conveniently make a response alone'. That is to say, a formal reply was out of the question. However, the cabinet felt that the feeler could not simply be ignored since this would 'hurt Soviet feelings'. It was therefore decided to send an emissary to Vladivostok to meet secretly with Vilensky with the message that 'in future, when other countries formally recognize the Soviet government, China will do likewise and will take the first four proposals as the basis for negotiation'. Meanwhile, China would ask for Soviet protection of Chinese nationals in Russia and respect for Chinese territorial sovereignty.[35]

As though Peking's disposition to act in step with the Western Allies was not enough to frustrate the Soviet initiative, it ran into the opposition of the coalition government at Vladivostok as well, a problem which could not be anticipated at the time of drafting the Karakhan Manifesto. The evidence suggests that the document was communicated to the Chinese without prior adjustment of views with Vladivostok.

It so happened that at this particular juncture, the Vladivostok government was taking an active interest in the railway and the Russians living in the area. The United Conference had declared its allegiance to that government which now took upon itself to safeguard the interests of the Manchurian Russians. It will be recalled that the general political strike on the Chinese Eastern Railway Zone in mid-March ceased only upon orders of the Vladivostok government to the United Conference.

Following the strike, as General Pao Kuei-ch'ing proceeded to take over provisional management of the railway and strip the C.E.R. Administration of political authority, Vladivostok government President Medvedev, in numerous conversations with High Commissioner Li Chia-ao, claimed an interest in the disposition of the Chinese Eastern question. He insisted that his government should appoint the managing director of the railway and at least one member to the reorganized board of directors, that police authority be entrusted to the United Conference, and that consular jurisdiction, i.e., extraterritoriality, be administered by the Harbin Consul-General Popov, a carryover from the previous government who had opted for Vladivostok. These demands coincided with the Karakhan Manifesto offering China an unconditional transfer of the railway.[36]

Soon after the publication of the manifesto in the *Krasnoe Znamiia*, the Vladivostok government issued a statement to the effect that it was an error. Li called on Medvedev to sound out his views, and reported to Peking as follows:

Medvedev spoke in general terms and said there was no differ-ence among Russian political parties concerning cordiality to-ward China. However, although the Vladivostok and Moscow governments feel that one was part of the other, numerous dip-lomatic questions remained to be harmonized by the Vladivostok government with Lenin's policy. Only after unity had been achieved could Vladivostok and Moscow revise Sino-Russian treaties. . . . On a number of urgent matters, Vladivostok had made concessions but others had to be postponed for considera-tion till later. Medvedev sounded as though he was prepared to abrogate consular jurisdiction, but recently a formal communi-que has been received proposing to put Russian nationals under the Harbin consul-general under supervision of the United Conference.[37]

The conversation took place on March 29, two days before Vilensky confirmed to Consul Shao that the Karakhan Man-ifesto was genuine. On April 1, in another conversation with Li, Medvedev again repudiated the document and made the remarkable statement:

I have read about the Karakhan Manifesto in the newspapers and I have also personally questioned Vilensky about it. Accord-ing to him, he is the only representative of Lenin and he has not heard of anyone else being sent to the east to make contacts. He fears this is an extremely dangerous act on the part of someone to deceive the Chinese.[38]

When Li's reports of Medvedev's repudiation of the Karakhan Manifesto reached the Wai-chiao Pu, the cabinet was in fact on the point of going a step further, as the result of a report from Ts'ao Yün-hsiang of the Chinese legation in Copenhagen. Litvinov had visited Ts'ao on April 2 and stated that British, French, Italian, and Japanese representatives had been in secret conference with him. The Soviet envoy had urged that Peking should similarly begin talks with Soviet representatives; the Chinese government consequently de-cided the lead of the Allied Powers should be followed and asked the Wai-chiao Pu to prepare an agenda for talks as Litvinov had requested.[39] Li Chia-ao's cables, however, caused the cabinet to return to its April 3 position. As prop-osed by the Wai-chiao Pu:

Regarding the Karakhan Manifesto, as reported in Li Chia-ao's telegrams, it has been repudiated by Medvedev. This shows disagreements among the Russians. Furthermore, in view of China's relations with other governments and the inconvenience to China if she were independently to express her attitude toward the document, it seems premature to respond to Litvinov's request for an agenda for talks.[40]

Meanwhile, Vilensky was still waiting for Peking's reply. Before Peking's emissary arrived, he met Consul Shao again on April 21. In the long and rambling conversation that ensued, he made several interesting points. He underlined his government's overriding concern over Japanese ambition and its need for friendship with China as one means of offsetting the threat. His government willingly renounced everything mentioned in the Karakhan Manifesto for the sake of 'consolidating frontiers, promoting Sino-Soviet friendship, and thwarting the ambitions of a common enemy'. He promised that all negotiations would be kept secret, and that the agreement would not have to be publicized until the Soviet government had won recognition from other governments. But, as firm evidence of Peking's intention to negotiate, an official reply would be necessary. Finally, he intimated that the Karakhan Manifesto had already encountered strong Japanese opposition and, if Peking should refuse to respond, the Soviet government might have no alternative but to give in to Japanese coercion and blandishments.[41]

Vilensky's meeting on May 22 with Fan Ch'i-kuang, the emissary designated by the cabinet to convey its reply, came as an anti-climax. Fan told Vilensky that the Chinese government appreciated 'the gesture of goodwill', but since the proposals involved not only China, the Soviet and various Siberian governments, but other governments as well, it could not conveniently respond alone. Vilensky tried to explain that the Siberian governments were only a formality to satisfy Japanese demands. Although they were not bound to obey the Soviet government, 'still, they will abide by any agreement reached between the Chinese and Soviet governments'.[42] In his last conversation with Ts'ao Yün-hsiang, Litvinov also made the same point and pressed once again for the talks to begin.[43] But the Peking government's mind was made up. The risks involved were too great, notwithstanding the promise of secrecy.

By the middle of June, Vilensky realized that his mission had failed. He turned up at Shao's office for a tourist visa to visit China 'to study Chinese industrial and commercial conditions' as a preparatory step for further Sino-Soviet trade. The visit of several weeks was an eye-opening experience for the Narkomindel Asian expert, who had spoken earlier on of a 'revolutionary' China. Years later, he recalled for his friend Trotsky the vivid disappointment he experienced during this first visit to China 'to make contacts'. He found in Shanghai and elsewhere a group of Chinese professors like Ch'en Tu-hsiu and Li Ta-chao leading a strong student movement, but 'there was not a single workers' cell' and hardly any proletarian movement to speak of.[44] The diplomatic failure, together with a more accurate appraisal of the Chinese scene, must have contributed to the switch in Moscow to the 'realist' position.

A third factor was the intransigence of the Vladivostok government. No sooner had Vilensky departed for China than Medvedev proclaimed on July 1 that his government 'is not bound by the Soviet government's declaration renouncing the old treaties, and does not hold itself responsible for the various offers made by the Soviet government in the telegram of March 26, 1920'.[45]

The new Soviet position was expressed in the so-called Second Karakhan Manifesto of September 27, handed to the Chang Ssu-lin Mission on October 2.[46] It took into account all the new factors not anticipated by the idealists who had drafted the first Karakhan Manifesto more than a year before. The new proposals put forward were more like a basis for negotiation than a statement of principles such as the earlier document was. These should now be summarized for their significance for subsequent diplomacy:

(1) The Soviet government to nullify all previous treaties with China, renounce all annexed territories, all concessions, and return 'without compensation and forever' all that had been extorted by Tsarist Russia.

(2) Both parties to establish regular commercial relations immediately.

(3) The Chinese government to undertake (a) not to assist anti-Bolsheviks or tolerate their activities inside China; (b) to disarm and deliver over to the Soviet government all White Guard forces, together with their arms and property.

(4) Russia to renounce extraterritoriality for Russian nationals in China.

(5) The Chinese government to discontinue recognition of the Russian legation, deport its personnel to Russia, and hand over all Russian property and archives.

(6) The Soviet government to renounce the Boxer Indemnity on condition that it be not paid to Russian consulates and organizations.

(7) Both parties to exchange diplomatic and consular representatives.

(8) The Russian and Chinese governments to agree to conclude a special treaty with respect to the rules and regulations governing the use of the Chinese Eastern Railway for the needs of Soviet Russia. In the making of the said treaty, the Far Eastern Republic shall also participate.[47]

Thus, the railway was no longer offered to the Chinese without compensation of any kind. Instead, it was to be subject to tripartite negotiation, the objective of which was a special agreement which would guarantee Russia's privileged use. According to Chang Ssu-lin, Karakhan was still willing to accept the principle that the railway, being inside Chinese territory, should be administered and policed by the Chinese. The Soviet government was prepared to leave it up to the Chinese as to when the transfer should take place. All that Russia wanted was convenient passage to Vladivostok at lower tariffs than those paid by other countries, which Karakhan justified on the grounds that the railway had been built out of funds from the Russian masses. Nothing was apparently said about whether the transfer was to be *gratis* or in the form of Chinese redemption.[48]

Despite his attempts, Karakhan could not prevail upon Peking to empower Chang Ssu-lin to negotiate and conclude an agreement. Direct contacts having proved fruitless, there remained the only alternative of indirect and equally uncompromising diplomacy via the Yurin mission of the Far Eastern Republic.

Peking's reception of the first Karakhan Manifesto therefore appears to have been remarkably restrained, and an opportunity for putting Sino-Russian relations on the most advantageous footing seems to have been lost. The constraints in Peking's policy were not self-imposed, however. On the contrary, restoration of relations was viewed with some urgency, on account of a number of compelling reasons.

First and foremost, the Peking government had been carrying out a policy of recovering sovereign rights during the recession of Russian power from China. This had been undertaken in the hope of formalizing the changes as *quid pro quo* for official recognition of the new Russian regime. Obviously, time was of the essence, since the weaker Russia was internationally, the more China could hope to have its terms accepted.

Secondly, the Peking government's sense of urgency derived from a fear of a Soviet-Japanese rapprochement. The old Russian regime had been hand-in-glove with Japan in the past in dismembering China. There was no reason why the two former predators would not get together again, given the new regime's tendency towards appeasement with Japan. The Peking leadership was therefore anxious that, no matter when China renewed ties with Russia, it should not be behind Japan.

Apart from the above considerations, there was a whole range of specific issues that awaited solution with the new Russian government. These had arisen simply because the two countries shared the longest land frontier in the world. Among these, two were particularly important. One was the question of trade. In the past, a profitable trade had been conducted, practically one-way in China's favor, which had been reduced to a mere trickle, owing to the political and monetary chaos in Russia.[49] The disruption in trade obviously affected large numbers of Chinese on both sides of the border, who were now clamoring to the government for assistance.

The other related problem was that some 700,000 Chinese nationals residing in Russia at the time had been subject to considerable hardship during the Russian upheaval. These may be divided into two categories, one being long-term migrants (*hua-ch'iao*), numbering about half a million by 1917, and the other being some 150,000 Chinese workers (*hua-kung*) who had been recently recruited by the Russian government for the war effort on the European front. About half of the *hua-ch'iao* were concentrated in eastern Siberian cities and settlements, and the rest scattered all over Russia. The *hua-ch'iao* were engaged in merchandizing textiles, tea, and foodstuffs imported from China, in vegetable gardening, or employed in other forms of work. Revolution and civil war hit them most severely for they suffered at the hands of both Reds and Whites. The Red policy of war communism meant forced requisition of goods and services, and confiscation of their private enterprises; the Whites robbed them of their merchandise and other possessions.

The *hua-kung* were stranded all over European Russia following the armistice, unable to return to China owing to difficulties of transport or suspicion, inspired by the Allied ministers in Peking, of their having been infected by the Bolshevik virus. As many as 50,000 subsequently enlisted in the Red Army, mostly out of despair for a living, and later appeared in Soviet literature of Sino-Soviet friendship as 'volunteers' to the Bolshevik cause. A considerable number were also found in the White armies.[50]

Large numbers of these Chinese domiciled in Russia, as well as those on the Chinese borderlands, were hard hit also by losses due to the Russian paper roubles. The roubles changed each time with the change of governments, central as well as local, and each change rendered those printed by the previous regime inconvertible and worthless. This had a particularly serious impact in north Manchuria and Outer Mongolia, where in the past the Romanov roubles had circulated freely by the billions, and gave rise to a persistently shrill cry for Peking's help. 'Indemnity of rouble losses' added to the many issues requiring negotiation with the new Soviet government.

Notwithstanding the urgent need to renew ties, the constraints in Peking were too strong for an independent initiative. Where the circumstances were right, however, the Peking government did not hesitate to act. An instance of this was the establishment of local relations between the Chinese authorities in Sinkiang and the Soviet authorities in Soviet Turkestan. Far away from the earshot of the foreign powers and conflicting foreign interests, the provincial government of Yang Tseng-hsin, in consultation with the Peking government, quietly entered into a series of negotiations bearing on local questions. The opportunity had arisen when the White forces were cleared out of Russian Turkestan in February 1920, and Soviet officials there asked the Sinkiang provincial government for the reopening of trade and the handing over of former Russian consuls and White Guard military officers.

The Chinese responded positively, and for their part raised a series of questions for negotiation. They wished the Soviet authorities to declare an amnesty and take back the Russian refugees, some 10,000 of whom had crossed the border; they raised the question of indemnity of losses suffered by Chinese due to the devaluation of the paper roubles. Most important of all, they wished the provision in the 1881 Treaty of St Petersburg, which gave Russian trade in Sinkiang duty-free privilege, to be set aside.

Signed on February 2, 1881, the St Petersburg Treaty permitted duty-free privilege on an 'experimental' basis, that is, until such time as increased trade warranted a levy by China. It was to have been reviewed after ten years, and China was to propose any revision six months in advance. Typically, at the end of three successive decades, the Tsarist government had brushed aside Chinese demand for the collection of duties. The Chinese estimated that they had lost well over 60,000,000 taels of revenue from Russian trade alone. The total loss was greater because other countries had claimed the same privilege when shipping goods to China via Sinkiang.

The year 1920 was the end of another decade, but without a legal government to negotiate with in Russia, the Peking government, bent on recovering sovereign rights, saw the overture from the Turkestan Soviet authorities as an opportunity finally to assert tariff autonomy over Russian trade in Sinkiang, and indeed all Russian trade with China. The Ili protocol, apart from solving various local problems, specifically provided for China's right to levy the standard import duties and thereby settled a long vexing question in previous Sino-Russian diplomacy.[51]

But when it came to the question of dealing with other problems and of doing so in the obvious manner of sending a mission to Russia or receiving a mission in the Chinese capital, the Peking government was unable to free itself from the constraints on its Russian policy posed by the attitude of the major powers towards Soviet Russia. Nowhere is this better illustrated than in the case of the Yurin mission.

Peking had two opportunities in 1920 for direct intercourse with the Soviet government, one through Vilensky at Vladivostok, and the other through Chang Ssu-lin in Moscow. But the Karakhan Manifesto was exciting too much international concern for the Peking government to make anything out of these opportunities. There followed a regression in Sino-Soviet intercourse to indirect contacts through the Yurin mission of the Far Eastern Republic.

The Yurin mission was named in May, 1920 upon the proclamation of the Far Eastern Republic at Verkhne Udinsk. The notion of a buffer state, spearheaded by the Transbaikal leaders, envisaged the unification of all of eastern Siberia under a central, nominally republican government, designed primarily to appease the Japanese, and secondarily to pave the way for direct political and economic relations between Soviet Russia and the outside world. Unification of Transbaikalia, Amur, Maritime Province, Kamchatka, and Sakhalin under one government did not occur until December 1920, when representatives of these regions accepted the Far Eastern government established at Chita. Being an instrument of Soviet foreign policy, the policies of the Far Eastern Republic were of course subordinated to those of the Soviet government. 'All diplomatic policies and declarations of the republic of a primary character', say the principles adopted by the Central Committee of the Russian Communist Party on January 12, 1921, 'must require the approval of the Narkomindel and the Central Committee of the RCP'.[52]

Led by Ignatius L. Yurin, the six-man delegation reached Kiakhta on June 10 and asked Chinese officials at Mai-mai-ch'eng, subordinates of the Commissioner for the Northwestern Frontier, General Hsü Shu-cheng, for permission to proceed to Peking. On June 21, Acting Foreign Minister Ch'en Lu, to whom the request was referred, sent a reply dissuading the delegation from undertaking the 'superfluous' journey to Peking and asking it to present whatever proposals it had to the local Chinese officials at Mai-mai-ch'eng instead.

Three reasons underlie the foreign minister's decision. First, to receive the delegation in the capital would be liable to give rise to international complications. The Yurin mission having set out for China without prior consultation between Peking and Verkhne Udinsk, its status was as yet undefined. Britain had, after all, set the precedent of receiving only a Soviet trade mission. Secondly, so long as Russian Minister Kudashev still enjoyed China's official recognition, Yurin's presence in Peking could only cause confusion. Thirdly, the Chinese government had dispatched a fact-finding mission, comprising three foreign presidential advisers—B. Lenox Simpson, John C. Ferguson, and George Padoux—to eastern Siberia to discover the nature of the various Siberian governments, and Ch'en Lu evidently wanted to wait for their report before taking a major initiative. However, the Yurin mission could not simply be ignored since useful discussions could be had on such questions as the plight of Chinese nationals in Transbaikalia. Besides, Verkhne Udinsk had just received the Chang Ssu-lin mission. Hence, Ch'en Lu thought it best to treat with the Yurin mission from a distance.[53]

Following the decision to hold talks on the Mongolian frontier, the Wai-chiao Pu and the Bureau of the Northwestern Frontier began to put together a joint delegation. The preparations were then overtaken by the Anfu-Chihli War. Fighting broke out on July 14 and was over in less than a week. Meanwhile, the foreign minister began to revise his previous position, being free now of General Hsü's interference and under various other stimuli.

By late July, the situation in eastern Siberia had noticeably improved in the favor of the Verkhne Udinsk government. Negotiations with the Japanese, begun in May, resulted in a ceasefire on July 17, followed by Japanese withdrawal from Transbaikalia and Amur. The foreign presidential advisers had returned on July 1 with a report that the Far Eastern Republic, despite its provisional character, should be seen by Peking as a hard political reality. Simpson, the leader, submitted the view that there would be no harm in Peking's initiating informal contact. The president, too, in a memorandum to the cabinet on July 7, observed that, in view of China's long common frontier with the republic, it would be unwise to refuse intercourse unreasonably. He suggested that another request from Yurin to come to Peking should be granted in order to cultivate friendly relations. As a result, on July 21, Ch'en Lu instructed Lu Pang-tao, the civil administrator at Mai-mai-ch'eng, to inform Yurin that he would be permitted to come to the capital provided that he accepted an unofficial status and designated himself as a commercial representative. Tired of the long wait, Yurin accepted the proposal without hesitation.[54]

The immediate problem the foreign minister faced was how to deal with queries about the Yurin mission which he expected from the foreign official community, and what matters could safely be raised for negotiation. Again, Simpson's advice was sought. In his memorandum of July 31, Simpson suggested that Peking should draw support from London's acceptance of the Krasin trade mission. If foreign opposition should nevertheless arise, the Wai-chiao Pu should appeal on the grounds that the long common frontier put China in a special position and matters arising from it could no longer be competently dealt with by Prince Kudashev. In any case, Yurin enjoyed no official status and was only a trade representative. As for what the agenda of talks might be, Simpson thought China should limit herself to questions bearing on the overland trade and postpone everything else until the conclusion of the Anglo-Soviet talks.[55]

Thus braced, Ch'en Lu received a flurry of visits from the diplomatic body. As expected, French Minister Boppé was the first to call. He had called before, on June 17, to warn that China would be out of line with Allied policy if it entered into political discussions with the Yurin mission. Now, on August 13, he reiterated his warning and further urged that, Yurin's objective being to promote foreign recognition of the Soviet government, China should treat him with caution. He was told that Yurin was only a trade representative and assured that China would follow other governments on the matter of official recognition. Asked why China was not free to act as she thought fit since the war had ended, the peace treaty been signed, and the notion of uniformity of policy become no longer valid, Boppé retorted with the argument that Germany had yet to carry out all the treaty provisions, and Allied unity was therefore still important.

Japanese Minister Obata called on August 15 to warn that China should follow the Allies and refrain from any form of intercourse with Yurin. Without ceremony, Ch'en Lu asked to know what the common Allied policy was towards Russia, and why a Soviet delegation had been received in London. Obata left in silence. In contrast, American Minister Crane advised the foreign minister, on August 18, to accord Yurin courteous treatment and expressed full sympathy for China's special geographical position. Ch'en Lu was quick to declare that Peking would be guided by Washington in its Russian policy.[56]

The Yurin mission finally entered Peking on August 26 and put up temporarily at Hotel de Pekin. Disunity in Allied policy gave the Wai-chiao Pu a sense of freedom. The prospects for the Yurin mission had never looked brighter. Indeed, in Moscow the Narkomindel felt so encouraged that it communicated the Second Karakhan Manifesto to General Chang Ssu-lin, expecting fruitful negotiations. Almost immediately, these hopes were dashed by a combination of circumstances.

Foreign Minister Yen Hui-ch'ing and his colleagues in the new post-Anfu-Chihli War cabinet, organized on August 9, were fresh in their posts, and zealous to make an energetic start. Yen felt the need to adopt a forward posture towards Russia. Concretely, the new policy meant discontinuing relations with the Tsarist diplomats, coupled with the abrogation of Russian extraterritoriality and recovery of Russian concession territories, and holding talks with the Yurin mission.

The Committee for the Study of Russian Treaties, headed by former minister to Russia, Liu Ching-jen, was organized within the Wai-chiao Pu for the purpose of preparing for treaty revisions with Russia. At its August 24 meeting, the committee was entrusted with formulating a proposal on how to proceed with talks with Yurin. It quickly arrived at the conclusion that China should not restrict negotiations to commercial matters only but explore with Yurin, secretly, other questions pertaining to the various rights and privileges the Soviet government had shown willingness to abandon as indicated in the First Karakhan Manifesto. However, the Chinese government had already publicly declared its intention of acting in concert with other countries regarding recognition of Russia; it therefore decided to refrain from official talks, and from recognition of the Far Eastern Republic until other countries had taken the lead.

These views were embodied in a memorandum by the Wai-chiao Pu's political affairs department for the foreign minister. It reads as follows:

> The reason for Yurin's designation as 'chief commercial representative' stems from our desire to act in accord with the Allies as well as obviate the objections of Japan and France. We must first find out whether he is empowered to represent all of eastern Siberia. When that has been established, we should then hold informal talks with him. Overtly, we should limit ourselves to commercial matters but, because China and Russia are adjoining states, we will have to raise political questions as well. For instance, we might exchange views with him on those rights and interests which the Soviet government has agreed to renounce in its manifesto. This will serve as a basis for negotiations when the Soviet government is subsequently recognized.[57]

On September 10, a polite meeting took place between the Wai-chiao Pu councillor, Chang Tsu-shen, and Yurin. Chang asked to examine Yurin's credentials and it became immediately apparent that Yurin possessed no letters of credence other than the one from Verkhne Udinsk. Yurin was informed that talks would begin as soon as he had received authorization from the other Siberian governments to represent them as well. The unification of eastern Siberia under one government was making promising progress and Yurin did not feel the Chinese to be unreasonable, since he claimed to represent the Far Eastern Republic of all eastern Siberia.[58]

In less than a month, however, these promising developments were cut short by the furore among the foreign official and private communities aroused by the abrogation of Russian extraterritoriality and the attempt to take over the Russian concessions. Foreign official opposition was fanned further by the publication of the Supplementary Agreement on the Chinese Eastern Railway on October 2. Foreign tolerance for Peking's steady impairment of Russian treaty rights in seeming disregard for international law was strained beyond limit.

In the minds of foreign governments, China's latest

moves were linked with Yurin's presence in Peking. Foreigners in general had been alarmed by the rising tide of rabid nationalism in China and blamed it in part on the Bolsheviks' inflammatory propaganda. Moscow's strident anti-imperialist pronouncements, evident in the Karakhan Manifesto, were matched by mounting anti-foreignism among the Chinese. To the foreigners, a re-enactment of the Boxer nightmare seemed to be in the making.

What proved decisive in dimming Yurin's prospects were foreign, especially Anglo-American, reactions communicated to the Wai-chiao Pu. The Japanese were of course seriously exercised by Peking's acceptance of the Yurin mission. In view of the large Tsarist debts to Japan for munitions, the Japanese minister said his government 'could not view with equanimity the renunciation of Russian assets, such as the Chinese Eastern Railway, Boxer indemnity, etc.'[59] But Peking could still ignore Tokyo's feelings if only it could count on American support which, in this instance, was not forthcoming.

On October 1, Assistant Secretary of State Bainbridge Colby told the Chinese minister, Wellington Koo, that while he was prepared to believe that China's actions were independent of Bolshevik instigation, he nevertheless felt it unwise for China to impair Russian treaty rights, however unjust they might be. He intimated having received a proposal from Tokyo for international management of Russian interests until the official government appeared in Russia; he feared he might not be able to resist Tokyo's pressure if China chose to provide the Japanese with the pretext. Striking against Russian rights, he said, might scare away foreign investment, thereby hinting that the promising discussions on loans from the foreign consortium then in progress, might be cut short. Chinese antiforeignism was precisely what the Bolsheviks were propagating and he suggested that China would be wise not to have anything to do with Yurin so as to quieten foreign fears.[60]

On the following day, Colby instructed Minister Crane to warn the Chinese government that its dealings with Yurin were giving rise to the impression that it was 'accepting the plans of the Russian Communists', that it was being used for aims opposed to the interests of the governments 'which in the past have shown themselves to be in sympathy with the nationalist desires of the Chinese'. By merely appearing to be 'subservient' to the Russian Communist influence, 'China would . . . lose the friendly regard of such nations'. Furthermore, the Chinese government's action would give an excuse for aggressions 'justified with a show of reason as being necessary to keep the rights of Russia from being confiscated by the Russian Reds who possibly would try to make use of them as a weapon against the interests and rights of other countries'.[61] In short, Peking's expectation that Washington would continue to exercise a restraining influence on Tokyo might be in jeopardy.

Simultaneously, the British Foreign Secretary, Lord Curzon, also instructed the British Chargé d'Affaires, Clive, to convey to the Chinese government 'a private and friendly warning' that its dealings with the Bolsheviks 'may lead to trouble with Russia in the future', and that the Bolshevik proposals 'would appear to be propaganda designed to stir up strife among foreign nations'. In communicating the warning, Clive added that in view of Yurin's obvious connection with Moscow, the Chinese government would do well to be on its guard.[62]

There remains the question of Britain's negotiations with the Bolsheviks. Unbeknown to Foreign Minister Yen, and probably to Minister Crane as well (who previously had advised courteous treatment of Yurin and now warned that it was 'liable to lend credence to the belief that the Chinese government was becoming a tool of the Bolsheviks') the Allied attitude of conciliation towards the Soviets had suddenly reverted in the summer to the militant and intransigent mood of 1919 when the Red Army had taken the offensive against Poland.[63] Anglo-Soviet talks in London had broken off in July and did not resume again until November. At least one of Foreign Minister Yen's problems was to synchronize his steps with those of Britain, however irrelevant the issues impinging on Anglo-Soviet relations might be to China. On October 15, Clive described to Lord Curzon Yen's unenviable position. He was hesitating as to what to do with Yurin. 'The Chinese Minister for Foreign Affairs fears, I think, that the Chinese Government has gone a little too far.'[64]

Yen's embarrassment was all the more profound when, on November 2, Yurin wrote to ask to begin talks, enclosing letters of credence from the Maritime Province, Amur, Sakhalin, and Kamchatka. On November 17, as instructed by Yen, Liu Ching-jen wrote Yurin a letter, unsigned and in the third person, to arrange a meeting for the next day. Yurin repaid what he saw as an insult by sending his second secretary, Kazanin.[65] Yurin must have observed, with wonder, how the Chinese government allowed itself to be bullied by the diplomatic body. He must have felt, too, that his colleagues in Moscow were dreaming when they spoke freely of a Sino-Soviet alliance against Japan and other imperialists. He could not have failed to note that upon encountering imperialist opposition, Peking simply ignored him while resisting as best it could when it was a case of recovering rights from Russia. His reports to the Narkomindel must have added weight to the cool-headed reappraisal of the China policy underway in Moscow.

Relations between Yurin and the Wai-chiao Pu had in fact been souring for some time. He was not permitted coded communication with his government. He was asked to remove the red flag on his limousine because French Minister Boppé was upset. His lease of premises was held up because Clive, the British Chargé, suspected irregularity in Yurin's purchase of large quantities of motor cars, chemicals, etc. to be shipped home.[66]

Foreign Minister Yen was of course also desperate. He told Minister Crane on November 26 that Yurin had presented his credentials, and that talks would soon have to begin. The very long common boundary, the absence of any means of protecting the numerous unrepresented Chinese in Siberia, and the need for commercial relations all made it imperative that something be determined upon. He said China was totally opposed to Bolshevism, and that there had been no reported increase of radicalism in the country. But Crane gave him no encouragement.[67]

That same evening, by private letter, Yen invited Yurin to his residence and the two met for the first time. Yurin was mollified and he agreed to meet Liu Ching-jen as his counterpart. Four days later, he presented a four-point agenda: (a) revision of the existing Sino-Russian treaties on the basis of equality; (b) exchange of consular representation to facilitate trade; (c) negotiation for a commercial treaty; and (d) settlement of the Chinese Eastern Railway question. The railway, he said, had 'colossal significance' for both countries and he proposed a suitable agreement 'whereby the interests, rights, and obligations of the two sides should find full security according to the principle of mutual fairness'. He categorically rejected the claim of the Russo-Asiatic Bank to have any say in the matter, thus firing the first shot against the Supplementary Agreement.[68]

His pace was faster than the Wai-chiao Pu had wished. On November 30, Liu Ching-jen told Yurin that Peking was ready to negotiate a commercial treaty but laid down four preconditions: that the Russian side should refrain from all political propaganda, indemnify Chinese losses in Russia, protect Chinese life and property in Russia, and settle all outstanding border incidents. Liu wanted Yurin's acceptance in writing. This was the Wai-chiao Pu's way of keeping the Yurin mission at arm's length until the way was clear for serious talks. Yurin had no choice: if he rejected them, talks would not begin; if he accepted them, talks still would not begin because he would have to demonstrate his 'sincerity' by implementing the conditions, some of which were time-consuming if not impossible or impractical. On December 13, he sent in his written acceptance; the Wai-chiao Pu then presented him with a list of claims for losses, etc.[69]

Yurin of course had no illusions about the Wai-chiao Pu's own sincerity. On February 2, in a long angry note, he accused the Chinese government of delaying negotiations deliberately, and warned that his government would not be to blame if Chinese interests in Russia continued to suffer. Furthermore, he accused the Chinese government of giving sanctuary to the White Guards or doing nothing to curb their movement and activity—pointing ominously to Baron Ungern von Sternberg's counterrevolutionary movement, just then appearing in Outer Mongolia.[70]

As if the Wai-chiao Pu's hands were not totally tied from the beginning of the talks, another deterrent was added. The ex-First Secretary of the Russian Legation, Grave, had somehow laid his hands on a copy of the Second Karakhan Manifesto, and with studied mischief, he omitted one clause and passed it on to the Japanese legation in Peking. The Japanese were taken in by the impression, as indicated in Obata's report to Tokyo, that a treaty carrying a secret clause had been signed in Moscow by Chang Ssu-lin. Grave's version was soon picked up by the Japanese and foreign press, to the great embarrassment of the Wai-chiao Pu.[71]

British Minister Alston came closest to depicting the mood of the Wai-chiao Pu when he wrote Lord Curzon on February 11, 1921:

> Faced with innumerable and urgent problems along her long and undefined Russian frontier, China is forced to stave off complications as best she may by unofficial missions and *pourparlers*, but it is unlikely that she will enter into serious negotiations until the anxiously awaited lead has been given her by one of the powers, or until her hand is forced by definite aggression on the part of Russia.[72]

The British minister's forecast turned out to be accurate in every detail. Only after the signature of the Anglo-Soviet trade agreement (March 16) did the Chinese government bestir itself once more to begin substantive talks with Yurin. The British precedent had opened the way for a commercial agreement but not for official recognition of the Far Eastern Republic until other powers took the lead. On April 30, Yurin deposited with the Wai-chiao Pu a draft agreement of commerce which the latter agreed to consider. Less than three weeks later, however, Yurin was suddenly recalled to Chita for consultations—no doubt in connection with the question of Outer Mongolia, on which Moscow and Chita were on the verge of a momentous decision. The Red Army's march into Outer Mongolia in June was to make direct talks with Moscow all the more imperative for Peking.

9

China's Loss of Outer Mongolia

The most important single event in Sino-Soviet relations in 1921 was Soviet military intervention in Outer Mongolia. In the summer of that year, Soviet and Far Eastern Republican troops moved in to put down Ungern Sternberg's White Guards, set up the Mongolian National Government, and effectively and permanently placed Outer Mongolia under Soviet control. The significance of the episode extends far beyond Sino-Soviet relations; Outer Mongolia was the first of many Soviet satellites, and the tactics employed here added up to a model that was to be followed elsewhere in later years.

At first glance, the events in Outer Mongolia represent a perfect example of the essential unity of the two basic objectives of Soviet external policy—safeguarding the security of the state and promotion of world revolution. That is indeed the view of Soviet historians. Kheifets, for example, while forthrightly defending Soviet armed intervention as self-defense, portrays the episode as 'the Mongol Revolution of 1921', a genuine national uprising in which Soviet forces assisted 'in the spirit of Leninist internationalism'.[1] But, whatever the revolutionary potential of the livestock-herding masses under a demanding feudal nobility, the fledgling Mongolian National Party, founded in March 1921 with Soviet assistance, played little more than a peripheral role in a political overturn that was executed largely by the Red Army.[2] Moreover, support of Mongol nationalism was not without difficulties, the most basic of which was the incompatibility among Pan-Mongolism, Chinese nationalism, and Soviet strategic interests.

The transformation of Outer Mongolia into a Soviet satellite took place against the background of a general shift in Soviet internal and external policies which began about this time. Without the benefit of immediate revolutionary aid from the European proletariat, the Soviet republic was forced to be reconciled to standing alone in the territory of the Russian empire. This meant a temporary retreat from world revolution to a policy of conciliation and compromise abroad, and from socialism to the New Economic Policy at home. The external policy henceforth acquired a new flavor of being tougher, less visionary, and more concerned with the preservation of the Soviet republic as a state surrounded by capitalist states.

In the Far East, this shift of emphasis to the defense of national interests merely reinforced the pre-existing trends. Here, years of confrontation with Japanese aggression had long cast the struggle as a patriotic effort. Japan continued to be the central concern of Soviet policy, which extended to China as well as Outer Mongolia. The ruse of the Far Eastern buffer had only been partially successful in that the Japanese troops withdrew in October 1920 from Transbaikalia and Amur to the environs of Vladivostok. There they were joined by disbanded Semenovites, and the intrigues and conspiracies that went on eventually proved fatal to Medvedev's socialist government. In May 1921 the Far Eastern Republic was subject to two synchronous assaults: one from the Maritime Province and one from Outer Mongolia, and both seen in Moscow as Japanese-inspired. Elsewhere, Japanese troops still occupied northern Sakhalin and both the eastern and southern sections of the Chinese Eastern Railway. In China, Chang Tso-lin's ascendancy after the Anfu-Chihli War of July 1920 signalled, in Moscow's view, a further advance of Japanese influence. But the immediate background of Soviet intervention in Outer Mongolia was the fall of Urga into the hands of Ungern Sternberg's White Guards.

In July 1920, the Anfu clique suffered a quick and crushing defeat by the allied Fengtien and Chihli cliques, and General Hsü Shu-cheng, Commissioner for the Northwestern Frontier, went down with it. Once more, Outer Mongolia was a power vacuum, and once again internal splits among the Mongols surfaced. Pro-Chinese Mongols seeking a return of enlightened Chinese rule probably still existed but were muted. The Jebtsun-damba and his camarilla, in position to take the lead again, approached the new situation with characteristic pragmatic realism, trying to regain autonomy from Peking and soliciting international support to maintain it. One Mongol delegation set out for Peking in July to discuss the restoration of autonomy. It also asked American officials, as another delegation had done the year before, to open an American consulate in Urga. Another group of youthful Mongol radicals, led by Sukhe Bator, headed for Moscow.[3]

Other Mongol groups were active meanwhile. Some Tushetu princes negotiated with the Japanese in Harbin for finance and arms purchase, using timber and mining concessions as security. They did this in the name of the Jebtsundamba, although he denied having given any authorization and denounced them for forging his seal and falsely acting in his name.[4] But the group which preempted the Mongolian scene for the next twelve months was the one which paved the way for the entry of Ungern's forces. It included certain Mongol 'bandit' leaders and the Buryats who had fled from Transbaikalia into Outer Mongolia since 1917. The Jebtsun-damba's group was not at first involved but, after further humiliation by the Chinese garrison, it too looked to Ungern for deliverance from the Chinese.

The delegation to Peking appears not to have been given a sympathetic hearing because on September 30 the Chinese government promulgated a set of statutes for the new office of Pacification Commissioner for Khalkha, Uliasutai, Kobdo, and Tannu Uryanghai (K'u-Wu-K'o-T'ang chen-wu shih). This was tantamount to the absorption of these regions into the Chinese provincial administration.[5] The former tu-hu shih, Ch'en I, was appointed to that post. He was invested with full civil and military authority (as General Hsü had once been) but, faced with the difficult situation in Outer Mongolia, he delayed his departure until December when the central government finally allocated some funds. The Chinese garrison in Outer Mongolia consisted of Ch'u Ch'i-hsiang's mixed brigade, sent in the summer of 1919, and Kao Tsai-t'ien's cavalry unit, sent in the summer of 1918, both at the request of the Urga government. They totalled a little over 3,000 men. Ch'u, an Anfu man, and Kao, a Chihli man, naturally did not see eye to eye, and their unpaid soldiers were resorting to extortion and plunder, adding fuel to smoldering Mongol resentment. The complete collapse of Anfu power left these men stranded in the distant and hostile Mongol grasslands as the only symbol of Chinese authority. That authority now came under a new challenge in August 1920 as Ungern's White Guards began to arrive.

A Russian officer of Baltic German extraction, Roman Nikolaus von Ungern-Sternberg the so-called 'Mad Baron', had been Semenov's faithful lieutenant throughout the Transbaikal fighting. Comrades-in-arms since early days, the two men had much in common. Both were autocrats, soldiers, and mystic dreamers, and both shared the credo of monarchy, anti-revolutionism, and anti-Westernism. By the summer of 1920, their position in eastern Transbaikalia was doomed by the Soviet and Far Eastern government forces surrounding them, and Japan's decision to withdraw from the area. At this point, the two men parted. Semenov thenceforth submerged himself in counterrevolutionary conspiracies in Tokyo, Peking, and Vladivostok. Ungern, on his part, made plans to move into Outer Mongolia and establish a base to continue the anti-Bolshevik crusade. He sought to use Pan-Mongolism to establish himself at Urga, a scheme that had been shelved temporarily the previous summer, but not completely abandoned.

The most detailed and possibly most reliable information on the origins, composition and objectives of the Ungern forces is found in Japanese military documents. Particularly useful is one report of early May 1921, submitted by Isomura Toshi, Chief of Staff of the Siberian Expeditionary Army at Vladivostok, to Vice Minister for War, Yamanashi Hanzō. It appears that when Semenov disbanded his Asiatic Division in August 1920, he placed his troops at Ungern's disposal. Ungern set out immediately from Dauria with two cavalry regiments and one infantry regiment, 1,500 men in all. Among them were about 50 Japanese irregulars led by one Sgt Hatakeyama Kōtarō, and an equal number of Chinese mercenaries led by Chang Shun. As the troops crossed the Tsetsen League border and headed for Urga along the Kerulen River, they were joined by the Inner Mongol 'bandit' T'ao-shih-t'ao and his so-called Mongol independence army. T'ao had been associated with the Pan-Mongolist Movement the year before and, earlier still, had been party to Balbojab's Manchu-Mongol independence conspiracy. According to the Isomura report, Ungern's forces were fairly well supplied with arms. One shipment had been secretly conveyed to Urga in August 1919 and then buried in the vicinity of the city when the attempt was called off; another shipment left ahead of Ungern's troops in August 1920. Together with those carried by his troops, Ungern possessed a total of 5,500 rifles, several machine-guns, and four artillery pieces.[6]

Ungern's advance was known to the Chinese garrison at Urga almost as soon as he crossed the border. The Chinese were able to make preparations in time so that when Ungern began his siege of the city on October 25 with a force of 3,000 men, he failed after ten days. He withdrew some distance from Urga to regroup before renewing attack.

Despite his initial reverse, the situation at Urga was in Ungern's favor, partly because of the Chinese garrison's lack of reinforcement, and partly because of the Jebtsun-damba's readiness to join up with Ungern after further humiliation by the Chinese. Chinese reinforcement was impeded by the very real problem of logistics. Distances between China and Outer Mongolia were enormous, communication lines few and easily cut. Between Kalgan and Urga lay 800 miles of trackless desert; it was another 250 miles from Urga to Mai-mai-ch'eng and 700 miles to Uliasutai. Since motor car transport was not sufficiently developed, the only alternative was to use oxen, camel and horse caravans, which was feasible only in spring· and summer. Winter was already setting in when the crisis broke, so no Chinese militarist was willing to send troops to the freezing, windswept lands in the far north.

The militarists were also influenced by important political considerations. The balance of power between the Chihli and Fengtien cliques was not yet stabilized after the Anfu-Chihli War. When the crisis was first reported, the Peking government asked the Chahar tutung, Wang T'ing-chen, to lead a relief column from Kalgan to Urga. Wang, a Chihli supporter with a strategic position *vis-à-vis* the capital, declined. This was seized by Chang Tso-lin as a pretext to put one of his own men, Chang Ching-hui, in Wang's place. But the Fengtien clique was no more inclined than Chihli to commit troops in Outer Mongolia. Of an entire division designated for the Mongolian expedition, Chang Ching-hui sent only a few hundred to Taolin, a long distance from Urga, and a still smaller number to the north, which Ungern drove back without any difficulty to the southern border.[7]

Denied reinforcement, the Chinese garrison commander Ch'u Ch'i-hsiang tried to forestall disaster by preventing contact between the Jebtsun-damba's group and the enemy. He had the Jebtsun-damba and his principal advisers removed from the palace and kept under guard. At the sacrilege the Mongols' anti-Chinese feelings intensified still more and many joined Ungern's ranks. The chen-wu shih, Ch'en I, arrived on the scene at this critical juncture. Deploring the garrison commander's action, he belatedly conciliated the Mongols by returning the Jebtsun-damba and his advisers to the palace and relaxing martial law.

Ungern began his second siege of Urga on January 31, 1921 with a considerably larger force, and took the city on February 3. The Chinese troops who escaped straggled northwards to Mai-mai-ch'eng. On March 24, Ungern proclaimed the independence of Outer Mongolia, and installed the Jebtsun-damba as the Bogdo-gegen and Primate of Mongolia and Tibet. In the cabinet, Jalakangja Khutukhtu served as Prime Minister, the Mongol 'bandit' leader T'ao-shih-t'ao as Minister for War, and Ungern as Chief of Staff. The 'Mad Baron' next instituted a reign of terror against Jews, suspected Bolshevik Russians and Chinese. Banner princes were ordered to supply recruits and provisions for an army which he intended soon to lead against the Bolsheviks in the north.[8]

According to the Isomura report, by April Ungern had organized an anti-Bolshevik force of 10,000 men, made up of 3,000 Russians, 4,000 Buryats, and about 3,000 followers of T'ao-shih–t'ao. Former units of Semenov still lurking in Transbaikalia were expected to join once the attack on the Far Eastern Republic began. The report also mentions certain potential conflicts between Ungern and the Jebtsun-damba's group. The Mongol leadership apparently felt it to be more realistic to aspire for autonomy guaranteed internationally than political independence, and demurred at Ungern's proposed drive against Soviet Russia. Late in May, disregarding the wishes of the Mongol leadership, Ungern and his forces began hitting Mai-mai-ch'eng and Kiakhta and pushing north into Transbaikalia. The Reds answered with a full-scale military intervention that ended in the destruction of the White Guards and the establishment of Soviet political predominance in Outer Mongolia.

Before leaving Ungern, the question of Japan's suspected support for his enterprise and Chang Tso-lin's alleged involvement in it deserves a brief comment as it figures prominently in Soviet justification for intervention and in noncommunist accounts. Just as in the case of Semenov's Pan-Mongolist Movement of 1919, a rash of rumors broke out in 1921 about Chang Tso-lin's intention to unite Manchuria and Mongolia and restore the Manchu monarchy and Japan's support of her Chinese and White Guard clients seeking a Manchurian-Mongolian-Siberian buffer against Bolshevism. The evidence for or against these assertions remains inconclusive and the truth is impossible to ascertain. Those who argue that Chang was in league with Ungern have pointed out that Chang could have detected and stopped the Ungern forces from crossing into Mongolian territory had he so wished. Other evidence brought forward to support this view are the sensational letters reportedly captured from Ungern by the Red Army, which suggest some connection between Chang and Ungern. On the other hand, Chang was said to have punished the garrison commander who was bribed to allow Ungern's troops in and permit supplies from the Hailar-Manchouli area to get through to Ungern. This can be regarded as evidence against Chang's connivance. The Chinese correspondents in Ungern's letters cannot be identified and in some cases were ascribed posts that were definitely held by others. In any case, even were the letters genuine, Ungern appears to be merely expressing the hope that Chang would lead an imperial restoration in conjunction with his effort in Russia, and the letters do not constitute conclusive evidence of an existing understanding between Ungern and Chang. Chang's reluctance to send a relief force to Urga has been cited also as circumstantial evidence for his connivance with Ungern but, as pointed out earlier, it can equally well be explained by logistical and political considerations. One is therefore inclined to agree with Chang's Japanese biographer, Sonoda Ikki, that no relationship whatsoever existed between Chang and Ungern.[9]

As in Semenov's Pan-Mongolist Movement of 1919, the question of Japan's involvement is not whether it existed but at what level. Given the army's assertion of autonomy from the Tokyo government and the capacity and propensity of field-grade officers for independent action, some Japanese involvement can be found in practically all White Guard plots during the Siberian intervention. Japanese involvement with Ungern is clearer than in the case of Semenov's Pan-Mongolist Movement. At least fifty Japanese irregulars were in Ungern's forces. These surrendered to the Chinese in October 1920 after participating in Ungern's first unsuccessful siege of Urga. According to the deposition of their leader Sargent Hatakeyama, a reservist army engineer, he was introduced to Semenov in 1919 by Captain Kuroki Shinkei, the Japanese liaison officer attached to Semenov's staff. In return for a timber concession in the Aksha region of Transbaikalia, he and his men agreed to join Semenov's Asiatic Division. In August 1920, they accompanied Ungern to Urga. Ungern's arms were also of Japanese origin, purchased from Japan via Captain Kuroki. The Isomura report speaks very favorably of Ungern's prospects for protracted warfare against the Bolsheviks and implicitly argues to higher military authorities for support of his crusade as one means of destroying Bolshevism.[10]

However, on April 1, 1921, gravely perturbed by rumors of Japan's support for Ungern and their effect on the Chinese government, the Japanese vice minister for war instructed a Japanese adviser to the Chinese president to declare that although Japanese adventurers (*rōnin*) might be involved, the Japanese government was not connected in any way with the incident. Since such measures were normally preceded by careful investigation and checking with local military officials lest contrary evidence surface later to cause embarrassment, it seems safe to assume that Japan's involvement with Ungern was limited to field-grade officers acting on their own initiative.[11]

But, whatever the reality, Soviet policy was based, like any other, on fear and suspicion. The notion that Japan and Chang Tso-lin were in league with Ungern worried the Soviet government and prompted it to take measures to safeguard its national security.

Responding to the threat to its self-interest, the Soviet government first sent its armed forces 20 miles within the Mongolian border in February 1921 in anticipation of a northward drive by Ungern. In March, working with the forces of change within Mongol society, it assisted in the formation of the Mongolian National Party and the Provisional Mongolian National Government at Kiakhta. Full-scale intervention was postponed until early July when a force of 10,000 men, made up of the Red Army, troops of the Far Eastern Republic, and 400 Mongol troops of the provisional government, descended on Urga. The White Guards were dispersed and progressively mopped up. The Mongolian National Government was formally and permanently proclaimed on July 10, with the Jebtsun-damba installed as a constitutional monarch though given a purely religious role. The Jebtsun-damba's leadership was expected to give the new government legitimacy and ensure maximum popular support. The Mongolian National Government on July 12 requested the Soviet troops to remain and they did not depart until March 1925.[12]

The train of events in 1921 constituted a major landmark in the evolution of Soviet policy towards Outer Mongolia since 1917. In the early days of the regime, anxious to unite with China against Japan, the Narkomindel hinted it was willing to renounce the Kiakhta Convention of 1915 and leave Outer Mongolia under Chinese tutelage. In the summer of 1919, anxious to unite with Outer Mongolia against Japan, it addressed a manifesto to the Mongols, at the same time as the Karakhan Manifesto to the Chinese, informing them it had renounced all the old treaties with China and Japan concerning Outer Mongolia. It said the Mongols were thenceforth an independent people, free to conduct their own foreign relations. Sensing difficulty in simultaneously championing Mongol independence and courting Chinese nationalism, the Karakhan Manifesto skirted the Mongolian question, vaguely stating that the Soviet government favored self-determination by national minorities within any state. In 1921, Soviet policy underwent another twist, calculated to further Soviet strategic goals at the risk of offending Mongol and Chinese nationalism.

According to the platform adopted by the Mongolian National Party, the immediate goal was set down as the restoration of the autonomous Mongolian state that had been suppressed by the Chinese militarist Hsü Shu-cheng, and the ultimate was the union of all Mongol tribes into a Pan-Mongol, independent state. In the first phase of Outer Mongolia's political evolution, the Mongolian National Party deemed some relationship with China desirable as a means, said the platform, of defending the area against foreign imperialism.[13] Whether the initial objective was formulated at Soviet behest or reflected the practical-mindedness of the Mongols, it fitted in with Soviet purposes. Indeed, after the proclamation of the Mongolian National Government when some Mongols were impatient to proceed to the next phase, they were told by the Soviet government to recognize Chinese sovereignty and be content with autonomy in order that 'unprofitable conflict' with China might be avoided.[14] And when the Soviet government consented to the Mongol request for Soviet troops to remain, the condition was that the Mongols should keep within their autonomous status.[15] Subsequent development shows that the Pan-Mongolist aspirations of the Mongolian National Party met with the same fate as they had in 1911-15, and for much the same reasons. A Pan-Mongolist, independent state would have involved Buryat separatism, sabotaged Soviet relations with China, and thrown the region open to influences other than those of Soviet Russia.

In short, the Soviet government wanted Outer Mongolia to limit its objective to returning, in form at least, to its former status, autonomous within the Chinese republic but under Soviet protection. This policy was clearly governed by certain tactical considerations related to Japan and China. It afforded Soviet military intervention the appearance that it was undertaken within the framework of the Kiakhta Convention of 1915, on the strength of which the Soviet government could claim a legally valid interest in Outer Mongolia. The Mongolian National Party's request of April 10, 1921 for Soviet military assistance, its request of July 12 for the troops to remain, and Ungern's actual forays into Soviet territory provided additional justification for Soviet intervention.

Whether Japan would tolerate the military intervention was one risk the Soviet government felt compelled to take in defense of its national security. It did everything it could, including delaying intervention for over six months, in order to preclude counteraction from Japan. Another measure taken with the same objective partially in mind was to seek China's understanding, if not cooperation, for Soviet action. Soviet policy in 1921 evolved against the background of significant and continual discussions between Moscow and Peking. The crux of the problem confronting the Soviet government was the incompatibility between its Mongolian and Chinese policies. In China it was seeking official recognition from the Peking government and the reinstatement of Russian interests, especially those in north Manchuria. In the longer term, it was courting Chinese nationalism in the hope of bringing about a unified, pro-Soviet China, independent of Japanese and other imperialists, with opportunities for promoting proletarian revolutionary movements. All these objectives were in danger of being sabotaged by Soviet action in Outer Mongolia. The decision to intervene highlights the accent of Soviet policy on short-term considerations, and the discussions between Moscow and Peking reveal a progressive hardening of Soviet policy towards China.

The Soviet government began contacting Peking during

Ungern's first assault on Urga. In a note to the Wai-chiao Pu on November 10, 1920, Chicherin characterized Ungern's activities as a common threat to China, the Far Eastern Republic, and Soviet Russia. He mentioned a request by Chinese troops near Urga to Soviet and Far Eastern military commanders for assistance and said the Soviet government was ready to comply. Corresponding orders had been given to Soviet troops to go to Mongolia as China's friends, and, upon destruction of the White Guards, to evacuate Chinese territory. On November 27, after Ungern was repulsed by the Chinese garrison, Chicherin sent the Wai-chiao Pu a second note, welcoming the Chinese victory. He was pleased that his government, which stood for the inviolability of foreign territory, found it unnecessary to send troops to Mongolia, and confident that China would take immediate and energetic measures for the complete liquidation of hostile White Guards. He nevertheless offered immediate military help if China considered it necessary.[16]

These early messages were cordial but they took Peking by complete surprise. To begin with, they did not reach Peking until December 21! The first was broadcast by Moscow radio but Peking received a garbled version of it on November 17 from the Chinese minister in London.[17] Both notes were sent to Irkutsk for relay to Peking, but the telegraph wires had been cut by Ungern and so the messages could not go through immediately. The Chinese government was also astounded by the mention of a request for Soviet assistance by local Chinese troops and dismissed it as a pretext fabricated by the Soviet government 'to meddle' in Outer Mongolia. The Wai-chiao Pu immediately instructed the Chinese minister in London and Ch'en I in Urga to inform Soviet officials that the alleged request for help was untrue and everything was being done to preclude the need for intervention by a third party. They were to warn also that the crossing of the border by Soviet troops would be considered by Peking as a violation of its territorial sovereignty.[18]

Early in February 1921, Ungern's second assault on Urga forced Chinese officials and troops to flee to the border towns of Mai-mai-ch'eng and Kiakhta. Soviet accounts assert that Ch'en I appealed to the Narkomindel official Makstenek on

February 19 for military assistance, and his deputy, Li Yüan, renewed the request on March 3.[19] But the exact circumstances of their actions were a great deal more complicated.

In fact, when Urga fell to Ungern, Soviet officials asked the Chinese civil administrator in Mai–mai–ch'eng, Lu Pang-tao, if he would consent to Soviet troops crossing the border to join with Chinese troops in suppressing Ungern. According to Lu, he rejected the proposal but Soviet troops nevertheless crossed the border in mid–February, taking up defensive positions 10 miles west and 20 miles south of Mai–mai–ch'eng. The Soviet officials gave Lu the undertaking that these troops would be promptly and unconditionally withdrawn at the end of the Ungern crisis.

The three principal Chinese officials, Ch'en I, Li Yüan, and Lu Pang-tao, confronted with the *fait accompli*, met in Mai–mai–ch'eng to take stock of the situation. They found the Chinese garrison had been reduced to about 1,000 stragglers incapable of further action and no relief from China was in sight. Pressed by the Whites in front and the Reds at the back, they decided a measure of cooperation with the Reds was desirable. The Reds had been transmitting their messages and liberally issuing visas and providing relief to Chinese refugees. The Chinese officials felt obligated and at the same time saw the necessity for a written agreement to limit the free movement of Soviet troops across the border. Hence, on February 19, Ch'en I proposed to Makstenek that, in the interest of joint defense of the border communities, Soviet troops would be allowed twenty miles inside the Mongolian border on the understanding that they would be promptly withdrawn after the crisis. But Makstenek counterproposed that joint operations be carried as far south as Urga and Ch'en I was compelled to seek instructions from Peking.[20]

The Chinese government endorsed Ch'en I's original proposal but rejected Makstenek's counterproposal as greatly harmful to China's sovereignty and prestige. This was conveyed to Makstenek by Li Yüan on March 3.[21] The Reds expressed keen disappointment and next took action in combination with the Mongolian National Party. On March 15, the party issued the Chinese with an ultimatum to leave Mai–mai–ch'eng, and when the Chinese refused the so–called

Mongolian People's Army of 400 men in conjunction with Soviet troops forced the Chinese to flee into Russian territory.[22]

In the next two months, the Soviet government assumed the role of an intermediary between the Mongolian National Party and the Chinese government. On April 7, Ch'en I learned from the Far Eastern Republican authorities at Verkhne Udinsk of the party's desire for an exchange of views with Peking. On its part, the Mongolian National Party favored unity with the Reds against the Whites and was opposed to a government led by the lamas and feudal despotism of the princes. Under the leadership of the party, Outer Mongolia would recognize China's sovereignty and would even accept a limited number of Chinese troops. The party had no intention of taking Outer Mongolia out of the Chinese republic but did want political autonomy.[23]

The Mongolian National Party's proposal to Peking was reinforced by a similar message from the Soviet representative in London to the Chinese minister there. On May 5, Krasin informed Koo that he had just received the vital information that Japan had instigated the Whites and the Jebtsun-damba to break relations with China and turn Outer Mongolia into a Japanese-dominated buffer between China and Russia. He said the Mongolian National Party's goal was an autonomous Mongolia within the Chinese republic, free from Japanese control. The Soviet government supported the party and its objectives and desired that China come to an agreement with the party before it was too late.[24]

These messages were placed before the Wai-chiao Pu's Committee on Russian Affairs for deliberations. They struck a familiar chord, unpleasantly reminiscent of the previous occasion in 1911-15 when the Tsarist government had acted as an intermediary between China and Outer Mongolia, with the Kiakhta Convention as the result. Although all vestiges of Chinese authority in Outer Mongolia had disappeared, the committee nevertheless deemed it unwise for the Chinese government to deal with the Mongolian National Party via the Soviet government, as it would mean allowing Russia to interpose between China and Outer Mongolia once again. The committee recommended that the government should, as a matter of policy, consider the Mongolian question as China's internal problem, tolerating no intervention from any third party. It proposed that the government, in reply, express the wish to send a commissioner to Kiakhta to study the Mongolian National Party before entering into discussions with Moscow. If the Soviet government agreed, it would in effect be bypassed and the Chinese commissioner would be able to contact the Mongolian National Party directly and win it over. The scheme was clever on paper but produced no practical results.[25]

In June, the Soviet decision to intervene ripened. For months, the Dal'buro (Far Eastern Bureau) of the Russian Communist Party in Irkutsk had been agitating for an immediate strike at Urga, pointing out that Ungern's counterrevolution in conjunction with Japan could deal a fatal blow to Soviet control of eastern Siberia.[26] But Moscow had remained cautious, still hopeful of joint operations with China to lessen international complications. China's rigid attitude combined with Ungern's actual forays into Russian territory late in May to produce the forward policy in Moscow. On the recommendation of the Red Army command in Irkutsk, the Politburo of the Russian Communist Party decided on June 16 that military operations begin forthwith and not end until the complete destruction of Ungern's forces and the occupation of Urga.[27] Chicherin promptly notified Peking of the decision. He said Ungern's attacks had forced the armies of the Far Eastern Republic and Soviet Russia to cross the Mongolian border. The Soviet government was guided solely by the principle of mutual respect for each other's territorial sovereignty. These military operations were beneficial to China since they would help in the preservation of China's sovereignty. He pledged that the troops would be withdrawn once the objective was accomplished.[28]

The Wai-chiao Pu was apparently lulled by Chicherin's profession of friendly intentions so that its reply two weeks later was cast in a softer vein than one would have expected. It said that although the proposed campaign against Ungern was evidently animated by a spirit of friendly cooperation, 'such a suggestion is very difficult for the Chinese Government to entertain inasmuch as it involves the territorial rights of

China'. It informed Chicherin that Chang Tso-lin had been named to lead an expedition to destroy the Ungern forces and preparations were underway. The Chinese government was entirely disposed to discuss the possibility of taking concerted action in regard to the disturbances along the Russo-Mongolian frontier as might be required from time to time.[29] In other words, the Chinese government had no objection to joint action in the border areas but preferred to deal with the situation in Urga with its own troops. But by the time the Wai-chiao Pu replied, the Soviet and Far Eastern troops were well on their way to Urga. In any case, the prospect of Urga being occupied by Chang Tso-lin's troops was repugnant in the extreme and Moscow would want to do everything to forestall it.

While his first note was being considered by the Chinese, Chicherin dispatched another, outlining a set of proposals on the future of Outer Mongolia. It said the Soviet government was most anxious to come to some definite arrangement with the Chinese government in regard to the area. The Soviet government recognized and supported the right of national self-determination of the Mongol people but wished also to uphold China's prerogatives in this question. The Mongolian National Government had proclaimed independence but, said the note, 'an independent Mongolia would become an easy prey to some White Guard adventurers and to Japan'. The Soviet government had already begun discussions with the Mongolian National Government and found the latter fully prepared to approach any proposal on its relations with China with an open mind. Therefore, the Soviet government proposed that a committee of representatives of the three governments concerned be formed to discuss the problem.[30]

Here is spelled out candidly the Soviet view that although Mongolian independence deserved support in principle, it was strategically undesirable to Soviet Russia. Chicherin obviously expected Peking to seize the oportunity for regaining some influence over Mongolian affairs. But Peking's reaction to Chicherin's open call for a tripartite settlement of the Mongolian question was as rigid as before. The proposal was contrary to China's policy, unchanged since 1919, of excluding Russian influence from Outer Mongolia. The Peking government chose to treat the Mongolian problem as its internal affair and sent no reply to Chicherin's note.[31] Yet, presented with a *fait accompli*, there was nothing that it could do to reverse the developments taking place in Outer Mongolia.

Soviet Russia's armed intervention proved to be far more successful than initially expected. It was a gamble that paid off handsomely for it was based on the uncertain assumption that neither Japan nor China would be able to take counteraction of a military kind. Japan was too much on the defensive internationally to respond with military force. As for China, her inaction during the many months prior to Soviet intervention stemmed entirely from the peculiar nature of warlord politics of the time. The specific question is why Chang Tso-lin's expedition to Outer Mongolia, referred to in the Wai-chiao Pu's reply to Chicherin, did not materialize.

The collapse of the Anfu clique in the Anfu-Chihli War of July 1920 brought the Chihli and Fengtien cliques to the forefront of warlord politics. The war had been waged and won largely by Wu P'ei-fu, a commander of the Chihli troops and subordinate of the Chihli clique leader, Ts'ao K'un. The Fengtien clique leader, Chang Tso-lin, had brought down from Manchuria a massive body of troops but did not enter the fray until a Chihli victory was clear. But in the postwar settlement, Chang quickly gained the upper hand over Ts'ao. The Fengtien faction was much more cohesive than the Chihli, and Chang easily outclassed Ts'ao in uncanny shrewdness and opportunism. The new cabinet formed in August 1920 with Chin Yün-p'eng as premier was virtually hand-picked by Chang, even though the real power in north China resided in Chihli hands. Division of Anfu territories, including Inner and Outer Mongolia, was postponed. Wu P'ei-fu, who began attracting Soviet attention as a possible ally at this time, was Chang's main source of worry. In these circumstances, Chang refused to be distracted by anything, such as a Mongolian expedition, that would undermine his influence in north China.[32]

The Chin Yün-p'eng Cabinet soon ran into a number of grave problems, including a dire need for money and the fall of Outer Mongolia into White Guard hands. Without funds, the cabinet could move no troops. Chang, who was able to send an expedition, laid down stiff terms: a generous allocation of funds and recognition of his authority over Inner and Outer Mongolia. Ts'ao K'un, who could spare no troops, did not wish Chang given the Mongolian assignment on those terms, unless the Chihli clique was suitably compensated. In short, the solution to the Mongolian question depended on how and when these super warlords decided on the distribution of Anfu territories.

In April and May 1921, Chihli's demand for a share of power in the cabinet, the Mongolian problem, and a looming cabinet crisis brought the super warlords together in Tientsin for a conference. The new cabinet announced in May, with Chin Yün-p'eng again as premier, was more balanced between Chihli and Fengtien than before. (It lasted no longer than December when Chang replaced it with one entirely of his own choice and thus lighted the fuse to the Fengtien-Chihli War of the spring of 1922.) The next order of business was the distribution of Anfu territories and the solution of the Mongolian problem. When the new government agreed to allocate funds and create a new office, called Commissioner for Mongolia (Meng-chiang ching-lüeh shih), Chang volunteered for the assignment. His opposite number consented after it was agreed that Shensi and Kansu should go to the Chihli clique.[33]

Chang returned to Mukden early in June, pleased that at long last Manchuria and Mongolia were under his sway. Late that month, after the Peking treasury had gathered with great difficulty 5,000,000 dollars for the Mongolian expedition, he began tackling the problem in earnest. The plan that he and his subordinates decided upon involved the dispatch of 30,000 men who would enter Outer Mongolia from Jehol, Hailar, and Kalgan. The Fengtien troops began to move just when Soviet and Far Eastern Republican troops were pouring in from the north.

Early in July, success of the Fengtien troops was reported on all three fronts. Chang Ching-hui's men, pushing northwards from Kalgan, routed small Mongol units in the way; Chi Chin-ch'un's men entering from Jehol similarly put Mongol troops to flight; and Wu Chun-sheng's column entering from Hailar succeeded in putting down the Hulunbuir malcontents. Then, Chang Tso-lin suddenly called a halt. The explanation lies in two political developments within China. In July, his Kwangsi allies were defeated by the Kwangtung forces of Sun Yat-sen and Ch'en Chiung-ming. Also, Wang Chan-yüan, Inspector General of Hunan and Hupeh, who was Chang's ally against Wu P'ei-fu, was driven out by Hunanese militarists and Wu stepped in and took over the two provinces for himself. With his political prosperity inside China thus threatened, Chang discontinued the Mongolian expedition and disavowed any further responsibility for Outer Mongolia.[34] The result was that Soviet Russia was given a completely free hand to do exactly as she pleased.

By mid-July 1921, therefore, all visible signs of Chinese sovereignty in Outer Mongolia had disappeared, and Soviet Russia, now in virtual political and military control of Urga was able to dictate her terms to Peking. This set the stage for years of diplomacy with Moscow that were filled with exasperation and despair for the Peking government.

10

The Yurin and Paikes Missions

When Yurin returned to his mission in China in mid-July 1921, Soviet political and military intervention in Outer Mongolia was already in full swing. His bargaining strength in Peking had undergone a marked change from what had prevailed only two months earlier. With the absence of Russian power following the October Revolution, the Chinese had tried to remove the incubus of Tsarist imperialism, in anticipation of a new order of relations with Russia. Although the effort to recover sovereign rights had not been a complete success, still the changes effected on the issues of Outer Mongolia, the Chinese Eastern Railway, Amur River navigation, and Russian extraterritorial privilege and concession territories had enabled China, by the second half of 1920, to look towards negotiating with a new Russia from a position of relative strength.

Blending revolutionary appeal with hard-headed power politics, Soviet policy throughout 1920 had tried to reach China and win an alliance with her against Japan. Generous offers notwithstanding, the Chinese did not respond positively, in part because they were not free to, and in part because of their conviction that the problem of Japan, common to both China and Russia, could be better met by China's acting in concert with the Western powers than with Bolshevik Russia. A flicker of hope flared in the autumn of 1920 with the admission of the Yurin mission to Peking, but it was quickly extinguished by foreign opposition. Thereafter, Yurin was shunted aside and ignored. This situation prevailed up to the early summer of 1921, when Yurin returned to Chita for important consultations.

As described in the previous chapter, one practical effect of these consultations manifested itself in a forward policy in Outer Mongolia. Soviet and Far Eastern Republican forces advanced into the territory in late June and installed the Mongolian National Government at Urga. The political and military control thereby gained by Russia in Outer Mongolia was to give Moscow a most effective diplomatic leverage in Peking. Furthermore, the Mongolian venture took place within the context of a rapid improvement in Russia's international position resulting from diplomatic gains in Britain and elsewhere. It came under the new conception of a foreign policy arrived at in early 1921 for Russia to build up her economic and diplomatic strength by all practical means and to take her place among the great powers of the world. The consequences of Peking's lack of diplomatic independence were becoming apparent: it could not negotiate until a major power provided the lead, by which time it was already too late.

From this point on, Peking's position of strength eroded rapidly. The power of initiative was passing into Russian hands. It was Russia's turn to state its terms, to be intransigent or flexible, to hasten or delay negotiations. For its part, China sustained the pattern of relations that existed up to the conclusion of the Sino-Soviet Treaty in May 1924, by incessant internal dissensions combined with diminishing central authority. Between Yurin's return to China in mid-July 1921 and the arrival of Karakhan in late 1923, the opportunity for serious negotiations arose but once—in the winter of 1921. It came out of Peking's desire for a settlement of the Chinese Eastern Railway question, prompted by Washington's call for an international conference on the Far Eastern question, and by the decision of Tokyo and Chita to convene the Dairen Conference, both of which had an important bearing on the Chinese Eastern Railway.

The Chinese were to find that, just as with the forward

policy in Outer Mongolia, Russian policy was stiffening on the Chinese Eastern Railway question as well. As in Outer Mongolia, Russia was seeking to return to another area where Tsarist Russia had once had vital interests, and for much the same reason as its preoccupation with Japan.

It will be recalled that in the course of 1920 the Chinese systematically de-colonized the C.E.R. Administration by carefully separating its political and economic aspects, and then, by the Supplementary Agreement of October 2, 1920, assumed temporary trusteeship of the enterprise on behalf of the future Russian government. The railway was now operated as a purely business concern by an administration staffed by Chinese and non-Soviet Russians. The problem of having eventually to reach an accord with Russia remained for the future, but the Chinese were determined to prevent a return to the pre-1917 situation where the railway had been a Russian state enterprise in everything but name. While being certain that Russia would be forced to accept decolonization as a *fait accompli*, the Chinese were by no means confident about the future arrangement concerning the railway itself. Of all the acts of Tsarist aggression in China, none was more difficult to undo than the laying of a railway within Chinese territory with funds supplied almost entirely by the Russian state treasury. The railway was only in China's temporary possession and nothing would alter the fact that it was a Russian state property. Just how the Soviet government proposed to dispose of the railway would obviously depend on how strong Soviet Russia became internationally.

Given the time factor and China's inherently weak position on the railway, it was natural that some Chinese officials should press for early negotiations. Most vigorous among them was Wang Ching-ch'un, a leading Chinese railway expert trained at Yale and Illinois, who in 1921 held three concurrent posts—counsellor to the Ministry of Communications, deputy manager of the Chinese Eastern Railway, and Chinese representative on the Inter-Allied Technical Board. His memorandum to the ministry in January was to form the basis of Chinese official thinking on this important matter. In it, he set forth three possibilities:

1. Transfer of the railway to China without compensation. Wang was aware that the Soviet government had equivocated on this point, still he felt it might be possible if China would sign a trade agreement, yield on other issues, and permit the Russians special privileges in the use of the railway as they had asked in the second Karakhan Manifesto.

2. If Russia insisted upon compensation, then China should issue government bonds to redeem it. He proposed that these bonds be distributed among Chinese and Russian nationals, with a portion made available to subjects of friendly powers. He felt this would appeal to the Russians, who were in dire need of funds, and moreover would put the railway on an international financial basis, thereby freeing it from the danger of seizure by Japan and international conflict.

3. If Russia refused to relinquish title rights, then the only remaining option would be joint ownership and management. In that case, China should contribute either 50 per cent or 100 per cent of the original capital, estimated to be 500,000,000 roubles, but insist on the original right to redeem the railway after 36 years and receive it free of charge after 80 years.[1]

It is clear that whichever option was eventually adopted would depend solely upon the new Russian rulers. From China's point of view, the first was of course the most desirable, but it was also the one the Chinese had least hope of obtaining. The remaining two, on the other hand, were fraught with difficulties. Redemption would involve a magnitude of resources beyond China's means, and moreover the bonds might fall into undesirable hands. Joint ownership would signify that a foreign *government* was legally permitted to own and operate a business enterprise on Chinese territory, a practice without precedent in China's foreign relations and a precedent that might be claimed by other powers. Three years later, this consideration, in view of Soviet insistence on retaining title rights and management, was to procure what was the only possible compromise whereby the railway was provisionally returned to the Soviet government and managed jointly.

Wang's proposals did not receive serious attention from the central government until the Anglo–Soviet trade agreement opened the way for substantive talks with Yurin. On April 30, the Wai-chiao Pu accepted a draft trade agreement. On the suggestion of Communications Minister Chang Chih-t'an, it was decided to couple the settlement of the railway question with trade. Hence, in his meeting with Yurin on May 13, Foreign Minister Yen raised the railway question for the first time. Yurin stated that he had been given no instructions on the subject but, personally, he saw two possibilities: either that the railway would be transferred to China or operated jointly as a purely business enterprise. Following Yurin's departure on May 18, the foreign minister pursued the matter by asking Minister Koo in London and Consul General Shen Ts'ung-hsun in Chita to elicit the views of the Soviet and the Far Eastern governments.[2]

The information received greatly distressed the foreign minister for it was evident that Russia's policy on the railway had evolved considerably away from an earlier position. It will be recalled that in March 1920 the first Karakhan Manifesto offered to transfer the railway unconditionally to China; in September, the second Karakhan Manifesto withdrew that offer and instead called for a tripartite agreement for special economic privileges for Russia in the use of the railway. In the latter document, nothing was said about the final disposal but, according to Chang Ssu-lin who received it, the offer to transfer title rights to China remained an open option at that time, although the conditions and procedure were unclear. Chang's impression was substantiated by a resolution passed by the Dal'buro on December 20 which stated: 'The conditions, procedure of transfer, and future direction of the Chinese Eastern Railway by the Chinese government should guarantee to Soviet Russia that the railway will not be used against its interests'.[3]

The updating of the above policy coincided almost exactly with the decision concerning Outer Mongolia. On June 21, after the Chinese had shown an inclination to widen trade talks to include the railway, the Soviet government formally empowered the Far Eastern government to negotiate in its name. A few days later, Consul General Shen was given the following reply:

Previously, the Soviet government did issue a declaration to China offering to transfer the Chinese Eastern Railway without any compensation. However, at that time, the Chinese government did not respond. At present, the Chinese Eastern question is complex. If the Far Eastern Republic took possession, it would be unacceptable to Peking; if transferred to China it would be beyond China's financial resources. Besides, the Japanese have long coveted the railway. Everything considered, however the railway is disposed of will cause inconvenience to both sides. It is therefore best to shelve this question and work out an appropriate method to be incorporated into the commercial treaty.[4]

Two weeks later, however, Yurin, now foreign minister of the Far Eastern government, instructed his secretary Kazanin in Peking to set forth the following basis for negotiation:

1. The Chinese Eastern Railway to be joint property of the governments of the Far Eastern Republic and China, and to be administered jointly as a strictly commercial transport line;
2. Abolition of all unequal rights and privileges formerly held by the Tsarist government, and abolition of the use of the railway for political purposes.[5]

Clearly, Chita was opting for the third course outlined by Wang Ching-ch'un earlier. This position meant that China was not to expect to redeem the railway, much less receive it free of charge. Here again as in the case of Outer Mongolia, the Russian policy was related to its preoccupation with Japan, in this case with Japanese ambitions concerning a former Tsarist sphere of interest. To begin with, about 3,000 Japanese troops still occupied the southern and eastern sections as of mid-1921. The Japanese government consented in January 1921 to a Chinese request for the Sino-Japanese Military Convention to be abrogated, but did so on the tacit understanding given by Peking that the troops would be allowed to remain, the purpose being to keep the line of communications open between south Manchuria and the Japanese expeditionary army in Vladivostok.[6] Hence, among Chita's terms was included the abolition of political use of the railway, by which the Russians, indirectly via China, sought to end the current military occupation of the railway by Japan while preparing for direct negotiations at Dairen to remove Japanese troops from Russian soil. Their own occupation of Outer Mongolia was powerful enough a leverage: they would not withdraw unless the Japanese did likewise.[7]

The play of international interests around north Manchuria also continued from where it started at the outbreak of the Russian revolution, only somewhat more subdued than before. In the earlier period, Japan had tried heavy-handedly to fill the vacuum with the overall objective of establishing an exclusive position in the entire Manchurian region, but had been frustrated by the United States. Now, the objective was pursued with subtler tactics but with no less persistence. Towards the end of 1920, for instance, War Minister Tanaka approached Chang Tso-lin with a set of far-reaching proposals designed to undermine the economic basis of the Russian railway system in Manchuria and to spread Japanese economic interest as widely as possible over Manchuria. He contrasted two ways of thinking about the Manchurian railways: America and Russia had thought in terms of east-west traffic whereas, he said, China and Japan should emphasize the north-south flow.

In order to block American-Russian ambitions, Tanaka set out three proposals. First, he asked for a narrowing of the gauge of the Harbin-Changchun line to conform with the South Manchurian and the Peking-Mukden. This had been one of Japan's most persistent objectives and all earlier attempts had been blocked by John F. Stevens of the Inter-Allied Technical Board. Now that the Chinese Eastern Railway was under China's and therefore Chang Tso-lin's control, Tanaka believed Chang to be in a position to decide without reference to the Americans. Secondly, he proposed an extension of the Harbin-Changchun line northwards to the Amur River city of Heiho. The Harbin-Heiho (Ping-hei) line would serve the dual purpose of developing the resources of north Manchuria and capturing the freight of the Ussuri Railway. Thirdly, he wanted the construction of a line from Kirin city to the Korean border town of Kanei. The Kirin-Kanei (Chi-hui) line was intended to open up the resources of Kirin province, bring order to a troublesome area, and of course tie Manchuria closely to Japan's Korean colony.[8]

However, Chang did not respond favorably to a project involving such expansion of Japanese interests and so fraught with international complications. When the Japanese pressed again in May for a change of the gauge they were again opposed by Stevens. Faced with the Inter-Allied Technical Board as the watchdog and Chang Tso-lin's obstructionism, the Japanese were kept within bounds while Chinese trustee-ship provided a semblance of stability. The net effect of this play of international interests around the railway was that it was preserved for the future Russian government. Motivated as it was by the desire to improve its economic and diplomatic strength, the Soviet government, not surprisingly, reclaimed possession of a line of such vital strategic and economic impor-tance. This it did in June 1921, indirectly through the Far Eastern Republic, since a direct claim would almost certainly have produced a confrontation with Japan.

Thus, in the second half of 1921, when Peking was finally ready for substantive talks, it faced a hard front on both the Chinese Eastern Railway and the Mongolian questions. Just at this time, two important developments in Far Eastern interna-tional relations further weakened Peking's position. One was Washington's call for an international conference that was designed to dispossess Japan of its wartime gains on the Asiatic continent. While the conference was welcome to China from the viewpoint of the Shantung question, it was a distinct cause for worry for the Chinese from the viewpoint of the Chinese Eastern Railway question. Washington had been persuading London and Paris to the view that the *status quo* of the railway be guaranteed by international control until the appearance of an official government in Russia. Washington's primary mo-tive was to prevent the railway from falling into Japanese hands, but the scheme meant that the Chinese would not be free to alter the status of the railway by negotiations with Russia until the latter had become vastly stronger through foreign recognition. It became a matter of great urgency in Peking to reach an agreement with Russia before the Washing-ton Conference was convened.

The American initiative also acted as a catalyst in bringing Tokyo and Chita together for diplomatic talks. By entering into negotiations with the Far Eastern Republic, Japan was hoping to avoid discussion of evacuation at the Washington Conference. This was welcomed by the Russians who faced the Japanese from a position of weakness, but unwelcome to the Chinese who faced the Russians also from a weak position. In the past, rapprochement between Japan and Russia had been always at China's expense, and, given Japan's interest in the Chinese Eastern Railway and Amur River navigation, the Chinese had every reason to think that Chinese interests would be compromised once again. If this danger was to be avoided, it was imperative that China should sign with Russia before Japan did. The Japanese, for obvious reasons, were just as anxious to see that the Russians did not sign with China first, hence their readiness to negotiate. Thus the Russians were in a position to play off China and Japan with considerable finesse.

On July 16, Yurin set out again for China, this time as foreign minister of the Far Eastern Republic, to settle all outstanding Sino-Russian issues, the most prominent being the Chinese Eastern Railway, Outer Mongolia, trade, and navigation. His second mission was not restricted to talks with the Chinese but included negotiations with the Japanese, scheduled to begin in the latter part of August at Dairen.

On his way to Peking, he stopped at Mukden on July 23-24 and outlined to the Manchurian warlord, Chang Tso-lin, a *quid pro quo*: withdrawal of Russian troops from Outer Mongolia in exchange for an agreement on trade and joint management of the Chinese Eastern Railway. Brushing aside the bargain, Chang took Yurin severely to task for the entry of Russian troops and demanded an immediate and unconditional withdrawal; otherwise, he would not be responsible for armed conflicts between his troops soon to be sent and the Russian troops in Mongolia. He declined to discuss other matters as they fell within the jurisdiction of the central government. Anxious to appear conciliatory, Yurin disavowed any aggressive intent in Outer Mongolia and declared it was the Far Eastern Republic's sincere intention to hand the territory back to China.

In Peking, at the meeting with Foreign Minister Yen on July 27, Yurin raised the railway question. Yen rejected

Yurin's demand for joint management, likening it to the past practice of Tsarist aggression. The railway being within Chinese territory, China wanted sole possession and management; in return, Russia would be compensated financially by an issue of bonds and given special privileges in the use of the railway by a special agreement. As far as the trade agreement was concerned, Yen told Yurin that a counterdraft had already been presented and negotiation on that matter could begin at any time.[9]

On August 1, Yurin departed again for Mukden, recognizing Chang's dominating influence in Peking, but the second visit did not change Chang's intransigence.[10] Yurin then went on to Dairen and began the parley with the Japanese on August 26. In a questionable attempt to undermine Yurin's position and hopefully bring him back to Peking, the Chinese provoked the diplomatic pouch incident. On August 19, Yurin's courier was searched at the Peking railway station and was found in possession of evidence incriminating Yurin with subversion. Among the documents seized were Yurin's recommendations to Moscow on the organization of a Comintern secretariat in China, formation of a military academy to give Chinese doctrinal and military training, and methods for creating a powerful Chinese communist party and organizing labor, student, and other social classes.[11] The incident did bring Yurin back to Peking but just long enough to lodge his protests before he returned again to Dairen.

Predictably, Chinese officials grew worried over the Russo-Japanese talks and felt helpless at the hard game that the Russians had chosen to play. The Manchurian warlord especially chafed at Yurin's 'insincere promises' about returning Outer Mongolia to China, and came to feel that the Mongolian responsibility was proving to be more of a burden than a gain. Accordingly, in early September, he relinquished it to the central government, signifying that he had no intention of undertaking a military expedition.[12]

Not the least of Peking's difficulties was the fact that Yurin possessed no authority to represent all of Russia. The Chinese found themselves dealing with two Russian governments, the Far Eastern and the Soviet; and the latter explicitly declared in July that Yurin was not its representative.

Moreover, to ensure that Soviet envoys would be received by Peking, Moscow and Chita shrewdly divided responsibility between themselves in such a way that the former would take a hard line on the railway question and seem soft on the Mongolian, while the latter would do exactly the reverse. This tactic also guaranteed maximal benefits in the two vital questions for Russia as a whole. Thus, sooner or later, Peking would have to consent to the visit of a Soviet mission if meaningful discussions were to take place at all.[13]

The first move of conciliation, however, came from Yurin and might have been related partly to his difficulties with the Japanese at Dairen. The Far Eastern delegation had begun by demanding Japan's consent to an immediate evacuation of troops before negotiations could begin on other matters. The Japanese had in turn countered with a demand for a general agreement to be signed first. On September 6, placating the Japanese, the Russian introduced a draft commercial treaty and offered to sign as *quid pro quo* for Japanese withdrawal within one month of the signature. At the end of September the Japanese replied, however, with a counterdraft of seventeen open and three secret clauses. Among the open ones were included a variety of economic and commercial rights and privileges, including free navigation on the Amur, a pledge by the Far Eastern government never to adopt communism as its social system, never to use Vladivostok as a naval base, never to keep naval forces in Pacific waters, and never to undertake military action in the area adjoining Korea and Manchuria. In addition, the Far Eastern government was to give Japan an eighty-year lease of northern Sakhalin as compensation for the Nikolaevsk massacre. The secret clauses bound the Far Eastern government to strict neutrality in case of armed conflict between Japan and a third power. The Japanese government agreed in principle to withdrawal from the Maritime Province but only at its own discretion, and at a time that it found suitable and convenient to itself, and from Sakhalin after the eighty-year lease had been consented to.[14]

Expecting a long-drawn conference with the Japanese, Yurin left for Peking on September 28, probably hoping that negotiations there would alarm them and wear down their intransigence. But other urgent business also awaited him: the embarrassing diplomatic pouch incident remained to be settled, and, more importantly, the Chinese Eastern Railway was becoming a pressing question for Russia. In the course of three talks in early October, a number of concrete points were agreed upon. The diplomatic pouch question was soon settled. Yurin surprised Yen with a proposal for a conference at Manchouli on the Mongolian question. He said his government had issued orders for evacuation and asked for a Chinese delegate to meet with Far Eastern and Soviet military commanders both to receive back the territory and to hold joint consultations on measures against the Ungernist remnants. Then, Yurin withdrew his opposition to Yen's proposal for China to redeem the Chinese Eastern Railway. He asked that special privileges in transportation and tariff be given to the Far Eastern Republic; the rolling stock of the Zabaikal Railway stranded on the Chinese Eastern Railway be returned; the existing Russian administrators of the Chinese Eastern Railway, suspected for counterrevolutionary leanings, be replaced by other Russians; and China should guarantee not to allow the railway to be used for military purposes. Moreover, in a conference soon to be convened to settle the railway question, the Soviet government should be allowed to participate. Foreign Minister Yen agreed to negotiate on the above basis and Yurin's mission was at an end.[15]

Thus there were to be two separate tripartite conferences, one on the Chinese Eastern Railway, and the other on the Mongolian question. To take up the railway conference first, agreement was reached in early November on Manchouli as the venue. To the terms outlined by Yurin on behalf of Chita, the Soviet representative, Alexander K. Paikes, added those of Moscow on November 5, as follows:

1. The Chinese government to take possession of the railway and all its appurtenances, and to receive the entire revenue without responsibility for the railway company's past debts to the Russian government;

2. Soviet Russia to receive the right to use the railway freely; the railway not to be transferred to a third party; and no third party to be allowed to interfere with the railway contract and finance;

3. Soviet troops to be allowed to be transported freely on the railway, but not troops hostile to Soviet Russia.[16]

These terms enable us to deduce Moscow's motives which, to a large extent, reflected its concern over Japan. The Chinese pledge not to transfer the railway to a third party was intended to prevent Japanese absorption. The pledge of non-interference in the railway contract and finance anticipated the American plan, due to be discussed at the Washington Conference, of international finance and control. An American official was told why both Chita and Moscow were opposed to international control: the reason being that the international guards would be mostly Japanese, as American troops would not be sent.[17] The demand that troops hostile to Soviet Russia not be allowed on the railway was clearly aimed at the Japanese troops still there. Free movement of Soviet troops, on the other hand, was necessary in order to outflank Merkulov's forces in the Maritime Province, just then attacking the Amur Province.[18] Whereas the Soviet terms were motivated entirely by political considerations, those of the Far Eastern government were both political and economic. By demanding replacement of the existing Russian administrators, Chita clearly sought participation in the railroad management.[19] Economically, Chita wanted special privileges. Moreover, whereas Moscow offered to restore the railway to China absolutely free of any financial and economic charges, Chita's position as understood by Foreign Minister Yen implied financial compensation. Yurin had stated his terms as a compromise on Yen's offer of redemption in place of Yurin's earlier demand for joint ownership and management.

Despite the stiffness of the ingeniously coordinated demands by Moscow and Chita, neither Foreign Minister Yen Hui-ch'eng nor Communications Minister Chang Chih-t'an appears to have been overly concerned, believing that the fundamental question was one of title rights. In due course, the Ministry of Communications worked out two negotiating positions. Among the maximal goals were Chinese ownership and control and exemption from responsibility for debts of the railway. In return China was prepared to grant tax exemption for goods in transit from one part of Russian territory to another, undertake never to transfer the railway to a third party, or permit a third party to interfere with the railway contract and finance. Coinciding closely with Soviet terms, the first Chinese position sought transfer of the railway without financial compensation.

The minimal position envisaged compensation, and set out the justifications for the assumption of ownership: the railway was located within Chinese territory; it had received land free of charge or at reduced cost, and was exempt from tax; the Russian government had in fact financed the construction and owned the share certificates, and was therefore free to dispose of the railway as it wished. The Chinese government agreed to pay 100,000,000 Chinese dollars, half of the sum being in old Romanov roubles in Chinese possession and the remainder in the form of 4 per cent interest-bearing bonds, due in seventy years.[20]

By mid-November, a six-man delegation made up of communications and foreign ministries personnel and led by Wang Ching-ch'un was ready to depart for Manchouli.[21] But at the last minute, the conference was abandoned, owing to the opposition of Chang Tso-lin.

Until now, Chang had been content to leave policy making concerning the railway in the hands of the central government, partly in order to take Japanese pressure off himself, and partly because only the central government had the expertise to handle a question of such technical and international complexities as the Chinese Eastern Railway. But he felt differently about a course of action that was liable to upset his delicate relationship with the Japanese. Since the latter part of 1920, the Japanese had grown increasingly concerned at Chang's consuming ambition in planting his power in north China, to the neglect of certain pressing problems closer to his home base. As Nagao Hampei, Japanese representative on the Inter-Allied Technical Board put it, he was paying more attention to the shifting power balance south of the Great Wall than to the pressing Bolshevik threat to north Manchuria. Japanese officials like Nagao had been endeavouring to persuade Chang to postpone his designs in north China, to turn his attention to where Japan would be in a position to assist a common interest, i.e. Manchuria, Outer Mongolia, and eastern Siberia.[22]

To abandon his ambitions in north China where a golden opportunity existed for their fulfilment was one thing that Chang would not do. On the contrary, in the latter part of 1921, he was more engrossed than ever in engineering a grand alliance against Wu P'ei-fu, which included former enemy Tuan Ch'i-jui, new friend Sun Yat-sen, and the Old Communications Clique. In December he replaced the 'neutral' Chin Yün-peng Cabinet with one headed by the Old Communications Clique chieftain, Liang Shih-i.

While prepared to risk displeasing the Japanese in pursuing his ambitions, Chang evidently felt it was dangerous to treat with the Bolsheviks. The Japanese themselves had been intransigent in opening talks with Moscow, and they could not be expected to countenance his approval for a conference with the Reds on a subject in which they themselves had a strong interest. The Sino-Soviet talks, moreover, would have brought in the very thing they were determined to keep out—Soviet influence in north Manchuria.

Foreign Minister Yen reported Yurin's proposed basis for negotiation to Chang on October 5, and, in his reply of October 12, Chang expressed a number of reservations, including special privileges for Russia, restrictions in the military use of the railway, change of the existing Russian personnel, whether an agreement with the unrecognized Chita government and without the Soviet government would be legally valid, and whether it would be opposed by the Russo-Asiatic Bank and its French backer. Still, he stated that 'Trade, the Chinese Eastern Railway, and navigation are matters for the central government to decide, not for a frontier official'. On October 22, Yen assured Chang that these reservations had been anticipated at the center, and his views would be borne in mind. Concerning the important question of legality, he said negotiations would be conducted with representatives of Chita and Moscow together; whether the agreement would have legal force would be treated as a separate question since any arrangement reached at this point would serve as a basis for a more advantageous agreement later. To clarify the central government's policy further, Yen sent Chang two Wai-chiao Pu members of the Chinese delegation, Hsü T'ung-hsin and Hsüeh Yung.

Upon Yen's mention of negotiating with Soviet representatives and his determination to go ahead with the conference, Chang decided to take a firmer stand. The Wai-chiao
Pu officials visiting him on November 17 found Chang intransigent. Making light of the Wai-chiao Pu's worry about
the Washington Conference, he declared that internationalization of the railroad would not be allowed so long as he was
alive. He did not think China had the necessary resources to
redeem the railroad and saw no benefit to Manchuria in the
scheme proposed by the center. Before Manchuria had been
compensated for vast amounts of worthless paper roubles,
there could be no negotiation on other matters. Then came the
clinching argument: 'Just now in Manchuria we are taking
precautions to keep the Reds out, hence we must proceed with
care in dealing with them'.[23]

Chang's block buster forced the Peking officials reluc-
tantly to abandon the negotiations. He had merely made ex-
plicit what had always been inherent in his total control of
Manchuria as a private domain. Yen Hui-ching, who remained as foreign minister after Chang's reorganisation of the
cabinet in December, assiduously avoided the subject in his
talks with the Soviet envoy Paikes. After the Fengtien-Chihli
War of April 28-May 4, in which Chang was defeated and
driven back into his home base, it became even less realistic for
the Peking administration to develop any policy on the railway. In any case, the initiative on that question rested almost
entirely with the Soviet government.

To turn now to the Mongolian question: upon receiving
Yurin's offer to hand the territory back to China, the elated
Foreign Minister Yen consulted Chang Tso-lin and had Li
Yüan designated as Commissioner in charge of receiving back
Outer Mongolia (Pan-li chieh-shou K'u-ch'ia shih-wu
wei-yüan). Anticipating direct negotiation with the Mongols,
Yen secured cabinet approval for a motion defining a new
relationship after Russian evacuation. In broad principle, the
Mongols were to be given autonomy in all matters other than
diplomacy and defense.[24]

By the beginning of November, the Chinese side was
ready to meet Far Eastern and Soviet military commanders at
Manchouli, and all that remained was for a date to be fixed.

Cruel disappointment awaited the Chinese, however. Despite successive inquiries to the Far Eastern Mission's office, the Chinese government got no reply. Finally, on November 19 the Far Eastern mission informed Foreign Minister Yen that since Yurin had made the proposal, 'important changes have taken place which have radically altered the situation'. The Far Eastern government had since then withdrawn its troops and therefore 'there is no further necessity for the convocation of such a conference'. The Russian forces still remaining in Mongolia were 'exclusively those of the Russian Socialist Federal Soviet Republic', and the question of their evacuation was now a 'matter of discussion between the Chinese Government and the Government of Soviet Russia'.[25]

One can only speculate on the motivation behind Yurin's proposal for the Mongolian conference and the subsequent change of mind. The proposal might have been made in order to get the railway conference started and was later withdrawn when it appeared that Chang would not consent to negotiate on the Chinese Eastern Railway. The withdrawal coincided closely with Chinese abandonment of the railway conference. Yurin might also have been playing for time to enable the higher quarters to ascertain Chang's intentions about Outer Mongolia. If Chang should send a military expedition as he told Yurin he would, an armed clash would have to be avoided at all cost, in view of both Chang's suspected Japanese backing and the thrust, also believed to be backed by the Japanese, being made by the White Guard Merkulov regime against the Amur Province. By mid-November, the Russians apparently had reached the conclusion that they had nothing to fear from the Manchurian warlord.[26]

In any event, the Chinese were left with the only alternative of direct negotiations with Soviet Russia, and were uncertain both as to when these would take place and what the Soviet position would be. Since Chicherin's June 25 note to Peking, Soviet policy on Outer Mongolia had been shifting increasingly against China's favor. Chicherin had demanded the convocation of a Sino-Soviet-Mongol conference for a tripartite agreement. Had Soviet policy stopped at this point, then there would have been a return to the framework of the 1915 Kiakhta Convention. But, two weeks later, Soviet

troops entered Outer Mongolia, set up the Mongolian National Government, and then, on November 5, the Soviet
government concluded a treaty with that Mongolian government. In line with Soviet national interests, the treaty recognized the Mongolian National Government as the legal government of Outer Mongolia, not as the government of an
independent country. Moreover, the preamble clearly abrogated all previous Russian treaties with Mongolia, including
the Kiakhta Convention which the Chinese, by General Hsü
Shu-cheng's action, had torn up themselves. However the
Peking government chose to define Sino–Mongol relationships, the treaty signified that the Mongolian National Government was already asserting 'autonomy' in diplomacy, and
that government, organized and recognized as legitimate by
Soviet Russia, was one which Peking would have to accept.[27]

Paikes served in Peking as Moscow's first direct envoy
for the better part of a year (December 1921–August 1922).
However, his main mission, which was to negotiate the
Chinese Eastern Railway, had ended even before his arrival.
His period of sojourn coincided with one of the most unstable
periods of warlord politics in north China. It was punctuated
by Chang Tso-lin's sudden seizure of the reins of the Peking
government in December, followed by sharpening frictions
between Chang and Wu P'ei-fu, culminating in the
Fengtien-Chihli War (April 29–May 4) and Chang's declaration of independence after defeat, followed by three provisional cabinets in rapid succession. The last appeared in September, after Paikes had been replaced by Joffe, and showed a
promising beginning, but soon dissolved in the dissensions
within the victorious Chihli clique.

Despite these unsettling conditions, Yen Hui-ching,
who remained the foreign minister to the end of the Paikes
mission, provided some continuity and attempted to conduct
discussions with the Soviet representative. Paikes tried to
press for negotiations on the railway, but Yen refused to
discuss any other issue until Soviet troops had withdrawn
from Outer Mongolia, a matter which Paikes had no authorization to discuss. Clearly, whatever discussions were held
were exercises in futility and exasperation for the Chinese side.

These are of interest to us only in so far as they clarified the Soviet position on Outer Mongolia, hence a brief summary will suffice.

In the course of the talks that Yen and Li Yüan had with Paikes in January, 1922, it was established that the Soviet position divided the Mongolian question into two separate parts. One concerned the presence of Soviet troops and the conditions under which they would withdraw. Paikes disavowed any aggressive intent on the part of his government and even handed over a written guarantee to that effect. The entry of Soviet forces was justified on the grounds of self-defense and by the request of the Mongolian government. They would not be withdrawn until the Soviet government was satisfied that the Mongolian and Chinese governments were capable of preventing the White Guards from using the area as a base for counterrevolution against Russia; and until a tripartite conference, attended by Chinese, Mongol, and Soviet delegates, was convened to settle Sino-Mongol relations.

The other part concerned the Soviet government's wish to act as an honest broker in bringing Outer Mongolia and China back together. Sino-Mongol relations were to be defined at a tripartite conference. The Chinese of course rejected this suggestion outright, declaring that Outer Mongolia was an internal question for China, and the mutual relationship was to be defined wholly between China and its sovereign territory. Anything more than friendly and informal mediation by Russia was unacceptable. That being the case, Paikes obligingly (and deceptively) yielded ground, stating that China should settle its relationship with Outer Mongolia alone, and that once this was achieved Soviet forces would withdraw.[28]

The Chinese were evidently taken in by what the cabinet interpreted to be a 'compromise', unaware that it was only a ploy by which Paikes hoped to get the Chinese to negotiate the railway.[29] They seriously believed that Russia's main concern was the White Guards, small bands of which were still roaming aimlessly on the Mongolian grasslands. In the course of the next few months, the Chinese followed a plan proposed by Li Yüan which combined force and persuasion. On the one hand, a military expedition was to be sent into Outer Mongolia to liquidate the White Guards and get Soviet troops to leave. On the other, commissioners were to be sent to convince the Mongols of China's conciliatory policy, to persuade them to nominate representatives to Peking for talks, and wean them away from foreign influence.[30]

The only man who could provide the necessary armed forces for the expedition was Chang Tso-lin. From February to April, Li Yüan visited Chang to persuade him to turn his attention to Outer Mongolia, but Chang was preparing for war against Wu P'ei-fu. On April 12, he informed the central government that he had long since resigned from the post of Commissioner for Mongolia, and that the Mongolian question was a matter entirely for the central government to handle.[31]

As to the remaining part of Li's plan, several approaches to the Mongols were made, of which only two need be mentioned. Two officials of long service in Outer Mongolia, Huang Ch'eng-hsü and Ch'en Wen-ts'e, set out in March with the instruction to offer the Mongols autonomy in everything but diplomacy and defense. They found themselves under constant surveillance, unable to contact those who might still be well-disposed towards China.[32] Subsequently, they returned empty-handed, with little else to report other than the fact that the Mongols wanted self-government and were relying for it on Soviet support.[33]

Another attempt to reestablish contact with the Mongols in Outer Mongolia was made through the Inner Mongolian banner princes. The episode may be reconstructed from a letter of reply, dated May 3, sent to these banner princes by the Mongolian government. It appears that emissaries of these princes had carried a message, explaining Peking's conciliatory policy, to the leaders of the Urga government. The resentful and defiant letter recounted how Outer Mongolia had broken free from China's oppressive rule and won autonomy through Tsarist mediation in 1911-15, how the Chinese had unilaterally torn up the Kiakhta Convention, and how the Ungernists coming after the Chinese had ravaged Mongolian territory. To end their misery, the Mongolian people had rallied together, appealed for Soviet assistance, and restored peace and order. The goal of the new government, the letter stated, was 'a completely democratic constitutional government' which would put internal affairs in order, and establish friendly relations with neighbours. Its policy was 'autonomy' (*tzu-chih*) and it would not tolerate interference from any quarter. The letter then heaped scorn on the notion of the five-race family republic, which the Chinese held so dear, pointing to the existence of Tibetan independence and the separate government in south China. 'The letter received exhorts us to place our defence and diplomacy in the hands of the Peking government. If this is a true indication of Peking's policy, then its lack of trust in us is worse than that of the Manchus who for centuries had given us those powers'.

Finally, the letter came to the point. No agreement signed between Urga and Peking would last, unless witnessed by a third party. Therefore, the Outer Mongolian government had asked the Soviet government to act as intermediary and guarantor of a peace treaty with the Chinese government.[34]

It should now be clear why Paikes, who was fully aware that the Mongolian National Government could not, or would not, negotiate with Peking alone, could afford to concede that the conference did not have to be tripartite. The message received from Urga also made clear the latter's rejection of the relationship as defined by Peking. In accord with Soviet strategic interests, the word 'autonomy' carried only one possible meaning: 'de facto independence from China'. Soviet avowal of recognition of 'Chinese sovereignty' amounted to no more than that.

There remains one other aspect of the Mongolian question which the Chinese raised with Paikes, namely, the Soviet-Mongol Treaty of November 5, 1921.[35] The Chinese of course knew about the treaty soon after a summary of it appeared in the leading Moscow daily and was picked up by the foreign press. Foreign Minister Yen had received verification on February 17 and the full text on March 11, from Consul General Shen Ts'ung-hsun at Chita. Yet, on two occasions of direct questioning, Paikes denied its existence.[36]

By late April, Foreign Minister Yen had come to realize that Paikes had lied to him. No troops could be sent to Outer

Mongolia and Urga's representatives would not come. He decided to appeal to international opinion by exposing the Soviet lack of faith at the Genoa Conference, then in progress, where the Soviet government sought to settle its relations with the capitalist world. He instructed Li Yüan to have another talk with Paikes to determine the final Soviet position.[37]

At the conversation of April 26, Paikes finally confirmed the existence of the Soviet-Mongol Treaty. He had left Moscow before the treaty had been concluded, he said, and had been informed only in mid-February, hence his earlier disavowals. But the Soviet government had never specifically stated that it proposed to abrogate the Kiakhta Convention which guaranteed Mongolian autonomy, whereas the Chinese had themselves been guilty of unilateral violation of that agreement. Then followed his tortured justification of Soviet action. The Soviet government considered the Kiakhta Convention to be still in force, hence the change of government at Urga was perfectly within the bounds of Mongolian autonomy; and since Russia was an intermediary in that convention, the Soviet-Mongol treaty was perfectly legitimate, constituting no violation of Chinese sovereignty. So far as Soviet evacuation was concerned, he reiterated that it would depend on how soon China and Outer Mongolia could adjust their mutual relations.[38]

Upon receipt of Li Yüan's report, Foreign Minister Yen in an indignant note, compared Soviet action to Tsarist imperialism and 'solemnly' protested that China would not recognize any treaty concluded between the Soviet government and Mongolia.[39] There was absolutely nothing else that Yen or anybody else could do.

It was not until June 29 that Li Yüan saw Paikes again. This was the final talk before Joffe's arrival and here Paikes put all his cards on the table. Nothing less than a tripartite conference to revise the Kiakhta Convention was acceptable as a condition for Soviet withdrawal, and until the tripartite agreement was reached, Chinese troops would be resisted by force.[40] Li's summation of China's position, submitted to the cabinet on July 5, was one of despair.

If we reject their demand for a tripartite conference, it means undertaking a military expedition, but this is out of the question. Our armed forces stationed on the Kiangsi-Hupeh front [against the southern dissidents] are already inadequate and therefore not available for transfer, and our border defence forces have not yet recovered full strength.

On the other hand, since our Mongolian vassal is far away in the distant frontier, unless we recover it soon, its orientation to Russia will in time become firmer and we shall have a great deal more difficulty in commanding its submission to the Center.

To accede to the Russian demand for a tripartite Conference is to jeopardize our sovereignty and expose ourselves to public derision.[41]

There is no better way to conclude this account of Paikes's mission and to preface the Joffe mission than with the conversation which took place in Berlin on August 4 between Commissar for Foreign Affairs Chicherin and Chinese Minister to Germany Wei Chen-chu. Acting on Wai-chiao Pu instructions Wei sought the views of the Narkomindel chief himself on the two issues which divided the two governments: Outer Mongolia and the Chinese Eastern Railway. In both cases, the Soviet commissar defended Soviet policy candidly. Concerning Outer Mongolia, he pointed out that the White Guards had, with Japanese assistance, been using that region as a base against Soviet Russia, and China had been too preoccupied with internal problems to suppress them. Besides, by their presence Soviet troops not only defended Soviet territory but rendered the essential service of maintaining peace and order. As for the Chinese Eastern Railway, the same menace had forced the Soviet government to demand that it be administered jointly by a Sino-Soviet committee. Asked whether the Soviet government was not breaking its earlier promises, Chicherin replied: 'We will remain true to our declaration but, for reasons of self-defence, we have no alternative but to adopt provisional measures (tsan-hsing pan-fa).[42]

Particularly noteworthy is Chicherin's statement of policy on the Chinese Eastern Railway. Foreign Minister Yen had not permitted Paikes to raise this question during their discussions, but it is clear that another shift in Soviet policy had occurred since Paikes had spoken with Consul General Shen Ts'ung-hsun on November 5, 1921. Presumably, this was in response to Chang Tso-lin's declaration of independence on May 12, 1922, which a member of Paikes's staff described as done on Japanese advice, 'a revival of the idea of a Japanese-Manchurian buffer' and 'spearhead of Japanese imperialism'.[43] Henceforth, Soviet policy on the railway was to remain firmly committed to the demand for resumption of ownership and control of the enterprise.

When we contrast Soviet thinking on these matters with Chinese, an enormous gulf becomes apparent. In August, anticipating negotiations with the new Soviet plenipotentiary Adolph Joffe, position papers were prepared on the Chinese Eastern Railway and Outer Mongolia by the Ministry of Communications and the Committee on Russian Affairs of the Wai-chiao Pu. Chinese fears of the railway question being compromised at the Washington Conference had proved to be exaggerated. Since the Washington Powers avowed respect for China's sovereign rights as one of their basic principles, they eventually shelved the American-inspired proposal for provisional international finance and control of the railway in the face of China's objection. Instead they passed a resolution warning China she would be held responsible for the obligations towards the various foreign interests in the railway.[44] The wish for an early settlement of the railway question now impelled the Ministry of Communications to assert, more firmly than ever, that the Russian government, not the Russo-Asiatic Bank, was the owner of the railway. Hence, China would be perfectly justified in negotiating with the Soviet government, whose durability none could now doubt. If Persia could stand up against the powers and sign with Soviet Russia, the ministry felt, China could surely do the same. As in the previous autumn, the ministry outlined a negotiating position whereby to insist on unconditional transfer first and, if refused by the Soviet side, to ask to redeem the railway. The important thing was for China to gain complete control and ownership. Just how the ministry proposed to secure Chang Tso-lin's consent to negotiating with the Soviet government is unclear.[45]

Whereas the Chinese Eastern Railway lay within China's effective jurisdiction and Peking was able to exercise some leverage on this question, the same cannot be said of Outer Mongolia. For more than a year, Chinese influence had disappeared from the region and Soviet Russia had established political and military predominance. The problem had been endlessly discussed within the Peking government and in the most abstract terms. It was generally agreed that the recovery of Outer Mongolia was predicated upon the Chinese government's ability to employ troops and the willingness of the Mongols to return to Chinese rule. Both these conditions were absent. The position paper on Outer Mongolia drawn up by the Committee on Russian Affairs on August 21 reflected this dilemma.[46]

The paper stated China should ask the Soviet government, as a gesture of friendship, to withdraw its troops in Outer Mongolia. If the Soviet side was agreeable, Chinese troops should be sent for the dual purpose of preserving peace and order and suppressing the White Guards. Should the Soviet government refuse on the pretext of the Mongol request for its services as guarantor of Outer Mongolian autonomy, China should insist, Outer Mongolia being Chinese territory, that all matters between China and Outer Mongolia should be decided by direct negotiations. For its part, the Chinese government would, in line with the world trend, respect the Mongolian desire for self-determination and was prepared to grant autonomy in everything except diplomacy, defense, justice, and communications. A further demand to the Soviet government was that both the Kiakhta Convention of 1915 and the recently concluded Soviet-Mongol Treaty should be abolished.

The Committee on Russian Affairs next outlined several steps the government should take with regard to Outer Mongolia. Mongolia being closely related to Manchuria, the Committee felt the government should obtain Chang Tso-lin's prior understanding concerning its Mongolian policy and seek his patriotic services. Before Chinese troops were sent, influential Mongol princes should be contacted and Peking's goodwill made known to them. The number of

Chinese troops to be sent after Russian withdrawal should be at least one mixed brigade together with artillery and machine-gun units, and the expenses should be borne by the central government.

To induce the Soviet side to be more forthcoming, the Committee recommended that a positive response to the Soviet request for a trade agreement be made as a friendly gesture. Soviet sincerity should be tested by preliminary talks. The Committee should meet again if the Soviet side should pose conditions for the withdrawal of troops. The Chinese government should strenuously resist the Soviet demand to serve as the guarantor of Mongolian autonomy. Only as the very last resort should it invite Soviet participation in any conference determining the future relationship between China and Outer Mongolia.

The differences between the Soviet and Chinese positions on the vital issues of Outer Mongolia and the Chinese Eastern Railway were so vast as to seem unbridgeable. It was a conflict between one state becoming ever more debilitated but nevertheless driven by the nationalistic imperative to recover sovereign rights, and another rapidly re-emerging in strength and propelled by *realpolitik* to return to the Pacific as a great power. These differences were destined to be bridged only by China's unilateral concessions.

11

The Joffe Mission

With the arrival of Adolf Abramovich Joffe, Soviet diplomatic pressure on Peking grew more intense. Unlike Paikes, who seems to have had authorization to discuss only the Chinese Eastern Railway question, Joffe came as a plenipotentiary, entrusted with the task of securing diplomatic relations and the reinstatement of Russian interests in China.

One of Moscow's ablest diplomats, Joffe had served with distinction in Germany where he combined diplomacy with revolution, a dual role that he also played in China with considerable skill. Like the Yurin and Paikes missions, that of Joffe was no ordinary diplomatic agency but, unlike theirs, its inordinate size of about 100 individuals indicated a stepped-up effort on Moscow's part to realize its manifold objectives. It may be surmised that together with still other Narkomindel and Comintern agents, Joffe and his staff of political and military experts were to work actively for a bourgeois democratic revolution which might give birth to a China, free of imperialism and ruled by bourgeois nationalists under Soviet influence. The bourgeois democratic revolution also contained the seeds of a Soviet revolution, born of a convenient wedlock between Chinese communists and bourgeois nationalists.

In addition to his varied tasks in China, Joffe was Moscow's plenipotentiary for Russo-Japanese talks as well. The Dairen Conference between the Tokyo and Chita governments had broken down in April over the former's refusal to fix a date for the evacuation of its forces. However, the second half of 1922 saw a dramatic improvement in Russia's position in the Far East. At the Washington Conference, the Japanese had promised evacuation from the Maritime Province and North Sakhalin, pending satisfactory arrangements with Russian authorities. Moreover, to prove their adherence to the 'Washington Conference spirit' of international cooperation, the Japanese government in June unilaterally decided to withdraw from the Maritime Province by the end of October, and issued a public statement to that effect. The about-face took the Russians by complete and pleasant surprise. By the end of July, agreement was reached between Tokyo and Chita to resume negotiations, with Japan consenting to Moscow's participation as well. On July 25, the Japanese were informed of the names of the chief Russian delegates: Joffe for Moscow and Yanson for Chita. The tone of Soviet policy in the Far East was epitomized in Karakhan's pointed instructions to Joffe: 'Make it understood that Russia has returned to the Pacific Ocean, and that all illusions about our weakness and the possibility of slighting us as an unequal power are fruitless'.[1]

Thus, when Joffe entered Peking in August, he actually had two irons in the fire, and time was on his side. Moving like a pendulum, he swung now in China's direction, now in Japan's, adroitly manipulating their fears. Joffe's turned out to be the briefest of the four Russian missions to visit Peking between 1920 and 1924, lasting about five months in all, but the fact that he achieved no concrete results on the diplomatic front should not be construed as a failure. Rather, this was due to intransigence on his part, born of a new confidence in exacting maximum terms from Peking and Tokyo.

Both officialdom and the public placed high hopes in the talks between Joffe and Chinese leaders. A new cabinet had been formed on August 5, replacing the two month old Yen Hui-ch'ing Cabinet. The young and able Wellington Koo now occupied the post of foreign minister, a redoubtable opponent for Joffe in the public polemics that soon replaced serious talks.

At the first meeting on August 15, after exchanging courtesies, Joffe put his best foot forward by asking to be allowed to present his credentials to the Chinese president, which Koo agreed to consider. Joffe then informed Koo of his concurrent mission to negotiate an end to Japanese military occupation and his wish to have some preliminary discussions in Peking first. Anticipating that the Mongolian question would be raised, he claimed Soviet foreign policy was completely different from Tsarist policy in promoting the achievement of independence by all nations capable of it. When Koo asked for Soviet voluntary evacuation as a gesture of friendship towards China, Joffe declared that the problem should be discussed along with other issues, and not be singled out for prior settlement. He also reiterated Chicherin's view that the troops were indispensable to local order and immediate evacuation would be contrary to the interests of all parties concerned.[2]

The second meeting on August 23 was still reasonably cordial. Joffe was told a private meeting with the president could be arranged but not a formal presentation of credentials. He was thus denied a propaganda coup. The two sides then got down to procedural aspects of negotiations. Joffe agreed to present a memorandum proposing a conference to resolve all questions of mutual interest between China and Russia, along the lines of the two Karakhan manifestoes. It was agreed that Koo should see the draft before the memorandum was presented. In the course of working out the procedure, however, important differences were highlighted. Koo's position was that important issues should be discussed one at a time until agreement was reached. In short, he made the settlement of such important questions as Outer Mongolia and the Chinese Eastern Railway part and parcel of official recognition of the Soviet regime. In sharp contrast, Joffe maintained: 'The Sino-Soviet conference should first discuss the basic principles of political and economic relations, sign the main treaty, resume diplomatic relations, and leave the details to be worked out by special committees'. In effect Joffe wanted official recognition to precede concrete solutions of outstanding issues.[3]

This procedure was incorporated in Joffe's memorandum of August 25 to Koo. In that document, moreover, Joffe recalled how the Soviet government at its inception had declared to the Chinese government and people its readiness to renounce Tsarist predatory acquisitions and establish a new relationship of political and economic equality. But the Chinese government had not only ignored these declarations but acted in a hostile manner by participating in the Siberian Intervention and sheltering White Guards in its territory. Still, the Soviet government held the greatest sympathy and friendship for the Chinese people struggling to free themselves. Joffe renewed the proposal to confer on all matters of mutual interest, confident that the establishment of political and economic relations accorded with the popular will of the two peoples. In conclusion he asked the Chinese government, if it was agreeable, to name the place and date for a Sino-Soviet conference.[4]

Joffe's August 25 memorandum gave Koo the first taste of what to expect from the Soviet envoy. Joffe was plainly attempting to revive the popular euphoria previously raised by the first Karakhan Manifesto, and put the Chinese government to the test of popular will. He completely ignored the content of the August 23 discussion, failed to show Koo a draft before communicating it, but, worse still, had simultaneously released the memorandum to the press. At Koo's insistence, Joffe furnished a revised proposal on September 2, which omitted reference to the procedure of negotiation and some of the more offensive passages. It was again simultaneously publicized, and was again intended more for the Chinese public than for the Chinese foreign minister. One point that appears in both the original and revised versions deserves close attention: a careful distinction Joffe made between the two Karakhan Manifestoes, the first embodying general principles, and the second, concrete proposals. This was Joffe's way out of the embarrassment expected over the Chinese Eastern Railway question.

To beat Joffe at his own game, Koo publicized his acknowledgment of September 7, naming Peking as the venue and asking Joffe, who had departed for Changchun on September 2 for the Russo-Japanese conference, not to delay the talks too long.[5]

Joffe clearly ran the risk of being hoist with his own petard. Wellington Koo was no run-of-the-mill Peking politician but a celebrity and patriot in the eyes of the Chinese public. Joffe had been given a warm reception by the Chinese public but the goodwill was based on certain expectations. As the revered chancellor of Peking University, Ts'ai Yüan-pei, observed in a widely reported statement, unlike the foreigners who were carrying on a vilification press campaign against Soviet Russia, the Chinese people had the greatest confidence in Russia, and were looking hopefully to her to show other countries the right conduct towards China.[6]

The Russo-Japanese conference which opened at Changchun on September 4 revived all the Chinese fears and suspicions that the Dairen Conference had previously aroused. Even Wu P'ei-fu and Chang Tso-lin, one through the central government and the other independently, detailed observers to Changchun, who would be ready to protest against any compromise of Chinese sovereign rights in Manchuria and Mongolia which might result from a Russo-Japanese rapprochement.[7] But Joffe chose to push a hard line, knowing that Russia had nothing to lose even if the conference broke down. The Japanese were surprised that Joffe and Yanson both represented Moscow and Chita, with Joffe playing the predominant role, since they intended to settle questions concerning only Japan and the Far Eastern Republic. Joffe insisted on the right to reopen all questions, whereas the Japanese expected that the draft discussed at Dairen would be signed now that they had fixed the evacuation date. Later on, a further obstacle emerged when the Japanese made plain that North Sakhalin would not be cleared of Japanese troops until the settlement of the Nikolaevsk massacre, which Joffe categorically rejected. The Russians appeared insincere and on September 23, the Japanese delegation was instructed by Tokyo to terminate the negotiations.

At the last minute, Joffe accepted a Japanese proposal that there be two consecutive treaties, one with Chita and one with Moscow, but on three further conditions: that the agreement with Chita contain an obligation for Japan to negotiate a treaty with Soviet Russia, that the Japanese pledge of non-aggression be extended to Soviet Russia, and that a date for evacuation of North Sakhalin be set. The Japanese could agree only to the second of these conditions; they were not ready for a general agreement with Soviet Russia, and they insisted upon compensation for the Nikolaevsk incident as the condition for evacuation of North Sakhalin. The conference collapsed on September 25 over these issues. But time was on Joffe's side. In November, Japan completed evacuation from the Maritime Province; and on December 30, the Far Eastern Republic formally merged with the Soviet Republic.[8]

Meanwhile, in the midst of its anxieties over the Changchun Conference, the Peking government had been carrying out a policy reassessment concerning Soviet Russia. The result was a bold reformulation of policy. The policy review was set off initially by a memorandum submitted by John C. Ferguson, the American adviser, to President Li Yüan-hung and Foreign Minister Koo, in which he outlined a number of reasons why he felt the Peking government would be ill-advised to engage in negotiations with Joffe. Ferguson appears to have acted entirely on his own initiative because there is no record of any foreign official, either formally or privately, expressing disapproval of Peking's negotiations with the Soviet envoy. Indeed, the only advice tendered to the Peking government by British, American, and other ministers was limited to precautionary measures against Joffe's propaganda activities.[9]

In his memorandum of early September, Ferguson referred, firstly, to the fact that Joffe was abusing China's hospitality by speaking disrespectfully of those governments with which China had treaty relations, and moreover by seeking to subvert China's social order. China had no significant trade with Soviet Russia, and Ferguson believed that a trade agreement with the Far Eastern Republic would more than suffice. It would be enough, he said, to enter into an agreement with Moscow after Britain and other powers had taken the initiative; to do so now, China would be aligning herself with Soviet Russia and Germany. By awaiting the action of Britain, France, and the United States, and following the lines laid down by these governments, China would be aligned with strong governments from which she might receive needed financial assistance. Ferguson recommended, therefore, that Joffe be informed that his return to Peking would not be welcome.[10]

These views were singularly out of touch with the mood

and preoccupations of the Peking government, and served only as a negative stimulus˙for policy rethinking. Early in October, Wellington Koo drew up a statement of his views which were subsequently adopted by the cabinet. In Koo's view, Joffe should be treated as an unofficial representative like his predecessors, but his movements should be closely watched. The Soviet government was permitting Chinese consular officials to be stationed in Russia and Koo felt the Chinese government should reciprocate by treating with the Soviet envoy.

More importantly, many outstanding issues awaited negotiations, the most urgent among these being Outer Mongolia, the Chinese Eastern Railway, Amur River navigation, trade matters, and demarcation of borders. In Outer Mongolia, Chinese political and military influence had long been barred and there were indications that Chinese economic influence was coming under increasing assault. Chinese trade was being crippled by exhorbitant levies, arbitrary detention, or confiscation by newly erected customs houses on the border. Freedom of travel by Chinese was being curbed by the new requirement of travel documents.[11] Since a military solution was out of the question, said Koo, diplomacy was the only course left open. Similarly, in the case of the Chinese Eastern Railway, numerous basic problems remained to be solved. The noncommunist Russians in control of the enterprise would not readily give up their interests while others, especially the Japanese, wanted to absorb it. The railway was becoming once more vulnerable to external aggression as the Inter-Allied Technical Board, which had served as a protective umbrella since 1919, was due to be disbanded upon Japan's military withdrawal from Russian territory. An agreement with the Soviet government on the railway question was obviously a matter of great urgency. Koo also felt that a trade agreement with the Soviet government was urgently needed to safeguard the livelihood of large numbers of Chinese. The agreement would be able to deal with the constant interference by Soviet officials with Chinese shipping on the Amur and with the problem of reopening railway traffic with Russia.

Since discussions with Soviet envoys in the past had produced no positive results owing to China's insistence on

the withdrawal of Soviet troops in Outer Mongolia as a precondition for negotiations, Koo proposed that the condition
be dropped. Previously, China had felt constrained to act in
concert with the Great Powers in her Russian policy but a
recent survey showed no uniformity of policies and attitudes
among the foreign governments. Each power was in fact
following a policy that suited its self-interest best. 'For our
part', Koo argued, 'China shares a long frontier with Russia
and many urgent problems await solution. It is quite natural
that we should establish relations as soon as possible. In our
Russian policy, therefore, we need not follow other powers
but should be careful not to fall behind. We should firmly
maintain a policy that accords with our own national
interests'.[12]

At long last, China's policy towards Soviet Russia had
come into its own. The Chinese government was ready to
recognize the Soviet regime ahead of the Great Powers, providing the outstanding issues were settled to mutual satisfaction. When the cabinet adopted the foreign minister's proposals, it also named a delegation, led by the chairman of the
Committee on Russian Affairs, Liu Ching-jen, to negotiate
with the Joffe mission.

On October 5, two days after Joffe's return to Peking, Liu
proposed to him that the Sino-Soviet conference should open
on November 10. Unexpectedly, Joffe's reaction was
lukewarm. He neither accepted nor rejected the proposal,
excusing himself on the ground of illness. In place of the
conference, there ensued a public war of words between him
and Foreign Minister Koo, which began before Joffe's return
from Changchun. The volleys of communiqués which
seemed to be an exercise of futility to the Chinese may actually
be seen as a mode of negotiation on the Soviet part, if highly
unconventional at the time. In all his notes, Joffe hammered
the point that the Karakhan Manifestoes of 1919 and 1920 did
not entitle Peking to any of the offers until juridical relations
between the two governments had been established. Hence,
on September 19, he issued two protests, one against Peking's
decision to float a short-term loan on the Russian share of the
Boxer Indemnity, and the other against the convocation of the
shareholders' meeting of the Chinese Eastern Railway.[13]

On September 25, before replying, Koo took the offensive on the Mongolian question. He accused the Soviet government of not keeping faith with the word of its representative, Alexander Paikes, who had stated that his government was ready to evacuate voluntarily to promote Sino-Soviet friendship. Not only had Soviet troops continued to occupy Outer Mongolia, but customs stations had been erected to cripple Chinese exports, and Chinese travel to Outer Mongolia had been restricted. Koo challenged the Soviet government to give concrete proof of its avowed respect for China's territorial sovereignty by withdrawing troops immediately and abolishing the customs stations.[14] On the next day, he answered Joffe's protests. He pointed out that the Chinese government had ceased payment of the Boxer Indemnity to Russia as early as August 1920 and the Soviet government had never protested before. As for the shareholders' conference, it concerned only the internal administration of the railway within the framework of Chinese provisional management. Until the railway question was settled, Koo insisted, the existing arrangement should continue.[15]

Since Outer Mongolia was already in Soviet possession, there was nothing that Joffe need discuss with Peking on that score. Public debate could only cast doubt on Soviet intentions. Hence, he penned the best reply he could on October 14, and avoided being drawn on the subject again. He reminded Koo of his previous rejection of singling out evacuation as a precondition for talks. 'Even the best elements among those Chinese fighting for freedom believe that withdrawal of Soviet troops at this time will be harmful to both China and Russia'. (As proof, he soon elicited a statement from Sun Yat-sen to that effect.) He further reminded Koo that before the Soviet government had dispatched the Red Army, it had forewarned Peking. Evacuation would take place as soon as Moscow judged the time to be ripe. Meanwhile, the threat of White Guard attack against Russia was believed to be increasing rather than diminishing, and north Manchuria was being used as a base for massing troops and supplies. He called Koo's attention to recent press reports of an agreement for mutual assistance between Chang Tso-lin and the White Guard General Dietrichs against Soviet Russia, whereby Chang was to receive large quantities of arms from Vladivostok.[16] He concluded with a long list of instances where the White Guards had allegedly been permitted to attack the territory of the Far Eastern Republic from Manchuria.[17]

The switch away from Outer Mongolia to north Manchuria was a clever move on Joffe's part. The latter was the Soviets' primary diplomatic objective. On September 17, the last Japanese troops on the Harbin-Changchun and Harbin-Suifenho sections withdrew to south Manchuria. The Inter-Allied Technical Board was dissolved on November 1. As the Japanese evacuated the Maritime Province, the Priamur Provisional Government of Merkulov was also dissolved, its members fleeing across the border into north Manchuria and elsewhere. The Chinese had come a long way in recovering sovereign rights in the railway zone, including the institution of a railway patrol, municipal administration, police, justice, postal communications, etc. The entire region was being organized into the Manchurian Special District, over which Chang Tso-lin's subordinate General Chu Ch'ing-lan ruled as Special High Administrator. The railway itself was under Chinese trusteeship, while being administered with the assistance of noncommunist Russians representing the Russo-Asiatic Bank interests.[18] What the Soviet government wanted most was to reintroduce Russian influence in an area that was in close proximity to the Japanese power base in south Manchuria. Moreover, the Chinese Eastern Railway was an indispensable political and economic link between the Maritime Province and the rest of Siberia.

Joffe followed up his October 14 note with one on October 19, another on November 3, and yet another on November 5, all concerning the railway. In the first two, he demanded the existing management be abolished, General Manager Boris V. Ostroumov be arrested and arraigned for mishandling funds and abetting anti-Soviet elements; and a Sino-Soviet provisional administrative organ be set up prior to the solution of the railway question at the Sino-Soviet conference.[19] In his November 5 note, he attempted to draw out Koo on the Karakhan Manifestoes, with the apparent purpose of dispelling any illusions that Peking might still be entertaining about receiving the railway unconditionally and making clear that the Soviet government considered the *second*

Karakhan Manifesto to be the proper basis for negotiation on that question. He deemed it necessary to stress that his government still stood by the two manifestoes in general and in the railway question in particular. But,

> it is quite wrong to infer from these declarations that Russia renounces all her interests in China. . . . These declarations do not annul Russia's legal and just interests. . . . Even if Russia vests in the Chinese people her title to the Chinese Eastern Railway, this will not annul Russia's interest in this line, which is a portion of the Great Siberian Railroad and unites one part of the Russian territory with another.[20]

Since November 10, the date proposed by the Wai-chiao Pu for the conference, was drawing near, Koo made a gesture of conciliation on November 6. In accordance with the new policy just adopted, he informed Joffe that prior evacuation of Soviet troops would no longer be insisted upon as a precondition for negotiations, on the understanding given in Joffe's October 14 note that Russia had no aggressive intent in Outer Mongolia, and that the withdrawal of Soviet troops would only be a matter of time.[21] The concession did not modify Joffe's attitude for it obviously suited Soviet purposes to procrastinate. November 10 passed and the conference did not start. On the next day, thoroughly exasperated by Joffe's delaying tactics, Koo rejected his demand for provisional joint management of the railway, and asked that the Soviet pledge of unconditional transfer, contained in the first Karakhan Manifesto, be honored. He moreover protested against the threatening massing of Soviet troops on the Manchurian border which was reportedly designed for an armed invasion of north Manchuria and scizure of the railway.[22]

Koo's reference to the offer of unconditional transfer was apparently what Joffe had hoped for. On November 14, he issued what he called the 'Third Manifesto' by which he proposed to clarify the point in question once and for all. He categorically denied that the offer was made at all in the first Karakhan Manifesto. The only concrete proposal ever made regarding the railway, he asserted, was contained in the second Karakhan Manifesto, in which the Soviet government clearly specified its wish for certain guarantees from China. In consenting to negotiate the railway question in the spirit of the manifestoes, he had had the second Karakhan Manifesto specifically in mind. He denied further that his government was intending to seize the railway by force, but warned: 'The Soviet government will not adopt any action contrary to the interests of the Chinese *people* unless the Chinese *government* by its hostile action compels the Soviet government to do so'.[23]

At this point, factionalism erupted within the ruling Chihli clique. The provisional cabinet (not approved by parliament) in which Koo held the foreign affairs portfolio, had been the third of its kind since the Fengtien-Chihli War. Dubbed at the time as the 'Able Men's Cabinet' (*hsien-jen nei-ko*), it had shown great promise with Wu P'ei-fu's backing and much public support. After defeating Chang Tso-lin in May, Wu had reinstated Li Yüan-hung as president in place of Hsü Shih-ch'ang, and restored the parliament of 1916. He had hoped by this 'return to legitimacy' to deprive Sun Yat-sen of the banner under which he had set up a separate regime in Canton, and to unify the country under Chihli leadership. But, following the victory that had been won largely by Wu, tensions and strains developed within the Chihli clique, between the major followers of Ts'ao K'un and his brother Ts'ao Jui on one hand and those of Wu P'ei-fu on the other. Resentment of Wu's ascendancy motivated the followers of the two Ts'ao brothers to try to remove his influence from the central government. This they did by starting a movement to put Ts'ao K'un in the presidency. Upon a suitable pretext, a confrontation was brought about between Ts'ao and Wu in mid-November which forced Wu, who shrank from breaking with his patron and superior, to step into the background. One consequence of the political in-fighting was the collapse of the cabinet on November 25, and with it went the able foreign minister, Wellington Koo.[24]

When C.T. Wang (Wang Cheng-t'ing) took over from Koo in late November 1922, it fell upon him to answer Joffe's November 14 'Third Manifesto'. Accordingly, on December 11, he did the inevitable by throwing the text which the Peking government had received in March 1920 in Joffe's face.[25] But Joffe had expected this to happen all along. In his reply on December 21, he feigned ignorance of the version which Peking had received, again categorically denied that the offer of unconditional transfer of the railway was ever included, and forwarded a copy of the 'authentic' text, which was identical with the one that appeared in the Soviet press in August 1919. And, more tŏ the point, he reminded Wang that the Chinese government had never acknowledged the manifesto at the time.[26] In this typically truculent manner, he cleared away what he deemed to be a 'misunderstanding' on the part of the Peking government.

By the end of December, the way had been quietly paved for Joffe to move on to greener pastures. Leaving matters with his deputy, J.C. Davtian, he departed for Shanghai on January 16, 1923, for talks with Sun Yat-sen and then sailed for Japan on January 27 to resume talks with the Japanese. His five-month long mission to Peking thus ended without concrete results. The Chinese side had been fully disposed to negotiate, but Joffe had not. He was unwilling to give the Chinese the opportunity to use formal recognition for the Soviet government in return for settling outstanding issues. In any case, the Chinese Eastern Railway, where Soviet interests principally lay, was under Chang Tso-lin's rather than the Peking government's effective jurisdiction. Furthermore, the general situation in the Far East was working steadily in favor of Russia, and Joffe evidently felt that he could afford to wait as far as talks with Peking were concerned. Instead of business-like talks, therefore, he had resorted to harassing the Peking government with a barrage of bellicose notes. Amidst the bluster, however, there did emerge a proposal in outline both as to the content of the treaty contemplated by the Soviet side and the procedure by which it was to be concluded. The procedure desired by Joffe was that the two parties should conclude an agreement restoring full diplomatic relations but it should consist of only the general principles by which the outstanding issues were to be settled later. Among the general principles were that the second Karakhan Manifesto should be taken as the basis for negotiations. The Soviet government recognized China's territorial sovereignty in Outer Mongolia but would not withdraw its troops until its national security was no longer threatened. Pending a definitive settlement of the Chinese Eastern Railway, a *modus vivendi* was to be worked out as part of the agreement whereby the railway would be temporarily managed jointly by Soviet Russia and China. It was precisely along these lines that the Sino-Soviet Treaty was concluded in 1924.

Two other matters remain to be dealt with before leaving the Joffe mission: the concentration of Soviet troops on the Manchurian border, allegedly for armed action against the Chinese Eastern Railway; and the joint communiqué issued by Joffe and Sun Yat-sen on January 26, 1923, and its implications for Sino-Soviet diplomacy. A discussion of these two problems requires a brief sketch of Soviet relations with the Chihli warlord, Wu P'ei-fu, and the Kuomintang leader, Sun Yat-sen.

Reports of Soviet troop movements along the Manchurian border actually began filtering into Peking as early as the beginning of 1922. During the winter of 1921-22, as the White Guards of the Maritime Province carried their offensive into the Amur Province, the armed forces of the Far Eastern Republic had counterattacked, retaking the city of Khabarovsk in mid-February. Instead of advancing into the Maritime Province against the White Guards, they decided to hold the line there so as to avoid an armed clash with the Japanese. In these circumstances, the railway zone in north Manchuria once again appeared likely to be embroiled in the Russian civil war, as clandestine White Guard groups were reported to be planning a second front, in conjunction with the Ungernist remnants, that would advance upon Transbaikalia from the western end of the Chinese Eastern Railway.[27]

Much of the Soviet military activity along the Manchurian border was no doubt connected with these White Guards. Later in the year, when Japanese troops left the Maritime Province, the Merkulov regime at Vladivostok disbanded, more White Guards crossed into north Manchuria and more Soviet troops movements took place in preparation for securing the Maritime Province and paving the way for its merger with the Soviet Republic. The great attention given to the railway question by the Yurin, Paikes, and Joffe missions was at least in part due to the threat posed by the White Guards ensconced in the railway zone.[28] But what interests us here is the fact that towards the end of April, the troop movements were rumored to be taken under a tacit understanding with Wu P'ei-fu. It was alleged that Soviet troops might be threatening Chang Tso-lin's rear while he prosecuted the war against Wu P'ei-fu.[29] The Fengtien-Chihli War lasted about a week (April 28 to May 4) and ended to the noticeable disappointment of the Soviets. Although Chang was defeated in the field, he was able simply to retire with many of his men and much of his material to the safety of his Manchurian home base. There he regrouped his forces for another round, generally expected in the spring of 1923.

Whether an understanding of some sort did in fact exist between the Soviets and Wu P'ei-fu about the time of the Fengtien-Chihli War remains shrouded in mystery. One man was absolutely certain of its existence: Sun Yat-sen, who had allied himself with Chang Tso-lin since before the war. His source of information, strangely enough, was none other than Joffe. So convinced was Sun of Soviet-Wu collaboration that he registered a strong dissent in a letter to Lenin on December 6, which reads in part:

> You can make Chang Tso-lin, within reasonable limits, do all that is necessary for the security of Soviet Russia. Following this policy, you will not only avoid the danger of a reaction against you in China but also help me create a situation that will facilitate and speed the joint work between Soviet Russia and China.[30]

He also informed his ally Chang Tso-lin of Soviet-Wu collaboration. His message to Chang is not available but, judging from Chang's acknowledgment of February 7, 1923, he seems to have told Chang that Wu intended to take advantage of a Soviet invasion to launch an attack from the south.[31] Later, in April, when the danger seemed to have passed, Sun also disclosed his conversations with Joffe to the American consul in Canton, Tenney. The latter's report of April 14 to Washington reads: 'Dr. Sun stated . . . that Wu was also supported by the Soviets, that when he saw Joffe recently at Shanghai he had learned that the Soviets had a plan whereby they were to cooperate with Wu in crushing Chang Tso-lin'.[32]

Leaving aside for the moment whatever Joffe had confided in Sun, the remaining evidence on whether a concrete understanding existed between Moscow and Wu is highly contradictory. On the positive side, there are many signs that Moscow had been looking upon Wu P'ei-fu as a potential ally as far back as 1920; in that year, Wu crushed the Anfu clique and became enormously popular with the young and progressive. Misinformed, Moscow had even expected a pro-Soviet orientation in Peking after the Anfu-Chihli War, only to learn with dismay later that Chang Tso-lin, another 'pawn' of Japanese imperialism, not Wu P'ei-fu, had come out of the melee on top.[33]

But, as enmity grew between Wu and Chang, Soviet strategists more than ever looked upon Wu as a possible ally, even at the cost of ideological purity.[34] In terms of dogma, Wu was necessarily a feudal militarist, the logical target of the bourgeois-democratic revolution. However, in Wu's case, ideology somehow did not fit. Wu combined military might with liberalism. He matched Chang Tso-lin in military power and Sun Yat-sen in ideas. To many Chinese and foreigners alike, Wu held out the best prospects for a unified, democratic China. The uncertainty of Wu's ideological status coupled with Moscow's strong need for allies in Asia resulted in Wu being portrayed in Soviet writings as a highly desirable ally. One Narkomindel commentator on the Chinese scene recommended that Moscow 'give special attention' to Wu 'whose liberalism is making him the most popular figure in the Yangtze Valley'.[35]

An alliance with Wu seemed both desirable and feasible in view of a natural convergence of mutual interests. To Moscow, Wu was not only boldly anti-Japanese, but the only force capable of challenging Chang Tso-lin, and thus checking the spread of 'concealed' Japanese influence in China. For his part, Wu was aware that Chang could be defeated but not destroyed so long as he was able to maintain an invincible base in Manchuria. Here, the Soviets held the key by being able to pose a threat to Chang's rear. This was precisely what Wu had in mind when he told Vilensky, who visited him at Loyang about the time of the Fengtien-Chihli War, that 'Chang cannot be so dangerous so long as he [Wu] had a natural ally like Soviet Russia at Chang's rear'.[36]

Vilensky left an all too brief description of the encounter, but what transpired may be gauged from the catalog of topics covered. Wu avowed great sympathy for Soviet Russia and regretted that domestic conflict had prevented him from taking necessary steps to effect friendly relations. He disclosed his plan for national reunification which consisted of reconvening the legitimate Old Parliament and the creation of a national army modelled on the Red Army. He favored an international alignment that put China in the camp of Soviet Russia and Germany. Internally, he intended to seek support from the broad democratic layers of Chinese society and promised labor legislation to protect the working masses. Vilensky came away from his visit visibly impressed. Writing soon after the Fengtien-Chihli War, he portrayed Wu as the symbol of Chinese national liberation, 'a spokesman of supra-class (*nadklassovyi*) national aspirations and moods'. He discerned a process of 'jointing' between 'the best militarist' and the Chinese bourgeoisie of the Yangtze Valley. 'Wu is popular in China', he wrote. 'He is a victor. He holds an army in his hands and moreover controls the Peking government. . . . In a word, Wu is the real power impossible for us to ignore. He is called to play an exceptionally great role in China's destiny'.[37] Vilensky's assessment of Wu is all the more remarkable since, as shall be shown later, he had come to China originally to hold talks with Wu's rival, Sun Yan-sen.

It is difficult to say whether on this visit Vilensky and Wu struck a bargain on joint action against Chang Tso-lin. On the other hand, there is some evidence affirming collaboration between Wu and the Chinese Communist Party. At the Fourth Comintern Congress in November, Karl Radek disclosed in a speech that during the Fengtien-Chihli War Chinese communists had assisted Wu on the Peking-Hankow Railway by preventing Old Communications Clique elements who were allied with Chang from impeding movement of Wu's troop trains for the north. This is corroborated by the Chinese communist, Teng Chung-hsia, who stated that, after the war, Li Ta-chao secured an agreement from Wu's minister for communications, Kao En-hung, whereby communists were employed as secret inspectors on the northern railway system; they were given free rein in organizing railroad workmen and ferreting out elements of the Old Communications Clique.[38]

In the military sphere, where Wu could have availed himself of Soviet military assistance at Chang's rear, Soviet troop movements were rumored but no troops crossed the border. This seems to suggest that the understanding, if one existed, had been a rather limited one, involving some CCP-Wu collaboration and the posing of a threat at Chang's rear without an actual invasion. It is probably closer to the truth that there was no full commitment between the Soviets and Wu. Indeed, it appears that up to the end of 1922, the Soviets had attempted to keep up relations with both Wu and Sun Yat-sen. Sun's attitude towards Wu was such that a clear-cut choice between him and Wu was required of Moscow and this Moscow tried to postpone as long as possible. The Soviet political analyst, A. Ivin, wrote at this time: 'If it were possible for Sun Yat-sen and Wu P'ei-fu to come to an agreement, this would not only be in their own interests but in China's interests as well'. His views were echoed by Joffe, Vilensky, and the Chinese communists.[39]

As it turned out, the Soviets were saved the embarrassment of deciding for one or the other by the factionalism that erupted within the Chihli clique. Wu withdrew from Peking politics and switched from a policy of peaceful unification to one of military force. In 1923, he concentrated his campaigns on the south, leaving Chang Tso-lin alone for the time being. Reconciliation developed between Ts'ao K'un and Chang. If coordinated military action with Wu had in fact been contemplated by the Soviets, the plan had to be temporarily shelved. Wu's capitulation to Ts'ao K'un also meant his going along with the latter's repressive policy towards the student and labor movements. The shooting of the Peking-Hankow railroad strikers in February 1923 ended the collaboration between Wu and the Chinese communists.[40]

In confiding the Soviet plan to Sun, Joffe's purpose may have been simply to induce Sun to influence Chang Tso-lin to accommodate Soviet wishes, especially with regard to the Chinese Eastern Railway. In an article in *Izvestiia*, Joffe in fact credited Sun with exercising an influence over Chang. To what effect he did not say, and details of the Sun-Chang correspondence on this point are not available. However, the fact that, in the joint communiqué of January 26, 1923, Sun came out in support of the Soviet position on the railway question is in itself an exercise of influence by Sun on the Soviets' behalf.[41]

Since Japan had been immobilized by the American attitude, it is not improbable, as Whiting has suggested, that an extremist group in the Soviets might have advocated a sudden military move against the railway.[42] A raid against Soviet territory by the White Guards, mounted from the railway area, could easily have served as a *casus belli*. But this would have assumed a change in the long-standing Soviet attitude of caution towards Japan to the extent of being ready to risk counteraction from the Japanese who had troops nearby in south Manchuria and Korea. That the prevailing mood of the Soviet leadership had not changed may be discerned in Vilensky's pamphlet *Rossiia na Dal'nem Vostoke* (preface dated November 1922), which was issued in Moscow by the supreme military editorial council in 1923.

In this booklet, Vilensky saw as the continuing dominant trend in the Pacific region the development of American-Japanese rivalry towards an eventual armed collision. Although both America and Japan were Soviet Russia's enemies, still *realpolitik* might cause either or both to seek an alliance with Soviet Russia which, if advantageous, should not be rejected. However, Japan was the greater enemy because, in the event of an American-Japanese conflict on Chinese soil, Japan would seize Russian territory for additional room for maneuvering. For this reason, northern Sakhalin had become 'the fighting question' for Japanese militarism, a springboard for seizure of the Russian Maritime Province. Vilensky warned against being deluded by Japanese evacuation of the Maritime Province as a victory; Japan, doing all it could to weaken Russia's position in the Pacific, still held 'the key to the mastery of the Russian Far East'. From northern Sakhalin, Korea, and Manchuria, the Japanese could employ 'strategic pincers' to put the fate of the Maritime Province in doubt. Against this potential danger, the Soviets had found allies among such Chinese nationalists as Wu P'ei-fu and Sun Yat-sen. Inspired by the Rapallo relationship between Soviet Russia and Germany, these Chinese leaders had conceived the notion of a triple alliance between China, Soviet Russia, and Germany as a means for China to free herself from imperialist domination. They had raised specifically the possibility of cooperation with Soviet Russia in evicting Japan from the Asian continent 'by the combined pressure of China from the south and Russia from the north so that Japanese imperialism will be denied its Manchurian base and expelled from Korea'.[43]

Vilensky's reactions to the scheme were as interesting as his analysis of Far Eastern politics. They suggest continuity in Soviet policy of avoiding any open or direct confrontation with Japan. He writes:

> Certainly, it is quite natural that Chinese nationalists should approach future Sino-Soviet relations from the viewpoint of adapting them to the needs of the struggle with Japanese imperialism. . . . But I doubt that Russia, at this juncture and especially in such an alliance with the Chinese nationalists, can take upon herself the task of armed struggle with Japan in the name of overthrowing Japanese imperialism in East Asia. Certainly, one may raise the question, but not in the immediate future.

He preferred Sino-Soviet relations to be placed on a different, less risky basis.

> At present, Sino-Soviet relations should be constructed in such a manner that, on the one hand, Russia should receive from China the necessary guarantee of the security of Russian interests in the Far East and, on the other, China may utilize the whole sum of the international significance that Russia possesses so that, relying on it, China can successfully carry out her struggle for liberation from the yoke of imperialism.

In short, for the time being, China should help Soviet Russia consolidate its position in the east by the immediate conclusion of a treaty of mutual recognition, a treaty of commerce, and especially by being reasonable about Russia's demands as regards the Chinese Eastern Railway and Outer Mongolia.[44]

Thus, along with the policy of temporary appeasement with Japan went a new rhetoric for the furtherance of Soviet interests in China. So that Soviet Russia might better prepare herself for the ultimate conflict with Japan, Chinese nationalists were called upon to sacrifice some of their national interests. This followed logically from the argument that, for the sake of the triumph of socialism, the Chinese Communist Party should put protection of the socialist fatherland in the forefront of its platform.

The Joffe-Sun joint communiqué is an excellent illustration of the dualism inherent in Soviet foreign policy where diplomacy and revolution meshed inseparably together. It shows how the Chinese nationalist leader was used for Soviet diplomatic purposes; it represents also a stage of a long and intricate process in which the Chinese nationalist revolution was harnessed for Soviet objectives. An extensive literature already exists on the origin of the alliance between Moscow and Sun Yat-sen's Kuomintang, and between the latter and the Chinese Communist Party. Less known is how Soviet diplomatic goals were thereby furthered by these revolutionary relationships.

As we know, it was Lenin who, long before the Bolshevik seizure of power, first conceived of an alliance between communism and bourgeois-democratic national movements. Significantly, in China, that alliance was forged after the Soviet state had survived the severe ordeal of civil and international war, and entered the phase of development in which it was compelled to postpone its domestic goal of communism and international goal of world revolution. Moscow entered into relations with Chinese nationalists at a time when it was putting Soviet national interests in the forefront of its foreign policy.

The real starting point of the evolution of the alliance may be put towards the end of 1921. Before this, there had been contacts between Soviet leaders and Sun, but they had been sporadic and various obstacles prevented them from developing into anything concrete. We know, for example, that in the spring of 1918, Sun had wired his good wishes to the Soviet regime as he had done a year earlier to the Provisional Government, but Chicherin's reverent acknowledgment of August 1, 1918 had failed to reach him.[45] Between December 1919 and April 1920, Bolshevik General A.S. Potapov saw him frequently in Shanghai, but to the former's dismay Sun was too timid to respond to the Karakhan Manifesto. The reason, according to Potapov, was that the detection of his relations with Moscow 'would have complicated his stay at the French Concession and the work being carried on by him in China'. Moreover, Sun was just then trying to regain Kwangtung from the Kwangsi militarists, who had squeezed him out of his south China base in 1918, and to that end had allied himself with the Anfu clique of militarists, the very forces considered in Moscow to be inimical to Soviet interests.[46]

On October 31, 1920, Chicherin sent Sun what must have been the second letter. In it, he expressed delight over the defeat of the Anfu clique, 'the extreme reaction' allied with Japanese imperialism. Yurin had just then entered Peking as a commercial representative of the Far Eastern Republic, and Chicherin desired that 'trade relations . . . be established immediately'. This letter did not reach Sun until June 14, 1921, and when Sun replied on August 28, 1921, another obstacle had arisen. He informed Chicherin that Chang Tso-lin had in fact become master of the Peking government.

> Chang . . . obeys Tokyo in all important matters which concern Japan. Peking, then, is Tokyo's tool in all questions of high politics that concern Japan's vital interests. Moscow must take this fact into serious account in all its dealings with Peking. Not before Peking is thoroughly cleansed (and that will be only when I enter it) can Russia hope for the restoration of favorable relations with China.

Interestingly enough, although Sun had regained Kwangtung at the end of 1920, assumed the presidency in the Canton government, and had been seeking foreign recognition without success, he carefully abstained from asking for Soviet recognition of his regime. In short, he was displeased at Soviet diplomacy with the Peking government, but would not recognize the Soviet government himself.[47]

It was with Maring's visit to Sun in December 1921 that contacts became more regular and directed to a more specific end. At that time, Sun was seeking a tactical alliance with Chang Tso-lin and preparing a northern expedition at Kweilin to crush Wu P'ei-fu and plant his influence in central China. There Maring and Sun held a series of discussions. Interestingly, many of the differences emerged that were to plague the subsequent Sun-Soviet alliance. The first was ideological. Sun apparently reacted favorably to Maring's proposal for the Kuomintang and the Chinese Communist Party to join cause. Such collaboration, placed on a proper basis, would have enabled him to harness the youthful energies of the CCP to the nationalist movement that he wanted to lead. However, Sun appears to have been quite firm on one point, namely, that revolutionary ideology perforce differed from country to country, depending on the conditions in each; he evidently believed that his own unique synthesis of the Three Principles of the People accorded with Chinese reality best. The New Economic Policy of the Soviet republic, which appeared to him like a page from his own Principle of People's Welfare, convinced him of the rightness of his ideas for China, and perhaps a degree of universality as well.[48]

Maring seems to have exerted himself in persuading Sun to reorganize his party, and put mass mobilization ahead of military matters. Such advice from Moscow became perennial. Years later, Maring ruefully recalled, 'Sun Yat-sen up to the very time of his death never really absorbed the idea of mass activity'.[49] Sun's eyes were always set on Peking, and a short cut seemed preferable to the time-consuming work of mass mobilization which was to be reserved for a time when he was not militarily preoccupied.

A further problem posed by Sun was the anomaly that the Chinese nationalist leader was not conspicuously anti-imperialistic in his utterances or program. Maring singled out the failure to conduct mass propaganda against foreign influence as 'the weak spot' of the KMT. Although anti-foreignism was widespread, wrote Maring, Sun and his party 'still have the naivete to hope that if only they do not provoke the foreigners with their propaganda, they will succeed in bringing about the revival of China without foreign intervention'.[50] Such complaints were to be echoed time and again by other ·Soviet agents.

The question of establishing formal relations between Canton and Moscow was also discussed. Sun told Maring that he wished to postpone the matter until he had carried the northern military expedition to Hankow. Otherwise, the British in Hong Kong could jeopardize the expedition. He seemed prepared meanwhile to initiate informal intercourse.[51] Just then, Chang Ch'iu-p'ai was leaving for Moscow as a KMT delegate to the Congress of the Toilers of the Far East, called in protest against the Washington Conference. Sun entrusted to Chang a letter to Chicherin, the text of which has never been made public.[52] But Chicherin's reply of February 7, 1922, to Sun indicates that the latter had spoken out strongly against Soviet diplomacy with the Peking government. It reads in part:

> I hope that very soon one of our friends from here can call on you personally and, if no obstacle arises, can remain with you constantly. During the meeting with the KMT representative, I discussed with him all the problems concerning our future relations. . . . I emphasize that our Government and people are the most genuine friends of the Chinese people and fervently wish that China would become a united progressive country, led by a popular government and fully free from external political and economic pressures. I underline, however, that our Government cannot interfere in China's internal affairs and encroach upon the complete and sole right of self-determination of the Chinese people, who themselves should decide their own destiny. All our sympathies certainly lie on the side of the popular, progressive, emancipated forces of China. But the Peking Government, whatever it is, is the official government of the Chinese state, and we are hoping to establish normal relations with it. In the course of our future conversations with the KMT representative and conversations of our friend who will visit you and your leading figures, we will define more clearly the extent of the ties which will unite us with you and your friends.[53]

The man selected to adjust relations with Sun Yat-sen was none other than Vilensky. He set out for China in April under the cover of councillor to the Paikes mission. Soon after arriving in China he was side-tracked into some enthusiastic conversations with Wu P'ei-fu in Loyang.[54] In his place, Sergei A. Dalin, secretary of the Far Eastern bureau of the Communist Youth International at Irkutsk, visited Sun and remained with him from April 27 until Sun's eviction in June from Kwangtung by Ch'en Chiung-ming. Under the joint auspices of the Narkomindel and Comintern, Dalin exchanged views with Sun on a wide range of subjects.[55] On the question of formal relations with Moscow, Sun reiterated the position stated to Maring earlier that he could not formally recognize the Soviet government until after he had reached Hankow. Like Maring, Dalin was also struck by Sun's fear of British intervention against his Canton government. 'This was the weightiest of his arguments. He detested and feared the British at the same time; he feared Hong Kong'.[56]

On the subject of ideology, Sun appears to have been still suspicious of Soviet intentions and made indirect soundings. As Dalin recalls:

> Sun knows that I am a Communist, that the Canton Communists are opposed to him, that the workers' movement is drawing away from him, and that I am connected with both the Canton Communists and the workers' movement. It is natural that Sun should have nourished some distrust towards me at first, wondering: 'Won't he organize a communist coup here?'[57]

Like Maring, Dalin took pains to explain that China was not yet ripe for the Soviet system, that a democratic revolution was the order of the day. The instrument of this was the KMT of which Sun was the leader, and the struggle would have the full support of the broad masses of Soviet Russia. 'I watched Sun's face and saw how it brightened up and how his eyes began to beam'.[58]

Another subject discussed was Manchuria and the question of the Chinese Eastern Railway, but Dalin gives no details. To Dalin's surprise, Sun inquired:

> Can't Russia carry out the same *coup* in Manchuria as she did in Outer Mongolia? We have a common enemy, Japan, which seized your Vladivostok . . . and our Manchuria with Chang Tso-lin's help. As soon as Wu P'ei-fu is defeated by me, we will go after Chang Tso-lin next. In this connection, Soviet Russia's assistance will be extremely important.[59]

What Sun's real motives were is impossible to tell. He might have been simply testing Soviet intentions, in view of the current rumors about Soviet military build-up on the Manchurian border. On the other hand, he could have meant what he said seriously. His alliance with Chang Tso-lin against Wu was after all a purely tactical one. Indeed, on this level, the only difference between him and Soviet political analysts was that the latter would rather see a Sun–Wu coalition instead.[60]

Finally, what transpired on the Mongolian question, again only fragmentarily disclosed by Dalin, is noteworthy. Dalin told Sun that in spirit Outer Mongolia much resembled revolutionary south China, and asked if Sun would agree to Mongolian independence. Sun's reply was resoundingly negative: Outer Mongolia was an integral part of China, there could be no talk of Mongolian independence. Dalin wryly reported: Sun the nationalist 'did not recognize the right of self-determination or autonomy for China's national minorities'.[61]

On June 23, taking refuge in a gunboat from Ch'en Chiung-ming's coup, Sun sent Dalin a letter addressed to Chicherin, referring to the political crisis.[62] After Dalin, Sun's next visitor was Maring again, who met Sun in Shanghai in August. Maring, who personally preferred Sun to Wu P'ei-fu and had been arguing that the Comintern abandon Wu in favor of Sun, had accompanied Joffe to China. As Maring recalled his second visit to Sun: 'Sun had himself been led, as a result of his defeat at Canton, to think along lines of modern mass activity and secondly in terms of aid from Russia'.[63] Dalin had accomplished the mission of exploring 'the extent of ties' possible between Sun and Moscow, and Maring now continued these conversations in close consultation with Joffe. Over the next five months (except for a brief journey to Moscow and talks with Chang Tso-lin en route about the railway question), Maring conducted earnest discussions with Sun on the reorganization of the KMT and collaboration with the CCP, and on a formal agreement of cooperation between the Soviets and the KMT.

Soviet aid being contingent upon it, agreement on party reorganization and KMT–CCP collaboration was reached quickly. Leading communists like Ch'en Tu-hsiu, Li Ta-chao, Ts'ai Ho-shen, and Chang T'ai-lei were formally admitted to the KMT at the beginning of September. This was followed immediately by a conference, with communist participation, to discuss party reorganization. On September 6, a nine-man committee, including Ch'en Tu-hsiu, was set up to draft the necessary documents.[64] On New Year's Day 1923, the party publicized its new manifesto, platform and regulations, embodying the new direction.[65] Not since the days of the T'ung-meng hui had the party taken an antiforeign stand. It now explicitly described China as 'a colony' of the foreign powers, and called for the abolition of unequal treaties—a short step from the strident anti-imperialist slogan of a year later.[66] In its economic policy, other than the old tenets regarding state regulation of capital and single-tax, the party called for limitation of landownership, and improvement of peasant life and landlord-tenant relations.[67]

Finally, the party structure was enlarged by the newly added departments of peasants, workers, and women, thus evolving towards a mass base. The significance of this innovation was explained by Sun himself in an address to a party conference on January 2, 1923. Political intrigues and military activities having proved ineffective, he said, the party should now become a vehicle of revolution, with mobilization of mass support through mass propaganda as its uppermost task.[68]

The preliminaries having now been effected, the time had come for a formal agreement between Soviet Russia and the KMT. To this end, Joffe came down to Shanghai on January 17. At the close of numerous talks, the two men issued a joint communiqué on January 26, comprising four points.[69] The document is a perfect illustration of the dualism inherent in Soviet policy towards China. First of all, it spells out, in Point One, the principle governing cooperation between Soviet Russia and the KMT, the vehicle of China's bourgeois nationalist revolution. Both parties agreed that neither Communism nor the Soviet system was applicable in China, since favorable conditions did not exist. 'China's most important and most pressing problems are the completion of national unification and the attainment of full national independence'. In this undertaking, Joffe assured Sun of Soviet 'willingness to lend support'. The urgent tasks were couched in the positive, no doubt on Sun's insistence, whereas Joffe would probably have preferred them in the negative strident slogans of antiwarlordism and anti-imperialism.

The remainder of the joint communiqué was closely related to Soviet diplomatic objectives. It embodied the Soviet diplomatic position exactly as it had been stated to the Peking government by Joffe. In Point Two, Joffe reaffirmed the principles enunciated by Russia in the second Karakhan Manifesto, underlining its important bearing on the Chinese Eastern Railway question. In Point Three, Sun came out in support of Joffe's demand that the railway question should be reserved for detailed consideration by a competent Sino–Soviet conference, but meanwhile 'a *modus vivendi* ought to be devised' through which the railway administration should be 'temporarily reorganized' without injury to 'the real rights and special interests' of either party. Sun also held that Chang Tso-lin should be consulted in this matter.

In Point Four, with respect to the Mongolian question, Joffe categorically declared (with Sun's complete agreement) that 'it is not, and never has been, the intention or the objective of the present Russian government to carry out imperialist policies in Outer Mongolia, or to work for Outer Mongolia's independence [in Russian, *otpadenie* or 'defection'] from China'. Sun, on his part, 'does not deem the immediate evacuation of Russian troops as urgently necessary or to the real advantage of China', the Peking government being too 'weak and impotent' to prevent recurrence of White Guard difficulties for the Soviet government. It is a matter of no small significance that under the Principle of Nationalism, enunciated in a revised form in the party platform of January 1924, Sun reversed his previous position by recognizing the right of self-determination for China's national minorities.

Both Joffe and Sun had good reason to be pleased with the entente. Joffe must have felt gratified that Sun had accepted, on paper at least, the Comintern strategy for bourgeois nationalist revolution, but especially that he had lent his prestige to the support of Soviet diplomatic goals. In the short run, the communiqué could be used at least to alarm Peking; and in the long run, it might even serve as the basis for a subsequent agreement with KMT China.

For Sun, the agreement probably signified Soviet commitment to render concrete aid to his party, although the details remained to be worked out. The assurance he had

received that his Three Principles, not communism or
sovietism, were to be the guiding ideology of the revolution
must have inclined him to view collaboration with the CCP in
a positive light. The CCP could be expected to expend its
youthful energies on behalf of the KMT and mobilize mass
support for it. The only perplexing aspect of the agreement
was his lending support to Soviet diplomatic goals from
which he appears to have had little else to gain unless to gratify
his desire to embarrass the Peking government.

It is impossible to say how much aid Sun was promised.
The subject was later pursued by Sun's agent, Liao
Chung-k'ai, who followed Joffe to Japan. Questions regarding Soviet supply of money, arms, military instruction, and
the organization of a military academy were reportedly discussed. As a result of these conversations, the Soviet government approved, in March 1923, a sum of two million Mexican
dollars in aid of the KMT, and agreed to dispatch an undis-
closed number of Soviet military advisers to Canton.[70] General A.I. Gekker, who was military attaché of the Joffe mission
and had been in consultation with Sun, brought out the first
group of four military experts in June; these were attached to
the Soviet mission in Peking as 'trainees' (hsüeh-hsi yüan).[71]
They proceeded to Canton three months later when Michael
M. Borodin also arrived there as representative of the Soviet
government and chief political adviser to the KMT. In January
1924, Borodin guided the KMT through its reorganization
and completed the preliminaries for the KMT-Soviet alliance.
Thus, a whole year elapsed between the Joffe-Sun joint
communiqué and the implementation of the pact. The delay
may have been for various reasons but chief among them was
probably the fact that what Moscow had gained in the KMT
was still a slippery toehold. The initial problems experienced
by the Comintern and the Soviet government during the
course of 1923 foreshadow the kinds of difficulties that beset
the partnership in subsequent years.

To begin with, the KMT reorganization at the end of
1922 would have amounted to a fundamental reorientation in
Sun's political strategy along Comintern lines, had it not been
for his propensity for backsliding. The change remained very
much on paper for quite some time. Maring recalled that in

1923 Sun was indifferent to mass activity. Vilensky noted that in the course of that year Sun was very cautious in expressing sympathy for Soviet Russia, fearful that 'an open orientation . . . could bring unpleasant consequences to south China in the form of a blockade, which he wished to avoid'.[72] Not until the Canton customs seizure episode at the end of the year—when Sun's attempt to seize the Canton customs surplus was met with a foreign naval demonstration—did he openly display a pro-Soviet orientation and the shrill slogan of anti-imperialism.

Nor was everything well with KMT-CCP collaboration. The entry of the communists into the KMT was greeted with suspicion by the faction-ridden party. This was exacerbated by the CCP's open criticism of the KMT. The resolutions of the third CCP congress of June, for instance, criticized the KMT for looking to the foreign powers for assistance, and for its exclusive preoccupation with military matters to the neglect of party and mass propaganda work. Sun reacted by warning Maring: 'Since the communists have joined the KMT, they should submit to party discipline and not openly criticize the KMT. If they disobey the KMT, I will expel them; and if Soviet Russia should render them covert protection, I shall oppose Soviet Russia'.[73] The Comintern had directed the communists to enter the KMT, on the basis of Maring's strategy that the communists should at the same time maintain their own organization and their own paper. Whether this was a case of Soviet and Comintern agents not having been sufficiently frank with Sun or of the CCP's recalcitrance, a common understanding of the basis for collaboration seems to have been lacking from the very start, with fateful consequences for the CCP.

In Sun's mind, his relationship with the Comintern was far less important than that with the Soviet government itself. It was the latter that was the real source of the concrete financial and military aid he needed for his unchanging quest for a speedy overthrow of the northern government and immediate access to power. Just how uncommitted he was to the Comintern line is illustrated by his proposal to shift his base of operations to Outer Mongolia, in order to be closer to the seat of power and Soviet aid. Fantastic as it might seem, he wrote Joffe on December 30, 1922, about leading a 100,000-strong army from Szechwan into Outer Mongolia for a subsequent drive against Peking. He asked for assistance in arms, equipment, instructors, etc. The plan received an unsympathetic hearing from Joffe who, in reporting to his superiors, referred to it as Sun's 'old dream'.[74] But, in the autumn of 1923, the persistent Sun sent Chiang Kai-shek to Moscow to renew the proposal to the Soviet leaders. On December 4, Chicherin was forced to put on the damper:

> We think that the fundamental aim of the KMT is to build up a great powerful movement of the Chinese people and that therefore propaganda and organization on the biggest scale are its first necessities. . . . The whole Chinese nation must see the difference between the KMT, a popularly organized mass party, and the military dictatorship of the various parts of China. The fraternal nations, such as the Mongolian people, the Tibetans, the various races of western China, must clearly understand that the KMT supports their right of self-determination, and their territories therefore cannot be used for your armed forces.[75]

One wonders whether, despite his lack of prospects for aid from any other quarters, Sun was genuinely prepared to follow the Comintern line, given the limited extent of the aid that Moscow was willing or able to give. Moreover, he continued to be vexed by the fact that the Soviet government persisted in dealing with the Peking government. He argued against it with Lenin and Joffe at the end of 1922, and did so again with Karakhan in 1923.[76]

The arrival of Borodin in Canton in the autumn of 1923 began a four-year relationship between the KMT and the Soviets that proved to be so full of unforeseen opportunities as well as problems, so disastrous to the CCP, and so fateful for China as a whole. The story does not fall within our compass, but the interaction between diplomacy and revolution in the initial phase already foreshadowed the tragedy ahead. Comparing the two areas of Soviet activity, it can be seen that, late in 1923, revolutionary activity was still unfolding rather tentatively, without much hope of immediate results. On the diplomatic front, on the other hand, Soviet strength swelled in the assertion of national interests in Outer Mongolia and north Manchuria. The conclusion of the diplomatic effort was the work of Leo Karakhan, who arrived in Peking to resume where Joffe had left off just as Borodin reached Canton to push forward the revolutionary effort.

12

The Karakhan Mission

Leo Karakhan's mission as Soviet plenipotentiary to China and Japan signalled the culmination of the long, arduous effort of the Soviet government to win formal acceptance by its Far Eastern neighbors. Author of the well-known manifestoes, Karakhan had long been regarded by the Chinese public as the Soviet spokesman of reborn Russia's revolutionary diplomacy of self-denial and sympathy towards China's nationalistic aspirations. During his stay in Peking, he spared no occasion to pander to these sentiments. He delighted his audience by constantly contrasting Soviet generosity with imperialist greed, and exhorted them to tear up the unequal treaties. In his more private talks with Chinese officials, however, he assumed a different role, a tough bargainer rigidly pressing for the reinstatement of Russia's interests, candidly declaring that Russia did not wish to be weaker in China than any other foreign power.

Karakhan's task was one of considerable delicacy: to enhance both Soviet national and revolutionary interests, to restore Russia's traditional position in north Manchuria and Outer Mongolia without undue blemish to the Soviet revolutionary image. In a little over a year, the Narkomindel deputy commissar succeeded in restoring Russia's traditional place in the northeast Asian triangle by a treaty that seemingly reconciled the irreconcilable principles of conventional diplomacy and revolutionary internationalism. Apart from his considerable diplomatic and oratorical skills, he owed his success in Peking to a superior bargaining position, to international developments favoring Russia, and to the Peking government's impotence and unpopularity at home. But the contradictions inherent in Soviet policy manifested themselves in a marked contrast between word and deed, principle and practice. This element of conscious deceit was to be the legacy of the Karakhan mission, leaving a lasting imprint on Sino-Soviet relations.

The period between Joffe's departure from Peking and Karakhan's arrival nine months later was one of anxieties and frustrations for the Peking government. Soviet diplomacy in the Far East, as the Joffe mission had clearly underlined, set a higher priority on negotiations with Japan than with China. Japan's evacuation from the Maritime Province in fall 1922 spurred the Soviet government on to seek normalization with Japan. To this end, Joffe was dispatched to China and, after the failure of the Changchun Conference, he was sent to Japan. Karakhan set out for China only when it was clear that Joffe's mission in Japan had failed.

Since October 1922, following the adoption of Foreign Minister Koo's proposals, Peking's Russian policy was freed once and for all from its earlier constraints of having to follow the lead of the Great Powers. To prove its readiness to negotiate, Peking even dropped its demand for the withdrawal of Soviet troops in Outer Mongolia as the precondition for diplomatic talks. Thenceforth, it made formal recognition of the Soviet regime conditional upon a definitive settlement of the outstanding issues. This was in line with its firm policy of recovering sovereign rights. But, as already noted, Joffe resorted to delaying tactics after some perfunctory talks with the Wai-chiao Pu, confident that time was on his side. Outer Mongolia was already under Soviet political and military control. Although the Chinese Eastern Railway was still in non-Soviet hands, it was not in any danger of being seized by Japan or any other power, thanks to Chinese and American vigilance. From Moscow's point of view, relations with Tokyo were far more important than with Peking. Success in Tokyo would mean not only the restoration of the old equilibrium with Japan but the capitulation of Peking to Soviet terms. When Joffe took leave of the Wai-chiao Pu in January 1923 he vaguely promised to be back in Peking by March to commence negotiations. Taking him at his word, the Peking government moved to set up the necessary machinery. To conduct complex diplomatic negotiations, it had lately developed the practice of instituting a special *ad hoc* organ with a full-time head and a complement of experts drawn from various ministries concerned. Where necessary, representatives of local interests could also be brought in. This practice had proved to be highly effective in the recent negotiations with Japan on the Shantung question and with Britain over the rendition of the Weihaiwei concession. The Sino-Soviet negotiations were expected to cover a wide range of issues which, by their very nature, required careful intra-governmental consultations and delicate liaison with local interests. In March, on the recommendation of Foreign Minister Huang Fu, the cabinet approved the organization of the Directorate of Sino-Soviet Negotiations (Tu-pan Chung-O chiao-she shih-i kung-shu) with C.T. Wang, Huang's friend, who had just completed negotiations on the Shantung question with distinction, as Director. Wang's appointment was formalized by a special presidential decree on March 26, which put him subordinate to the cabinet as a whole rather than to the Wai-chiao Pu.[1]

When informed of Peking's decision, Joffe replied saying he was pleased that the Chinese government—'contrary to its former policy of delaying negotiations'—was at last ready to start them. He said he would hasten to Peking as soon as he was well enough to travel and after he had finished his business in Japan.[2]

While Joffe procrastinated, Wang spent the months of April and May in Manchuria to cultivate Marshal Chang Tso-lin and his leading subordinates and secure their cooperation with the Directorate. There was in fact no disagreement of substance between Peking and Mukden over how the Sino-Soviet issues concerning Manchuria should be settled, but the pride of the Old Marshal, avowedly independent of Peking, was involved. Wang's task was to reassure Mukden that the Directorate was nonpartisan and that it would act in Mukden's interest. Typically, Chang did not commit himself at this early stage. Within his entourage, there were some who were motivated purely by partisan considerations and would have nothing to do with the Chihli-dominated Peking administration, but there were others who were realistic enough to perceive the limitations of the autonomous Manchurian government in the conduct of diplomacy and were prepared to leave the Manchurian issues to Peking to negotiate. Wang was able, meanwhile, to set up a liaison office at Harbin and station a representative at Mukden.

As his second objective Wang sought to acquaint himself with the actual situation of the Chinese Eastern Railway and Amur River navigation. During his visit the Soviet side provoked a crisis over Chinese navigation of the Amur River.

Chinese mercantile shipping in the north Manchurian waterways, as noted earlier, received an important impetus from the collapse of Russian dominance over the Amur River system as a result of the Russian upheaval. On the basis of a local and provisional agreement with the Blagoveshchensk Bolsheviks in May 1918, Chinese vessels gained access to the common section of the Amur for the first time. Until the end of 1922, Chinese steamships based at Harbin were able to navigate and trade between Khabarovsk and Moho and along the Ussuri. This shipping activity still lacked a firm basis. It was yet to be regulated definitively by a formal instrument with Russia; and it was effectively bottled in, since access to the sea via the Lower Amur was denied by Soviet authorities. Moreover, the Chinese Eastern Railway shipping department, active both before and after China's assumption of trusteeship of the railway, enjoyed a favorable position, being able to outdo the Chinese by its superior organization, larger fleet, and technical skill.[3]

When the sailing season opened in spring 1923 Sino-Soviet controversy arose over mutual exclusion of the one's vessels from the other's national waterways. Since 1920, reacting against Russia's exclusion of Chinese navigation of the Lower Amur, a right the Chinese still claimed on the basis of the 1858 Treaty of Aigun, an effort was begun by the Chinese to assert progressively the exclusive use of their internal Manchurian waterways. By early 1923, the situation had evolved to a point where non-Chinese vessels were restricted to the section from the Sungari-Amur junction to Harbin. The Chinese allowed into their national waters only those vessels displaying the old Russian tricolor flag. Even so, as the Chinese suspected, vessels originating from Soviet territory simply hoisted the old flag at the Amur-Sungari junction before entering the Sungari, thus navigating in Chinese waters despite the absence of official relations.

As part of a broad campaign waged by the Soviet government to demoralize the Chinese in the future negotiations, Soviet authorities banned Chinese vessels from the Amur River altogether in May 1923 by instituting a blockade at the Sungari-Amur junction.[4] The Chinese found themselves back where they had been before 1917.

The incident brought the Manchurian officialdom and the Chinese shipping community together to draft a provisional agreement for discussion with Soviet officials. The sailing season was short and the Chinese were anxious to prevent undue losses. The draft differed little in substance from previous ones; it envisaged two alternatives, either free navigation of each other's national waterways or mutual exclusion. The Chinese naturally favored the principle of reciprocity and were prepared to admit Soviet vessels displaying the Soviet flag into the Sungari prior to the resumption of normal relations. They decided to regard vessels flying the tricolor flag as those of a third nation and to ban them from the Amur and the Sungari. As the Chinese saw it, the draft agreement had the virtue of being in accord with the Aigun Treaty, conciliatory to the Soviets, and guaranteeing Chinese shipping access to the sea. Alternatively, if the Soviet authorities should prove intransigent, they saw no alternative but to ban all Russian ships, communist or noncommunist, from the Sungari.[5] The negotiating position of the Chinese on the navigation question had clearly weakened: for access to the common section of the Amur as well as the Lower Amur, the Chinese relied solely on the Sungari as their bargaining point.

When C.T. Wang placed the draft before Davtian in Peking in June, the acting head of the Soviet mission was distinctly uncooperative. It was not possible, he said, to admit

Chinese vessels freely into the Amur, much less the Lower Amur, 'since the Japanese may falsely fly the Chinese flag and gain free navigation'. His government's policy was mutual exclusion from each other's national waters. Before the Sino-Soviet conference, he was unwilling even to consider a provisional agreement on navigation, saying it should be discussed between the local authorities concerned. Asked if China was free to detain vessels which changed from the Soviet to the old Russian tricolor flag at the Amur–Sungari junction, Davtian ingeniously replied that although the shipping company involved was a Soviet one, its administration had not yet submitted to Soviet authority.[6]

After protracted prevarication, the Chinese finally regained access to the common section of the Amur late in the sailing season. Retaliating against the continuing ban by Russia of Chinese navigation of the Lower Amur, the Manchurian authorities instituted a ban from the Sungari against all vessels flying the tricolor flag as well as those operated by the Chinese Eastern Railway shipping department.[7]

The Chinese Eastern Railway was an issue of far greater consequence than navigation. The Chinese effort to decolonize the railway zone had met with considerable success and was gathering further momentum. By 1923 Chinese sovereign rights pertaining to municipal administration, guarding of the railway, police, and justice had been recovered. However, the extent of the control of the railway itself gained by the Chinese left a great deal to be desired. As C.T. Wang discovered to his acute dismay, Chinese trusteeship and control was quite nominal. In 1920 the Peking government had encouraged General Pao Kuei-ch'ing to execute a thorough-going take-over of the enterprise. Peking's assurances of moral and material support notwithstanding, Pao had adopted a cautious course of action, no doubt at Chang Tso-lin's behest, in order not to antagonize the Japanese. In essence, changes to the railway were effected, as far as possible, within the legal framework of the original railway concession, and they were formalized by an agreement supplementary to the 1896 Contract, with the original signatory, the Russo-Asiatic Bank, which was now under French protection. By 1923 the Chinese had reasons to regret the supplementary agreement for the bank had never been anything more than a dummy used by the Tsarist government to camouflage a state enterprise. Moreover, the agreement was now providing France with the pretext to claim an interest in the railway even though her creditor's right was one step removed.

A more serious shortcoming of the agreement was the manner in which the power of management was distributed between the bank and the Chinese. Each side had five members on the board of directors. In case of even ballot, the Chinese tupan had the casting vote, in addition to his consulting vote, but no decision was binding unless approved by at least seven. The two groups on the board naturally formed two opposing blocs and the resulting paralysis of the board caused power to devolve entirely on the Russian chief executive, General Manager Ostroumov. A man of strong will, Ostroumov was a Russian patriot to boot. He ran the enterprise in the clear conviction that it was Russian-owned and therefore should be entirely Russian-controlled. He resisted the Chinese as strenuously as he did the French. Hence, once assured that the railway was in no danger of being seized by a foreign power, the Soviet government was content, public statements to the contrary, to leave the railway in Ostroumov's hands before an agreement was reached with Peking.

Unlike the case of Amur River navigation, Wang felt that China was still in a position to improve her position on the railway since it was entirely within Chinese territory. Consultations with Peking and Mukden resulted in a plan for the reorganization of the railway administration. Essentially Wang proposed to suspend the board of directors, put a Chinese in Ostroumov's place, and replace the various Russian chiefs of departments with Chinese. Mindful of the Washington resolutions, he based the proposed changes on the argument of giving substance to China's trusteeship of the railway. The plan received the Chang Shao-tseng Cabinet's approval in May.

Before acting on it, however, Wang apparently hoped to minimize complications by seeking some prior understanding from the Soviet side, especially since rumors of an intended seizure of the railway by Soviet troops were still rampant. Dressing up the proposal as attractively as possible, he asked Davtian for a list of names of people whom the Chinese tupan might co-opt to the management or employ as his personal advisers. He explained that the change was purely temporary but it meant that China was prepared to admit a degree of Soviet influence on the railway even before the establishment of formal relations. Davtian was only too quick to see Wang's ulterior motives and replied in an equally calculated vein. Since the railway was Soviet property and the Soviet government wanted control of it, any change short of giving Moscow the right to appoint its nationals directly to the railway administration was unacceptable. Unless Wang could agree to this counterproposal, Davtian said, it would be better to postpone the railway question to the Sino-Soviet conference.[8]

Before Wang could decide whether to go ahead with the plan regardless of the Soviet attitude, Peking was plunged into new political turmoil. In June the Paoting and Tientsin factions of the Chihli clique ousted Li Yüan-hung (whom the Loyang faction of Wu P'ei-fu had made president only twelve months before) in preparation for the elevation of Ts'ao K'un to the presidency. The Chang Shao-tseng Cabinet, which had approved Wang's plan only weeks before, dissolved and intense in-fighting ensued among Chihli politicians for cabinet posts. The political instability in the capital forced Wang to shelve the plan entirely. This was to be the last opportunity for Peking to gain control of the railway and strengthen its bargaining position *vis-à-vis* the Soviet government.[9]

Marshal Chang Tso-lin, for reasons of his own, had apparently declined to assume final responsibility for Wang's project, but he was not averse to taking drastic actions of another kind. So far the recovery of each sovereign right from Russia had entailed financial liability to the Manchurian treasury. In summer 1923 Mukden decided to launch an assault on the enormous land-holdings of the railway. Of some 1300 km² of land owned by the railway, partly received free of charge from the Ch'ing government and partly purchased from private Chinese owners, less than half was actually used in connection with the railway operations. The railway leased out its surplus land to others at considerable profit. Mukden demanded that the surplus land be handed over, threatening violence. The attack on the railway's assets brought into question the Washington resolutions which accorded China the position of a trustee of the railway. General Manager Ostroumov had little difficulty in mobilizing the consuls of the four powers which had passed the resolutions to block Mukden's move. The consuls sealed off the land office where files of the land leases were kept.[10] The attitude of the consuls underlined to the Chinese once again the international complexities that surrounded the railway question and their very limited freedom of action in this regard.

Faced with the large number of issues awaiting negotiation and with its inability to improve its bargaining position by further unilateral action, the Peking government became increasingly apprehensive about the outcome of future negotiations. Its quiet despair was greatly compounded by the spectre of a Soviet-Japanese rapprochement as Joffe continued to delay his return to Peking. For six anxious months, Chinese officials watched intently his activities in Japan.

It is instructive to follow Joffe's fortunes in Japan because during the next phase of Sino-Soviet diplomacy, Soviet tactics in Peking bore a striking resemblance to Tokyo's tactics towards Joffe. This affinity derived simply from the fact that the Soviet position was weak in Tokyo but strong in Peking. In each case the strong occupied some territory of the weak, insisted on the continuing validity of the old treaties, freely decided to keep the talks at an informal, exploratory level or upgrade them to an official level.

Joffe's visit to Japan was arranged by Lord Mayor of Tokyo Viscount Gotō Shimpei, an ardent advocate of Russo-Japanese cooperation, after being cleared with Premier Katō Tomosaburō.[11] Initially, the talks were confined to a private exchange of views between Joffe and Gotō. Joffe renewed the demand for Japanese troops to withdraw from North Sakhalin and sought a full resumption of normal diplomatic relations. Gotō, reflecting Tokyo's official position, made evacuation conditional on the settlement of the Nikolaevsk incident, and official recognition conditional on the same plus the honoring of Tsarist debts to Japan. While rigid on the debt question,

Joffe offered economic concessions in North Sakhalin as compensation for the Nikolaevsk massacre. To conciliate Japan further, Soviet officials in Vladivostok signed an agreement with Japanese fishing interests.

By early May, everything that could be accomplished by informal preliminary talks had been accomplished and the stage was set for the negotiations on an official level. The premier was agreeable but his cabinet was divided. Most notably, one reason for hesitation derived from Japan's Great Power status: to set the precedent of recognizing Soviet Russia without a settlement of the debt question would have offended the other Great Powers whom Japan was anxious to conciliate. The Japanese foreign ministry then empowered a representative to hold informal discussions with Joffe so as to explore the prior conditions for a third Soviet-Japanese conference. At twelve sessions, Joffe went over the same ground with Kawakami Toshitsune and reached much the same position as with Gotō before. It was clear to Joffe that the Japanese government would not risk entering into official talks at this time. On July 19, the Narkomindel decided to force the issue. Joffe was instructed to propose the commencement of formal negotiations. On July 26 Joffe did so but Tokyo refused to be rushed and the talks were broken off. Joffe's departure coincided with Karakhan's arrival in China.

The announcement of the Karakhan Mission to the Far East was timed closely to the Narkomindel instructions to Joffe to prod the Japanese into official negotiations. When the Wai-chiao Pu was notified on July 21 of Karakhan's appointment it was still possible that he might delay talks with Peking and negotiate with Tokyo instead. But that probability ceased to exist when on August 2 he actually started the journey from Moscow. After his arrival in China, he called on the Japanese minister and wrote to Viscount Gotō in order to get negotiations started; but the Japanese continued to dally. In sharp contrast, Karakhan's attitude towards Sino-Soviet talks was as frigid as Tokyo's towards Soviet-Japanese talks. Had Tokyo been more forthcoming he would have killed two birds with one stone, and the Chinese would have been thoroughly demoralized. Instead, he had to deal with the Peking government without that crucial assistance, muster whatever personal resources he could to harass the Chinese, bludgeon them into a less demanding attitude, and hope that his success in Peking would have the desirable impact on Tokyo.[12]

For some weeks, both Chinese officialdom and public awaited Karakhan's arrival with great expectation, the one under the misapprehension (which was quickly dispelled) that Karakhan, the man who made those generous offers, would be easier to deal with than had been the case with Joffe, and the other reliving the euphoria of spring 1920 when the Karakhan Manifesto was publicized. Karakhan arrived in Harbin on August 13 to a rousing welcome from the Manchurian officialdom and popular organizations. It was a homecoming in one sense. As a young Menshevik wanted by the Tsarist police for his involvement in the 1905 Revolution he had once found refuge in Harbin. There he continued his education and engaged in radical journalism until 1911 when he enrolled in a school at Vladivostok and subsequently entered the University of St Petersburg to study law. At thirty-seven, he had risen to be a Narkomindel deputy commissar, billed as an expert in Far Eastern affairs.[13] After a few days in Harbin, on August 18 he moved on to his second stop—Mukden, headquarters of Chang Tso-lin.

He remained in Mukden for two weeks, an extraordinarily tense period for C.T. Wang and the Peking government. As his chief object was the Chinese Eastern Railway he naturally sought an agreement with Chang Tso-lin, the de facto authority in Manchuria. The crucial moment had arrived —would Chang act strictly in partisan terms and thus undermine Peking's prestige or unite behind C.T. Wang's Directorate. At first, despite Wang's appeals for unity, Mukden entered into preliminary talks with the Soviet envoy. But the difficulties encountered during the exploratory talks combined with Wang's tact produced a change of attitude in Mukden. On September 1, a disappointed Karakhan set out for Peking.[14]

Following Mukden's change of heart, Wang cabled Chang his appreciation and asked that a team of Manchurian representatives be attached to his Directorate to assist in the negotiations in the capital. Chang promptly obliged by sending a four-man delegation and told Wang to use his own discretion about formal recognition of the Soviet government.[15] Surpassing Wang's initial expectations, Mukden cooperated fully with the Directorate.

Mukden cooperated partly because of Wang's firm assurance that Manchurian interests would be safeguarded but mainly because of the difficulties inherent in separate negotiations with Karakhan. What those obstacles were are easily guessed. Separate negotiations as such imposed severe limitations on both sides. Mukden attached great importance to three issues in particular. First was the railway question, concerning which Mukden had three options: to insist on unconditional transfer as previously promised by Karakhan, immediate redemption, or equal ownership and control. While no longer hopeful that Karakhan would honor the pledge, Mukden was determined to secure an agreement for the immediate redemption of the railway by China. Only as the last resort would it be satisfied with equal partnership and control. In addition, it wanted the eighty-year stipulation for free transfer in the original 1896 Contract to be reduced by half. Mukden's second concern was to obtain indemnity of official and private losses incurred during the Russian Revolution and civil war, including those due to an enormous quantity of inconvertible Romanov paper roubles in Chinese hands. There was, finally, the question of Amur River navigation: Mukden offered Soviet navigation of the Sungari as a *quid pro quo* for Chinese access to the Lower Amur. Mukden's difficulty was that it had nothing to give in exchange since diplomatic recognition, the only bargaining point held by the Chinese side, was the sole prerogative of the Peking government.

From Karakhan's point of view, a favorable outcome of the separate negotiations depended heavily on the right circumstances. In autumn 1923 Mukden did not feel strongly enough to act in a fit of pique against Peking. Nor were war clouds gathering south of the Great Wall threatening Chang Tso-lin's political fortunes to oblige him to secure his rear by concessions to Moscow. Furthermore, given Moscow's firm policy of restoring Russian power in northeast Asia, Karakhan could not accommodate Mukden's demands in any way. He was prepared at most to grant the Chinese a degree of nominal partnership in the Chinese Eastern Railway. He could not agree to compensation for Chinese losses during the Russian upheaval as a matter of principle as this could give rise to incalculable claims from other quarters. Nor could he allow the Chinese on the Lower Amur lest the precedent be seized upon by the Japanese. Hence, during the preliminary talks, he adamantly refused to discuss any question except the Chinese Eastern Railway. The exploratory talks ended with both sides wide apart.[16]

Wang-Karakhan Talks: Phase One

Without the leverage of a Soviet-Japanese rapprochement or positive results from the negotiations at Mukden, Karakhan's prospects in Peking were not as promising as he had wished. But the handicap was short-term in that time was on his side. Initially, he concentrated on the propaganda front. The choice was a wise one in view of the difficulties inherent in his mission. He was faced with the dilemma of having to press uncompromisingly for the restoration of Russian interests without at the same time endangering the alliance with Chinese nationalism that Soviet revolutionary policy sought to foster. More immediately he confronted a government in Peking with a determination to champion China's sovereign rights and keep Soviet influence out. To overcome these problems he endlessly projected an image of Soviet Russia as the champion of China's national aspirations. A recurrent theme in his public utterances was that the Peking government, oblivious to China's national interests, was deliberately delaying negotiations in deference to foreign pressures.

On the more obscure diplomatic front the old tactics of procrastination and harassment continued. Relations between Karakhan and the Wai-chiao Pu opened on a discordant note. For a start, he feigned grievance over the fact that back in April Foreign Minister Koo, upon resuming his portfolio, had made courtesy calls on all foreign legations except the Soviet mission—a fact easily explained by the mission's unofficial status. Although Koo's personal secretary was among those welcoming him at his arrival, Karakhan nevertheless insisted that it was Koo who should call on him first. The first few days were taken up by altercations over this question. When

Karakhan finally called at the Wai-chiao Pu on September 6, his first demand was a formal presentation of credentials to the Chinese president. This was another cause for prolonged argumentations.[17]

It was two weeks before C.T. Wang was able to persuade Karakhan to get down to business. The first meeting on September 14 immediately ended in a deadlock. Wang proposed negotiations of all outstanding issues as a condition for official recognition whereas Karakhan demanded just the reverse. Told that he was putting the cart before the horse, Karakhan declared he had no other instructions, and warned that he might be directed to Tokyo unless his demand was met.[18]

At subsequent sessions, this impasse remained. Karakhan was determined that if any side should give way it would be Wang. Between the two positions lay a compromise: to agree on the general principles for settling the outstanding issues, restore formal relations, and negotiate definitive agreements later. This had been the formula proposed by Joffe and rejected by Foreign Minister Koo the year before, but Wang was anxious to break the deadlock. Writing to Koo on September 20, Wang argued it was necessary to convince Karakhan of Peking's independence of the foreign powers; he had full confidence in the Soviet envoy and averred that unless the negotiations were pushed forward Karakhan's successor might prove even less conciliatory.[19]

The personal relationship between Wang and Koo was to figure as a factor of some importance in complicating the negotiations, although never to the extent claimed by Soviet and other historians. This was nevertheless unfortunate for the Peking government, especially since those circumstances which had previously bedeviled the prospects of negotiations with Soviet Russia were now conspicuously absent. Mukden was prepared to join Peking in a united front; the political turmoil of the summer in the capital was subsiding as the Paoting and Tientsin factions of the Chihli clique succeeded in installing Ts'ao K'un in the presidency backed by a parliament under their control. A comparatively strong cabinet, headed by the respected veteran statesman Sun Pao-ch'i, was in office, and over the months of the negotiations the political situation was singularly quiet. Furthermore, foreign opposition to Peking's independent recognition of the Soviet regime, whatever Karakhan might say, had long since ceased; some opposition was expected especially from the French to be sure but it concerned only the matter of the railway, and the Peking government was in any case braced for it.

As two prominent statesmen of wide public acclaim, a degree of rivalry between Koo and Wang seemed inevitable. This was compounded by differences of background, possibly political affiliations, and perhaps even age. C.T. Wang (B.A., Yale; hon. LL.D., St John's), aged forty-two, son of a Methodist pastor, was primarily a politician. Like Koo he had been catapulted to fame by Versailles. He also had the distinction of having led the negotiations with Japan which resulted in the return of the Kiaochow leased territory and the Tsingtao-Tsinan Railway. Wang's method was the conventional one of give-and-take based on the equally conventional assumption that formal promises were made to be honored. As a man of few reverses he prided himself in the expeditious discharge of any official task. During his negotiations with Karakhan he acted as though his personal prestige depended on a quick and successful outcome. It should, however, be said in his defense that he had little else besides *de jure* recognition to bargain with. He viewed the approaching negotiations with pessimism and diffidence and was easily outclassed by Karakhan in skill and staying power.

Wellington K.V. Koo (Ph.D., international law, Columbia), five years younger than Wang, son of a wealthy tax collector, was a seasoned professional diplomat. He showed increasing misgivings about Wang's suitability for the Sino-Soviet negotiations but it was too late to do anything about it. The relationship between the two men was characterized by a lack of trust, for if Koo suspected Wang of a desire for quick glory Wang probably reciprocated by attributing Koo's attitude to envy at his leading part in negotiating what was generally expected to be an epoch-making treaty.

Before answering Wang's confidential letter, Koo committed the first act of what Wang must have taken as a personal insult. To commence negotiations Wang needed a certificate of full power from the cabinet. Drafted by Koo, the certificate

Wang received empowered him 'to conduct negotiations and reach conclusions'. Only after the results had been ratified by the government would he be issued another certificate empowering him to sign. In short, Wang was issued a certificate of limited power. This caused such a stir in the Directorate of Sino-Soviet Negotiations that even Karakhan, ever ready to foment rivalries between Wang and Koo, was to make disparaging references to it.[20]

It was not until October 8 that Koo expressed an opinion on Wang's proposed solution to the deadlock. He strongly implied that he did not share Wang's faith in the sincerity of Soviet intentions. He told Wang he fully appreciated the urgent need for China to restore official relations with Soviet Russia, but *de jure* recognition was China's only bargaining point. The formula of exchanging diplomatic recognition for an agreement of general principles on the settlement of outstanding issues provided China with no guarantee against Soviet bad faith. Even if not all the issues could be definitively negotiated right away, he pointed out, concrete agreements should at least be secured on the most essential ones such as Outer Mongolia and the Chinese Eastern Railway. To safeguard against false pretenses on Karakhan's part Koo further suggested that Wang should insist on the unconditional transfer of the railway being written into the treaty.[21]

Koo's instinct was as sound as his remarks were prophetic. The history of Sino-Russian relations before and after the October Revolution had been littered with broken promises. An agreement of mere principles put too high a premium on Soviet good faith which Koo felt to be unjustified in view of the Wai-chiao Pu's experience with Karakhans's predecessors. But it remained to be seen how the contest between Peking's determination to roll back Soviet influence beyond its northern frontiers and Moscow's opposite determination would unfold.

Reacting to Koo's comments Wang did not dispute the wisdom in the alternative outlined by Koo. Later he proceeded in the negotiations with Karakhan accordingly. But he felt Koo was being unreasonable about the railway. The railway was Russian state property, he wrote, and nothing had happened to give it the character of spoils of war. Besides, as early as 1921, the then foreign minister, Yen Hui-ch'ing, had already proposed redemption by China as the solution.[22]

Amidst these private consultations with Koo, Wang had meanwhile proposed his solution to the deadlock to Karakhan. The latter reacted as one who had successfully laid a trap and asked that he be furnished with a draft. The compromise formula was just the thing that would enable him to bridge the gap between his diplomatic and propaganda objectives. In return for the desired concessions from China all he had to do was to fill the agreement with high-sounding principles.

On October 13, Wang sent Karakhan a draft prepared at the end of the consultations with Koo and reflecting a modified position. It read as follows:

In accordance to the Soviet declarations of 1919 and 1920, the Government of the Republic of China proposes as the basis for the resumption of formal relations as follows:

1. All treaties, conventions, agreements, protocols concluded between China and the Tsarist regime shall be null and void. The two parties shall conclude new agreements based on the principles of justice and equality.

2. The Soviet government agrees to withdraw all troops at present stationed by it in Outer Mongolia and to complete such withdrawal not later than six months after the signing of this agreement. China shall independently dispatch troops to garrison Outer Mongolia.

3. The Soviet government agrees to consider null and void all its treaties and agreements concluded with Outer Mongolia.

4. Both parties mutually undertake within their own respective territory not to permit the existence and/or actions of any organs or organizations created to plot against their respective governments; not to carry on propaganda inimical to their respective public order or to the system of their respective social organization.

5. Matters concerning the delimitation of frontiers are to be regulated in accordance with the 1919 declaration renouncing the policy of aggrandizement practised by the former Tsarist regime.

6. Vessels of only China and Russia are permitted to navigate the Argun, Amur, Ussuri, and Sungari River and waters of Hanka Lake common to both China and Russia. Chinese vessels shall be free to navigate the lower reaches of the Amur River

between Khabarovsk and Nikolaevsk as well as load and unload merchandize and passenger therein.

7. The Soviet government agrees to restore completely to the Chinese government the Chinese Eastern Railway together with all other properties appurtenant thereto.

8. The Chinese government agrees to conclude a special agreement with the Soviet government for extending to Russia facilities for transportation on the Chinese Eastern Railway.

9. The Soviet government agrees to renounce the concessions, military barracks, and parade grounds, leased as well as established by the former Russian government in China, to relinquish the rights of extraterritoriality, and to forgo the indemnity of the Boxer protocol.

10. The Soviet government agrees to settle equitably the Chinese public and private claims for losses sustained during the revolutionary period in Russia.

11. The two parties agree to regulate matters concerning trade and commerce by an equitable agreement to be speedily concluded between them, and to adjust customs duties on the basis of equality and reciprocity.

12. The Soviet government agrees to reimburse to China all expenses incurred by it in connection with the internment and repatriation as well as furnishing of supplies to Russian refugees.

13. After the signing of the present agreement, both parties shall immediately constitute a Joint Sino-Russian Commission to arrange the details of the preceding articles.[23]

In his reply on October 17 Karakhan resumed a rigid stance, dismissing Wang's draft entirely. He counterproposed that except for an immediate agreement on a *modus operandi* concerning the Chinese Eastern Railway, all other matters be discussed in good time after resumption of diplomatic relations.[24] During the course of the next two weeks, Wang sat out one session after another, putting up with Karakhan's demands, insults, and rigidities. At the end of the eighth he found it necessary to take a break. The state of negotiations as they stood then may be gauged from a resumé that Wang prepared on November 8.[25]

Concerning procedure, it was agreed to sign in the first place an agreement on general principles making resumption of official relations automatic. Negotiation on details was to begin immediately thereafter and be completed within six months.

As to matters of substance, Karakhan was reported as having consented without much discussion to Articles 4, 5, 6, 9, and 11 of Wang's draft. There followed several points listed as requiring further consideration. First, concerning the abolition of the old treaties (Art. 1), Karakhan made exception of those governing the Sino-Russian frontiers. Secondly, as to the indemnity of losses (Art. 10), he would consider only losses incurred by private Chinese citizens during the period of severance of relations (i.e. since September 1920) and caused by Russian officials and people in violation of Soviet laws and decrees. Thirdly, in regard to Outer Mongolia (Art. 2 and 3), he agreed to recognize Chinese territorial sovereignty and withdraw Soviet troops, but declined to specify the date and procedure of evacuation in the agreement on general principles.

On the Chinese Eastern Railway disagreement was total. Karakhan agreed for the present only to give China the title over the railway. For this title China was to pay a redemption price entirely out of Chinese capital. The conditions of such reimbursement, including the date and mode of transfer, were to be negotiated at a future conference. During the interim the Soviet government was to retain for itself all the rights on the railway, with the original contract and statutes of 1896 intact. This provisional arrangement provided for due observance of Chinese political sovereignty in the railway zone and a degree of Chinese participation in the railway administration.

For his part, Wang counterproposed that all the rights, title, and privileges concerning the railway be vested in China at once, in name and in fact. China, in return, would reimburse the Soviet government the actual value of the railway property. As an additional concession, the reimbursement would take the form of Chinese treasury notes, secured on the railway property, so that pending the redemption of these notes by China, the Soviet government could retain for itself the rights of a creditor.

The positions formulated by Karakhan and Wang on this question corresponded in fact to the respective positions of 1921, but the possibility that had existed then for the Soviet side to entertain the proposal from China no longer existed in 1923.

In early November the talks came to a standstill. This was

followed by a test of nerves and a sporadic war of words over the next three months. Karakhan let it be known that he was getting ready to depart, perhaps for Canton and then Tokyo. Wang had the more reason to go on leave, since he had to avoid being shown to be weak. A visit to Tokyo was arranged so that he could convey Peking's formal condolences for the earthquake disaster of September and make quiet inquiries on how close Tokyo was to formal recognition of Moscow.[26]

Accordingly, on November 21, Wang notified Karakhan by letter of his temporary absence on official business in Japan, making it appear that the resumption of talks would depend on Karakhan's attitude towards formal negotiations.[27] In his reply two days later Karakhan slipped back to his original demand for *de jure* recognition to precede formal negotiations, as though the previous sessions had never taken place.[28] When Wang pointed out on November 28 that this was contrary to the understanding reached,[29] Karakhan rejoined on November 30, the day of Wang's departure, with a public letter which was a masterpiece of propaganda. Since its inception, wrote Karakhan, the Soviet government had sought to restore relations with the Chinese government. However, the Peking administration had ignored the new principles enunciated in his 1919 and 1920 declarations. Although these principles were without precedent in China's foreign relations, the Peking government had nevertheless acted contrary to the wishes of every honest Chinese loving his motherland. It had been prevented from acting in China's national interest because its policy had been coordinated with the policy of the imperialistic Great Powers. It had manifested its subservience to foreign interests by joining in the Allied Intervention against the Russian Revolution, supported the White Guards with Russia's share of the Boxer Indemnity, and sheltered and patronized these White Guards in Mongolia and Manchuria against the Soviet Republic. Despite all this, Karakhan continued, the Soviet government had remained true to the new principles and would not settle a single question 'without full regard for the legal interests and rights of the Chinese people'. However, the Peking government must show proof of its independence of the imperialist powers by immediate restoration of normal relations.[30]

On January 9, 1924, Wang retaliated with a public reply of his own from Shanghai, whither he had retired after his visit to Japan. The main line of his attack was on Soviet good faith, as evidenced in the Soviet disavowal of the Karakhan Manifesto received by Peking, and continuing occupation of Outer Mongolia by Soviet troops.[31] In his retort of January 17, by a show of righteous anger, Karakhan questioned the Peking government's right to the promises made by the Soviet government in view of its hostile acts against Soviet Russia. He was careful to separate Chinese official guilt and Chinese popular innocence, and challenged Peking once more to act in China's national interest instead of bowing to foreign pressure.[32]

Chinese public opinion had at no time been hostile to formal recognition of the Soviet government. The most vocal segments, such as academic, student, and certain parliamentary circles, had in fact been in favor of immediate and unconditional recognition. Karakhan's charges, manifestly a mixture of half-truths asserted for a polemic purpose, could not fail to have a ring of authenticity in the ears of these Chinese. To them, the central government was an object of opprobrium, given to incompetence, venality, and perpetual infighting, and dominated by self-serving militarists impervious to the nation's true interests. Owing to this profound alienation, the complex premises and constraints under which the Peking government operated met with as little comprehension as its efforts at recovering sovereign rights met with incredulity.

But the worst blow to Peking's Soviet policy was still to come. On February 2, the new British Labour government of Ramsay Macdonald extended full diplomatic recognition to Moscow. This precedent, set by the greatest of world powers, and followed immediately by Italy and others, decisively eroded the last modicum of Peking's bargaining strength. Public clamor for immediate recognition, dignified by a petition of forty-seven eminent Peking University professors to the cabinet, reached a new pitch.[33] Pressure of a potentially more serious kind also came from Wu P'ei-fu from Loyang. Alarmed by the recrudescence of reports that Karakhan was preparing to leave for Canton, Wu urged a speedy conclusion of the negotiations.[34]

Wang-Karakhan Talks: Phase Two.

On February 2, the very day of Britain's recognition of Soviet Russia, Karakhan began prodding the Wai-chiao Pu into resuming talks. He intimated that he was still prepared to proceed in accordance with Wang's formula, but made it clear that his position on the Chinese Eastern Railway and Outer Mongolian questions remained unchanged.[35]

In mid-February, the Peking government recalled C.T. Wang to the capital. Crestfallen, Wang entered into a series of sessions with Karakhan. On February 22, he put forward a draft agreement on the provisional management of the Chinese Eastern Railway, and on February 25, a draft agreement on general principles. From Karakhan's comments on them, which were often long and abusive, he drew up parallel drafts which reflected Karakhan's precise position. On March 1, these drafts were finalized with Karakhan, and it was agreed that in a week's time, after Wang had had consultations with the government, there would be another meeting.[36]

A comparison between the two sets of drafts shows that Wang and Karakhan agreed on certain issues, and were far apart on others. To begin first with the areas of agreement, the two governments were to resume normal relations by concluding an agreement of general principles for the settlement of outstanding questions, to hold a conference within one month after the signing of the agreement and to complete the detailed arrangements not later than six months after the opening of the conference. Among the principles agreed upon was that, at the conference, the two parties were to annul the old treaties and replace them with new ones 'on the basis of equality, reciprocity, and justice, as well as the spirit of the 1919 and 1920 declarations'. Again, 'on the principles of equality and reciprocity', they were to redemarcate their national boundaries, but pending such redemarcation, to maintain the existing ones; to discuss the navigation of rivers; to conclude a commercial treaty together with a customs tariff; and to discuss Chinese claims for the compensation of losses. The Soviet government was to renounce concession territories, indemnities, and extraterritoriality. And there was the usual security clause against propaganda and subversion.

As to be expected, the unagreed issues concerned Outer Mongolia and the Chinese Eastern Railway. Wang's draft wanted the Soviet government to recognize Outer Mongolia as an integral part of the Chinese republic, immediately to withdraw all troops, and to declare null and void all treaties concluded with Outer Mongolia. Karakhan's draft, on the other hand, reads: 'The Soviet government recognizes Outer Mongolia as an integral part of the Chinese Republic, and declares that as soon as the conditions—namely, as to the time limit of the withdrawal and guarantee of suppression of the White Guards—are agreed upon at the Conference, it will effect the complete withdrawal of all the Soviet troops from Outer Mongolia'. It was silent on Soviet-Mongol treaties.

On the Chinese Eastern Railway question, there was agreement that the railway was a purely commercial enterprise, Chinese authorities were to administer those rights which properly belonged to the Chinese national and local governments, such as justice, civil administration, military administration, police, and municipal government. It was agreed that China should be allowed to redeem the railway, and that a special agreement was to be concluded at the conference, concerning the amount of compensation, the procedure of payment, and the transfer of the property. Pending the final settlement of the question, an arrangement for the provisional management of the railway was to be drawn up.

Significantly, disagreements developed mainly over how the provisional management should be organized. Since 'provisional' really meant 'indefinite' in Karakhan's terms, each side wanted control of the management. With the supplementary agreement of October 2, 1920, as the basis, it was agreed that each side should appoint five directors to form a board of ten, seven should constitute a quorum, and six votes should be required for any decision to be valid. Since the supplementary agreement had not worked because of bloc voting, Wang wanted both the president and vice-president of the board to be appointed by the Chinese government. But Karakhan insisted that these two posts be elected by the board and the election subject to both governments' approval. The equal balance of strength in the board could, and in fact did, lead to paralysis, so that the power of management could easily devolve into the hands of the chief executive, i.e. the general manager. The contest between the two governments for control of the railway, therefore, centered around this post. Wang's draft wanted the management to consist of the Russian manager plus an assistant Chinese manager, both to be appointed by the Chinese government, and under the direction of the president and the vice-president. Karakhan's draft, on the other hand, provided for one Russian manager, another Russian assistant manager, and one Chinese assistant manager; all three officers were to be appointed by the board, with the appointments subject to the approval of their respective governments; and they were to function under the direction of the board as a whole.

The above drafts and counterdrafts make clear that the Chinese Eastern Railway and Outer Mongolia constituted the two primary points of disagreement. But, unlike in the autumn of 1923, Wang felt unequal to the bitter tug of wills. Britain's recognition of the Soviet government, fear of being overtaken by a Soviet-Japanese rapprochement, public pressure, and Karakhan's threat to depart for Canton combined to rob him of any will to resist further.

After long and strenuous debates, he finally gave in on the railway question. At the first session on February 19, he had retreated from his original position that China redeem the railway immediately to a demand for equal partnership and management. That, too, had not been acceptable to Karakhan. Karakhan's counterdraft made the Soviet position loud and clear: until China was able, or allowed to, redeem the railway, it was to be Soviet-owned and controlled, with a nominal degree of Chinese participation in its management. Dropping all pretenses, Karakhan had declared at one point: 'We do not wish to be weaker than other powers in China, and we intend that our *political* influence on the railway should be preserved'. In the face of Karakhan's rigid attitude Wang felt that he had no alternative but to recommend to the Peking government and the Mukden authorities that Karakhan's demands be accepted *in toto*. In submitting the two sets of drafts to the president, the cabinet, and the Manchurian leadership on March 1, he reminded them of the loss of an opportunity in the previous summer to assert a more substantial degree of trusteeship over the railway. The only hope now, he said, lay in the future conference where the date and conditions of Chinese redemption would be determined. With that hope, both Peking and Mukden also acquiesced to the inevitable.[37]

The only area where Wang had some will left to debate was Outer Mongolia. He proposed to obtain from Karakhan an agreement that Soviet troops be withdrawn over four stages, and the Soviet-Mongol Agreement of 1921 be nullified.[38]

On March 6 the cabinet met to hear an extended report from C.T. Wang and to go over the drafts. It was decided in the end that the matter was too important so that copies should be distributed to each ministry for detailed consideration and amendments. The volume of annotations that were submitted over the next few days suggest that the mood of the cabinet was despondent rather than jubilant. At the March 6 meeting, on the suggestion of Foreign Minister Koo, it was decided to add a new clause to the agreement on general principles. With the semi-public Russo-Japanese conventions of 1906-16 in view, it required the Soviet government to declare null and void all agreements concluded in Tsarist times with any third party affecting China's sovereign rights and interests; and the two parties were to pledge not to conclude in future any treaty prejudicial to the sovereign rights and interests of either party.

Beyond this, two main objections regarding the drafts were voiced. The first concerned the fact that much of the agreement was in the nature of pledges, yet to be negotiated at a future conference. Foreign Minister Koo was skeptical as before about Soviet good faith. He was joined by the minister for agriculture and commerce, Yen Hui-ch'ing, whose experience in dealing with Yurin and Paikes had similarly failed to inspire any confidence in Soviet words. Although a six-month time limit was stipulated for the completion of detailed negotiations, there was nothing to prevent the Soviet side from stalling. As the key to the whole problem, it was suggested that Wang should insist that the abolition of the old treaties should take immediate effect rather than wait until the conference. On this point the cabinet was unanimous.

The other major criticism concerned the provisions on Outer Mongolia. The cabinet was unanimous in the demand that the Soviet-Mongol Agreement be annulled; concerning evacuation about half of the cabinet members still felt strongly that a date should be fixed.[39]

On March 8 Wang met Karakhan again. He had no trouble getting the latter's consent for the new clause to be included. The condition on the abrogation of extraterritoriality was modified so that it was understood that Russian nationals would henceforth be entirely amenable to Chinese jurisdiction, even though 'equitable provisions' would be made at the conference. In regard to the Boxer Indemnity, it was agreed that, following the American formula, a commission of two Chinese and one Russian should administer the funds for the promotion of education.

The two principal questions raised by the cabinet, however, ran into serious difficulties. Karakhan felt that in the case of the old treaties it was not possible to invalidate agreements signed over several hundred years in one stroke. Under Wang's further pressure he agreed to supplement the clause with a protocol to the effect that 'prior to the conclusion of new treaties, etc., all existing treaties, etc., concluded between the Chinese and Tsarist governments, that contradict the spirit of the 1919 and 1920 Declarations or affect China's sovereign rights and interests, shall cease to be operative upon the signing of the present Agreement'. The concession was minimal as the old treaties were not specified; in any case they were to be made inoperative, not invalid.

On the Mongolian question Karakhan yielded no ground whatsoever. The Soviet-Mongol Agreement, he said, would remain in effect until the conclusion of an agreement at the conference to follow between China and Soviet Russia, as well as the adjustment of the relationship between China and Outer Mongolia in the future. The Soviet government did not expect China to recognize the agreement, he said. The meeting ended without the question of evacuation being even raised.[40]

At the next cabinet meeting on March 11 the various ministers brought forth detailed amendments to the drafts which they had had time to digest. Wang was again present to report the results of his latest talk with Karakhan. It became clear that the two main objections raised by the cabinet on March 8 remained the stumbling block. The cabinet persisted in the demand that the old treaties be definitely invalidated in the agreement on general principles and the Soviet-Mongol Agreement be annulled. While the majority was disposed to accept Soviet military withdrawal at some future date the terminology of the clause was found offensive because evacuation was conditional upon China's 'guarantee of suppressing White Guard activity in Outer Mongolia'.[41]

After the cabinet meeting Wang immediately called on Karakhan again. The encounter appears to have been curt and brief, which probably explains why no transcript exists. Wang was forced to come away empty-handed.[42]

The cabinet met again on March 12 and again on the 13th. It is not clear what transpired at these meetings. According to Wang's account, the cabinet still felt strongly that he should persist in obtaining the immediate invalidation of the old treaties. In addition, it wanted the clause on evacuation rephrased by substituting 'measures to be adopted in the interests of the safety of the frontiers' for 'guarantee of suppressing White Guard activity in Outer Mongolia'. The demand for the cancellation of the Soviet-Mongol Treaty was apparently not raised, and Wang himself never took the matter up again with Karakhan. Wang was of the opinion that it was unnecessary to raise the question further, given Soviet recognition of China's territorial sovereignty and Karakhan's statement that China's recognition of the agreement was not expected by Moscow. Most of the cabinet members appear to have been satisfied by this line of argument. But, as Wang himself indicates, these views were only those of the majority. That Foreign Minister Koo was not included in it was to be the source of difficulties.[43]

On the two points raised by the cabinet Wang entered a marathon session with Karakhan, lasting from 8 p.m. on March 13 to 4 a.m. on March 14. Unfortunately no transcript can be found but the outcome was that Karakhan agreed to amend the condition regarding evacuation. However, he still would not consent to the immediate invalidation of the old treaties; he was prepared only to amend the protocol so that all the old treaties, without exception, were to become inoperative. For reasons not readily apparent, the protocol was made a secret document.

In the small hours of the morning of March 14 the two negotiators initialed the texts agreed upon. Around this act broke a turbulent dispute which rocked Peking during the spring and put the drafts in abeyance. Without the transcript it is difficult to explain the circumstances that led Wang to initial the drafts. According to Karakhan it was his understanding that the negotiations were now concluded and formal signature was to take place later in the day when clean copies were prepared. Wang on his part seems to have felt also that the marathon session was final. He already had had numerous consultations with the cabinet and, given his standing, he had no reason to believe that cabinet approval and the presidential mandate empowering him to sign would not be automatic.

The rupture that followed has always puzzled historians who, in attempting to explain it, have advanced various theories.[44] Most popular among these was the belief that the Peking government disavowed Wang's signature on account of foreign intervention. The notion was first actively fostered by Karakhan and it was entirely in line with his persistent effort of discrediting the intransigence of Peking as a sign of subservience to foreign pressures. French Minister A. de Fleuriau's warning to the Peking government on March 12, so close to the time of the rupture, came as handy proof and the suspicion sown by Karakhan gained no small ground in the Chinese public mind.

The French ministers's protests, it should be noted however, produced no effect on the cabinet. France's main concern was to hold the railway as hostage to salvage some of the Tsarist debts whereas the Chinese were determined that the railway was a question between China and Russia alone. The Chinese had expected the French protest all along (as did Karakhan himself) and were ready for it. In spring 1924 Peking had even less reason to accommodate French wishes; it was incensed, as were other powers, that France should allow a petty squabble over the gold franc question to hold up ratification of the Washington resolutions on extraterritoriality and tariff autonomy. The Wai-chiao Pu's reply on April 7 firmly rejected the French protest.[45] The Chinese were equally firm when subsequently France, Britain, and the U.S., warned that the Washington resolution required China to observe the rights of foreign stockholders and creditors in the disposal of the railway question. They declined such responsibility since these rights had originated from loans by these governments to the Chinese Eastern Railway to make it operational for the Siberian Intervention, during which China occupied a relatively passive position.[46]

Japan, whose attitude on the railway had mattered so much before, now posed no problem whatsoever. In fact, the Army General Staff, which had much say in matters concerning Manchuria, wanted to see the Sino-Soviet negotiations go forward. Under the illusion that Peking would indeed be allowed by Moscow to redeem the railway, it formulated a plan to enable the Chinese to purchase the railway one section at a time with secret Japanese funds. To strengthen its hand, the Army General Staff proposed to the Japanese government that the latter register reservations on certain rights and interests of Japan and her nationals in the railway. Hence, the Japanese note to Peking, seemingly in line with those of other powers, was not delivered until the Sino-Soviet Treaty had been concluded. Japanese army records also show that when Mukden sought to elicit Japanese views on negotiation of the railway question with Moscow it was told to go ahead. Unfortunately for Japan, the Soviet government was thinking along lines diametrically opposed to her own.[47]

Clearly, the Peking administration's disavowal of the initialed drafts could not have been due to foreign pressures as it is often alleged. The available British, American, and Japanese official records in fact uniformly credit the rupture to internal Chinese politics. Indeed, the very foreign officials suspected of exerting pressure on the Peking government were explaining to their principals that the rupture stemmed from 'political and personal rivalries in the Chinese government', or 'jealousy of Dr. Wang prevailing in high official circles', or, most specifically, antagonism between Foreign Minister Koo and C.T. Wang.[48]

Much of the mystery of the episode disappears if the consequence of events is traced in detail. On the morning of March 14 Wang presented Premier Sun Pao-ch'i with the initialed drafts and asked that a special meeting of the cabinet be convened. The cabinet had not been insensitive to the loud public clamor and most of its members were impatient to garner popular support for the administration by concluding the treaty with Soviet Russia. At this point, however, the interplay of personalities between Foreign Minister Koo and C.T. Wang assumed central importance, although other lines of conflict cannot be ruled out. Comparing his own annotations to the initialed drafts, the foreign minister could not have failed to see that his own views had not been taken into sufficient consideration by Wang. On his part, Wang must have reciprocated with the feeling that Koo was being insensitive to the frustrations involved in the negotiations with Karakhan. In any case, having been specially commissioned by the president, Wang evidently felt he was directly responsible to the president and the cabinet as a whole.

But when the initialed drafts were reviewed by the cabinet the foreign minister asserted his position. With his sharp legalistic mind he faulted the drafts on three counts. First, the Soviet refusal to cancel the agreement with Outer Mongolia clearly belied its recognition of Chinese territorial sovereignty. Second, the revised wording concerning Soviet military withdrawal still employed the word 'condition' which, in Koo's mind, put the very principle of the inviolability of sovereign territory in jeopardy. Third, as Koo belatedly discovered among the numerous appendices, the transfer of the Russian Orthodox Mission buildings and landed property to the Soviet government, to which Wang had agreed, was a breach of the existing laws and regulations which permitted only *private* foreign property-holding inland. At these objections from the foreign minister, a man respected by his colleagues, the cabinet wavered in indecision.[49]

At this point, desparing a victory so close within grasp, Karakhan tried to stampede the Chinese into signing. He issued a three-day ultimatum on March 16 for the drafts to be ratified. Otherwise, China would be held responsible for all ensuing consequences. Towards the end of the negotiations Karakhan had found himself maneuvered into the reverse position of having to make one concession after another to satisfy the Chinese cabinet. Obviously, he felt he could not afford to remain there for very long. Certainly he could not entertain the demand for the Soviet-Mongol Agreement to be invalidated without dangerous repercussions in Urga as well as publicly admitting that the Soviet government had violated Chinese sovereignty, respect for which he had so noisily professed.

The Chinese cabinet, on the other hand, felt it had had enough of Karakhan's insults. With the ultimatum it moved from indecision to intransigence. Out of self-respect alone it felt the ultimatum had to be rejected, although it did so only after a personal appeal by Premier Sun to Karakhan had failed. On March 19, in a long and denunciatory letter which he made public, Karakhan declared that thenceforth the Chinese government was not to reopen discussions before resumption of diplomatic relations 'unconditionally and without treaties'. Returning to the earlier tactic of discrediting the Peking administration he showed up the latter as incapable of acting in China's national interests. He accused the Chinese government of bad faith in dishonoring the signature of its own negotiator because of its subservience to foreign pressures. As proof, he alluded to the French note of March 12. Using all leverages available, Soviet troops on the Manchurian border carried out various maneuvers and Soviet overtures to Japan were prominently reported in the press.[50]

Faced with an agitated public the Peking government tried to explain its position in a statement which was also meant as a reply to Karakhan's note of March 19. Drafted by Koo, the statement said the Chinese government declined to consider the negotiations concluded and listed three points as being still in dispute. To refute Karakhan's point that the initialing of the drafts made them final, the statement maintained that for Wang's initials to be valid in that sense he would have had to receive another presidential mandate empowering him to sign. The blame for the rupture lay rather with Karakhan who had persistently refused to place the talks on an official footing; had he done otherwise there would have been a mutual exhibition of powers and the misunderstanding would have been avoided. Since the negotiations were unofficial, the statement concluded, the Chinese government felt itself no more bound by the results than Karakhan did.[51]

Back and forth went charges and countercharges but Karakhan was not engaged in an exercise to prove who was right. Rather, it was a contest with the Peking government for the hearts and minds of the Chinese public. The cabinet might have had right on its side but it had been cornered into the position of putting forth arguments that sounded legalistic, abstruse, if not petty. When Karakhan played the trump card by releasing the text of the agreement on general principles on March 21, the cabinet was besieged for days by a storm of wrathful protests in favor of immediate recognition of the Soviet government. To a public oblivious to fine print and uninformed about Soviet diplomatic conduct in Peking in recent years, the document plainly represented the ultimate fulfillment of the first Karakhan Manifesto. The response was sensational.

Popular agitation was only one problem for the cabinet, and ultimately less important compared to what the rupture caused among the super-warlords. The Sino-Soviet question suddenly ceased to be nonpartisan. First to intrude into the dispute was Wu P'ei-fu who had divorced himself from capital politics but remained a powerful force within the Chihli clique. Convinced that Karakhan would soon be Canton-bound, he cabled the cabinet from March 18 almost daily over the next two weeks urging it to sign. He was soon joined by his numerous tuchün allies: Hsiao Yao-nan (Hupeh), Lu Hung-t'ao (Kansu), Tseng Shih-ch'i (Shantung), Chang Fu-lai (Honan), Lin Chen-hua (Shensi), Ch'i Hsieh-yüan (Kiangsu), Sun Ch'uan-fang (Fukien), and Yang Tseng-hsin (Sinkiang).[52] Chang Tso-lin for his part reacted by recalling his representatives at the end of March from Peking, letting it be known that the drafts were unacceptable to the Autonomous Government of Manchuria. He had backed Wang's efforts to the end but he could not adopt an identical stand with Wu P'ei-fu.[53]

The Sun Pao-ch'i Cabinet quivered under the castigations of the Wu P'ei-fu faction, the noisy demonstrations of various public bodies in sympathy with Karakhan, and a revolt within the parliament. Eventually, it rode out the storm. It dissolved the Directorate of Sino-Soviet Negotiations and charged the Wai-chiao Pu to conduct future negotiations. A curtain of silence fell over Karakhan and Foreign Minister Koo for nearly two months. In fact, the test of will had resulted in a complete discontinuation of contacts after April 1.

Then, quite suddenly on May 20, for reasons that will shortly become clear, Karakhan made a tactical retreat. During the next ten days, secret meetings took place twice daily, and the three issues were finally ironed out. The disposal of the Orthodox Mission property was modified in comformity with Chinese laws and regulations. The offensive word 'condition' in the evacuation clause was deleted. Finally, concerning the Soviet-Mongol Agreement, Karakhan consented to add a declaration to the effect that China 'will not and does not recognize as valid any treaty, agreement etc. concluded between Russia *since* the Tsarist regime, and any third party or parties affecting the sovereign rights and interests of the Republic of China'. In return, Karakhan obtained from Koo a declaration, with an equal measure of implied insult, that China would not transfer to any third party, in part or in whole, the concession territories renounced by Soviet Russia.

The documents comprising the Agreement on General Principles, the Agreement on the Provisional Management of the Chinese Eastern Railway, seven declarations, one exchange of notes, and one secret protocol were approved by the cabinet and the president on May 30, and signed by Koo on the following day.[54]

Once concluded, Karakhan had reason to be pleased with the agreement. The winning of diplomatic recognition from China was a distinct victory for him personally, not least because he had had to give away nothing essential to Soviet interests in return for it. Moreover, the agreement meant a big step forward in the Soviet effort to repossess the Chinese Eastern Railway for the agreement established beyond a doubt Soviet Russia's legal ownership of the railway, even though actual repossession still awaited further diplomacy with Mukden.

The Chinese public saw in the agreement, so generously studded with 'equality and reciprocity', a fulfillment of Soviet revolutionary principles. The true mark of adroitness of Soviet diplomacy lay in fashioning an agreement which, on the one hand, appeared to give China more than it actually did, and, on the other, conceded what the Washington Powers had promised China but had yet to fulfill. If the promises were written off, as they were indeed meant to be, the Soviet side had in fact returned China nothing that the Peking government and the Manchurian authorities had not already recovered during the recession of Russian power: abolition of extraterritoriality for Russian subjects, retrocession of the Russian concession territories in Tientsin and Hankow, cancellation of the Boxer Indemnity, recovery of the right of navigation of common waterways, and decolonization of the Chinese Eastern Railway Zone.

For the Peking government the agreement brought a sigh of relief, now that the controversy had ended. It was less pleased than Karakhan with the substance of the agreement and indeed looked forward to the future Sino-Soviet conference with great misgivings. But the Peking officialdom put on a brave front, an appearance of jubilation for the benefit of the Washington Powers in the hope that the unfavorable contrast would goad them on to fulfill their promises of renouncing extraterritoriality and restoring to China her tariff and the concession territories.

As already noted, one effect of the rupture in mid-March was Mukden's prompt dissociation from the negotiations conducted in Peking. Karakhan had plainly overplayed his hand by recourse to the ultimatum. Mukden's rejection of the drafts meant, in effect, that negotiations on issues affecting Manchuria had to start all over again. Since the main thrust of Wu P'ei-fu's messages to the cabinet was its insensitivity to the nation's interests by not endorsing C.T. Wang's signature, Chang Tso-lin decided to prove his greater patriotism by doing better. This determination to seek more concessions from Karakhan coupled with the fact that Chang was the *de facto* master of Manchuria had the effect of putting Mukden in a comparatively strong bargaining position.

Karakhan found himself bereft of any alternative but to initiate negotiations with Mukden. These negotiations cannot be traced in detail without the relevant records, but predictably Mukden made rigid demands concerning the Chinese Eastern Railway, Amur River navigation, and the indemnity of losses. It appears that the first of the negotiators Karakhan sent to Mukden was Michael Borodin, the Soviet political adviser to Sun Yat-sen in Canton. Karakhan did so apparently in the hope that Sun Yat-sen's connections with Chang Tso-lin would help expedite matters. The general political line-up among the contenders for power in China had remained substantially unchanged since 1922: the Chihli clique being the target of a coalition, if only an *ad hoc* and limited one, among Sun Yat-sen's Kuomintang, Tuan Ch'i-jui's Anfu clique, and Chang Tso-lin's Fengtien clique. One may assume that Borodin was instructed to seek Mukden's acceptance of terms similar to those formulated in the unratified drafts, but he apparently made no headway. It was in these circumstances that, in the latter part of May, Karakhan made his next adroit move: concede a little to Koo, conclude the agreement with the Peking government, and then confront Mukden with it.

The sudden conclusion of the Sino-Soviet agreement therefore took Mukden by complete surprise. On June 2 Chang Tso-lin decreed that his Autonomous Manchurian Government was not bound by the agreement, and that the *status quo* of the Chinese Eastern Railway was to remain unchanged until completion of the negotiations at Mukden.[55] The agreement signed in Peking thus produced no immediate capitulation from Mukden which Karakhan must have fully expected, but it had greatly strengthened his bargaining position. Mukden's repudiation now provided Karakhan with one of countless pretexts to delay holding the conference that was to follow immediately upon signature of the Sino-Soviet agreement. Karakhan's attitude together with Peking's opposition to a separate agreement in Mukden in turn produced pressures on Chang Tso-lin for the acceptance of the terms as negotiated by the central government. It turned out that Karakhan did not have to wait long. Early in fall 1924 the continued rivalry between the Chihli and Fengtien cliques culminated in open warfare. On September 20, as Manchurian troops were heading south of the Great Wall, Chang Tso-lin's representatives put their signatures on the Soviet-Mukden Agreement alongside that of Karakhan's first secretary, Nikolai K. Kuznetsov.

Two points are especially noteworthy about this latter

agreement. Firstly, it did contain a number of concessions not to be found in the Peking agreement. While the terms relating to the provisional management of the Chinese Eastern Railway duplicated those of the Peking agreement verbatim, the general principles were different in two respects:

(a) whereas in the Peking agreement both the date of redemption and the method of computing the redemption price remained to be discussed at the Sino–Soviet conference, the Mukden agreement provided for China's right of redemption immediately upon signature; and the redemption price was specified as 'actual and fair cost', i.e., not any prohibitive price that the Soviet government might choose to name but at the actual value of the property at the time of redemption;

(b) the eighty-year concession period, after which the property was to pass free of charge to China as stipulated by the 1896 Contract, was reduced to sixty years, with the possibility of further reduction by mutual consent.

The article governing navigation was also more tightly formulated than in the Sino–Soviet Agreement. Whereas C.T. Wang never got beyond an agreement to regulate the navigation of waters common to Sino–Soviet frontiers, the Mukden Agreement specified that, within two months of signature, a joint commission was to discuss Chinese mercantile traffic 'on the Lower Amur down to the sea' and Soviet shipping on the Sungari up to Harbin on the principles of equality and reciprocity. But, as in the case of much of the Peking agreement, it remained to be seen whether the Mukden agreement, together with its novel features, would be faithfully implemented or remain as mere principles on paper.

The Mukden agreement is noteworthy, secondly, in that it was intended by Mukden as more than just a local arrangement. It appears that formal ratification at the highest level was one of Mukden's uncompromising demands and a stumbling block for some time. There was even a secret declaration accompanying the agreement whereby, in accordance with Mukden's wish, it was understood that the contracting party named 'China' in the various provisions meant the Autonomous Manchurian Government of the Republic of China until such time as Mukden recognized Peking as the official government of China. In short, the agreement was envisaged by Mukden at the outset not as an independent, local document but a supplement and future annex to the Peking agreement.[56]

Two weeks after the signing of the Mukden agreement the railway management was reorganized. The fateful railway entered a new era of Sino-Soviet joint management. Almost immediately, a broad range of conflicts ensued as Chinese participation was quickly rendered purely nominal. The railway came under sole Soviet management in fact, and became once more the instrument for the entrenchment of Soviet power in north Manchuria. The traditional balance against Japan was finally and fully restored.

Karakhan had done his job well. But the new relationship had been constructed on so large an element of conscious deceit that, instead of normalized relations, the various agreements inaugurated a period of prolonged crisis in Sino-Soviet official relations after 1924.

13

Epilogue

By the end of 1924, Karakhan had accomplished his two main diplomatic objectives in China—restoring full diplomatic relations and repossessing the Chinese Eastern Railway. In exchange, he had renounced extraterritoriality, the Hankow and Tientsin concessions, and the Boxer Indemnity, recognized China's tariff autonomy, and agreed that henceforth the Chinese Eastern Railway would be operated as a business enterprise without political privileges. However, all these points had been secured by the Peking government during the temporary waning of Russian power. The Sino-Soviet agreements merely formalized what had existed since 1920. The more important concessions sought by Peking were stated in the agreements only as principles, which might not be honored. These comprised Soviet recognition of China's territorial sovereignty in Outer Mongolia, China's right of redeeming the Chinese Eastern Railway, navigating on the Amur River to the sea, and indemnity for losses incurred during the Russian upheaval.

A conference was to have begun within one month of the signing of the Sino-Soviet treaty and definitive agreements concluded within six months of the opening of the conference. However, as Foreign Minister Koo had foreseen, the Soviet envoy once again resorted to delaying tactics. He declined to open the conference until the Peking government had carried out all its obligations, such as the immediate transfer of the

Russian legation premises, the premises of the Orthodox Mission, and the Chinese Eastern Railway.[1]

By the time these difficulties had been overcome by the Peking government in the autumn, civil war broke out once again between the Fengtien and Chihli cliques. The war was more than just a convenient pretext for Karakhan to delay negotiations. It was a moment for the decisive trial of strength between Chang Tso-lin and Wu P'ei-fu, and the outcome had significant implications on Soviet strategic interests. Soviet political analysts had ceased commenting on Wu P'ei-fu for over a year. In the middle of 1924, they resumed portraying Wu as a nationalist, one most responsible in influencing the Peking government during the negotiation of the Sino-Soviet treaty. Chang Tso-lin, on the other hand, continued to be seen as a feudal militarist tied to Japanese interests. There was no doubt as to which side Moscow wished to see worsted.[2]

But the war unfolded contrary to Soviet expectations. The main development was that one of Wu's associates, General Feng Yü-hsiang, who was to have advanced on Manchuria through Jehol to outflank the Fengtien forces, abandoned the march midway and executed a coup in the capital. Early in November, the Chihli front collapsed under Fengtien onslaught, and Wu was reduced to a fugitive.

In Peking, the president was deposed and the cabinet dissolved. A regency government took office until late November when the old Anfu leader, Tuan Ch'i-jui, came out of retirement to assume the post of provisional chief executive. He served in that position until the spring of 1926, uneasy frontman for the two antagonistic victors, Feng and Chang.[3]

These political changes had a direct bearing on Sino-Soviet diplomacy in that Peking and Mukden were once again speaking with one voice. Chang clearly had the upper hand over Feng in postwar north China. This particularly alarmed Russia, suggesting a fresh line of Soviet approach, initiated in 1925, rendering aid to Feng and fostering a connection between him and the Kuomintang.[4]

During the first two months of 1925, the new government in Peking set about making preparations for the long-overdue Sino-Soviet conference. Unity between Peking and Mukden was achieved when the latter submitted the Soviet-

Mukden Agreement to the central government to be annexed to the Sino–Soviet Treaty. Peking further decided that the central government should be responsible for negotiation of issues that concerned the nation as a whole, and Mukden should handle those concerning Manchuria. To this end, the Directorate of Sino–Soviet Conference (Tu-pan Chung-O hui-i kung-shu) was organized, with C.T. Wang as director, empowered to negotiate *and* to sign. His deputy was Cheng Ch'ien, nominated by Mukden.[5]

The Chinese government was determined to get the conference started, and the public clearly expected results. It was against this background that Karakhan made his next astute move. He informed the Chinese government on March 6 that his government had completed withdrawal of troops from Outer Mongolia. But his motives were transparent, for having accomplished everything he had set out to achieve, he had nothing more to gain from further negotiations with the Chinese. The Chinese Eastern Railway was too valuable, strategically and economically, and the Soviet government was not about to allow the Chinese to redeem it immediately. The shipping department of the railway was already navigating on the Sungari River as in the past, so there was no necessity to allow the Chinese through the Lower Amur in exchange for that. Nor could the Soviet government afford to discuss indemnity for Chinese losses, for fear of setting a dangerous precedent.

But in the face of Peking's relentless pressure for negotiations and suspicions about Soviet intentions in some public quarters, Karakhan obviously had to do something. Evacuation of Outer Mongolia was a sop that might assuage the Chinese government and pacify anti-Soviet critics for a time, at no real sacrifice to Soviet or Mongolian interests.

Chinese authority disappeared from Outer Mongolia after 1921 and the Peking government was helpless about the loss of the territory to Soviet influence. In the search for a solution, armed intervention and diplomacy were seen as alternatives rather than complements. Military action was never seriously contemplated because of seasonal and logistic problems, the reluctance of any militarist to assume responsibility, and the fear of armed conflict with Soviet and Mongol troops. The only alternative, then, was diplomacy.

To no one's surprise, diplomacy (not backed by force) produced no results. One overture after another was made by Chinese officials and various intermediaries, surreptitiously at first to the secular nobility, and later openly to the Urga leadership itself. The princes, though favorably disposed, dared not openly assume a pro-Chinese orientation, and the Urga leadership, being the Mongolian National Party and its Soviet advisers, maintained a frigid stance against disclosing its attitude until Peking made an official declaration of its intentions.[6]

The Mongolian People's Party meanwhile advanced the Mongol revolution with speed and depth. After expelling the Chinese, it proceeded to subjugate the old ecclesiastical and secular élites, build a Mongol army, and reconstitute the politics and economy with socialism as the recognized goal. It proclaimed the Mongolian People's Republic soon after the death of the Jebtsun-damba Khutukhtu in May 1924. Thus Soviet recognition of Chinese territorial sovereignty did not alter in the least the hard reality of Outer Mongolia's *de facto* independence from China. The Sino-Mongolian relationship was something that the Soviet side was content (and could afford) to leave to the two parties to decide, so long as Urga was amenable to Soviet advice.

The question that remained was the presence of Soviet troops. The Sino-Soviet conference was to decide the date of withdrawal and the measures for mutual frontier security. Karakhan's notification of March 6, 1925 therefore came as a sudden, and unpleasant, surprise for the Chinese government, which regarded the act as a device to allay Chinese public suspicions. It found the tone of the note both offensive and ominous. The Peking government was blamed for the necessity of Soviet intervention in the first place, and for the delay in the opening of the Sino-Soviet conference. After advertising Soviet magnanimity to the Chinese people, the note expressed the hope that 'those circumstances which made it necessary to bring the Red Army into Outer Mongolia will no longer occur in the future'. It expected a *peaceful* solution to the Sino-Mongolian problem.[7]

After sending Karakhan a curt reply, the Chinese government next contacted the Urga government. It was a moment desired for years, and how Urga would respond was an anxious question. The decision was taken that the director of the bureau of Mongolian and Tibetan affairs, Prince Gungsang-norbu, would send an emissary to Tsereng-dorji, the Mongol premier. A message drafted by the Wai-chiao Pu welcomed the withdrawal of Soviet troops and urged that the opportunity for the adjustment of the Sino-Mongolian relationship be seized. It said the central government was sworn to strengthen the spirit of a family of five races. As one of the races, Outer Mongolia had in the past shared equally in the family's joys and sorrows. The central government would support any plan that benefitted the Mongol people, and Urga was asked to send representatives to Peking to discuss all matters so that all misunderstandings might be removed and mutually satisfactory solutions arrived at.[8]

The Peking government's views at this time were not very different from the policy decided in 1921. The Wai-chiao Pu submission adopted by the cabinet in March 1925 gave the Mongols the autonomy of local government, reserving diplomacy, defense, communications, and justice for Peking. But the Chinese government did not entertain great hopes of a favorable response, and foresaw the need to coerce the Mongols into submission.[9]

Urga's reply was long in coming. When it arrived in June, it confirmed Peking's fears. The Mongolian People's Republic had longed in vain for an early settlement of Sino-Mongolian differences, wrote Tsereng-dorji, but the delay had been due not to the presence of Soviet troops but to the incessant internecine strife within China. Moreover, the Chinese government had yet to state its policy towards Outer Mongolia. 'Our only wish is that the Chinese government should end domestic strife immediately, act in concert with us to throw off the yoke of imperialism, reform itself to give substance to a truly democratic republic, and work for the happiness of our four hundred million Chinese brethren and the equality among the races'. Otherwise, the Chinese government should adopt the policy of self-determination for its national minorities. After a clear declaration of those intentions by

China, the letter concluded, the Mongolian government would send its plenipotentiaries to negotiate in Peking.[10]

Urga's attitude left the Chinese government as helpless as it had ever been. Again, the use of force was entirely out of the question. Neither Chang Tso-lin nor Feng Yü-hsiang, who possessed the troops, would intervene since they were too busy vying for supremacy in north China.

Karakhan had disposed of the Mongolian question neatly. With public goodwill partially restored, he could afford to keep putting off the Sino-Soviet conference. Many points of friction arose over the Chinese Eastern Railway after reorganization, providing him with the pretexts he needed. In August, 1925, Karakhan suddenly requested the conference be convened immediately. It was, thus preserving the public image that he sincerely desired negotiations, but just as suddenly he slipped away to begin a three-month furlough.

During his absence, a half dozen joint committees were set up to look into individual issues. The Soviet delegates were interested in a commercial agreement, but the work of other committees was obstructed by their refusing to decide during Karakhan's absence. These committees sat for almost a year, and Karakhan was able to move the negotiations forward or stall them as he pleased. Finally, in July 1926, C.T. Wang asked to be relieved; the directorate was dissolved, and the issues transferred back to the Wai-chiao Pu as outstanding questions.[11]

The frustrations of Chinese officials in the capital were mild, however, compared to those experienced by the Manchurian officialdom. No sooner had Soviet personnel been substituted for the Russo-Asiatic Bank appointees in the C.E.R. Administration than protracted conflicts developed.

It would be too tedious to detail the multitude of conflicts that followed the return of Russian influence in north Manchuria.[12] But underlying them was the harsh reality of the Soviet pursuit of reestablishing predominance in the region. The 'provisional' arrangement concerning the railway became permanent by the Soviet delay in discussing Chinese redemption. Control of the enterprise as an exclusive Soviet state property was secured simply by a monopoly of management powers. Moreover, in Chinese eyes, the Soviet side was seeking not only to assert economic rights but to turn the railway into a political arm, both as the front line of defense against Japan and as an invaluable instrument for the attainment of its broad political objectives in China.

At first, protracted conflicts developed over the unequal distribution of power between Chinese and Soviet directors on the management. The principle of equal representation quickly produced a deadlock in the board, and sole power of management devolved on Soviet manager A.N. Ivanov. His dictatorial methods became the most frequent of Chinese charges. The Manchurian Chinese did everything they could, including using mobs, to unseat him or limit his powers, but to no avail.

This latter day General Horvath became the center of recurrent storms of Chinese protests as he stubbornly advanced Soviet political influence. The Chinese were dissatisfied with inequality of employment, in numbers, positions, and salaries. They claimed that 75 per cent of the railway land bore no direct relationship tò the railway enterprise itself. They saw the trade unions and educational institutions as agencies of Soviet propaganda and subversion. The Chinese railway patrol and police force, which symbolised Chinese sovereignty in the railway area, were undermined when Ivanov stopped paying subsidies.

Numerous and intense as the conflicts were, the Manchurian Chinese did not go to the extreme. Chang Tso-lin was preoccupied with the political struggle south of the Great Wall and evidently felt it wise to limit these conflicts, however intense and protracted, short of war.

But beginning with the Kuo Sung-ling rebellion in late 1925, the Soviet-Mukden feud took on a new complexion. In November 1925, Kuo, one of Chang's officers in Tientsin, revolted in conspiracy with Chang's rival, Feng Yü-hsiang. Marching northward, and winning victory after victory, his forces entered Manchuria on December 1 to destroy Chang. To help meet the crisis, Chang sent for the Heilungkiang troops. In the past, the railway had transported Manchurian troops on credit, but Ivanov declared on November 28 that from December 1, prepayment would be required. He also warned that Soviet troops would be brought in if disorders occurred. The Heilungkiang troops made their way south on the Taonan-Angangki line. This episode impressed on the Fengtien warlord the Soviet's capability of using the railway to undermine his position.

At the end of December, after the rebellion had been put down, hostility flared between the returning Heilungkiang troops and the Soviet manager. When Ivanov persisted in asking for prepayment, some units commandeered several trains at Changchun and made their way to Harbin. Ivanov retaliated by shutting down the Harbin-Changchun section and was in turn arrested by the Chinese troops on January 22, 1926. Then came Karakhan's ultimatum, followed by prompt negotiations at Mukden. The problem was settled without loss of face to either side: for transporting Chang's troops, the railway was to charge against the amount due to the Chinese government.[13]

Chang now was fully aware that Soviet influence was festering within his own domain like a cancerous growth, beyond his powers to expel. Worse still, Soviet Russia was actively engaged in the power struggle in north China. Soviet aid was flowing to Chiang Kai-shek in the south and to Feng Yü-hsiang in the northwest, and together they posed a deadly challenge to himself. During the next two years, while avoiding the ultimate act of seizing the railway, Chang vented his vengeance against Karakhan by campaigning for his removal. After the Soviet government agreed to recall Karakhan in September 1926, Chang followed with other measures, such as forcibly closing down the shipping department of the railway, seizing the Soviet vessels in the Sungari, and asserting his authority over the education department of the railway. The next April, while the Northern Expedition was in progress, he instituted a raid against the Soviet embassy and exposed Soviet subversion. This caused a rupture of the official relationship that had been restored only three years before.

Still, the Soviet position in north Manchuria remained substantially unaffected until 1935 when the Soviet Union was forced to sell the Chinese Eastern Railway to the Japanese puppet state, Manchukuo. During this period, the Sino-Soviet feud continued unabated, culminating in the Chinese seizure of the railway in 1929, followed by Soviet land and air bombardment of the Manchurian border communities, and China's subsequent capitulation.

The significance of this story up to this point may be assessed in terms of Soviet official policy over the period 1917-26 and the nature of Warlord China's response. The principal argument is that Soviet Russia's China policy should be seen as a part of her policy towards the Far East as a whole, and in that policy Japan occupied the central position. The blend of hard-headed power politics and revolutionary appeal found in the China policy was closely related to the necessity for the Soviet republic to come to terms with the principal enemy, Japan.

In the early days of the October Revolution, the Bolsheviks made a single, desperate attempt to seize control of the Chinese Eastern Railway Zone, which was a likely hotbed of counterrevolution and the most logical area of Japan's first advance against Bolshevik Russia. After the collapse of the Harbin Soviet, Soviet policy next took the form of a holding operation. It sought appeasement and avoidance of conflict with Japan at all cost. Towards China it showed a markedly conciliatory attitude and tried, with calculated concessions, to win Chinese official and popular friendship as an indirect means of countering Japan. But this policy of accommodation with Japan also failed when the Allied Intervention began in fall 1918, and Soviet power was steadily rolled back beyond the Urals.

During the next twelve months, the Soviet republic struggled for survival, threatened by enemies on all sides. In the summer of 1919, an opportunity presented itself for a fresh initiative in China, where resentment against the Versailles settlement erupted into mass protests and demonstrations. The Chinese outbursts were all the more welcome because of the anti-Japanese sentiment which prompted them. Moscow acted by issuing the Karakhan Manifesto of July 25, 1919, which contained every concession previously offered to China. It also offered an unconditional transfer of the Chinese Eastern Railway instead of asking China to redeem it, as had been done before. This last offer appears not to have been a unanimous decision, however. One segment of the Soviet policymaking body evidently hoped to secure an alliance with Chinese nationalism against Japan by means of generous appeals. Others apparently favored a more cautious approach, so that in the end the option of reclaiming old Russian interests in north Manchuria was kept open.

By the time the Karakhan Manifesto was actually communicated to the Chinese in spring 1920, Soviet Russia had emerged from the period of complete isolation, steadily gaining initiative in foreign policy. Although Japan was an unremitting threat, motivated as she was by ideological hostility and territorial aggrandizement, other foreign troops were being withdrawn, civil war was coming to an end, and Soviet Russia could find some comfort in the developing American-Japanese rivalry. From this still relatively weak position, the Soviet government reintroduced the two-pronged policy that had been applied without success before the Siberian intervention. It appeased Japan by creating the Far Eastern Republic as a buffer, and conciliated China by means of the Karakhan Manifesto. After the failure of the Vilensky mission in mid-1920, Soviet policy towards China switched to one looking towards reclamation of various Tsarist interests deemed essential to the security of the Soviet state.

There now emerged a clear outline of the Far Eastern policy that was to be followed to 1926 and beyond. While continuing to appease Japan, the Soviet government simultaneously sought to foster its influence in China as a means of strengthening its general position. This preoccupation with external security in the Far East coincided with the domestic change of front signified by the New Economic Policy of March 1921. By its new policy, the Soviet government acknowledged that no immediate aid would be forthcoming from the proletariat, recognized the necessity to postpone reaching its domestic and international goals and concentrate meanwhile on strengthening its national security against the encircling hostile world.

In China, this emphasis on national security found expression in the Soviet claims to treaty rights in Outer Mongolia and north Manchuria. White Guard activity coupled with Peking's weakness in the summer of 1921 provided the setting for Soviet military intervention in Outer Mongolia. In north Manchuria no such direct action was feasible, partly because the Japanese power base was too close, and partly because the area was effectively ruled by Chang Tso-lin. But the Chinese Eastern Railway was being preserved for Soviet Russia, thanks to a convergence of American and Soviet strategic interests. In the end, Soviet Russia was able to restore what was in fact the prerevolutionary line of power balance with Japan.

The diplomatic record thus underlines a very basic continuity between Soviet and Imperial Russian policies, deriving from the continuity of the external environment. The traditional imbalance between Russia and Japan together with Chinese vulnerability shaped Soviet as much as did Tsarist policies. And the continuity was accentuated when the new regime found it easiest and most desirable to reclaim the old interests on the basis of the existing Sino-Russian treaties. Despite Moscow's incessant profession of a new diplomacy towards China, its policy had all the familiar resonances of the old diplomacy of imperialism to Peking's ears.

Moscow's China policy in 1926 is best illustrated by a set of resolutions passed by a special commission of the Politburo. The principal elements of Soviet policy are found in them—detente with Japan, fostering of Soviet influence on China's borderlands, and manipulation of the Chinese revolution for the narrow goal of national security. The commission met on March 25, 1926, with Trostky as chairman, and its resolutions were formally approved by the Politburo a week later. The resolutions were an attempt to come to grips with newly arisen challenges to Soviet influence in various parts of China.

In Canton, the Kuomintang since 1924 had been fashioned with Borodin's assistance into the bearer of the bourgeois democratic revolution. With the CCP as a bloc within it, the party had raised anti-imperialism as the immediate goal for the national revolution. The tide of antiforeignism and radicalism had grown, especially after the May Thirtieth Incident in Shanghai and the June twenty-third massacre in Canton in 1925. A nationwide movement of protests against Japanese and British acts was in full swing. However, this outburst of Chinese mass energies, which had

been longed for by Moscow, was greeted not with total jubilation but mixed feelings. Although the opportunity to carry
out a revolutionary policy of great historical scale was welcome, the commission nevertheless feared that antagonizing
both Britain and Japan would destroy the Chinese revolution
and, worse still, endanger the safety of the Soviet republic. It
assessed the situation as follows:

> The international conditions are becoming extremely difficult
> in view of the stabilization in Europe, the Locarno Treaties, and
> especially the imperialist powers' grave concern over the China
> problem. Under these circumstances, the leading revolutionary
> forces of China, and more so, the Soviet government should do
> everything in order to hamper the creation of a united imperialist
> front against China. Japan can become extremely dangerous for
> the Chinese revolution at present, owing to both its geographical
> position and its lively economic and military interests in
> Manchuria. . . . It is necessary to try and gain a respite, and this
> means in effect setting aside the question of the political fate of
> Manchuria, i.e. actually being reconciled to the fact that south
> Manchuria will remain in Japan's hands in the immediate
> future.[14]

Until new revolutionary waves appeared in Europe and
Asia, neither the Soviet republic nor the Chinese revolution
could afford a united front against the imperialists. In short,
the Soviet tactic was to divide the imperialist camp by isolat-
ing Britain as the chief target of antiforeignism and buying off
Japan at China's expense. The commission resolved that the
Canton government should for the time being absolutely
abstain from armed expeditions of an aggressive nature and
from all actions that might push the imperialists on the road of
armed intervention. The launching of the Northern Expedition by the KMT, less than three months after this directive,
highlights the still tenuous influence that Moscow exercised in
Canton; it may be seen as the beginning of the end of the first
phase of Soviet intervention in the Chinese revolution.

Of greater interest are the consequences of the continuing
Soviet policy of accommodation with Japan as it affected the
Chinese borderlands. In January 1925, Karakhan duplicated
his truimph in China by restoring diplomatic relations with
Tokyo. The crucial point of the Soviet-Japanese Convention

was that the Treaty of Portsmouth of 1905 was recognized as being still valid, thereby reaffirming the division of Manchuria into two mutually exclusive spheres of interest. Karakhan made the agreement notwithstanding his undertaking to Peking not to conclude agreements with any third party that were injurious to China's sovereign rights.[15]

The next step for Soviet Russia was to consolidate and further develop her interests in north Manchuria, while at the same time promoting stable relations with Japan. Chang Tso-lin appeared to Moscow likely to remain a key factor in the Manchurian vortex for some time to come and some kind of understanding with him seemed essential for achieving Soviet objectives. The Trotsky commission gave its closest attention to these problems.

The commission envisaged a tripartite agreement between Soviet Russia, Japan, and Chang, which would put railway construction and economic development in Manchuria on the basis of full respect for mutual rights and interests. It resolved to establish with Chang 'a strict business-like regime' for the Chinese Eastern Railway, including precise procedures for resolving all issues of controversy and conflict. The Soviet manager Ivanov was to be replaced, and all Soviet personnel were to be warned against acting one-sidedly over the heads of the Chinese authorities. To promote better Soviet–Mukden relations, the commission called for broad measures of a cultural and political character for the sinicization of the railroad, such as bi-lingualism in the railway administration, creation of Chinese schools for railwaymen, and cultural and educational institutions for Chinese workmen and the general population in the railway zone.

But there was no change in the basic Soviet objectives in north Manchuria. The commission resolved that the Chinese Eastern Railway was to remain in Soviet hands, which alone could guard it against being seized by the imperialists. Indeed, the commission even mooted the possibility of excluding the Chinese from the management altogether, if such a step could be accomplished without excessive complications with Chinese officials and public. Chang was to be told that the Soviet government would not tolerate independent railway construction by him and to ask him to accept a plan for the further expansion of the Chinese Eastern Railway, including the building of feeder lines and macadam roads and the development of shipping. More generally, an undertaking was to be sought from Chang not to encroach on Outer Mongolia and, if possible, not to intervene in the internal affairs of China proper.

To promote better relations with Japan in Manchuria, the commission proposed a Soviet-Japanese conference to resolve controversies and disputes arising from their Manchurian interests. Also, it resolved that the Soviet government oppose, by all possible means, Japanese construction of railways linking up with the eastern or the western section of the Chinese Eastern Railway or north of it, scare Japan off by rumors of Soviet intention to route a line from Chita through eastern Inner Mongolia, and construct as soon as possible railways from Verkhne Udinsk to Urga and Kalgan, and from Khabarovsk to a Soviet port.

The task of securing the various agreements from Chang and Japan was entrusted to the deputy commissar for communications, L.P. Serebriakov, who visited the Far East in spring and summer 1926. He approached Chang with far-reaching demands but negligible concessions at a time when the Manchurian warlord was showing marked animosity towards the Soviet government. Serebriakov therefore met with a cold rebuff.[16] What success he had in Tokyo is difficult to say. But the overture could not have been rejected out of hand since, in Japanese military circles, the United States had replaced Soviet Russia as Japan's foremost imagined enemy. Over the next two years, other Soviet feelers followed, and Soviet-Japanese coexistence in Manchuria remained remarkably quiet, despite many opportunities for tension.

But Russo–Japanese equilibrium in Manchuria was upset once again in 1931 by the explosive militarism of the Japanese Kwantung Army. The basic imbalance between Russia and Japan in the Far East was underlined when, in 1935, faced with Hitlerism in the west and Japanese militarism in the east, Moscow appeased Japan by bowing out of Manchuria altogether. However, at the end of World War II, with a tenacity that has characterized the entire history of her encroachment on Manchuria, Russia returned to wield her influence in the region for almost another decade, even though the old triangular relationship between Russia, Japan, and China had changed beyond recognition.

Warlord China existed much like a deformed offspring of the republican revolution. The driving force of that revolution, as Mary Wright has noted, was nationalism expressed in a threefold thrust: resistance to imperialism, as seen in the watchword 'recovery of sovereign rights'; the aspiration for a strong, modern, centralized nation-state capable of warding off foreign aggression and overriding the centrifugal tendencies that weakened the Chinese state; and, less importantly, the overthrow of Manchu rule.[17] But Republican China was quickly forced to come to terms with the foreign omnipresence. Loss of sovereign rights within China and foreign encroachment of the frontiers continued as before. In the vacuum created by the demise of the Confucian monarchy, military men became the arbiters of Chinese society, too deficient in political beliefs and too limited in actual power to rise above the regional level and organize a new national order.

From 1917 to 1926, the government in Peking functioned fictitiously as the legitimate national government. In fact, warlordism rendered it perpetually unstable and also vastly limited its power. Within the brief span of nine years, there were four changes of president and more than a dozen changes of cabinet. And these changes were always the result of the constant fluctuations in the balance of power among the Peiyang warlord cliques. Over the various domains of the competing cliques the central government exercized little or no power; where the power of these cliques did not extend, as in the case of the half dozen southern and southwestern provinces, it had even less.

In foreign relations, the situation of the central government was somewhat more complex. This was due to the fact that the Wai-chiao Pu, which was responsible for foreign policymaking, was relatively immune from warlord interference. There was a common desire among the warlord cliques for the legitimacy conferred upon their power by foreign recognition of Peking as the official government of China. This in turn required that acceptable diplomatic relations be conducted with the foreign powers. Moreover, the warlords seemed to realize that, given the complexity of China's foreign relations, only the foreign affairs experts who staffed the Wai-chiao Pu and its various offices abroad possessed the knowledge and adroitness to fashion policies to maximum advantage.

The result of the Wai-chiao Pu's unique position was that it became the repository of the aspirations for a freer China, more independent of foreign control. It was staffed by professionals with the requisite training in Western learning, and throughout this period it maintained a greater degree of continuity in personnel than most other agencies.

Moreover, there was a consistency in the evolution of the Wai-chiao Pu's policy towards Soviet Russia. This policy consisted of two parts: one concerned the whole complex of former Russian interests in China and on the borderlands, the other with relations with the new regime in Russia. By far the most dominant and persistent theme in the Wai-chiao Pu's attitude was that the Russian upheaval was an opportunity to be hurriedly seized for sweeping away the Tsarist incubus. The watchword of its Russian policy was 'recovery of sovereign rights', and its strategy was to effect changes unilaterally as far as possible and then to bargain official recognition of the Soviet government for the latter's acceptance of these changes. Before the end of 1920, the Wai-chiao Pu had reasserted China's right of navigation of the Amur River system (leaving access to the sea as an issue to be negotiated), done away with Russia's protectorship of Outer Mongolia (although its policy was completely undermined by the Anfu militarist Hsü Shu-cheng), reduced the Chinese Eastern Railway to a purely business enterprise from the colonial administration that it once had been, abrogated extraterritoriality for Russians, and recovered the concessions in Hankow and Tientsin.

The other half of the Wai-chiao Pu's Russian policy concerned the attitude China might safely adopt towards Bolshevik Russia, how and when might relations be renewed with minimal international complications. There was in fact never any reluctance on the Wai-chiao Pu's part to deal with the Soviet government. The sooner it negotiated with a weaker Russia, the more it could hope to gain in the final settlement; the earlier an agreement with Moscow was reached, the less danger there would be of a Soviet-Japanese rapprochement at China's expense. In the end, the policy of trading off official recognition for Soviet concessions proved to be abortive owing to Moscow's determination and capacity to retain Tsarist gains in north Manchuria and Outer Mongolia, the insubordination of the warlords to the central government, and, less importantly than generally believed, the influence of the foreign powers.

The insubordination of the warlords graphically underlines the limited nature of the central government's power. It can be seen in General Hsü Shu-cheng's disruption of the Chin Yün-p'eng Cabinet's Mongolian policy in 1919. It was evident in Chang Tso-lin's sudden discontinuation of the Mongolian expedition in the summer of 1921, due to his preoccupation with the domestic struggle for supremacy. It was again evident in his successive declarations of the autonomy of his Manchurian domain when the rival Chihli clique controlled Peking, a fact which complicated the Wai-chiao Pu's diplomatic effort with Moscow.

Even where government-warlord cooperation was close, recovery of sovereign rights did not occupy the same priority in warlord thinking as in that of the central government. Local powerholders were less inclined to accept risks inherent in the official policy, and this inevitably affected its implementation. Thus, General Pao Kuei-ch'ing's handling of the Chinese Eastern Railway problem in 1920 was not as thorough-going as the central government wished. And Chang Tso-lin's opposition in the winter of 1921 effectively barred the Wai-chiao Pu from negotiating the Chinese Eastern Railway question at the proposed Manchouli conference.

It is widely believed, as communist historians have persistently claimed, that Peking's Soviet policy in this period was strongly influenced by the foreign powers. This problem may be approached on two levels: foreign influence on the government itself and on the warlords. Up to the spring of 1921, when Britain took the lead in beginning *de facto* recognition of Moscow, Peking was compelled to act in concert with the Great Powers, particularly the Allied Powers of World War I.

It did so with some reluctance, being anxious not to antagonize the new regime in Russia and also being aware that the passing of time would make Russia stronger and more difficult to negotiate with. Peking's view of its own prerogatives was not timid because it was only some years after the war that the Allied Powers stopped acting in concert with regard to the Soviet government. Peking could not afford to antagonize the Great Powers because it needed their countervailing influence against Japan. Its effort to recover various sovereign rights to the extent of unilaterally tearing up the existing Sino-Russian treaties shows that it clearly had a mind of its own.

After Britain had provided the lead, the Peking government felt considerably freer to deal with Moscow on its own terms. Thereafter, the delay in negotiations was not due to foreign influence on Peking but to the unbridgeable gap between the Chinese and Soviet positions and Moscow's determination to outwait the Peking government. Britain's official recognition of the Soviet government in February 1924 removed the main prop of Peking's policy, which together with the fear of a Soviet-Japanese rapprochement forced Peking to capitulate to Soviet demands.

Foreign influence on the warlords, and through them on Peking's Soviet policy, is more difficult to assess. Certainly, some warlords did associate themselves, whether out of choice or necessity, with certain foreign interests, but those connections were probably imbued with no less a degree of pragmatic opportunism than alliances among the warlords themselves. The connections varied greatly, depending on the warlord and the foreign power concerned, and on the contingencies confronted by a warlord at a given time that required him to take the foreign interests into account.

In view of Japan's hostility towards Bolshevik Russia, one would expect that her influence on the Anfu and the Fengtien cliques would affect Sino-Soviet relations. However, there is considerable evidence to the contrary. America's military involvement in Asia from autumn 1918 and the intensified American-Japanese rivalry seem to have given the so-called pro-Japanese cliques of Chinese militarists considerable room to maneuver. The Anfu clique did not voluntarily conclude the Sino-Japanese joint defense pact in 1918, and it did not hesitate to obstruct its implementation, including the use of American restraining influence on Japan. China's involvement in the Siberian Intervention was motivated by the need to be associated with the inter-Allied effort so as to avoid being dragged into Japan's separate, unilateral intervention in Siberia. The Anfu clique dissociated itself from the pact by discontinuing the intervention in spring 1920 like the Western powers, while the Japanese army remained on Russian soil for another one and a half years. It even acted independently of Japan by sending the Chang Ssu-lin mission to Moscow in the summer of 1920. General Hsü Shu-cheng's activities in Outer Mongolia are generally interpreted as furthering Japan's interests but this assertion has yet to be supported by hard facts.

As for Chang Tso-lin, leader of the Fengtien clique, his relationship with Japan seems to have varied even more, depending on the circumstances. Given the entrenchment of Japan's influence within his economic and military base, he was bound to maintain peaceful and stable relations with the Japanese. In 1917, busy as he was with Manchurian unification, he was anxious to please the Japanese since their support was essential to the success of his ambitions. In the early 1920s, when the Japanese made persistent demands regarding former Russian interests in north Manchuria, he was far from subservient. Indeed, it is by no means rare to find in Japanese official records complaints about his intractability. As Akira Iriye has pointed out, although Chang was inevitably dependent on Japan, this did not mean that he did not share the vision of a freer Manchuria, more independent of foreign control.[18] He resisted the Japanese demands by leaving responsibility for the Chinese Eastern Railway in the hands of the Peking government. The Western powers' interest in the railway, moreover, was a pretext on which he could conveniently fall back.

More research will be necessary before the enormously complex relationships between the government and the warlords, and between the warlords and the foreign powers can be fully unravelled. But enough has been said to justify a more positive appraisal of the government's conduct of foreign affairs at least. The Wai-chiao Pu, as an agency of government in charge of foreign relations, had more power and independence, more continuity, better personnel, more positive policies and nationalistic motivations than most people realize.

There remains the compellingly urgent question: Why was the Chinese public, nationalistic though it was, relatively unappreciative of the Wai-chiao Pu's efforts and unconcerned about the paradoxes of the Soviet posture in China? It is practically impossible to characterize precisely the opinion held by so variegated a body as the public on the Chinese government and on Soviet Russia, but a number of ingredients may be clearly identified. Although there always existed a number of groups hostile to Soviet Russia, the public appears, by and large, to have been pro-Soviet. The pro-Soviet tide rose with the first Karakhan Manifesto, timed and directed at the upsurge of nationalism. Each successive envoy thereafter worked assiduously to preserve the pro-Soviet attitude of the Chinese public. In resisting the return of Russian power, therefore, the Peking government fought a lonely battle, without the public's understanding or support. The government was slow to understand and make capital out of the dilemmas inherent in Soviet policies. By the time it awoke to the necessity to make similar use of the press, it was already in a supplicant's position, more anxious to befriend than expose, fearful of being overtaken by a Soviet-Japanese rapprochement.

The public was not uniformly hostile to each cabinet or to all the warlords. Thus, Wu P'ei-fu was favorably regarded for a time and the Wang Ch'ung-hui Cabinet backed by him enjoyed much public support while it lasted. Nevertheless, an unbridgeable gulf seemed to separate the government from the public for the most part. Political chaos, perpetuated by recurrent civil wars among the warlords and in-fighting among self-seeking politicians, so alienated the public that the government, more often than not, was castigated for its incompetence or impotence. Among the intelligentsia, the government was regarded by the national and social revolutionaries as a target of political revolution, and by liberals in their academic retreat as the object of occasional criticism and protest. Some moderate conservatives were in sympathy or worked with the government, but the amount of public influence they commanded was probably minimal.[19] In the vital area of destroying foreign imperialism, an obsession of the public at large, the government's investment of effort and talents was unreflected in positive achievements. The nationalistic public turned from indifference to profound suspicion and cynicism.

In addition to this basic disaffection between the government and the public, there were differences of views in regard to both Soviet Russia and the crucial issues of Sino-Soviet diplomacy, differences which stemmed from the different images each perceived of Russia. The Peking government saw Russia as an aggressive power, to be resisted along with all other imperialists. This image, as already seen, was rooted in reality as well as experience. Hence, the government acted with swiftness and determination in recovering sovereign rights from a momentarily weak Russia and held on to a policy of exclusion of Russian interests and influence at China's borders as the basis for renewed relations. But what the government had to show in the way of concrete results in this case seemed to have mattered least to the public. Thus, the Soviet government received fervid demonstrations of gratitude for a revolutionary, equal treaty with China even though it actually gave away nothing the Chinese government had not already regained. The effort and achievement of the official nationalists went practically unnoticed.

For a good cross section of Chinese public attitudes towards Soviet Russia, one can do no better than refer to a little-known controversy among the Peking intellectuals in the latter part of 1925, in the supplements of two major Peking newspapers, *Ch'en pao (Morning Post)* and *Ching pao (Peking Press)*. The controversy, which rapidly turned into polemics, began with the question whether imperalism could be distinguished between 'Red' and 'White', and became more explicitly centered around the question whether Soviet Russia was a friend or foe to China. The debate opened with the stating of two extreme positions. Ch'en Ch'i-hsiu, a Marxist academic, argued in a learned discourse that 'Red Imperialism' was impossible in terms of dialectic materialism. But, as others were quick to point out, Ch'en seems to be saying that to call Russia imperialist and thus lump her together with other imperialist powers would be playing into the hands of the real enemy. He seems to feel that China should conserve her energies for the struggle against the real imperialists.[20] Ch'en was countered by the political philosopher Chang Hsi-jo, who deemed Russia to be worse than the imperialists. Chang was particularly concerned with the subversion of China's internal order by the Soviet propagation of communism which, he said, corrupted not only the body but the soul of the nation. Russia was the greater enemy because of her reckless pursuit of self-interest at the expense of a helpless China.[21]

The term 'Red Imperialism' (*ch'ih-she ti-kuo chu-i*) itself had been coined by anti-Soviet detractors. Of these, two groups were particularly prominent in the 1920s and their anti-Soviet attitude was in direct response and criticism to the alliance between the Kuomintang and Soviet Russia, launched in 1923. One consisted of the advocates of narrow nationalism (*kuo-chia chu-i*) and they exercised an influence out of proportion to their numbers. They had organized themselves into the Young China Party (Shao-nien chung-kuo tang, later named the Chinese Youth Party or Chung-kuo ch'ing-nien tang), with the influential organ *Hsing-shih (Awakened Lion)*. They were, at one and the same time, fervently anti-imperialist and anti-communist, rejecting class struggle as too ruthless and divisive. Li Huang, a leading member of the group, contributed to the controversy by arguing that Soviet Russia was retreating from communism to state capitalism at home and was pursuing her national self-interest abroad. He was unusually mild in discussing Soviet conduct, declaring it was quite natural for Soviet Russia to act in her self-interest, because he wished to reserve the strongest criticism for China. Both the government and the revolutionary groups were to blame, he said, one for being so weak as to be taken advantage of, as in Outer Mongolia, and the other for allowing themselves to be used by Soviet revolutionary policy.[22]

The other major anti-Soviet group was the Chinputang (Progressive Party) together with its descendant, the Yen-chiu hsi (Study Clique). Old rivalries with the Russian-allied Kuomintang probably accounted in part for the group's anti-Soviet attitude. Some members apparently believed that political capital could be made out of the bolshevization (*ch'ih-hua*) of the Kuomintang. The leader of the group of moderate conservatives was the famous journalist and reformer Liang Ch'i-ch'ao, who in the 1920s had given up practical politics in favor of cultural reforms. Immensely influential a generation before, Liang had been superseded by others as leaders of students and other young intellectuals. Liang himself contributed an interesting piece to the debate on friendship or enmity with Russia.

Liang quickly dismissed Ch'en Ch'i-hsiu's argument about the non-existence of 'Red Imperialism' as specious, since imperialism could have non-economic foundations as well. Communism with its doctrine of class struggle, he argued, was unsuited to Chinese economic conditions because what the country needed most was to promote productivity under protective tariffs and harmonious industrial relations. Russia, which propagated class warfare, was therefore as great an enemy as the imperialists who denied China her tariff autonomy. He denounced Russia unequivocally as 'the quintessence of imperialism'. It was in the Russian national character, he said, to be ruled by a dictatorship and to be imperialistic. In a fervent appeal, he exhorted the bright and romantic youthful converts of Marxism-Leninism to wake up, see the selfish purposes of Soviet Russia, and watch against being used and duped.[23]

Apart from the moderate conservatives and the advocates of *kuo-chia chu-i*, there was a third miniscule group opposed to Soviet Russia, namely, the anarchists. The anarchists drew their inspiration from Russian anarchism and, like their Russian counterparts, opposed the Bolsheviks for their pyramidal structure and monopoly of power. Their representative in the debate was Pao P'u, a journalist who had written extensively on the October Revolution. Like Liang Ch'i-ch'ao, Pao believed Russia to be no less imperialistic than the other imperialist powers. Russia, he said, was not a communist, workers' state but ruled by the Russian Communist Party. She promised autonomy and equality to her national minorities on one hand, and then trampled on those principles on the other. She declared herself to be anti-imperialist but acted in an imperialist manner, as evident in her position in Outer Mongolia, her delaying the opening of the Sino-Soviet conference, and in her activities in Canton.[24]

Finally, there was the right wing splinter group within the Kuomintang, which had always been a party composed of many different elements. Members of the right wing were anti-Soviet because they shared some if not all the views held by other anti-Soviet groups enumerated above.

Still, all these hostile groups probably added up to a very small number of individuals and commanded limited public attention, compared to the pro-Soviet. The latter included many liberals and the vast number of student organizations influenced by them, the mainstream of the Kuomintang, and of course the communists. Except for the communists, whose ideological link with the Russians set them apart, the predominant tendency was to view Russia as an essential ally in the struggle against imperialism. Faced with a concerted bloc of imperialist powers, they were delighted that there should be one foreign power ready to lend if only moral support to the all-consuming cause of anti-imperialism. How then did their views on Soviet ambitions in China's borderlands differ from those of the Peking government?

On the question of Outer Mongolia, there was a clear divergence of views between the government and the pro-Soviet groups. For the government, as for Soviet Russia, Outer Mongolia's internal status was always a secondary question to its external significance as a buffer. The crucial issue for both governments was who should control the defensive screen. For the pro-Soviet, noncommunist Chinese, the issue of Outer Mongolia was one of considerable ambiguity, in that they had difficulty seeing the Soviet activity there as a straightforward case of aggression. Many were prepared to condone the act as one of defending threatened self-interests and were more inclined to castigate the government for allowing the situation to reach such a pass.[25] Many liberals were cynical about China's past policies and actions in Outer Mongolia and, as nationalists, felt constrained by their own convictions about national self-determination for the Mongols. To the vast majority of the pro-Soviet Chinese, Outer Mongolia seemed rather distant and, bearing in mind the recent history, they appeared to regard the territory as one more morsel fought over by competing warlords and desired by the Japanese.

Similarly, in the case of north Manchuria, the pro-Soviet

Chinese saw the area as part of the domain of one of the most hated warlords, Chang Tso-lin. The pragmatic-minded did not fail to see the virtue of having Russian influence there to counterbalance that of Japan, the most hated imperialist power.[26] The government no doubt shared this view when there was no alternative, but during the negotiations with Russia it had sought, with little public sympathy, to eliminate Russian influence in north Manchuria as a desirable end in itself, and as a means of putting pressure on the Japanese in the south.

In any case, the vast majority of the Chinese public, in their obsession with anti-imperialism, seemed to want friendship with Soviet Russia even at some price. The liberal political scientist Ch'ien Tuan-sheng probably spoke for them when he wrote:

> Imperialism is our enemy. . . . Being dominated by Britain, Japan, America, etc., our most urgent task in foreign affairs is to destroy imperialism and free ourselves from its shackles. I have stated . . . that it is possible for Soviet Russia to turn imperialist, but I have not said she has. Besides, Soviet Russia is the enemy of Britain, Japan, and other imperialist powers. We need not be overly concerned about how much strength she actually possesses because, in our struggle against imperialism, her help will bring more advantages than disadvantages. Hence, each day that she opposes the principal imperialists, we should unite with her. We should even tolerate some small advantage that she takes of us.[27]

Thus, though not oblivious to the paradoxes of the Soviet posture, the centrality of anti-imperialism and Russia's position in that public concern, combined with the anti-government attitude to produce a tolerance of Soviet conduct and widen the gap between the public and the government.

The Janus-like figure of Russia became a deeply divisive issue in Chinese society in the 1920s. The question of friendship or enmity with her was to be debated again and again among Chinese policymakers and in Chinese society in later years.

Now, fifty years after conclusion of the first Sino-Soviet Treaty, those radical revolutionaries who had dismissed 'Red Imperialism' as an invention of the reactionaries in league with imperialism and as ideologically preposterous have coined the new term 'Socialist Imperialism'. Peking's early diplomacy with Moscow and its fruits are part of their inheritance. They voice grievances in much the same vein as the Peking government of the old days. Despite the attritions of history, some of the old issues seem remarkably alive. Once again, the Soviet position in Outer Mongolia and the presence of Soviet troops there constitute a major exacerbating factor. Though superseded by technological change, Amur River navigation is the subject of continuing discussion. Whereas in the past the Chinese communist leaders repeatedly hailed Soviet Russia as having signed the first, equal treaty with China—a fact that the Russians often quote to embarrass them—now, as if the scales have suddenly dropped from their eyes, they point to the fact that the provisions of that treaty have yet to be carried out. The key issue now concerns the boundaries between the two states which the Chinese maintain are still governed by unequal treaties. In this instance, the Chinese position tallies with the historical record. As already shown, the old treaties were declared, in a separate, secret protocol, to be inoperative, though not invalid. It was agreed to maintain the existing boundaries pending the conclusion of new treaties. This is one of many questions that the Russians have consigned to historical oblivion. Though under no illusion that any significant shift in the boundaries can ever be achieved with Moscow, the Peking leadership nevertheless has raised the question to maximum polemical advantage.

Notes

Introduction

1. Sino-Soviet relations of this period are the topic of two earlier studies, Allen S. Whiting, *Soviet Policies in China, 1917-1924* (New York, 1954) and Wang Yü-chün, *Chung-Su wai-chiao ti hsü-mo* (The first phase of Sino-Soviet diplomacy; Taipei, 1963). Whiting's volume has had the well-deserved reputation of an indispensable work. A fine model of scholarly analysis, it examines Soviet policies in China through policy debates in Moscow and traces Soviet diplomacy in Peking. The present book approaches the subject from the Chinese side and is therefore complementary to his. The use of Chinese official records will make it possible to substitute facts for conjecture and offer fresh interpretations, which will be noted in their appropriate places. Wang's book, on the other hand, draws on the same documentary records as mine but to a more limited extent. It is a chronicle of the Yurin, Paikes, and Joffe missions, covering the period 1920 to 1923, with extensive citations of documents. Its principal usefulness lies in reflecting the Nationalist Chinese perspective on the subject.

2. Whiting, *Soviet Policies in China*, p. 32.

3. Ibid., p. 249.

4. Ibid., p. 252.

5. The most significant work in this area is being done by Andrew Nathan; see his 'Factionalism in early republican China: the politics of the Peking government, 1918-1920', Ph.D. thesis, Department of Government, Harvard University, 1970.

I. North Manchuria on the Eve of the Russian Revolution

1. The best studies of the first phase of Russian expansion in Manchuria are Andrew Malozemoff, *Russian Far Eastern Policy, 1881-1904* (Berkeley, 1958), B.A. Romanov, *Rossiia v Manzhurii, 1892-1906* (Leningrad, 1928) and *Ocherki diplomaticheskoi istorii Russko-Iaponskoi Voiny, 1895-1907* (Mos-

cow, 1947). For the Sino-Japanese agreement concerning the Portsmouth Treaty, see John V.A. MacMurray, ed., *Treaties and Agreements with and concerning China, 1894-1919*, 2 vols. (New York, 1921), I, 549-53.

2. On the three Russo-Japanese conventions, see Ernest Batson Price, *The Russo-Japanese Treaties of 1907-1916 concerning Manchuria and Mongolia* (Baltimore, 1933). An excellent study based on Japanese official documents is Yoshimura Michiō, *Nihon to Roshiya* (Japan and Russia; Tokyo, 1968).

3. MacMurray, *Treaties and Agreements*, II, 1220-8.

4. Yoshimura, *Nihon to Roshiya*, pp. 292-4, 301-3, 311-16.

5. The most detailed and thoroughly documented account of the build-up of Russian interests in north Manchuria and their decline is Ishihara Shigetaka, comp., *Tō-Shi tetsudō o chūshin to suru Rō-Shi seiryoku no shōchō* (The rise and fall of Russian and Chinese influence on the Chinese Eastern Railway; Dairen, 1928). Less detailed and reflecting the official Russian point of view is the specially commissioned volume E. Kh. Nilus, *Istoricheskii obzor KVZhD, 1898-1923*, tom 1 (Harbin, 1923). An interesting personal account by the man most closely involved in the development of Russian interests is Dmitri L. Horvath, 'Memoirs', a manuscript in English deposited in the Hoover Library, Stanford University.

6. For the railway contract, see MacMurray, *Treaties and Agreements*, I, 74-5.

7. Horvath, 'Memoirs', Chap. I.

8. For the agreements on the expropriations of land, see MacMurray, *Treaties and Agreements*, I, 663-71; Nilus, *Istoricheskii obzor*, pp. 410-19.

9. Horvath, 'Memoirs', Chap. II; Ishihara, *Tō-Shi tetsudō*, Chap. I; Nilus, *Istoricheskii obzor*, Chap. XVIII.

10. Ishihara, *Tō-Shi tetsudō*, pp. 207-8; Nilus, *Istoricheskii obzor*, Chap. XIX.

11. MacMurray, *Treaties and Agreements*, I, 274-8, 321-4.

12. Ishihara, *Tō-Shi tetsudō*, pp. 195-206; Nilus, *Istoricheskii obzor*, Chap. XVII.

13. Nilus, *Istoricheskii obzor*, Chap. XXI.

14. MacMurray, *Treaties and Agreements*, II, 1185-6.

15. *COKH, Chung-tung t'ieh-lu, 1920* (Chinese Eastern Railway 1920), comp. T'ao Ying-hui et al. (Taipei, 1969), pp. 327-30, Doc. 424, Tung Shih-en to Wai-chiao Pu (hereafter abbrev. WCP), Sept. 20, 1920.

16. Horvath, 'Memoirs', Introduction.

II. The Harbin Soviet

1. Ishihara, *Tō-Shi tetsudō*, pp. 277ff.

2. *COKH, O cheng-pien yü i-pan chiao-she, 1917-1919* (Russian Revolution and general intercourse, 1917-1919), 2 vols., comp. Wang Yü-chün (Taipei, 1960), I, 85-6, Doc. 150, Kuo Tsung-hsi to WCP, Apr. 14, 1917.

3. The comparative strength in the Soviet was 80 moderates against 53 Bolsheviks, according to Seki Hiroharu, *Gendai Higashi Ajia kokusai kankyō no tanjō* (The birth of the international environment in contemporary East Asia; Tokyo, 1969), p. 77.

4. Ibid., p. 105, n.69.

5. *COKH, OCP 1917-1919*, I, 81, Doc. 139, Meng En-yuan and Kuo Tsung-hsi to Cabinet, Apr. 10, 1917; Ishihara, *Tō-Shi tetsudō*, pp. 395ff.

6. What follows is based partly on Seki's study of the events as found in his *Gendai Higashi Ajia*, pp. 21-194. Unlike Seki, who is interested in the Harbin Soviet as a whole, I focus attention primarily on Chinese official reactions, which may be more clearly delineated now than before by using recently available Chinese official documents.

7. *Papers Relating to the Foreign Relations of the United States, 1918, Russia*, 3 vols. (Washington, D.C., 1930-2), II, 2-4, Moser to Reinsch, Nov. 17, 1917.

8. A.N. Kheifets, *Sovetskaia Rossiia i sopredel'nye strany vostoka v gody grazhdanskoi voiny, 1918-1920* (Moscow, 1964), p. 320.

9. Seki, *Gendai Higashi Ajia*, pp. 52-5.

10. Ibid., pp. 70-3.

11. Ibid., pp. 73-7.

12. *COKH, Chung-tung t'ieh-lu, 1917-1919* (Chinese Eastern Railway, 1917-1919), 2 vols., Li Kuo-ch'i, comp. (Taipei, 1960), I, 6, Doc. 15, WCP to Meng En-yuan and Kuo Tsung-hsi, Dec. 7, 1917.

13. Kheifets, *Sovetskaia Rossiia*, p. 323.

14. Ibid., p. 324; Seki, *Gendai Higashi Ajia*, pp. 90-3.

15. Sonoda Ikki, *Chang Tso-lin* (Tokyo, 1923), pp. 373-88.

16. Ibid., Chaps. 2-4.

17. Ibid., Chaps. 5-6.

18. Ibid., pp. 145-52.

19. Ibid., pp. 153-63.

20. *COKH, CTTL 1917-1919*, I, 3, Doc. 8, WCP to Meng En-yuan and Kuo Tsung-hsi, Dec. 5, 1917; pp. 6-7, Doc. 16, WCP to Chang Tso-lin and Pao Kuei-ch'ing, Dec. 7, 1917.

21. Seki, *Gendai Higashi Ajia*, pp. 115, 120-1, 123-4.

22. Ibid., pp. 61-3, 114-16, 121-3.

23. *COKH, CTTL 1917-1919*, I, 11-12, Doc. 31, Meng En-yuan to WCP, Dec. 18, 1917.

24. Ibid., p. 14, Doc. 36, Meng En-yuan to WCP, Dec. 20, 1917.

25. Ibid., p. 16, Doc. 38, Ho Tsung-lien and Chang Tsung-ch'ang to WCP, Dec. 20, 1917; p. 19, Doc. 46, Meng En-yuan and Kuo Tsung-hsi to WCP, Dec. 24, 1917; p. 27, Doc. 64, Meng to WCP, Dec. 27, 1917.

26. *COKH, OCP 1917-1919*, I, 77-8, Doc. 132, Meng En-yuan and Kuo Tsung-hsi to Cabinet, Apr. 7, 1917; *COKH, CTTL 1917-1919*, I, 55, Doc. 29, Liu Ching-jen to WCP, Dec. 13, 1917; Seki, *Gendai Higashi Ajia*, p. 188.

27. *COKH, CTTL 1917-1919*, I, 43-5, Doc. 8, Communications Ministry to WCP, Jan. 3, 1918; pp. 117-18, Doc. 127, Kuo Tsung-hsi to WCP, Feb. 21, 1918.

28. Ibid., pp. 40-1, Doc. 4, Meng En-yuan to Cabinet, Jan. 1, 1918; pp. 45-7, Doc. 12, War Ministry to WCP, Jan. 7, 1918; p. 81, Doc. 68, Ch'en Lu-Kudashev conversation, Jan. 26, 1918; p. 85, Doc. 74, Meng En-yuan and Kuo Tsung-hsi to WCP, Jan. 26, 1918; pp. 57-8, Doc. 36, Meng and Kuo to WCP, Jan. 13, 1918.

29. *Dokumenty vneshnei politiki SSSR* (Moscow, 1957-   ), I, Doc. 26.

30. The legation's statement appeared in *Izvestiia*, Feb. 3, 1918; Kheifets, *Sovetskaia Rossiia*, p. 329.

31. Ibid., pp. 327-8.

32. *COKH, OCP 1917-1919*, I, 244-5, Doc. 79, Liu Ching-jen to WCP, Jan. 19, 1918; *COKH, CTTL 1917-1919*, I, 105-6, Doc. 110, Liu to WCP, Jan. 19, 1918.

33. *COKH, CTTL 1917-1919*, I, 86-7, Doc. 77, Liu Ching-jen to WCP, Jan. 26, 1918; *COKH, OCP 1917-1919*, I, 266-71, Doc. 126, Liu to WCP, Feb. 2, 1918.

34. George Alexander Lensen, *Japanese Recognition of the USSR:Soviet-Japanese Relations, 1921-1930* (Tokyo, 1970), pp. 6-7.

35. *COKH, CTTL 1917-1919*, I, 94, Doc. 90, Liu Ching-jen to WCP, Feb. 3, 1918; pp. 97-8, Doc. 95, Liu to WCP, Feb. 5, 1918; p. 98, Doc. 96, Liu to WCP, Feb. 5, 1918.

36. Kheifets, *Sovetskaia Rossiia*, pp. 332-4.

37. S.S. Khuseinov, 'Vmeshatel'stvo imperialisticheskikh derzhav v Sovetsko-Kitaiskie peregovory, 1917-1918', *Narody Azii i Afriki*, 5 (May, 1962), 83-91; Kheifets, *Sovetskaia Rossiia*, pp. 326ff.

38. *DVP*, I, 109-11, Doc. 71.

39. *Izvestiia*, July 5, 1918, p. 7.

III. China and the Siberian Intervention

1. The Allied Intervention in Siberia has been the subject of some of the best historical scholarship. To mention only recent studies, there are Morley, *The Japanese Thrust*; Hosoya Chihiro, *Siberia shuppei no shiteki kenkyū* (A historical study of the Siberian expedition; Tokyo, 1955); Kennan, *The Decision to Intervene* (Princeton, 1958); and Ullman, *Intervention and the War* and *Britain and the Russian Civil War* (Princeton, 1968). China played a puzzling but not insignificant role that has never been investigated. Seki's study of the negotiations for the Sino-Japanese joint defense agreement of May 1918 is concerned primarily with policymaking of the Terauchi Cabinet, though it sheds a great deal of light on the Chinese side as well. In this chapter, I am concerned with Chinese policymaking in Peking, work on which has been made possible by recently available Chinese official documents. Seki's study is found in his *Gendai Higashi Ajia*, pp. 197-395.

2. A succinct treatment of Japan's response to the October Revolution is found in Morley, *The Japanese Thrust*, Chap. III.

3. Seki, *Gendai Higashi Ajia*, pp. 285-8.

4. *COKH, CP*, p. 19, Doc. 26, WCP to Chang Tsung-hsiang, Feb. 22, 1918; *COKH, OCP 1917-1919*, I, 252-3, Doc. 97, Office of the President to WCP, Feb. 19, 1918.

5. On Lu Cheng-hsiang, see Howard L. Boorman, ed., *Biographical Dictionary of Republican China*, 4 vols. (New York, 1967-71), II, 441-4.

6. *COKH, OCP 1917-1919*, I, 264-5, Doc. 123, WCP motion, Feb. 27, 1918.

7. *FRUS, 1918, Russia*, II, 81-2, Morris to Secretary of State, Mar. 19, 1918; pp. 45-6, Secretary of State to the British ambassador, Feb. 13, 1918.

8. *COKH, TPPF 1917-1919*, I, 89, Doc. 39, Wellington Koo to WCP, Feb. 27, 1918.

9. *COKH, CP*, pp. 19-20, Doc. 29, Chang Tsung-hsiang to WCP, Feb. 23, 1918; p. 20, Doc. 30, Chang to WCP, Feb. 23, 1918.

10. Ibid., pp. 22-3, Doc. 37, Chang Tsung-hsiang to WCP, Feb. 26, 1918.

11. On May 23, several days after the negotiations were completed, Foreign Minister Lu Cheng-hsiang explained to the French minister Peking's rationale for concluding the pact. 'This government believes', he said, 'that in future when Japan should decide to dispatch troops to Siberia, it is bound to ask this country for passage through Chinese territory. Moreover, the disorders in Siberia will affect Chinese borders directly. Hence, it is felt wise to conclude an agreement for joint action'. *COKH, CP*, pp. 161-2, Doc. 318, Boppé-Lu conversation, May 23, 1918.

12. Seki, *Gendai Higashi Ajia*, p. 30; *COKH, CP*, p. 25, Doc. 45, WCP to Chang Tsung-hsiang, Mar. 2, 1918.

13. Morley, *The Japanese Thrust*, p. 119; *COKH, CP*, pp. 30-1, Doc. 61, Chang Tsung-hsiang to WCP, Mar. 8, 1918. The English text is derived from *Wai-chiao wen-tu* (Diplomatic documents; Peking: Ministry of Foreign Affairs, 1921), Sino-Japanese military agreements for joint defense, Doc. 10.

14. *COKH, CP*, pp. 32-3, Doc. 65, WCP to Chang Tsung-hsiang, Mar. 11, 1918.

15. Ibid., pp. 35-6, Doc. 71, Chang Tsung-hsiang to WCP, Mar. 12, 1918; pp. 37-8, Doc. 77, Chang to WCP, Mar. 13, 1918.

16. Ibid., pp. 40-1, Doc. 88, Chang Tsung-hsiang to WCP, Mar. 16, 1918.

17. Ibid., pp. 41-2, Doc. 89, WCP to Chang Tsung-hsiang, Mar. 17, 1918; *Wai-chiao wen-tu*, Doc. 21.

18. *COKH, CP*, p. 44, Doc. 98, Chang Tsung-hsiang to WCP, Mar. 19, 1918.

19. Ibid., p. 51, Doc. 116, Chang Tsung-hsiang to WCP, Mar. 25, 1918.

20. Morley, *The Japanese Thrust*, p. 120; Seki, *Gendai Higashi Ajia*, pp. 379ff; *COKH, CP*, p. 50, Doc. 113, Japanese Legation to WCP, Mar. 25, 1918.

21. The Japanese draft is given in Morley, *The Japanese Thrust*, pp. 162-4.

22. Seki, *Gendai Higashi Ajia*, p. 389; *COKH, CP*, p. 83, Doc. 198, Naval Ministry to WCP, Apr. 12, 1918.

23. This particular draft of the military agreement is not available but the naval draft, similar in format and approved by the Cabinet on May 2, is found in *COKH, CP*, pp. 131-3, Doc. 284, Naval Ministry to WCP, May 11, 1918.

24. Ibid., pp. 110-12, Doc. 249, Saitō-Lu Cheng-hsiang conversation, Apr. 17, 1918; pp. 129-30, Doc. 283, Yoshizawa-Lu Cheng-hsiang conversation, May 11, 1918.

25. Morley, *The Japanese Thrust*, pp. 188-9.

26. *COKH, CP*, pp. 165-7, Doc. 327, Cabinet Secretariat to WCP,

May 27, 1918; pp. 140-2, Doc. 292, Naval Ministry to WCP, May 14, 1918; p. 146, Doc. 302, WCP to Naval Ministry, May 17, 1918; pp. 171-4, Doc. 328, Naval Ministry to WCP, May 27, 1918.

27. Morley, *The Japanese Thrust*, pp. 101-6, 277-8.

28. Ibid., Chap. VII.

29. *COKH, TPPF 1917-1919*, I, 252-63, Doc. 318, WCP to Wellington Koo, July 1, 1918.

30. Kennan, *The Decision to Intervene*, Chaps. XV, XVII.

31. Ibid., pp. 396ff.

32. Ibid., Chaps. XII, XIII.

33. *COKH, CP*, p. 209, Doc. 407, WCP to Shih Chao-chi, July 20, 1918.

34. Ibid., pp. 211-12, Doc. 413, Hayashi-Liu Ts'ung-chieh conversation, July 20, 1918; p. 220, Doc. 434, Hayashi-Liu conversation, July 24, 1918; *FRUS, 1918, Russia*, II, 297-8, Polk to Morris, July 19, 1918; p. 298, MacMurray to Lansing, July 20, 1918; p. 299, MacMurray to Lansing, July 20, 1918; pp. 300-1, Morris to Lansing, July 23, 1918.

35. *COKH, CP*, p. 227, Doc. 447, Koo to WCP, July 29, 1918; p. 234, Doc. 463, Koo to WCP, Aug. 2, 1918; *FRUS, 1918, Russia*, II, 299-305, Long-Koo conversations on July 23, 25, and 26, 1918.

36. *FRUS, 1918, Russia*, II, 314, Polk to Morris, July 29, 1918; pp. 321-2, Morris to Secretary of State, Aug. 1, 1918.

37. *COKH, CP*, p. 323, Doc. 652, War Participation Bureau to WCP, Sept. 6, 1918; for the agreements mentioned, see MacMurray, *Treaties and Agreements*, II, 1434-40, 1445-52.

38. The Saitō-Tuan Chih-kuei letters are found in *COKH, CP*, pp. 348-54, Doc. 689, War Ministry to WCP, Sept. 23, 1918.

39. The Japanese maintained the premier's reply was sufficient approval for Japan's dispatch of troops, while Premier Tuan maintained his verbal reply was a 'casual and unspecific' remark only; *COKH, CP*, pp. 301-2, Doc. 611, Hayashi-Ch'en Lu conversation, Aug. 27, 1918.

40. Ibid., p. 299, Doc. 605, Hayashi-Liu Ts'ung-chieh conversation, of uncertain date.

41. *COKH, CTTL 1917-1919*, I, 180-5, Doc. 248, War Ministry to WCP, Sept. 6, 1918.

42. Ibid.

43. *FRUS, 1918, Russia*, II, 330, Morris to Secretary of State, Aug. 5, 1918; pp. 343-4, Morris to Secretary of State, Aug. 13, 1918.

44. Ibid., pp. 345-6, Ishii to Secretary of State, Aug. 14, 1918.

45. Ibid., pp. 334-5, MacMurray to Secretary of State, Aug. 8, 1918; pp. 348-9, MacMurray to Secretary of State, Aug. 15, 1918; p. 353, MacMurray to Secretary of State, Aug. 21, 1918; *COKH, CP*, p. 264, Doc. 532, WCP to Koo, Aug. 19, 1918.

46. *COKH, CP*, p. 294, Doc. 595, Chang Tsung-hsiang to WCP, Aug. 26, 1918.

47. Ibid., p. 304, Doc. 616, WCP to Koo, Aug. 29, 1918; p. 309, Doc. 622, WCP to Chang Tsung-hsiang, Aug. 30, 1918; *COKH, CTTL 1917-1919*, I, 180-5, Doc. 248, War Ministry to WCP, Sept. 6, 1918.

48. *COKH, CP*, p. 298, Doc. 603, Joint Commission of War Ministry and General Staff to WCP, Aug. 27, 1918; pp. 323-4, Doc. 652, Joint Commission to WCP, Sept. 6, 1918.

49. Ibid., p. 237, Doc. 469, Joint Commission of War Ministry and General Staff to Shao Heng-chün, Aug. 5, 1918.

50. *FRUS, 1918, Russia*, II, 391, Secretary of State to MacMurray, Sept. 25, 1918; p. 396, MacMurray to Secretary of State, Sept. 28, 1918; p. 462, Polk to Morris, Dec. 12, 1918; *COKH, CP*, p. 364, Doc. 700, WCP to MacMurray, Sept. 26, 1918; pp. 366-7, Doc. 704, MacMurray-Ch'en Lu conversation, Sept. 30, 1918.

51. *COKH, CTTL 1917-1919*, I, 185-6, Doc. 250, MacMurray-Ch'en Lu conversation, Sept., 1918; *FRUS, 1918, Russia*, III, 243-5, MacMurray to Secretary of State, Sept. 7, 1918.

52. *COKH, CTTL 1917-1919*, I, 261-2, Doc. 20, Liu Ching-jen to WCP, Jan. 16, 1919.

53. Ibid., p. 279, Doc. 57, WCP to Liu Ching-jen *et al.*, Jan. 26, 1919; p. 283, Doc. 65, Reinsch-Tiao Tso-ch'ien conversation, Jan. 27, 1919.

IV. Amur River Navigation

1. Lucian W. Pye, *Warlord Politics* (New York, 1971), pp. 151-2.

2. Biographies of Lu, Ch'en, Yen, and Koo are found in Boorman, *Biographical Dictionary of Republican China*, II, 441-4; I, 211-13, IV, 50-2; and II, 255-9.

3. Ishihara, *Tō-Shi tetsudō*, pp. 857-67; *COKH, TPPF 1917-1919*, II, 489, Doc. 58, Fu Chiang to WCP, May 5, 1919.

4. G.E.P. Hertslet, comp., *Treaties, etc. between Great Britain and China, and between China and Foreign Powers, etc.*, 2 vols. (3rd ed., London, 1908), I, 454-5, 461-2, 483-92.

5. *COKH, TPPF 1917-1919*, I, 46, Doc. 55, Kudashev to WCP, Oct. 26, 1917; see also items listed in ibid., subject index, p. 3.

6. Ibid., p. 161, Doc. 173, Pao Kuei-ch'ing to WCP, Aug. 12, 1918.

7. Ibid., pp. 193-4, Doc. 234, Cabinet to·WCP, May 11, 1918; p. 199, Doc. 244, Cabinet to WCP, May 17, 1918.

8. Ibid., pp. 187-8, Doc. 224, Pao Kuei-ch'ing to WCP, May 7, 1918; pp. 238-9, Doc. 301, Kudashev to WCP, June 22, 1918; pp. 374-5, Doc. 445, Wu P'ei-kuang and WCP, Aug. 12, 1918.

9. Ibid., II, 564, Doc. 186, Kudashev to WCP, Aug. 2, 1919; p. 520, Doc. 111, Pao Kuei-ch'ing to WCP, May 22, 1919; *Documents on British Foreign Policy*, ed. E.L. Woodward and Rohan Butler; 1st ser., Vol. 6 (London, 1956), p. 743, Doc. 510, Jordan to Curzon, Oct. 1, 1919.

10. *COKH, TPPF 1917-1919*, II, 461-2, Doc. 34, Statement of the War Ministry's views, Apr. 17, 1919; p. 500, Doc. 75, Pao Kuei-ch'ing to WCP, May 14, 1919; p. 462, Doc. 35, Statement of Naval Ministry's views, undated.

11. Ibid., II, 561, Doc. 181, Liu Ching-jen to Fan Ch'i-kuang, Aug. 1, 1919; p. 566, Doc. 190, Liu to Fan, Aug. 6, 1919; pp. 591-2, Doc. 207, Kudashev-Chu Ho-hsiang conversation, Aug. 15, 1919. The Russian fear was of course fully justified. Included among 'Principles of Japan's Russia

Policy, decided at the Cabinet Meeting of January 26, 1919' was one which stated that it should be Japan's objective to obtain 'free navigation on the Amur River'; see Hosoya Chihiro, 'Japanese Documents on the Siberian Intervention, 1917-1922', *Hitotsubashi Journal of Law and Politics*, I:1:52-3 (Tokyo, Apr. 1960).

12. *COKH, TPPF 1917-1919*, II, 568, Doc. 194, Liu Ching-jen to WCP, Aug. 9, 1919.

13. See items listed in ibid., I, subject index, pp. 83-5.

14. See items listed in ibid., I, subject index, pp. 87-91.

15. See items listed in ibid., I, subject index, pp. 66-9.

16. *COKH, Tung-pei pien-fang 1920* (Manchurian-border defense 1920), comp. T'ao Ying-hui *et al.* (Taipei, 1969), pp. 49-50, Doc. 63, Tung Shih-en to WCP, Mar. 15, 1920; p. 54, Doc. 71, Chi Ching to WCP, Mar. 30, 1920; p. 57, Doc. 76, WCP to Chi, Apr. 3, 1920.

17. Ibid., pp. 52-3, Doc. 68, Li Chia-ao to WCP, Mar. 15, 1920.

18. Ibid., pp. 142-3, Doc. 207, WCP to Communications Ministry, Nov. 6, 1920; pp. 147-9, Doc. 212, Naval Ministry to WCP, Oct. 22, 1920.

V. China's Recovery of Outer Mongolia

1. John K. Fairbank, Edwin O. Reischauer, and Albert M. Craig, *East Asia: The Modern Transformation* (Boston, 1965), pp. 786-8.

2. MacMurray, *Treaties and Agreements*, II, 992-6.

3. Ibid., II, 1178-80.

4. Ibid., II, 1066-7, and 1239-44.

5. Ibid., II, 1247-9.

6. Robert A. Rupen, *Mongols of the Twentieth Century* (Bloomington, 1964), p. 75.

7. Ibid., pp. 74-5.

8. *COKH, Wai Meng-ku, 1917-1919* (Outer Mongolia, 1917-1919), comp. Li Yü-shu (Taipei, 1959), p. 162, Doc. 14, WCP to Ch'en I, Feb. 14, 1918; p. 166, Doc. 26, Ch'en I to WCP, Feb. 23, 1918; pp. 166-7, Doc. 27, Ch'en I to WCP, Feb. 23, 1918.

9. Ibid., p. 178, Doc. 53, Chang Ch'ing-t'ung to WCP, Mar. 24, 1918; p. 183, Doc. 66, Ch'en I to WCP, Apr. 19, 1918; pp. 187-90, Doc. 73, Ch'en I to WCP, Apr. 28, 1918.

10. Ibid., p. 206, Doc. 88, En-hua to WCP, May 7, 1918; pp. 220-1, Doc. 111, Ch'en I to WCP, May 29, 1918; p. 235, Doc. 138, War Ministry to WCP, June 26, 1918.

11. Ibid., pp. 241-2, Doc. 151, Ch'en I to WCP, July 22, 1918; pp. 262, Doc. 191, Russian Legation to WCP, Sept. 6, 1918; p. 285, Doc. 223, Joint Commission of War Ministry and General Staff to WCP, Oct. 17, 1918.

12. Ibid., p. 305, Doc. 1, WCP to Ch'en I, Jan. 5, 1919; pp. 325-7, Doc. 35, Ch'en I to WCP, Feb. 22, 1919.

13. Ibid., p. 219, Doc. 108, Ch'en I to WCP, May 27, 1918; pp. 266-7, Doc. 195, Li Yüan to WCP, Sept. 13, 1918; p. 269, Doc. 200, Ch'en I to WCP, Sept. 19, 1918; pp. 279-80, Doc. 211, Ch'en I to WCP, Oct. 2, 1918.

14. Rupen, *Mongols*, p. 67.

15. *COKH, WMK 1917-1919*, pp. 308-10, Doc. 6, Ch'en I to WCP, Jan. 20, 1919.

16. Ibid., p. 321, Doc. 28, Ch'en I to WCP, Feb. 16, 1919; p. 389, Doc. 116, Ch'en I to WCP, Apr. 30, 1919.

17. Ibid., pp. 325-7, Doc. 35, Ch'en I to WCP, Feb. 22, 1919; p. 310, Doc. 8, WCP to Ch'en I, Jan. 21, 1919; pp. 336-7, Doc. 45, WCP to Cabinet Secretariat, Mar. 5, 1919.

18. Rupen, *Mongols*, pp. 129ff.

19. *COKH, WMK 1917-1919*, pp. 451, Doc. 237, Ch'en I to WCP, Aug. 4, 1919.

20. Ibid., p. 316, Doc. 16, WCP to War Ministry, Feb. 7, 1919.

21. S. Jagchid, 'Wai Meng-ku ti tu-li, tzu-chih, ho ch'e-chih' (Independence, autonomy, and cancellation of autonomy of Outer Mongolia) in Wu Hsiang-hsiang *et al.*, eds., *Chung-kuo hsien-tai shih ts'ung-k'an* (Collection of essays on modern Chinese history; Taipei, 1962)́, IV, 100, n. 82.

22. *COKH, WMK 1917-1919*, pp. 561-5, Doc. 373, Ch'en I to WCP, Oct. 17, 1919; pp. 342-3, Doc. 55, Ch'en I to WCP, Mar. 13, 1919.

23. Ibid., pp. 561-5, Doc. 373, Ch'en I to WCP, Oct. 17, 1919.

24. Ibid., p. 368, Doc. 92, Ch'en I to WCP, Apr. 10, 1918.

25. Ibid., pp. 386-7, Doc. 111, Ch'en I to WCP, Apr. 19, 1918; pp. 405-6, Doc. 143, Ch'en I to WCP, June 8, 1919.

26. Ibid., pp. 415-16, Doc. 159, Ch'en I to WCP, June 20, 1919; pp. 444-5, Doc. 220, Ch'en I to WCP, July 26, 1919.

27. Ibid., pp. 386-7, Doc. 111, Ch'en I to WCP, Apr. 19, 1919; pp. 419-20, Doc. 171, Ch'en I to WCP, June 29, 1919.

28. Ibid., p. 414, Doc. 158, Cabinet to WCP, June 19, 1919; p. 419, Doc. 170, Ch'en I to WCP, June 29, 1919; pp. 419-20, Doc. 171, Ch'en I to WCP, June 29, 1919.

29. Ibid., p. 365, Doc. 89, WCP to Lu Cheng-hsiang, Apr. 5, 1919; Li Chien-nung, *The Political History of China*, pp. 392-3.

30. *COKH, WMK 1917-1919*, pp. 380-4, Doc. 108, Cabinet to WCP, Apr. 17, 1919, enclosing Hsü Shu-cheng's proposals.

31. Ibid.

32. Ibid., p. 414, Doc. 158, Cabinet to WCP, June 19, 1919.

33. Ibid., p. 455, Doc. 243, Ch'en I to WCP, Aug. 7, 1919; p. 473, Doc. 267, Ch'en I to WCP, Aug. 21, 1919.

34. Examples are Tang, *Russian and Soviet Policy*, p. 359; Rupen, *Mongols*, p. 135; Li Yü-shu, *Wai Meng-ku ch'e-chih wen-t'i* (The issue over the cancellation of autonomy in Outer Mongolia; Taipei, 1961), Chap. 6; Weigh Ken Shen, *Russo-Chinese Diplomacy, 1689-1924* (Shanghai, 1928), p. 189.

35. For a detailed study of the Hara Cabinet's Siberian policy, see Hosoya Chichiro, 'Nihon to Kolchak seiken shōnin mondai' (Japan and the question of recognition of the Kolchak regime), *Hōgaku kenkyū*, 3:13-135 (Tokyo, 1961).

36. *Documents of British Foreign Policy*, VI, 671-5, Doc. 467, Robertson to Jordan, Aug. 8, 1919.

37. *Nihon gaikō bunshō, 1919*, I, 504-5, Doc. 480, Furusawa to Uchida,

May 15, 1919. Uchida's instruction was prompted by a conversation with the Russian minister in Tokyo, Krupensky, who implied that Japanese agents were behind Semenov's Pan-Mongolist activity. Ibid., pp. 501-2, Doc. 477, Uchida to Furusawa, Apr. 27, 1919.

38. *COKH, WMK 1917-1919*, pp. 451-2, Doc. 237, Ch'en I to WCP, Aug. 4, 1919; p. 502, Doc. 322, Kuo Tsung-hsi to WCP, Sept. 29, 1919.

39. Hosoya, 'Japanese Documents on the Siberian Intervention', p. 52.

40. *COKH, WMK 1917-1919*, pp. 308-10, Doc. 6, Ch'en I to WCP, Jan. 20, 1919; p. 449, Doc. 230, General Staff to WCP, July 30, 1919.

41. Ibid., pp. 461-2, Doc. 253, Ch'en I to WCP, Aug. 16, 1919.

42. Ibid., pp. 471-2, Doc. 262, WCP motion on Outer Mongolia to the Cabinet, Aug. 20, 1919; pp. 472-3, Doc. 265, WCP to Ch'en I, Aug. 21, 1919.

43. Ibid., p. 500, Doc. 318, Ch'en I to WCP, Sept. 27, 1919; pp. 516-18, Doc. 353, Ch'en I to WCP, Oct. 22, 1919.

44. Ibid., p. 506, Doc. 333, Ch'en I to WCP, Oct. 6, 1919; p. 514, Doc. 345, Cabinet to WCP, Oct. 15, 1919; p. 560, Doc. 371, Ch'en Lu to Tseng Chü-tseng, Oct. 28, 1919.

45. Ibid., p. 518, Doc. 356, WCP to T'ien Chung-yü, Oct. 22, 1919.

46. Ibid., pp. 578-9, Doc. 393, Jebtsun-damba to President Hsü Shih-ch'ang, Oct. 10, 1919.

47. Ibid., pp. 573-4, Doc. 386, Jebtsun-damba to President Hsü Shih-ch'ang, Oct. 24, 1919.

48. Ibid., p. 572, Doc. 382, Ch'en I to WCP, Oct. 31, 1919.

49. JMA, Japan, Defence Agency, War History Division, Taishō 10-nen (1921), Vol. 6, Diplomacy #4, Aoki shōshō ni kansuru ken (Concerning Lt General Aoki), Banzai to Tanaka, Aug. 6, 1919.

50. *COKH, WMK 1917-1919*, p. 514, Doc. 352, Ch'en I to WCP, Oct. 22, 1919; pp. 584-5, Doc. 404, Hsü Shu-cheng to WCP, Nov. 11, 1919.

51. Ibid., pp. 574-6, Doc. 387, Hsü Shu-cheng to WCP, Nov. 4, 1919; pp. 584-5, Doc. 404, Hsü to WCP, Nov. 11, 1919; pp. 586-7, Doc. 408, Hsü to WCP, Nov. 12, 1919.

52. Ibid., p. 576, Doc. 388, WCP to Ch'en I, Nov. 4, 1919; p. 607, Doc. 450, Hsü Shu-cheng to WCP, Nov. 13, 1919.

53. Ibid., pp. 601-2, Doc. 439, Presidential Decree, Nov. 22, 1919.

54. Ch'en Ch'ung-tsu, *Wai Meng chin-shih shih* (Recent history of Outer Mongolia; reprint, Taipei, 1965), Pt 3, pp. 17-19.

55. Ibid., Pt 3, pp. 12-15.

56. Ibid., Pt 2, pp. 114-31.

57. *COKH, WMK 1917-1919*, pp. 173-5, Doc. 45, En Hua to WCP, Mar. 19, 1918; pp. 298-9, Doc. 244, Ch'en I to WCP, Oct. 21, 1918; p. 442, Doc. 214, Yen Shih-ch'ao to WCP, July 22, 1919; pp. 450-1, Doc. 235, Yen to WCP, Aug. 2, 1919.

58. *COKH, Wai Meng-ku 1920* (Outer Mongolia, 1920), comp. T'ao Ying-hui *et al.* (Taipei, 1969), items listed in subject index, p. 1.

VI. Decolonization of North Manchuria

1. *Documents of British Foreign Policy*, VI, 644, Doc. 440, Jordan to

Curzon, July 24, 1919; pp. 647-8, Doc. 443, Jordan to Curzon, July 26; Sonoda, *Chang Tso-lin*, pp. 204-22.

2. *COKH, O cheng-pien 1920* (Russian Revolution, 1920) comp. T'ao Ying-hui *et al*. (Taipei, 1968), pp. 27-8, Doc. 54, Pao Kuei-ch'ing to Cabinet, Jan. 20, 1920.

3. *COKH, CTTL 1920*, p. 34, Doc. 56, Pao Kuei-ch'ing to Cabinet, Feb. 2, 1920; M. Kolobov, 'Bor'ba s Bol'shevikami na Dal'nem Vostoke', Chap. XXIII, pp. 7ff.

4. *COKH, OCP 1920*, p. 27, Doc. 53, Pao Kuei-ch'ing to WCP, Jan. 21, 1920; pp. 27-8, Doc. 54, Pao to Cabinet, Jan. 20, 1920; p. 37, Doc. 71, Chang Tso-lin to Cabinet, Jan. 24, 1920; *COKH, CTTL 1920*, p. 18, Doc. 31, WCP to Pao, Jan. 26, 1920.

5. *COKH, CTTL 1920*, pp. 108-9, Doc. 141, Communications Ministry to WCP, Mar. 18, 1920; p. 112, Doc. 146, Hsu Nai-lin to WCP, Mar. 23, 1920; *COKH, OCP 1920*, pp. 84-5, Doc. 154, Cabinet to WCP, Feb. 14, 1920.

6. *COKH, CTTL 1920*, p. 35, Doc. 58, Pao Kuei-ch'ing to WCP, Feb. 4, 1920.

7. Ibid., p. 35, Doc. 58, Pao Kuei-ch'ing to WCP, Feb. 4, 1920; pp. 38-9, Doc. 65, Cabinet to Pao, Feb. 7, 1920; pp. 43-4, Doc. 70, Pao to Cabinet, Feb. 13, 1920.

8. Ibid., p. 34, Doc. 56, Pao Kuei-ch'ing to Cabinet, Feb. 2, 1920.

9. Ibid., pp. 43-4, Doc. 70, Pao Kuei-ch'ing to Cabinet, Feb. 13, 1920.

10. Kolobov, 'Bor'ba s Bol'shevikami', Chap. XXIII, pp. 3-7; *COKH, CTTL 1920*, pp. 229-30, Doc. 286, Directorate of C.E.R. to WCP, June 5, 1920; *COKH, OCP 1920*, pp. 403-4, Doc. 634, Cabinet to WCP, June 11, 1920.

11. *COKH, CTTL 1920*, pp. 43-4, Doc. 70, Pao Kuei-ch'ing to Cabinet, Feb. 13, 1920.

12. *COKH, CTTL 1917-1919*, II, 713-17, Doc. 451, Pao Kuei-ch'ing to WCP, Sept. 9, 1919.

13. *COKH, CTTL 1920*, pp. 43-4, Doc. 70, Pao Kuei-ch'ing to Cabinet, Feb. 13, 1920; p. 52, Doc. 85, Pao to Cabinet, Feb. 26, 1920; p. 53, Doc. 87, Pao to Cabinet, Feb. 29, 1920.

14. *COKH, OCP 1920*, pp. 139-140, Doc. 245, Li Chia-ao to WCP, Mar. 12, 1920; pp. 154-6, Doc. 280, Directorate of C.E.R. to WCP, Mar. 15, 1920; *COKH, CTTL 1920*, p. 87, Doc. 106, Pao Kuei-ch'ing to Cabinet, Mar. 15, 1920.

15. *COKH, CTTL 1920*, p. 105, Doc. 137, Pao Kuei-ch'ing to Cabinet, Mar. 23, 1920; pp. 105-6, Doc. 138, Pao to Cabinet, Mar. 22, 1920; *COKH, OCP 1920*, p. 152, Doc. 274, Pao to Cabinet, Mar. 17, 1920.

16. Ibid., pp. 123-4, Doc. 162, Communications Ministry to WCP, Apr. 6, 1920; p. 135, Doc. 172, Chang Tso-lin to Cabinet, Apr. 10, 1920.

17. On Pimenov, see Kolobov, 'Bor'ba s Bol'shevikami', Chap. XXIII, pp. 20ff.

18. *COKH, CTTL 1920*, pp. 123-4, Doc. 162, Communications Ministry to WCP, Apr. 6, 1920; p. 149, Doc. 196, Pao Kuei-ch'ing to Cabinet, Apr. 22, 1920; Ishihara, *Tō-Shi tetsudō*, pp. 384-5.

19. Ishihara, *Tō-Shi tetsudō*, p. 385.

20. *COKH, CTTL 1920*, p. 128, Doc. 166, Boppé-Ch'en Lu conversation, Apr. 7, 1920; pp. 153-4, Doc. 205, Boppé to WCP, Apr. 26, 1920; pp. 212-14, Doc. 272, Communications Ministry to WCP, May 29, 1920.

21. Ibid., pp. 312-14, Doc. 406, Communications Ministry to WCP, Aug. 28, 1920.

22. The text of the Supplement is found in *China Year Book 1923*, ed. H.G. Woodhead (Tientsin and London, 1924), pp. 660-2.

23. *COKH, CTTL 1920*, pp. 370-1, Doc. 466, Sung Hsiao-lien to WCP, Nov. 13, 1920.

24. Ostroumov's stewardship of the Chinese Eastern Railway is fully discussed in Ishihara, *Tō-Shi tetsudō*, pp. 519-41.

25. *COKH, CTTL 1920*, pp. 322-5, Doc. 419, Communications Ministry to WCP, Sept. 11, 1920; pp. 325-6, Doc. 420, Cabinet to WCP, Sept. 15, 1920; pp. 379-86, Doc. 475, Hsia Wei-sung to WCP, Nov. 27, 1920.

26. Ibid., pp. 338-43, Doc. 441, Office of the President to WCP, Oct. 13, 1920; pp. 397-9, Doc. 493, Ministry of Interior to WCP, Dec. 15, 1920.

27. Ibid., p. 404, Doc. 505, Ministry of Interior to WCP, Dec. 30, 1920; Ishihara, *Tō-Shi tetsudō*, pp. 664-7.

28. *COKH, CTTL 1920*, p. 334, Doc. 431, Pao Kuei-ch'ing to Cabinet, Oct. 2, 1920; *China Year Book, 1921-1922*, pp. 626ff. and 638ff.

29. BGD, FO 405.228.9, Jordan to Curzon, Feb. 8, 1920.

30. BGD, FO 405.228.23, Curzon to Geddes, Feb. 28, 1920; USDS 861.77/1493, Davis to Secretary of State, Apr. 28, 1920; USDS 861.77/1534, Davis to Secretary of State, May 22, 1920.

31. USDS 893.51/2773, Tenney to Secretary of State, Apr. 15, 1920; USDS 893.51/2788, Secretary of State to Tenney, Apr. 22, 1920; USDS 861.77/1534, Davis to Secretary of State, May 22, 1920.

32. BGD, FO 405.228.43, Eliot to Curzon, June 14, 1920.

33. *COKH, CTTL 1920*, pp. 322-5, Doc. 419, Communications Ministry to WCP, Sept. 11, 1920.

34. Ibid., p. 336, Doc. 437, Yen-British chargé conversation, Oct. 6, 1920; pp. 336-7, Doc. 438, Yen-Crane conversation, Oct. 7, 1920.

VII. Extraterritoriality and Concession Territories

1. *COKH, OCP 1917-1919*, I, items listed in subject index, pp. 23, 60-4; *China Year Book, 1921-1922*, pp. 624-5.

2. *COKH, OCP 1920*, pp. 29-30, Doc. 57, Cabinet to WCP, Jan. 23, 1920; *COKH, CTTL 1920*, pp. 51-2, Doc. 84, Cabinet to WCP, Feb. 26, 1920.

3. *COKH, T'ing-chih O shih-ling tai-yü* (Discontinuation of relations with Russian minister and consuls), comp. T'ao Ying-hui et al. (Taipei, 1968), pp. 2-5, Doc. 5, Minutes of 6th meeting of the Committee for the Study of Russian Treaties, Aug. 24, 1920; pp. 7-11, Doc. 9, Minutes of meeting of Wai-chiao Pu councillors and department heads, Aug. 30, 1920.

4. Ibid., p. 1, Doc. 2, WCP to Chinese ministers in Britain, France,

USA, Italy, Belgium, and Holland, Aug. 19, 1920; pp. 15-16, Doc. 21, WCP to Chang Tso-lin, Sept. 2, 1920.

5. Ibid., pp. 2-5, Doc. 5, Minutes of 6th meeting of the Comimittee for the Study of Russian Treaties, Aug. 24, 1920.

6. For the Kalmykov episode, see *COKH, OCP 1920*, items listed in subject index, pp. 29-36.

7. *COKH, TCTY*, p. 13, Doc. 14, WCP memorandum on the Russian minister and consuls, Sept. 2, 1920.

8. Ibid., p. 12, Doc. 11, WCP to Chang Tso-lin, Sept. 1, 1920; p. 14, Doc. 15, Chang Tso-lin to WCP, Sept. 3, 1920.

9. *China Year Book, 1921-1922*, p. 625.

10. *COKH, TCTY*, p. 39, Doc. 50, WCP to President, Sept. 23, 1920; pp. 39-40, Doc. 51, Presidential Decree, Sept. 23, 1920; *China Year Book, 1921-1922*, p. 626.

11. *COKH, TCTY*, pp. 44-5, Doc. 64, WCP to all Chinese ministers and consuls, Sept. 24, 1920.

12. Wesley R. Fishel, *The End of Extraterritoriality in China* (Berkeley, 1952), p. 35. Chap. II gives an excellent account of the early effort of the Chinese to abolish extraterritoriality.

13. *COKH, TCTY*, pp. 2-5, Doc. 5, Minutes of 6th meeting of the Committee for the Study of Russian Treaties, Aug. 24, 1920.

14. *China Year Book, 1921-1922*, p. 622.

15. *COKH, TCTY*, pp. 57-9, Doc. 86, Yen-Crane conversation, Sept. 24, 1920; pp. 76-8, Doc. 132, Yen-Clive conversation, Sept. 29, 1920; pp. 89-90, Doc. 155, WCP to Wellington Koo, Oct. 7, 1920.

16. *China Year Book, 1921-1922*, pp. 628-9; *COKH, TCTY*, p. 94, Doc. 170, Dean of Diplomatic Body to WCP, Oct. 11, 1920; p. 130, Doc. 232, WCP to Dean of Diplomatic Body, Oct. 22, 1920.

17. *COKH, TCTY*, p. 96, Doc. 172, Cabinet to WCP, Oct. 6, 1920; *China Year Book, 1921-1922*, pp. 644-5.

18. *China Year Book, 1921-1922*, p. 637.

19. Ibid., pp. 645-6; *COKH, TCTY*, pp. 186-7, Doc. 298, Yen-Clive conversation, Nov. 10, 1920; p. 191, Doc. 305, WCP to Hsu Yüan, Nov. 18, 1920.

20. *COKH, TCTY*, pp. 66-7, Doc. 105, Yen-Boppé conversation, Sept. 25, 1920.

21. Ibid., pp. 18-28, Doc. 31, Huang Jung-liang to WCP, Sept. 11, 1920; p. 29, Doc. 35, Wu Chung-hsien to WCP, Sept. 13, 1920.

22. Ibid., pp. 35-8, Doc. 47, Ministry of Interior to WCP, Sept. 23, 1920; pp. 49-50, Doc. 76, Ministry of Interior to WCP, Sept. 25, 1920; pp. 62-3, Doc. 95, WCP to Ministry of Interior, Sept. 29, 1920.

23. Ibid., p. 45, Doc. 66, Huang Jung-liang to WCP, Sept. 25, 1920.

24. Ibid., pp. 96-8, Doc. 174, Huang Jung-liang to WCP, Oct. 7, 1920; pp. 85-6, Doc. 147, Crane to WCP, Oct. 5, 1920; pp. 116-18, Doc. 204, Huang to WCP, Oct. 12, 1920; p. 129, Doc. 230, WCP to Huang, Oct. 22, 1920; *China Year Book, 1921-1922*, pp. 635, 646.

25. *China Year Book, 1921-1922*, p. 646.

VIII. The Karakhan Manifestoes

1. For a general characterization of Soviet foreign policy of 1919, see E.H. Carr, *The Bolshevik Revolution, 1917-1923*, 3 vols. (London, 1950-3; reprint, Harmondsworth, 1966), III, Chap. 23.

2. Allen S. Whiting, 'The Soviet Offer to China of 1919', *Far Eastern Quarterly*, X:355-64; *Soviet Policies in China* (New York, 1954), Chap. II.

3. M.S. Kapitsa, *Sovetsko-Kitaiskie Otnosheniia* (Moscow, 1958), p. 35.

4. Cited in N.A. Popov, *Oni s nami srazhalis' za vlast' sovetov* (Leningrad, 1959), pp. 180-1.

5. *Pravda*, Nov. 6, 1918, p. 3, cited in Whiting, *Soviet Policies in China*, p. 107.

6. *Izvestiia*, Sept. 14, 1919, p. 2, cited in Whiting, *Soviet Policies in China*, p. 38.

7. 'Resolutions passed by the Communist Mussulmans of Turkestan, telegram from Tashkent to Zinoviev', *Communist International*, 5:60 (Sept. 1919).

8. Kapitsa, *Sovetsko-Kitaiskie Otnosheniia*, p. 35; Vilensky, 'Dal'nevostochnyi uzel', *Vestnik N.K.I.D.*, 2:20-6 (Aug. 13, 1919).

9. V.D. Vilensky, *Kitai i Sovetskaia Rossiia* (Moscow, 1919), p. 14.

10. The Peking government did not remain ignorant of the Karakhan Manifesto for long. The text as it appeared in the Soviet press on August 26 was soon picked up by the Japanese in Paris. On September 12, Major General Tanaka, the military attaché of the Japanese embassy in London, then visiting Paris, forwarded a copy of the gist of the document to the Japanese adviser to the Chinese president, Higashi Otohiko. Tanaka advised that the Chinese government be told of the Soviet document and warned that the Bolsheviks were paying special attention to China, 'seeking to plunge China into the whirlpool of social disorders'. He recommended a strict investigation of Bolshevik subversive activities in China. Tanaka's communication is found in *Shun-t'ien shih-pao (Shun-t'ien daily)*, Oct. 5, 1919, p. 7.

11. Whiting, *Soviet Policies in China*, pp. 32-3.

12. Ibid., p. 32.

13. V.D. Vilensky, *Za velikoi Kitaiskoi stenoi* (Moscow, 1923), p. 6.

14. Trotsky Papers, T444. Houghton Library, Harvard University.

15. Trotsky Papers, T446. As early as December 15, 1919, Lenin had warned the Omsk Revolutionary Military Council: 'Remember, it is a crime to go excessively far into the East'. Cited in M.A. Persits, *Dal'nevostochnaia Respublika i Kitai* (Moscow, 1962), p. 28.

16. White, *The Siberian Intervention*, pp. 366-8.

17. Persits, *Dal'nevostochnaia Respublika*, p. 33.

18. P.S. Parfenov-Altaiskii, *Bor'ba za Dal'nii Vostok, 1920-1922*, (Moscow, 1928), p. 69.

19. Cited in Lensen, *Japanese Recognition*, p. 7.

20. *Documents of British Foreign Policy*, VI, 1055-6, Doc. 790, Hodgson to Curzon, Mar. 23, 1920.

21. *COKH, O tui-hua wai-chiao shih-t'an* (Preliminary Soviet diplomatic feelers to China), comp. T'ao Ying-hui *et al*. (Taipei, 1968), p. 18, Doc. 34, 'Letter from the Plenipotentiary of Siberia and Far East to the Chinese Consul General at Irkutsk, brought back by Consul Wei Po', Apr. 9, 1920.

22. Leong Sow-Theng, *Sino-Soviet Relations: The first phase, 1917-1920* (Canberra, 1971), p. 27, n. 25.

23. *COKH, WCST*, pp. 15-16, Doc. 30, Cabinet to WCP, Apr. 2, 1920. Kushnarev is identified in Persits, *Dal'nevostochnaia Respublika*, p. 15.

24. *COKH, WCST*, p. 11, Doc. 23, Shao Heng-chün to WCP, Apr. 1, 1920.

25. *Shun-t'ien shih-pao*, Mar. 25, 1920, carries a relay from Vladivostok.

26. *COKH, OCP 1920*, p. 120, Doc. 208, WCP to Shih Chao-chi, Mar. 3, 1920.

27. The Japanese government was fully apprised of these developments by Minister Obata Yūkichi and instructed him to act in concert with the Allied ministers in Peking; see Japanese Foreign Ministry Archives, MT 16324.16/1594-1595, Obata to Uchida, Dec. 20, 1919; MT 16324.16/1695-1698, Uchida to Obata, Dec. 31, 1919; MT 16324.16/1808-1810, Obata to Uchida, Jan. 21, 1920.

28. *COKH, OCP 1917-1919*, II, 578-81, Doc. 1006, Cabinet to WCP, Nov. 14, 1919; pp. 635-6, Doc. 1097, President to WCP, Dec. 10, 1919.

29. Ibid., p. 640, Doc. 1104, Cabinet to WCP, Dec. 15, 1919.

30. *COKH, OCP 1920*, p. 127, Doc. 221, Cabinet to WCP, Mar. 7, 1920. The Wai-chiao Pu's three-point motion cannot be found, but from other documents it is clear that the proposal for *de facto* intercourse was included. COKH, *I-pan chiao-she* (General intercourse), comp. T'ao Ying-hui *et al*. (Taipei, 1968), p. 82, Doc. 123, Li Chia-ao to WCP, Mar. 30, 1920. The decision for Chinese troops to be withdrawn was made in March by Tuan Ch'i-jui's Border Defence Bureau 'with a view to obviating Bolshevik suspicion of China's intentions'. The evacuation was completed in May. In Tuan's view, China's withdrawal automatically caused the Sino-Japanese military pact to lapse. *COKH, OCP 1920*, pp. 131-2, Doc. 230, Li Chia-ao to WCP, Mar. 9, 1920; p. 294, Doc. 473, Border Defence Bureau to WCP, May 10, 1920; *COKH, CTTL 1920*, pp. 154-6, Doc. 207, Cabinet to WCP, Apr. 28, 1920, enclosing views of the Border Defence Bureau.

31. *COKH, WCST*, pp. 7-8, Doc. 13, Cabinet to WCP, Mar. 26, 1920.

32. Ibid., pp. 13-14, Doc. 26, Shao Heng-chün to WCP, Apr. 2, 1920.

33. Leong, *Sino-Soviet Relations*, pp. 7-9.

34. Ibid., p. 9.

35. Ibid.

36. Ibid., pp. 12-13; *COKH, CTTL 1920*, pp. 130-4, Doc. 169, Li Chia-ao to WCP, Apr. 10, 1920.

37. *COKH, CTTL 1920*, pp. 125-6, Doc. 164, Cabinet to WCP, Apr. 6, 1920.

38. Cited in Leong, *Sino-Soviet Relations*, p. 13.

39. Ibid., p. 11.

40. Ibid., p. 13.

41. Ibid., pp. 13-14.
42. Ibid., p. 14.
43. Ibid., p. 15.
44. Ibid., pp. 29-30, n. 50.
45. Ibid., p. 16.
46. Ibid., pp. 16-19.
47. WCPA, P1783/644, War Ministry to WCP, Jan. 17, 1921; the Russian text is found in *Sovetsko-Kitaiskie Otnosheniia 1917-1957: Sbornik documentov* (Moscow, 1959), pp. 51-3, Doc. 15.
48. WCPA, UE/- , Chang Ssu-lin's memorandum, recalling conversations with Karakhan, dated early 1923.
49. Persits, *Dal'nevostochnaia Respublika*, pp. 217-19.
50. *COKH, IPCS*, items listed in subject index, pp. 2-8, 13-19, 21-2.
51. Ibid., items listed in subject index, pp. 8-13.
52. Persits, *Dal'nevostochnaia Respublika*, pp. 40-3.
53. *COKH, WCST*, items listed in subject index, pp. 6-8.
54. Ibid., items listed in subject index, p. 8.
55. Ibid., pp. 70-1, Doc. 109, Simpson's views, July 31, 1920.
56. Ibid., p. 78, Doc. 120, Boppé-Ch'en Lu conversation, Aug. 13, 1920; pp. 84-6, Doc. 133, Crane-Ch'en conversation, Sept. 18, 1920.
57. Ibid., p. 89, Doc. 142, Memorandum of the WCP political affairs department, Sept. 2, 1920; *COKH, TCTY*, pp. 2-5, Doc. 5, Minutes of 6th meeting of the Committee for the Study of Russian Treaties.
58. *COKH, WCST*, pp. 94-6, Doc. 155, Yurin-Chang Tsu-shen conversation, Sept. 10, 1920.
59. BGD, FO 405.228.111, Clive to Curzon, Sept. 20, 1920, recounting a conversation with Obata.
60. *COKH, TCTY*, pp. 73-4, Doc. 125, Wellington Koo to WCP, Oct. 1, 1920.
61. *FRUS 1920*, I, 768-70, Colby to Crane, Oct. 2, 1920.
62. BGD, FO 405.228.118, Curzon to Clive, Sept. 25, 1920; FO 405.225.122, Clive to Curzon, Oct. 2, 1920; *COKH, TCTY*, pp. 76-8, Doc. 132, Clive-Yen Hui-ch'ing conversation, Sept. 29, 1920.
63. Carr, *The Bolshevik Revolution*, III, 167-9.
64. BGD, FO 405.228.149, Clive to Curzon, Oct. 15, 1920.
65. *COKH, WCST*, pp. 126-9, Doc. 189, Yurin to Yen Hui-ch'ing, Nov. 2, 1920; pp. 132-4, Doc. 194, Kazanin-Shih Chao-tseng conversation, Nov. 18, 1920.
66. Ibid., items listed in subject index, pp. 9-12.
67. *FRUS 1920*, I, 779, Crane to Secretary of State, Nov. 26, 1920.
68. Persits, *Dal'nevostochnaia Respublika*, pp. 137-9.
69. *COKH, WCST*, pp. 143-5, Doc. 201, Yurin-Liu Ching-jen conversation, Nov. 30, 1920; p. 149, Doc. 206, Yurin to Yen Hui-ch'ing, Dec. 13, 1920; pp. 146-9, Doc. 205, WCP to Yurin, Dec. 13, 1920.
70. WCPA, P2452/- , Yurin to Yen, Feb. 2, 1921.
71. Japanese Foreign Ministry Archives, MT 16324.4/80-81, Obata to Uchida, Jan. 31, 1921.
72. BGD, FO 405.231.16, Alston to Curzon, Feb. 11, 1921.

IX. China's Loss of Outer Mongolia

1. A.N. Kheifets, *Sovetskaia Diplomatiia i narody vostoka*, *1921-1927* (Moscow, 1968), Chap. 1.

2. For an opposite view, see Murphy, *Soviet Mongolia,* Chaps. 1-2.

3. USDS 893.00/3555, Crane to Secretary of State, Sept. 9, 1920; Jagchid, 'Wai Meng-ku', pp. 133-4.

4. *COKH, WMK 1920*, items listed in subject index, pp. 3-4.

5. The statutes are given with comments in Pi Kuei-fang, *Wai Meng chiao-she shih-mo chi* (An account of negotiations concerning Outer Mongolia; Peking, 1928), pp. 62-70.

6. JMA, T1062 (Reel 117, F29274-87), Isomura to Yamanashi, May 5, 1921; see also T1061 (Reel 117, F29259-73).

7. *COKH, WMK 1920*, p. 60, Doc. 85, Chang Tso-lin to Cabinet, Oct. 28, 1920; Sonoda, *Chang Tso-lin*, pp. 328-31.

8. Pi, *Wai Meng chiao-she*, pp. 72-4.

9. Ibid., p. 72; Sonoda, *Chang Tso-lin*, pp. 304-25, 348.

10. Same as note 6 above; see also JMA, Japan, Defence Agency, War History Division, Taishō 10-nen (1921), Miscellanies #81, Higashi to Tanaka, May 5, 1921.

11. JMA, T544 (Reel 101), F07396-9, Yamanashi to Banzai, Apr. 1, 1921.

12. Rupen, *Twentieth Century Mongols*, pp. 143-4.

13. Ibid., pp. 136ff.

14. WCPA, P2509/- , Shen Ts'ung-hsun to WCP, July 28, 1921, enclosure.

15. Cited in Whiting, *Soviet Policies in China*, pp. 168-9.

16. These two notes are filed in WCPA, P2534/4945 and P2534/8610, respectively.

17. *COKH, IPCS*, p. 319, Doc. 489, Shih Chao-chi to WCP, Nov. 15, 1920.

18. WCPA, P2534/7851, Cabinet to WCP, Dec. 24, 1920; P1845/3036, WCP to Ch'en I, Dec. 24, 1920; P1845/3037, WCP to Shih Chao-chi, Dec. 24, 1920. The Chinese records shed no light whatsoever on the Soviet claim that local Chinese commanders and officials had appealed to Soviet authorities for military assistance.

19. For example, see Kapitsa, *Sovetsko-Kitaiskie Otnosheniia*, p. 65.

20. WCPA, P2315/- , Ch'en I to Cabinet, Mar. 1, 1921.

21. WCPA, P2315/- , Cabinet to Ch'en I, Mar. 3, 1921.

22. A detailed eye-witness account of the expulsion of the Chinese from Mai-mai-ch'eng is found in WCPA, P2305/- , Li Yüan to the President, exact date not given but sometime in March 1921.

23. WCPA, P2428/543, Cabinet to WCP, Apr. 12, 1921, enclosing Ch'en I's report to Cabinet, Apr. 7.

24. WCPA, P2563/- , Koo to WCP, May 5, 1921.

25. WCPA, P2563/- , Memorandum on the Mongolian question, prepared by the Committee on Russian Affairs for submission to Cabinet, May

12, 1921; P2564/824, Cabinet to WCP, May 17, 1921, giving approval to memorandum.
26. Hoover Library, Stanford University, Vw Russia G394, Dal'buro to the Central Committee, RCP, Apr. 11, 1921; Vw Russia G394, Narkomindel of Far Eastern Republic to Narkomindel of Soviet Republic, May 6, 1921. The origins of these documents are not clear.
27. Kheifets, *Sovetskaia Diplomatiia*, pp. 23–30.
28. WCPA, P2315/- , Chicherin to WCP, June 15, 1921, rec'd via London on June 25.
29. WCPA, P2428/1254, WCP to Chicherin, June 30, 1921.
30. WCPA, UC/- , Chicherin to WCP, June 25, 1921.
31. WCPA, P2563/- , Premier Chin Yün-p'eng's comments on Chicherin's note of June 25, 1921.
32. Pye, *Warlord Politics*, pp. 147–8; Sonoda, *Chang Tso-lin*, pp. 266–82.
33. Sonoda, *Chang Tso-lin*, Chap. 14.
34. WCPA, P2315/- , Chang Tso-lin to Cabinet, Sept. 5, 1921; Li, *The political history of China*, pp. 405–8, 415–16; Sonoda, *Chang Tso-lin*, Chap. 15.

X. The Yurin and Paikes Missions

1. WCPA, P2519/- , Communications Ministry to WCP, Jan. 6, 1921.
2. WCPA, P2509/- , Yurin-Yen Hui-ch'ing conversation, May 13, 1921; P2430/1464, WCP to Wellington Koo, June 13, 1921.
3. Persits, *Dal'nevostochnaia Respublika*, p. 166.
4. Ibid., pp. 151–2; WCPA, P2509/1720, Shen Ts'ung-hsun to WCP, June 25, 1921.
5. WCPA, P1233/- , Kazanin-Yen Hui-ch'ing conversation, July 8, 1921.
6. JMA, T546 (Reel 101, FO 7474–7498), Gunji kyōtei haishi ni kansuru ken (Abrogation of the Sino-Japanese military agreement).
7. The Japanese military attaché in Peking, Higashi Otohiko, argues quite plausibly that Japan's military occupation of north Manchuria was one reason for Soviet military intervention in Outer Mongolia; see JMA, Japan, Defence Agency, War History Division, Taishō 10-nen (1921), Miscellanies #83, Higashi's China Report, July 26, 1921.
8. JMA, Japan, Defence Agency, War History Division, Taishō 10-nen (1921), Vol. VI, Diplomacy #5.
9. WCPA, P2509/- , Chang Tso-lin to Cabinet, July 24, 1921; P2432/- , Yurin-Yen Hui-ch'ing conversation, July 27, 1921; P2434/1422, Cabinet to Chang, July 28, 1921.
10. USDS 893.00/4114, Schurman to Secretary of State, Sept. 16, 1921.
11. Ibid.
12. WCPA, P2315/- , Chang Tso-lin to Cabinet, Sept. 5, 1921.
13. WCPA, P2428/382, WCP to Chang Tso-lin, Aug. 4, 1921.
14. Lensen, *Japanese Recognition of the U.S.S.R.*, Chap. 1.
15. WCPA, P2432/- , Yurin-Yen Hui-ch'ing conversations on Oct. 3, 4, 5, 1921.
16. WCPA, P1233/4430, Shen Ts'ung-hsun to WCP, Nov. 5, 1921.
17. USDS 861.77/2382, Warren to Hughes, Jan. 17, 1922.

18. WCPA, P2519/- , Paikes-Yen Hui-ch'ing conversation, Jan. 9, 1922.

19. The American official was told the Far Eastern Republic also wanted complete control and administration to be vested in Soviet Russia and China and the railway to be guarded by troops which these countries approved; see USDS 861.77/2382, Warren to Hughes, Jan. 17, 1922.

20. WCPA, P1233/989, Communications Ministry to WCP, Nov. 24, 1921.

21. WCPA, P1233/3835, WCP to Communications Ministry, Nov. 10, 1921; P1233/601, Communications Ministry to WCP, Nov. 15, 1921.

22. JMA, T551 (Reel 101 FO 7521-7529), Nagao to Tanaka, Dec. 16, 1920.

23. WCPA P1233/1093, Chang Tso-lin to Yen Hui-ch'ing, Oct. 12, 1921; UF/- , Yen to Chang, Oct. 22, 1921; P1233/4630, Hsü T'ung-hsin to Yen, Nov. 20, 1921; P1233/881, Hsü to Yen, Nov. 22, 1921; P1233/4596, Chang to Yen, Nov. 18, 1921.

24. WCPA, P2314/- , Chang Tso-lin to WCP, Oct. 11, 1921; UF/- , WCP to Chang, Oct. 22, 1921; UF/- , WCP motion on Outer Mongolia, Nov. 1, 1921.

25. WCPA, P2654/781, Far Eastern Republic mission to WCP, Nov. 19, 1921.

26. It is not improbable that Yurin was insincere all along and acted out of personal vengeance towards Foreign Minister Yen for a fruitless mission, and especially for the diplomatic pouch incident which reportedly cost Yurin his career. Said to have been upbraided by Soviet leaders for his failure, Yurin was found in early 1922 living in obscurity in Moscow, ignored by the Narkomindel. WCPA, P2705/1231, Wu Chun-sheng to WCP, Oct. 25, 1921; Yu-che (pseud. Huang Shih-lung), *Hsin-O hui-hsiang lu* (Recollections on new Russia; Peking, 1925), p. 101.

27. The text is found in WCPA, P2301/498, Shen Ts'ung-hsun to WCP, Feb. 21, 1922.

28. WCPA, P2426/- , Paikes-Yen Hui-ch'ing conversation, Dec. 16, 1921; UD/428, Paikes-Yen conversation, Jan. 12, 1922; P2314/- , Li Yüan to WCP, Jan. 14, 1922.

29. WCPA, P2314/- , Cabinet to WCP, Jan. 18, 1922.

30. WCPA, P2301/- , Li Yüan to Cabinet, Jan. 13, 1922.

31. WCPA, P2315/- , Chang Tso-lin to WCP, Apr. 12, 1922.

32. The American consul in Kalgan, Samuel Sokobin, who was detailed to Urga to observe the situation, reported on March 28 that Mongolian politics was divided into three currents: (a) establishment of an independent Mongolian government, absolutely free from all interference; (b) a government in which Russian advisers would participate; and (c) a Mongolian government with some relationship with China. USDS 893.00/4347, Sokobin to Secretary of State, Mar. 28, 1922.

33. WCPA, UF/56, Cabinet to WCP, Mar. 2, 1922.

34. WCPA, P2314/- , Li Yüan to Liu Ching-jen, June 12, 1922, enclosure.

35. Cf. Whiting, *Soviet Policies in China*, pp. 176-8. Contrary to Whit-

ing, no opportunity existed for a Sino-Soviet rapprochement at this time, nor did Paikes's 'blunder' of withholding the treaty from the Chinese destroy that opportunity. Paikes did not hastily leave Peking but remained until late in August, after Joffe's arrival.

36. WCPA, P2547/146, Cabinet to WCP, Nov. 23, 1921, enclosing a memo from the President's office concerning Reuters's Nov. 15 wire about the treaty and urging ascertainment of the truth. P2314/- , Cabinet to WCP, Jan. 18, 1922; P1845/- , Shen Ts'ung-hsun to WCP, Feb. 17, 1922; P2301/498, Shen to WCP, Feb. 21, enclosing the text of the Soviet-Mongol Agreement.

37. WCPA, P2314/308, Li Yüan to WCP, Apr. 8, 1922.

38. WCPA, UF/3, Li Yüan to WCP, May 1, 1922.

39. WCPA, P2314/- , WCP to Soviet mission, May 1, 1922.

40. WCPA, P2301/- , Paikes-Li Yüan conversation, June 29, 1922.

41. WCPA, P2314/188, Li Yüan to WCP, July 5, 1922; P2314/- , Li to Cabinet, July 5, 1922.

42. WCPA, P2423/4, Chinese Legation (Berlin) to WCP, Oct. 1, 1922.

43. A.E. Khodorov, 'Manchzhurskaia problema', *Novyi Vostok*, 2:560-7 (1922).

44. BGD, FO 405.236.155, Balfour to Lloyd George, Feb. 4, 1922.

45. WCPA, P2519/- , Communications Ministry to WCP, Aug. 1, 1922.

46. WCPA, P2451/- , Minutes of Committee on Russian Affairs, Aug. 21, 1922; see also P2301/- , Minutes of Committee on Russian Affairs, July 17, 1922.

XI. The Joffe Mission

1. Lensen, *Japanese Recognition of the U.S.S.R.*, p. 63.

2. WCPA, P2314/- , Joffe-Koo conversation, Aug. 15, 1922.

3. WCPA, P2418/533, Joffe-Koo conversation, Aug. 23, 1922.

4. WCPA, P2423/- , Joffe to Koo, Aug. 25, 1922.

5. WCPA, P2423/116, Joffe to WCP, Sept. 2, 1922; P2423/112, Koo to Joffe, Sept. 7, 1922.

6. *Peking and Tientsin Times*, Sept. 1, 1922, enclosed in USDS 893.00B/29.

7. WCPA. P2472/- , Wu P'ei-fu to Koo, Aug. 28, 1922; P2474/3148, T'ung Chao-yüan to WCP, Sept. 6, 1922.

8. The Changchun Conference is fully described in Lensen, *Japanese Recognition of the U.S.S.R.*, Chap. 2.

9. WCPA, P2426/- , Alston-Koo conversation, Aug. 30, 1922; P2433/830, Schurman-Koo conversation, Sept. 19, 1922.

10: WCPA, P2423/446, Ferguson to Koo, Sept. 11, 1922, enclosing Ferguson's memo to the President.

11. WCPA, P2672/738, Agriculture and Commerce Ministry to WCP, Sept. 16, 1922.

12. WCPA, UE/- , Koo to President, prepared on Sept. 27, presented on Oct. 7, 1922.

13. WCPA, P2493/123, Joffe to WCP, Sept. 19, 1922; P2493/- , Joffe to WCP, Sept. 19, 1922.

14. WCPA, P2672/- , Koo to Joffe, Sept. 25, 1922.

15. WCPA, P2493/117, Koo to Joffe, Sept. 26, 1922.

16. JMA, T560 (Reel 101 FO 7660-7672), Chief of Police, Korean Governor Generalcy, report on White Russians joining Chang Tso-lin's army.

17. WCPA, P2672/735, Joffe to Koo, Oct. 14, 1922.

18. Ishihara, Tō-Shi tetsudō, pp. 773-6.

19. WCPA, P2423/706, Joffe to Koo, Oct. 19, 1922; P2423/- , Joffe to Koo, Nov. 3, 1922.

20. WCPA, P2423/- , Joffe to Koo, Nov. 5, 1922.

21. WCPA, P2541/- , Koo to Joffe, Nov. 6, 1922.

22. WCPA, P2541/- , Koo to Joffe, Nov. 11, 1922.

23. WCPA, P2423/553, Joffe to Koo, Nov. 14, 1922.

24. James E. Sheridan, Chinese Warlord: The career of Feng Yü-hsiang (Stanford, 1966), pp. 124ff.

25. WCPA, P2541/- , C.T. Wang to Joffe, Dec. 11, 1922.

26. WCPA, P2429/1069, Joffe to WCP, Dec. 21, 1922.

27. WCPA, P2706/452, Wu Chun-sheng to Cabinet, Mar. 10, 1922.

28. WCPA, P2423/- , Davtian-Chu Ho-hsiang conversation, Dec. 28, 1922.

29. WCPA, P2708/1593, Wu Chun-sheng to Cabinet, May 4, 1922; P2708/1707, Wang Hung-nien to WCP, May 14, 1922; P2708/1150, Directorate of C.E.R. to WCP, May 23, 1922.

30. Cited in A.I. Kartunova, 'Sun' Iat-sen—drug Sovetskogo naroda', Voprosy Istorii KPSS, 10:27-38 (Oct. 1966), p. 32.

31. Cited in Chiang Yung-ching, Pao-lo-t'ing yü Wuhan cheng-chüan (Borodin and the Wuhan regime; Taipei, 1963), pp. 2-3.

32. USDS 893.00/4988, Tenney to Secretary of State, Apr. 14, 1923.

33. Vilensky, Kitai: Politiko-ekonomicheskii ocherk, pp. 24-7.

34. Whiting has ably shown the lengths to which Soviet writers were prepared to go in order to justify an alliance with Wu P'ei-fu in terms of Marxism-Leninism; see Soviet Policies in China, Chap. VII.

35. G. Kizul', 'Kitai', Vestnik N.K.I.D., 1-2:154-60 (Mar. 15, 1920).

36. Vilensky, Za velikoi Kitaiskoi stenoi, pp. 81-8.

37. Ibid.

38. Teng Chung-hsia, Chung-kuo chih-kung yün-tung chien-shih (A short history of the Chinese labor movement; Peking, 1957), pp. 24-7; Protokoll des Vierten Kongresses der Kommunistischen Internationale (Hamburg, 1923), p. 630.

39. A.A. Ivin, 'Sovremennyi Kitai', Novyi Vostok, 2:552-69 (1922), p. 558; Teng, Chung-kuo chih-kung yün-tung chien-shih, p. 27; Adolph Joffe, 'Kitaiskii Kavdak', Izvestiia, Jan. 5, 1923, datelined Dec. 12, 1922, Peking; Vilensky, 'Novoe politicheskoi obstanovke Kitaia', Izvestiia, Jan. 27, 1923.

40. H. Maring, 'Krovavyi epizod v istorii Kitaiskogo rabochego dvizheniia', Kommunisticheskii Internatsional, 26-7:7455-66, p. 7461.

41. Adolph Joffe, 'Nachalo', *Izvestiia*, Feb. 22, 1923; Whiting, *Soviet Policies in China*, p. 202.

42. Whiting, *Soviet Policies in China*, pp. 194ff.

43. V.D. Vilensky, *Rossiia na Dal'nem Vostoke* (Moscow, 1923), pp. 63-6.

44. Ibid., p. 67.

45. Leong Sow-Theng, 'Sun Yat-sen and the Bolsheviks', *Transactions of the International Conference of Orientalists in Japan*, XIV:39-53 (Tokyo, 1969).

46. USDS 893.00/3376, 'Confidential Memorandum on Conditions in Canton', by George Sokolsky, May 18, 1920.

47. *DVP*, V, 718, n. 24; Eudin and North, *Soviet Russia and the East*, pp. 219-21, Doc. 61.

48. Wang Ching-wei, 'Political Report to the Second KMT Congress', in *Wang Ching-wei yen-chiang lu* (Speeches of Wang Ching-wei; n.p., 1927), pp. 36-7.

49. Harold R. Isaacs, 'Notes on a Conversation with H. Sneevliet: The Chinese Question', *China Quarterly*, 45:102-9 (Jan.-Mar., 1971), p. 108.

50. H. Maring, 'Revoliutsionno-natsionalisticheskoe dvizhenie v Iuzhnom Kitae', *Kommunisticheskii Internatsional*, 22:5803-16 (Sept. 13, 1922), p. 5808.

51. Dov Bing, 'Sneevliet and the early years of the CCP', *China Quarterly*, 48:681-3 (Oct.-Dec., 1971); Isaacs, 'Notes on a Conversation with H. Sneevliet', pp. 102-9; Ch'en Kung-po, 'Wo yü Kung-ch'an tang' (I and the CCP), *Ch'un-ch'iu tsa-chih* (Historical miscellany), 204:1:3-6 (Hong Kong, Jan. 1, 1966), p. 4; Lo Chia-lun, ed., *Ko-ming wen-hsien* (Documents of revolution), 22 vols. (Taipei, 1953-60), IX, 1409-11. According to the Chinese Communist historian Ting Ming-nan, the plan for a military academy was mooted by Maring in 1922; see 'Soviet aid to China during the First Revolutionary War, 1925-1927', *Current Background*, No. 194 (July 24, 1952; American Consulate General, Hong Kong).

52. Some idea may be gained from a cryptic exchange between Chicherin and Lenin over Chang and Sun's letter. In a note to Lenin, Chicherin said: 'Here is the representative of his party, the KMT; we will establish *de facto* intercourse. They do not desire much'. *DVP*, II, 63.

53. *DVP*, V, 83-4.

54. Kartunova, 'Sun' Iat-sen', p. 31.

55. Sergei Dalin, *V riadakh Kitaiskoi revoliutsii* (Moscow, 1926). Dalin's book is an untapped source for the study of the Sun-Soviet alliance and KMT-CCP collaboration. Though it does not reveal the agreement reached on a variety of questions discussed, it nevertheless sheds some light on what transpired. The section dealing with his visit to Canton has been reproduced by Dalin in a revised form in L.S. Tikhvinsky, ed., *Sun' Iat-sen, 1866-1966: K stoletiiu so dniia rozhdeniia* (Moscow, 1966), pp. 255-85. As an example of the political uses to which history is put in the Soviet Union, the revised version emphasizes how his visit to Sun produced the turning point in Sun's career: turning from the United States to Soviet Russia for assistance.

56. Dalin, *V riadakh*, pp. 94-5.

57. Dalin, *V riadakh*, pp. 88-9. Why the Canton communists and the labor movement were against the KMT at this time is explained in my 'The Soviets and China: Diplomacy and Revolution, 1917-1923', Ph.D. dissertation (Harvard University, 1968), pp. 287-9.

58. Dalin, *V riadakh*, p. 89.

59. Ibid., p. 95.

60. The KMT military strategy as conceived by Sun Yat-sen's chief of staff Chiang Kai-shek is outlined in *Min-kuo shih-wu-nien i-ch'ien chih Chiang Chieh-shih hsien-sheng* (Chiang Kai-shek before 1926), ed. Mao Szu-ch'eng (Reprinted, Hong Kong, 1965), pp. 112-14. Simply, it called for a tactical alliance with the Fengtien clique against the Chihli clique, and upon the latter's destruction a struggle for supremacy with the Fengtien clique. The strategy is interesting in that Chiang Kai-shek was thinking, as early as January 1921, in terms of obtaining Soviet aid.

61. In a personal message to Hsü Shu-cheng shortly after the latter's cancellation of Mongol autonomy, Sun praised him highly for performing a meritorious deed. See *Kuo-fu ch'üan-chi* (Complete works of Sun Yat-sen; 3 vols., Taipei, 1965), III, 444.

62. Dalin, *V riadakh*, p. 115; *DVP*, V, 718, n. 23.

63. Isaacs, 'Notes on a Conversation with H. Sneevliet', p. 107.

64. Chang Kuo-t'ao, 'Wo ti hui-i' (My reminiscences), *Ming-pao yüeh-k'an* (Light monthly), 1:8:73-89 (Aug. 1966), p. 86; *Ko-ming wen-hsien*, VIII, 1040-3.

65. *Ko-ming wen-hsien*, VIII, 1044-57.

66. Ibid., VIII, 1044-7.

67. At the Twelfth Party Congress of the RCP in April 1923, Bukharin justified cooperation with the KMT on its agrarian program, denouncing 'some of our comrades' who still viewed the KMT as just another militarist group. The KMT's agrarian platform, said Bukharin, showed the party to have a petty bourgeois foundation and therefore different from that of all other groups. *Kommunisticheskaia partiia Sovetskogo Soiuza 12 s'ezd* (Moscow, 1923), pp. 243-4.

68. *Ko-ming wen-hsien*, VIII, 1053-4.

69. The text of the Sun-Joffe joint communiqué used here is that given in Conrad Brandt, Benjamin I. Schwartz, and John K. Fairbank, eds., *A Documentary History of Chinese Communism* (Cambridge, Mass., 1952), pp. 70-1.

70. Kartunova, 'Sun' Iat-sen', p. 34.

71. A.I. Cherepanov, *Zapiski voennogo sovetnika v Kitae* (Moscow, 1964), pp. 11-17.

72. V.D. Vilensky, *Sun' Iat-sen: otets Kitaiskoi revoliutsii* (Moscow, 1924), p. 34.

73. Brandt, Schwartz, and Fairbank, *A Documentary History of Chinese Communism*, pp. 71-2; Ch'en Tu-hsiu, 'Kao ch'üan-tang t'ung-chih shu' (A letter to all comrades) in *Kung-fei huo-kuo shih-liao hui-pien* (Collection of historical materials on how the Communist bandits brought about a national calamity; 3 vols., Taipei, 1964), I, 427-44.

74. Kheifets, *Sovetskaia Diplomatiia*, pp. 148-9.

75. Cited in Whiting, *Soviet Policies in China*, pp. 245–6. An illuminating account of Chiang Kai-shek's mission to Soviet Russia is given in Kartunova, 'Sun' Iat-sen', pp. 34–6. The American minister, Jacob Schurman, learned in August 1922, that Sun was negotiating with Wu P'ei-fu for a tactical reconciliation and one of Sun's conditions was his appointment as Commissioner for the Northwestern Frontier which would give him authority over Outer Mongolia; see USDS 893.00/4598, Schurman to Secretary of State, Aug. 14, 1922; USDS 893.00/4601, Schurman to Secretary of State, Aug. 19, 1922.

76. In his letter to Lenin on December 6, 1922 protesting against alleged hostile Soviet military action in north Manchuria, Sun wrote: 'I must again reiterate that the negotiations with the present government in China are not only a waste of time but are dangerous as well. Peking is now the servant and the weapon of the imperialist powers, and that is why to deal with Peking means in fact dealing with these powers. This is dangerous because there is always the possibility that Peking and those powers by their manoeuvres will put you in an unfavorable position in front of the Chinese people'. Kartunova, 'Sun' Iat-sen', p. 32. For Sun's complaints to Joffe, see L.S. Tikhvinsky, *Sun' Iat-sen: Vneshnepoliticheskie vozzreniia i praktika* (Moscow, 1964), p. 264. By the autumn of 1923, Sun appears to have become somewhat more resigned to Soviet diplomacy with Peking. On September 16, he cabled Karakhan: 'Your most formidable difficulty lies in negotiating with a political group which, besides being wholly unrepresentative of the Chinese people, has ceased even to bear the simulacrum of a national government'. On the next day, in another cable, he said: 'In case you find it hopeless to negotiate with Peking . . . you may have to consider the expediency of coming to Canton and negotiating with my new Government, now under formation, instead of returning to Moscow empty-handed'. Both telegrams are given in *DVP*, VI, pp. 435–6.

XII. The Karakhan Mission

1. WCPA, UA/- , WCP memo to Cabinet, March 1923; P723/231, WCP to Wang, Mar. 26, 1923.

2. WCPA, UA/71, WCP to Soviet Mission, Mar. 27, 1923; UA/32, Soviet Mission to WCP, Mar. 31, 1923.

3. Ishihara, *Tō-Shi tetsudō*, pp. 864–5, 875–85.

4. A detailed account may be found in ibid., pp. 866–75.

5. Ibid., pp. 870–1.

6. WCPA, UB/- , Davtian-Wang conversation, June 1, 1923; Davtian-Chao Ch'üan conversation, June 15, 1923; Davtian-Wang conversation, June 18, 1923.

7. Ishihara, *Tō-Shi tetsudō*, pp. 885–8.

8. WCPA, UB/- , Davtian-Wang conversation, June 1, 1923; UB/- , Davtian-Wang conversation, June 4, 1923.

9. WCPA, P2557/- , C.T. Wang to Chu Ch'ing-lan and C.C. Wang, June 25, 1923; P2557/492, C.T. Wang to President, Mar. 1, 1924.

10. Ishihara, *Tō-Shi tetsudō*, pp. 782–811.

11. For a full account of Joffe's talks in Tokyo, see Lensen, *Japanese Recognition of the U.S.S.R.*, Chaps. III–IV.

12. WCPA, P2429/10, Kuznetsov-Chu Ho-hsiang conversation, July 21, 1923; for Karakhan's overtures to Japan, see Lensen, *Japanese Recognition of the U.S.S.R.*, pp. 141–53.

13. WCPA, P2558/127, Ts'ai Yün-sheng to C.T. Wang, Aug. 3, 1923; P2558/75, Ts'ai to Wang, Aug. 20, 1923; P2558/78, Ts'ai to Wang, Aug. 20, 1923.

14. WCPA, P2557/41, C.T. Wang to Chang Tso-lin, Aug. 20, 1923; P2557/82, Chang to Wang, Aug. 22, 1923; P2558/61, K'ung Yung-chih to Wang, Aug. 29, 1923; P2557/45, Wang to K'ung, Aug. 29, 1923; P2558/92, K'ung to Wang, Aug. 30, 1923; P2557/134, Wang to K'ung, Aug. 30; P2558/95, K'ung to Wang, Aug. 31, 1923; P2558/103, K'ung to Wang, Sept. 1, 1923.

15. WCPA, P2557/49, C.T. Wang to Chang Tso-lin, Aug. 31, 1923; P2558/102, Chang to Wang, Sept. 3, 1923; P2558/123, K'ung Yung-chih to Wang, Sept. 14, 1923; P2557/73, Wang to Chu Ch'ing-lan, Sept. 17, 1923; P2558/144, Ch'i Ta-p'eng to Wang, Sept. 27, 1923.

16. WCPA, P2558/81, Ts'ai Yün-sheng to C.T. Wang, Sept. 5, 1923.

17. WCPA, UB/– , Kuznetsov-Chao Ch'üan conversation, Sept. 2, 1923; UB/– , Karakhan-Chu Ho-hsiang conversation, Sept. 13, 1923; UB/– , Karakhan-Wang conversation.

18. WCPA, UB/– , Karakhan-Wang conversation, Sept. 14, 1923.

19. WCPA, UB/710, C.T. Wang to Wellington Koo, Sept. 20, 1923.

20. WCPA, P723/1063, Koo to President, Sept. 26, 1923; P723/201, Wang to Koo, Oct. 6, 1923; UB/– , Karakhan-Chao Ch'üan conversation, Oct. 2, 1923; P2431/135, Ch'i Ta-p'eng to Wang, Oct. 1923, no exact date given.

21. WCPA, P2431/738, Koo to Wang, Oct. 8, 1923.

22. WCPA, P2447/763, Koo to Wang, Oct. 26, 1923; P2557/397, Wang to Koo, Nov. 7, 1923; P2431/433, Koo to Wang, Nov. 30, 1923.

23. P2447/763, Koo to Wang, Oct. 26, 1923, with Wang's draft enclosed.

24. Karakhan's reply to Wang's draft cannot be found, but its content is alluded to in WCPA, UB/– , Karakhan-Wang conversation, Feb. 25, 1924.

25. WCPA, UB/– , Wang to Koo, Nov. 8, 1923, with the resumé enclosed. For Karakhan's refusal of an exhibition of powers, which would have put the talks on a formal level, see UB/– , Karakhan-Wang conversation, Oct. 4, 1923; P2557/84, Wang to Chang Tso-lin, Oct. 4, 1923.

26. WCPA, P2557/97–100, Wang to Chang Tso-lin, Oct. 31, 1923; P2557/45, Directorate of Sino-Soviet Negotiations to Ch'iu Fen-ling, Dec. 5, 1923; P2557/492, Wang to President, Mar. 1, 1924.

27. C.T. Wang's letter to Karakhan of Nov. 21 is given in *China Year Book, 1924*, p. 876.

28. WCPA, UB/249, Directorate of Sino-Soviet Negotiations to WCP, Jan. 10, 1924, enclosure.

29. Ibid.

30. WCPA, P245/7618, Karakhan to Wang, Nov. 30, 1923.

31. WCPA, P2519/- , Wang to Karakhan, Jan. 9, 1924.

32. WCPA, P2438/474, Karakhan to Wang, Jan. 17, 1924.

33. WCPA, P2478/553, Petition of Peking University professors to Cabinet, Feb. 15, 1924. Among the professors were Chiang Mon-lin, Hu Shih, Li Ta-chao, Chou Tso-jen, and Li Shih-tseng. Despite Foreign Minister Koo's personal standing with the Peking intellectuals he seems to have had difficulty in gaining their sympathetic understanding of the government's objectives; see P2478/773, Chiang Mon-lin et al. to Koo, Feb. 27, 1924; P2478/495, Chiang et al. to Koo, Mar. 14, 1924.

34. WCPA, UE/66, Koo to Wu P'ei-fu, Feb. 25, 1924; UE/601, Wu P'ei-fu to Koo, Feb. 27, 1924.

35. WCPA, P2478/210, Karakhan-Chu Ho-hsiang conversation, Feb. 2, 1924; P2478/314, Karakhan-Chu conversation, Feb. 10, 1924.

36. These drafts are found in WCPA, UB.

37. WCPA, UB/- , Karakhan-Wang conversations of Feb. 19, 22, 25, 1924; P2557/492, Wang to President, Mar. 1, 1924; P2557/493, Wang to Cabinet, Mar. 3, 1924; P2519/713, C.C. Wang and Yü Jen-feng to C.T. Wang, Mar. 12, 1924; P2557/71, C.T. Wang to Ch'i Ta-p'eng, Mar. 10, 1924; P2431/216, Ch'i to C.T. Wang, Mar. 13, 1924; P2557/121, C.T. Wang to Chang Tso-lin, Mar. 15, 1924.

38. Ishihara, Tō-Shi tetsudō, pp. 985-7.

39. Annotations of various ministries are found in WCPA, P2456, as are collated views on the Draft Agreement on General Principles.

40. WCPA, P2443/- , Karakhan-Wang conversation, Mar. 8, 1924.

41. WCPA, P2456/- , Collated views on the Draft Agreement on General Principles.

42. Shun-t'ien shih-pao, Mar. 12, 1924 (7180), p. 2.

43. Ibid., Mar. 23, 1924 (7190), p. 2, gives Wang's public statement of self-defense in which he recounted in detail his numerous consultations with the cabinet. Some information on the March 13 cabinet meeting may be obtained from ibid., Mar. 15, 1924 (#7183), p. 2.

44. For instance, Kapitsa, in his Sovetsko-Kitaiskie Otnosheniia, pp. 109-12, maintains that Peking's failure to sign was due, in part, to foreign pressure, and, in part, to rivalry between Koo and Wang for the honor of signing the agreement. The first reason originated with Karakhan, and the second appears to have been widely believed in Chinese public circles at the time. Whiting, in Soviet Policies in China, p. 224, believes it 'probable that Wang was made a scapegoat for errors of judgment within the Wai-chiao Pu'. O. Edmund Clubb, in China and Russia: The 'Great Game' (New York, 1971), p. 266, thinks Wang was made a scapegoat by the government in the hope of getting further concessions. Both Whiting and Clubb give some credence to foreign pressure as well.

45. WCPA, P2457/- , A. de Fleuriau to WCP, Mar. 12, 1924; P2457/- , WCP to de Fleuriau, Apr. 7, 1924.

46. FRUS 1924, I, 484-95.

47. A mimeo. copy of the Army General Staff's document, entitled

'Rō-Shi kōshō ni motozuku Tō-Shi tetsudō mondai ni kansuru iken' (Views concerning the Chinese Eastern Railway question on the basis of Sino-Soviet negotiations), is found in Tōyō Bunkō, Tokyo. Dated July 1924, it was originally printed as a confidential document for official use, and classified 'secret'. See also JMA, T582 (Reel 101/8030-8037), Hayashi to Vice Minister for War, July 9, 1924.

48. *FRUS 1924*, I, 482, Schurman to Secretary of State, Mar. 17, 1924; BGD, FO 371.10955, Annual Report (China), 1924, p. 27; JMA, T581 (Reel 101/8024-8029), Hayashi to Vice Minister for War, Apr. 5, 1924. A search through USDS 761.93 of the relevant periods has failed to turn up anything to indicate that foreign pressure, apart from the kind already mentioned, was at work.

49. Wang later refuted these objections publicly, after being ignominously cashiered and replaced by Koo as chief negotiator on March 21; see *Shun-t'ien shih-pao*, Mar. 25, 1924, p.4.

50. WCPA, P245/550, Karakhan to Wang, Mar. 16, 1924, enclosing the ultimatum; P2474/930, Karakhan-Sun Pao-ch'i conversation, Mar. 17, 1924; P2457/509, Wang to Karakhan, Mar. 18, 1924, relaying the Cabinet's rejection of the ultimatum; P245/1037, Karakhan to Wang, Mar. 19, 1924.

51. WCPA, P2474/116, Karakhan-Koo conversation, Mar. 19, 1924; P2457/- , Koo to Karakhan, Mar. 22, 1924; P2457/- , Karakhan to Koo, Mar. 25, 1924.

52. These telegrams are found in WCPA, P2457, as are the cabinet's circular telegrams endeavoring to explain the situation.

53. For Mukden's reactions to the Peking agreement, see Ishihara, *Tō-Shi tetsudō*, pp. 1009-10.

54. WCPA, P2471/- , Koo to President, May 30, 1924; P2457/- , cabinet circular telegram to all provincial authorities, May 31, 1924. Transcripts of the Karakhan-Koo negotiations are not found in the archives. Complete texts of the agreements are found in P2471.

55. For Chang Tso-lin's reactions, see Ishihara, *Tō-Shi tetsudō*, p. 1033. The early stages of the Soviet-Mukden talks are recounted by Chang in his telegram to Generals Chu Ch'ing-lan and Chang Huan-hsiang on June 14, cited in ibid., pp. 1033-4.

56. The texts of the Soviet-Mukden Agreement, together with the secret declaration, are found in WCPA, P2458.

XIII. Epilogue

1. Transcripts of numerous discussions on the subject are found in WCPA, P2456 and P2471.

2. Vilensky, 'Sino-Soviet Agreement', *Izvestiia*, June 12, 1924.

3. The best account of these events is found in Sheridan, *Chinese Warlord*, Chap. 6.

4. Ibid., pp. 163-71.

5. WCPA, P2408/536, Chang Tso-lin to WCP, Jan. 19, 1925; P2456/- , Chang to WCP, Feb. 2, 1925; P2471/16, WCP to C.T. Wang, Feb. 28, 1925; P2408/- , WCP motion to the cabinet, Feb. 28, 1925; P2408/- , WCP to

Chang, Feb. 28, 1925; P2408/33, Office of Provisional Chief Executive to WCP, Mar. 2, 1925; P2471/125, WCP to Office of Provisional Chief Executive, Apr. 18, 1925.

6. Records of discussions of various government bodies in 1923 and 1924 are filed in UF, P2341, P2557, and P2565.

7. WCPA, P2318/278, Karakhan to WCP, Mar. 6, 1925.

8. WCPA, P2408/72, WCP to Karakhan, Mar. 21, 1925; P2408/14, Bureau of Mongolian and Tibetan Affairs to Tsereng-dorji, Mar. 27, 1925.

9. WCPA, P2408/- , WCP motion on Outer Mongolia, Mar. 11, 1925; P2318/- , Transcript of a conference on Outer Mongolia, Mar. 9, 1925; P2318/- , Transcript of a conference on Outer Mongolia, Mar. 11, 1925.

10. WCPA, P2408/325, Mongolian People's Republic to the Bureau of Mongolian and Tibetan Affairs, June 13, 1925.

11. WCPA, P2408/14, WCP to Karakhan, May 22, 1925; P2456/1143, Karakhan-Chu Shao-yang conversation, May 30, 1925; P2456/- , Cabinet to WCP, July 14, 1926.

12. A full treatment is given in Ishihara, Tō-Shi tetsudō, Chaps. 14-22.

13. Ibid., pp. 1165-232; Sheridan, Chinese Warlord, pp. 181-5.

14. Trotsky Archives, T870, Trotsky to Chicherin et al., 'Voprosy nashei politiki v otnoshenii Kitaia i Iaponii', Mar. 25, 1926.

15. Lensen, Japanese Recognition of the U.S.S.R., Chap. 5. For Chinese protests, see WCPA, P2456/925, Chicherin-Li Chia-ao conversation, Jan. 24, 1925; P2471/815, Karakhan to WCP, Feb. 26, 1925; P2408/11, WCP to Karakhan, Apr. 29, 1925.

16. See Ishihara, Tō-Shi tetsudō, pp. 1233-314 for full details of Serebriakov's mission.

17. Akira Iriye, After Imperialism: The Search for a New Order in the Far East, 1921-1931 (Cambridge, Mass., 1965), p. 161.

18. See her 'Introduction: The Rising Tide of Change' in Mary C. Wright, ed., China in Revolution: The First Phase, 1900-1913 (New Haven and London, 1968), pp. 1-63.

19. Chow Tse-tsung, The May Fourth Movement: Intellectual Revolution in Modern China (Cambridge, Mass., 1960), p. 217.

20. Chang Chin, comp., Lien-O yü ch'ou-O wen-t'i t'ao-lun chi (The debate on friendship or enmity towards Russia; Peking, 1927), pp. 1-6.

21. Ibid., pp. 8-10.

22. Ibid., pp. 47-51.

23. Ibid., pp. 117-21.

24. Ibid., pp. 106-10.

25. Ibid., pp. 15-22, 43, 45.

26. Ibid., p. 173.

27. Ibid., p. 163.

Bibliography

I. Chinese Foreign Ministry Documents, 1917–1926

1. Published for the years 1917–1920 under the general title *Chung-O kuan-hsi shih-liao* 中俄關係史料 (Historical materials on Sino-Russian relations) by the Institute of Modern History, Academia Sinica, Republic of China.

COKH, CP	*Ch'u-ping Hsi-pei-li-ya* 出兵西北利亞 (Siberian expedition), comp. Li Nien-hsüan 李念萱 *et al.* (Taipei, 1962).
COKH, CTTL 1917–1919	*Chung-tung t'ieh-lu* 中東鐵路 (Chinese Eastern Railway), 2 vols., comp. Li Kuo-ch'i 李國祁 (Taipei, 1960).
COKH, CTTL 1920	——— comp. T'ao Ying-hui 陶英惠 *et al.* (Taipei, 1969).
COKH, IPCS	*I-pan chiao-she* 一般交涉 (General intercourse), comp. T'ao Ying-hui *et al.* (Taipei, 1968).
COKH, OCP 1917–1919	*O cheng-pien yü i-pan chiao-she* 俄政變與一般交涉 (Russian Revolution and general intercourse), 2 vols., comp. Wang Yü-chün 王聿均 (Taipei, 1960).

COKH, OCP 1920　　　　*O cheng-pien* 俄政變 (Russian Revolution), comp. T'ao Ying-hui *et al.* (Taipei, 1968).

COKH, TCTY　　　　　*T'ing-chih O shih-ling tai-yü* 停止俄使領待遇 (Discontinuation of relations with the Russian minister and consuls), comp. T'ao Ying-hui *et al.* (Taipei, 1968).

COKH, TPPF 1917–1919　*Tung-pei pien-fang* 東北邊防 (Manchurian border defence), 2 vols., comp. Teng Ju-yen 鄧汝言 (Taipei, 1960).

COKH, TPPF 1920　　　——— comp. T'ao Ying-hui *et al.* (Taipei, 1969).

COKH, WCST　　　　　*O tui-hua wai-chiao shih-t'an* 俄對華外交試探 (Preliminary Soviet diplomatic feelers to China), comp. T'ao Ying-hui *et al.* (Taipei, 1968).

COKH, WMK 1917–1919　*Wai Meng-ku* 外蒙古 (Outer Mongolia), comp. Li Yü-shu 李毓澍 (Taipei, 1959).

COKH, WMK 1920　　　——— comp. T'ao Ying-hui *et al.* (Taipei, 1969).

2. Unpublished, deposited in the Wai-chiao Pu Archives at the Institute of Modern History, Academia Sinica, Republic of China. The following lists two categories of files, those with numbers and those without. Only files that are cited in this study are listed.

WCPA,　P245　　O tai-piao-t'uan yang-wen lai-chien 俄代表團洋文來件 (Communications in Russian received from the Soviet Mission).

　　　　　P723　　Fa-kei ts'ou-pan Chung-O chiao-she shih-i cheng-shu　發給籌辦中俄交涉事宜証書 (Issue of certificate of powers to the Directorate of Sino-Soviet Negotiations).

　　　　　P1233　Yü Yüan-tung kung-ho-kuo chiao-she 與遠東共和國交涉 (Diplomacy with the Far Eastern Republic).

　　　　　P2156　10-nien, 11-nien Chung-tung t'ieh-lu an 十年，

十一年中東鐵路案 (Chinese Eastern Railway, 1921, 1922).

P2301 O Meng shih t'iao-ch'en chi shuo-t'ieh 俄蒙事條陳及說帖 (Suggestions and submissions on the Mongolian question).

P2305 Wai-Meng ch'ing-hsing pao-kao shu 外蒙情形報告書 (Reports on conditions in Outer Mongolia).

P2314 Wai-Meng wen-t'i 外蒙問題 (The Outer Mongolian problem).

P2315 Meng-an ch'ao-tang 蒙案抄檔 (Copied file on Outer Mongolia).

P2318 Chung-O 13-nien hui-i kuan-yü Wai-Meng chih chiao-she 中俄十三年會議關於外蒙之交涉 (Negotiations on Outer Mongolia at the Sino-Soviet talks of 1924).

P2341 Shou-fu Wai-Meng chün-pei chi shou-hui Wai-Meng k'uang ch'üan 收復外蒙軍備及收回外蒙礦權 (Recovery of the rights of defence and mining in Outer Mongolia).

P2408 Chung-O hsieh-ting fu Feng-O hsieh-ting 中俄協定附奉俄協定 (Sino-Soviet Agreement, with Soviet-Mukden Agreement appended).

P2418 Yüan-tung kung-ho-kuo chi Lao-nung tai-piao lai-hua an 遠東共和國及勞農代表來華案 (Far Eastern Republic and Soviet missions to China).

P2423 Lao-nung cheng-fu hsüan-yen chi tui Lao-nung cheng-fu chiao-she 勞農政府宣言及對勞農政府交涉 (Declarations of the Soviet government and negotiations with the Soviet government).

P2426 Su-lien chu-hua tai-piao-t'uan an 蘇聯駐華代表團案 (The Soviet mission in China).

P2428 Lao-nung chün-tui t'ung-kuo Meng-ching 勞農軍隊通過蒙境 (Crossing of Soviet army into Mongolian territory).

P2429 Lao-nung O-kuo p'ai-chu Chung-kuo wei-yüan an 勞農俄國派駐中國委員案 (Dispatch of Soviet commissioners to China).

P2430 Same designation as P2429.

P2431 Ts'ou-pan Chung-O chiao-she kung-shu hui-wu ch'u shou-wen 籌辦中俄交涉公署會務處收文 (Documents taken over from General Affairs Section of the Directorate of Sino-Soviet Negotiations).

P2432 Hui-wu Yurin an 會晤優林案 (Conversations with Yurin).

P2433 Lao-nung tai-piao Joffe 勞農代表越飛 (The Soviet representative Joffe).

P2434 Chita tai-piao Yurin lai-hua an 赤塔代表優林來華案 (Arrival of Chita's representative Yurin in China).

P2438 Yü Lao-nung tai-piao chiao-she Chung-O wen-t'i lai-wang wen-chien 與勞農代表交涉中俄問題來往文件 (Communications with the Soviet representative in the course of negotiating Sino-Soviet problems).

P2443 Chung-O chiao-she, t'an-hua ti-kao 中俄交涉, 談話底稿 (Draft transcripts of Sino-Soviet negotiations).

P2447 Chung-O hui-i an 中俄會議案 (Sino-Soviet negotiations).

P2451 Wai-Meng ch'e-chün chiao-she 外蒙撤軍交涉 (Negotiations on withdrawal of Soviet troops from Outer Mongolia).

P2452 Kuan-yü Chung-O hui-i t'iao-ch'eng chi ts'o-i wen-chien hui-an 關於中俄會議條陳及磋議文件彙案 (Documents arising from suggestions and deliberations concerning Sino-Soviet negotiations).

P2456 Chung-O hui-i chüan 中俄會議卷 (Sino-Soviet negotiations).

P2457 Chung-O hui-i ko-hsiang wen-chien 中俄會議各項文件 (Various documents concerning Sino-Soviet negotiations).

P2458 Chung-O hui-i ko-hsiang yin-shua-p'in 中俄會議各項印刷品 (Printed documents of Sino-Soviet negotiations).

P2471 Chung-O hsieh-ting 中俄協定 (Sino-Soviet Agreement).

P2472 Jih-O chiao-she 日俄交涉 (Soviet-Japanese negotiations).

P2474   Chung-O hui-i chüan 中俄會議案 (Sino-Soviet negotiations).

P2478   Ch'eng-jen Su-lien an 承認蘇聯案 (Recognition of the USSR).

P2493   Chung-O i-pan chiao-she 中俄一般交涉 (Sino-Soviet general intercourse).

P2509   10-nien Chung-tung t'ieh-lu chiao-she an 十年中東鐵路交涉案 (Negotiations on the Chinese Eastern Railway in 1921).

P2511   11-nien Chung-tung t'ieh-lu chiao-she an 十一年中東鐵路交涉案 (Negotiations on the Chinese Eastern Railway in 1922).

P2519   12-nien, 13-nien Chung-tung t'ieh-lu chiao-she an 十二年,十三年中東鐵路交涉案(Negotiations on the Chinese Eastern Railway in 1923 and 1924).

P2534   O lao-nung cheng-fu ch'ing p'ai-ping tao Meng ch'ü-chu hsieh-tang an 俄勞農政府請派兵到蒙驅逐謝黨案 (Request of the Soviet government to send troops into Outer Mongolia for the expulsion of the Semenovites).

P2547   Kuan-yü O-kuo ko-chung shih-chien 關於俄國各種事件 (Various matters concerning Soviet Russia).

P2557   Ts'ou-pan Chung-O chiao-she shih-i kung-shu fa-wen 籌辦中俄交涉事宜公署發文 (Communications sent to the Directorate of Sino-Soviet Negotiations).

P2558   Ts'ou-pan Chung-O chiao-she kung-shu hui-wu ch'u ch'ao-chuan Wai-chiao Pu Chung-O hui-i wen-chien 籌辦中俄交涉公署會務處抄轉外交部中俄會議文件 (Documents on Sino-Soviet negotiations transcribed by General Affairs Section of the Directorate of Sino-Soviet Negotiations for the Wai-chiao Pu).

P2563   Chu O-ching Moscow pao-kao wen-tien 駐俄京莫斯科報告文電 (Telegraphic reports from Chinese representative in Moscow).

P2564   K'u-luan an 庫亂案 (Disturbances in Outer Mongolia).

P2565   Wai-Meng t'ao-lun hui chi-lu 外蒙討論會記錄

(Transcripts of conferences on Outer Mongolia).

P2706 Tung-sheng pao-kao 東省報告 (Reports from Manchuria).

P2708 Tung-sheng pien-fang 東省邊防 (Manchurian border defence).

WCPA, UA Chung-O hui-i chüan: hsieh-ting ch'ien-ting ch'ien liang-kuo hu-p'ai tai-piao chieh-hsia chih ching-kuo 中俄會議卷：協定簽訂前兩國互派代表接洽之經過 (Sino-Soviet negotiations: meetings of representatives of both nations prior to the signature of the Sino-Soviet Agreement).

UB Chung-O hui-i: ts'ou-pan Chung-O chiao-she shu ch'eng-li i-hou hui-i chin-chan ch'ing-hsing 中俄會議：籌辦中俄交涉署成立以後會議進展情形 (Sino-Soviet negotiations: progress of talks after the establishment of the Directorate of Sino-Soviet Negotiations).

UC Kiakhta Chung-O-Meng hsieh-yüeh an 恰克圖中俄蒙協約案 (The Sino-Mongol-Russian Convention of Kiakhta).

UD K'u-lun shih-hsien chi hung-chün chan-ling K'u-lun 庫倫失陷及紅軍佔領庫倫 (Loss of Urga and the occupation of Urga by the Red Army).

UE Chung-O hui-i chüan: pen pu yü ko-sheng chi chu-wai shih-ling tui Chung-O chiao-she chih chu-chang 中俄會議卷：本部與各省及駐外使領對中俄交涉之主張 (Views on Sino-Soviet negotiations submitted by Wai-chiao Pu and ministers and consuls stationed abroad).

UF Shou-hui K'u-Ch'ia yü ch'e-t'ui chu-Meng hung-chün chih chiao-she 收回庫恰與撤退駐蒙紅軍之交涉 (Recovery of Urga and Kiakhta and negotiations for the withdrawal of Soviet troops in Outer Mongolia).

II. Others

Banno Masataka 坂野正高, 'Dai-ichiji taisen kara go-sanjū made: Kokken kaifuku undō shi oboegaki' 第一次大戰から五・卅

まで：国権回復運動史覚書 (From World War I to the May 30th incident: A study of the rights recovery movement), in Ueda Toshio 植田捷雄, ed., *Gendai Chūgoku o meguru sekai no gaikō* 現代中国を続る世界の外交 (World diplomacy and China), pp. 1–67 (Tokyo, 1951).

Bing, Dov, 'Sneevliet and the Early Years of the CCP', *China Quarterly*, 48: 677–97 (Dec. 1971).

BGD, British Government Documents, Foreign Office Files 1917–24.

Boorman, Howard L., ed., *Biographical Dictionary of Republican China*, 4 vols. (New York, 1967–71).

Brandt, Conrad, Benjamin I. Schwartz, and John K. Fairbank, *A Documentary History of Chinese Communism* (Cambridge, Mass., 1952).

Carr, Edward Hallett, *The Bolshevik Revolution, 1917–1923*, 3 vols. (London, 1950–3).

—— *Socialism in One Country, 1924–1926*, 3 vols. (London, 1954–64).

Chang Chin 章進, comp., *Lien-O yü ch'ou-O wen-t'i t'ao-lun chi* 聯俄與仇俄問題討論集 (The debate on friendship or enmity towards Russia; Peking, 1927).

Chao Chung-fu 趙中孚, *Ch'ing-chi Chung-O Tung-san-sheng chieh-wu chiao-she* 清季中俄東三省界務交涉 (Sino-Russian negotiations over the Manchurian Border Issue, 1858–1911; Taipei, 1970).

Ch'en Ch'ung-tsu 陳崇祖, *Wai-Meng chin-shih shih* 外蒙近世史 (Recent history of Outer Mongolia; reprint, Taipei, 1965; [Shanghai, 1924]).

Ch'en, Jerome, 'Defining Chinese warlords and their factions', *Bulletin of the School of Oriental and African Studies*, 31: 563–600 (1968).

Chi, Madeleine, *China Diplomacy 1914–1918* (Cambridge, Mass., 1970).

China Year Book (London and Tientsin, 1921–6).

Chu Ch'ing-lan 朱慶瀾 comp., *Tsui-chin shih-nien Chung-O chih wai-chiao* 最近十年中俄之外交 (Sino-Russian diplomacy over the last decade; Harbin, 1923).

Clubb, O. Edmund, *China and Russia: The 'Great Game'* (New York and London, 1971).

Dalin, Sergei A., *V riadakh Kitaiskoi revoliutsii* (Moscow, 1926).

Documents on British Foreign Policy, 1919–1939, ed. E.L. Woodward and Rohan Butler; 1st ser., Vol. 3 (London, 1949); Vol. 6 (London, 1956).

DVP: Dokumenty vneshnei politiki SSSR (Moscow, 1957–).

Eudin, Xenia Joukoff, and Robert C. North, *Soviet Russia and the East, 1920–1927: a documentary survey* (Stanford, 1957).

Fischer, Louis, *The Soviets in World Affairs: A history of relations between the Soviet Union and the rest of the world*, 2 vols. (New York, 1930).

Fishel, Wesley R., *The End of Extraterritoriality in China* (Berkeley, 1952).

FRUS: Papers Relating to the Foreign Relations of the United States (Washington, D.C.).

Fujii Shōzō 藤井昇三, '1920-nen An-Chih sensō o meguru Nit-Chū kankei no ichi kōza'１９２０年安直戦争を続る日中関係の一考察 (The Anfu-Chihli War of 1920 and Sino-Japanese relations), in *Nihon gaikō shi kenkyū*, ed. Kokusai seiji gakkai (Japan Association of International Relations; Tokyo, 1961), pp. 56–70.

Hertslet, Godfrey E.P., *Treaties, &c., Between Great Britain and China; and Between China and Foreign Powers; &c.*, 2 vols., 3rd ed. (London, 1908).

Horvath, Dmitri Leonidovich, 'Memoirs', Hoover Library, Stanford University.

Hosoya Chihiro 細谷千博, *Siberia shuppei no shiteki kenkyū* シベリア出兵の史的研究 (A historical study of the Siberian expedition, Tokyo, 1955).

—— 'Japanese Documents on the Siberian Intervention, 1917–1922: Part 1, Nov. 1917–Jan. 1919', *Hitotsubashi Journal of Law and Politics*, 1.1: 30–53 (Apr. 1960).

—— 'Nihon to Kolchak seiken shōnin mondai' 日本とコルチャク政権承認問題 (Japan and the question of recognition of the Kolchak regime), *Hōgaku kenkyū* 法学研究(Journal of Legal Studies), 3:13–135 (1961).

Iriye, Akira, *After Imperialism: The Search for a New Order in the Far East, 1921–1931* (Cambridge, Mass., 1965).

Isaacs, Harold R., 'Notes on a conversation with H. Sneevliet: The Chinese Question', *China Quarterly*, 45:102–9 (Mar. 1971).

Ishihara Shigetaka 石原重高, comp., *Tō-Shi tetsudō o chūshin to suru Rō-Shi seiryoku no shōchō* 東支鉄道を中心とする露支勢力の消長 (The rise and fall of Russian and Chinese influence on the Chinese Eastern Railway; Dairen, 1928).

Jagchid, S. 札奇斯欽, 'Wai Meng-ku ti tu-li, tzu-chih, ho ch'e-
chih', 外蒙古的獨立自治和撤治 (Independence, autonomy,
and cancellation of autonomy of Outer Mongolia), in Wu
Hsiang-hsiang 吳湘湘 et al., eds., Chung-kuo hsien-tai shih
ts'ung-k'an 中國近代史叢刊 (Collection of essays on modern
Chinese history), IV, 39–141 (Taipei, 1962).
Japanese Foreign Ministry Archives, microfilmed by the Library
of Congress: Meiji-Taishō Documents
    MT1.6.3.24 Rōkoku·Kakumei ikken 露国革命一件 (Docu-
    ments relating to the Russian Revolution).
    MT1.6.3.24-4 Bessatsu: Kakkoku no taidō, Shina no bu 別冊：
    各国ノ態度, 支那ノ部 (Separate volume: Attitudes of
    various countries, China, Jan. 1922–Dec. 1922). Reel 185.
    MT1.6.3.24-16 Bessatsu: Teikoku oyobi rekkoku no tai-Rō
    saku 別冊：帝国及ビ列国ノ対露策 (Separate volume:
    The policies of Japan and of other nations with regard to
    the USSR, Jan. 1918–Sept. 1924). Reels 194-7.
Papers of Matsumoto Tadaō, Parliamentary Vice-Minister
    PVM12-51 Rōkoku no Shina sekka ni kansuru hōkoku 露国
    ノ支那赤化ニ関スル報告 (Reports on the communiza-
    tion of China by Russia). 'Chūo shikkō iin tokubetsu
    kaigi sekijō ni okeru Karakhan no Shina ni kansuru kōtō
    hōkoku' 中央執行委員特別会議席上ニ於ケルカラハンノ
    支那ニ関スル口頭報告 (Karakhan's oral report to a
    special session of the Central Committee; Sept. 11–14,
    1925). Reel P32–P33.
JMA: Japanese Military Archives
    Microfilmed by the Library of Congress
    T544 (Reel 101, FO7396–7399), Gaimō no henran o Nip-
    p'onjin enjōshi aritaru ken 外蒙ノ変乱ヲ日本人援助シ
    アリタル件 (Japanese assistance to the rebellion in Outer
    Mongolia).
    T546 (Reel 101, FO7474–7498), Gunji kyōtei haishi ni kan-
    suru ken 軍事協定廃止ニ関スル件 (Abrogation of the
    Sino-Japanese military pact).
    T551 (Reel 101, FO7521–7529), Tōsanshō Jun'etsushi Chō
    Saku-rin shōgun ni kansuru hiken, Nagao Hanpei 東三
    省巡閲使張作霖将軍ニ関スル卑見 (Opinions of Nagao
    Hanpei regarding the Inspector General of Manchuria,
    General Chang Tso-lin).
    T560 (Reel 101, FO7660–7672), Hakugun Chō Saku-rin no
    kika ni hiran to suru ken 白軍張作霖将軍ノ麾下ニ入ウ

ントスル件 (White Russians joining Chang Tso-lin's army).

T581 (Reel 101, FO8024–8029), Rō-Shi kaigi yori mitaru tai-Shi heiwateki gaikō shudan ni tsuite 露支会議ヨリ見タル対支平和的外交手段ニ就テ (Japan's peaceful diplomatic measures towards China in view of the Sino-Soviet Conference).

T582 (Reel 101, FO8030–8037) Nichi-Rō-Shi sankoku no teikei o hakaru tame tekitō no kikai ni oite Nippon shusai no motoni sankoku kōshō o kaisai suru o yōsuru ken 日露支三国ノ提携ヲ図ル為適当機会ニ於テ日本主宰ノ下ニ三国交渉ヲ開催スルヲ要スル件 (The necessity of holding, at an appropriate opportunity, tripartite negotiations under Japanese auspices between Japan, Russia, and China for the purpose of promoting cooperation among the three nations).

T1061 (Reel 117, FO29259–29273), Baron Ungern kōdō narabini Gaimō keisei no shōrai ni kansuru kansatsu バロンウンゲルン行動並ビニ外蒙形勢ノ将来ニ関スル観察 (Observations on the activities of Baron Ungern and the future situation of Outer Mongolia).

T1062 (Reel 117, FO29274–29287), Baron Ungern gun sentōryoku narabini jikyū nōryoku no handan ni kansuru shiryō バロンウンゲルン軍戦争力並ビニ持久能力ノ判断ニ関スル資料 (Materials for evaluating the military power and stamina of Baron Ungern's army).

Defence Agency, War History Division, Archives, Tokyo

Taishō 10-nen (1921), Vol. 6, Diplomacy #4, Aoki shōshō ni kansuru ken 青木少将ニ関スル件 (Concerning Lt General Aoki).

Taishō 10-nen (1921), Vol. 6, Diplomacy #5, Yü Ch'ung-han to no kaidan ni kansuru ken 于冲漢トノ会談ニ関スル件 (Conversations with Yü Ch'ung-han).

Taishō 10-nen (1921), Vol. 6, Diplomacy, #21, Henbōgun ni zokusuru waga shōkō ni kansuru ken 辺防軍ニ属スル我将校ニ関スル件 (Concerning our officers in the Border Defence Army).

Taishō 10-nen (1921), Miscellanies #81, Chōhō bukan teishutsu shōrui sōfu no ken 諜報武官提出書類送附ノ件 (Documents forwarded by intelligence officers).

Taishō 10-nen (1921), Miscellanies #83, Shi jōhō 支常報 (China report).

Kapitsa, M.S., *Sovetsko-Kitaiskie Otnosheniia* (Moscow, 1958).

Kartunova, A.I., 'Sun' Iat-sen—drug Sovetskogo naroda', *Voprosy Istorii KPSS*, 10:27–38 (Oct. 1966).

Kazanin, Mark I., *Zapiski sekretaria missii: stranichka istorii pervykh let Sovetskoi diplomatii* (Moscow, 1962).

Kennan, George F., *Soviet-American Relations, 1917–1920:* Vol. 1, *Russia Leaves the War* (Princeton, 1956); Vol. 2, *The Decision to Intervene* (Princeton, 1958).

Kheifets, A.N., *Sovetskaia Rossiia i sopredel'nye strany Vostoka v gody grazhdanskoi voiny, 1918–1920* (Moscow, 1964).

———— *Sovetskaia Diplomatiia i narody vostoka, 1921–1927* (Moscow, 1968).

Khodorov, A.E., 'Manchzhurskaia problema', *Novyi Vostok*, 2:560–7 (1922).

Khuseinov, S.S., 'Vmeshatel'stvo imperialisticheskikh derzhav v Sovetsko-Kitaiskie peregovory, 1917–1918', *Narody Azii i Afriki*, 5:83–91 (1962).

Kizul'G., 'Kitai', *Vestnik N.K.I.D.*, 1–2:154–60 (Mar. 15, 1920).

Kolobov, M., 'Bor'ba s Bolshevikami na Dal'nem Vostoke'. Hoover Library, Stanford University.

Kurdiukov, I.F., 'Iz istorii Sovetsko-Kitaiskikh otnoshenii, 1920–1921', *Sovetskoe Kitaevedenie*, 1:141–3 (1958).

Lensen, George Alexander, *Japanese Recognition of the U.S.S.R.: Soviet-Japanese relations, 1921–1930* (Tokyo, 1970).

Leong, Sow-Theng, *Sino-Soviet Relations: the First Phase, 1917–1920* (Canberra, 1971).

Li Chien-nung, *The Political History of China, 1840–1928*, tr. Teng Ssu-yü and Jeremy Ingalls (New York, 1956).

Li Yü-shu 李毓澍, *Wai Meng-ku ch'e-chih wen-t'i* 外蒙古撤治問題 (The issue over the cancellation of autonomy in Outer Mongolia; Taipei, 1961).

MacMurray, John V.A., ed., *Treaties and Agreements with and concerning China, 1894–1919*, 2 vols. (New York, 1921).

Malozemoff, Andrew, *Russian Far Eastern Policy, 1881–1904* (Berkeley, 1958).

Mirovitskaia, R.A., *Dvizhenie v Kitae za priznanie Sovetskoi Rossii, 1920–1924* (Moscow, 1962).

Morley, James W., *The Japanese Thrust into Siberia, 1918* (New York, 1957).

Murphy, George G.S., *Soviet Mongolia: A study of the oldest political satellite* (Berkeley and Los Angeles, 1966).

Nihon gaikō bunshō, Taishō 8-nen 日本外交文書，大正八年 (Japanese diplomatic documents, 1919), Vol. I (Tokyo, Japanese Foreign Ministry, 1970).

Nilus, E. Kh., *Istoricheskii obzor KVZhD, 1898–1923*, tom I (Harbin, 1923).

Parfenov-Altaiskii, P.S., *Bor'ba za Dal'nii Vostok, 1920–1922* (Moscow, 1928).

Persits, M.A., *Dal'nevostochnaia Respublika i Kitai* (Moscow, 1962).

Pi Kuei-fang 畢桂芳, *Wai Meng-ku chiao-she shih-mo chi* 外蒙古交涉始末記 (An account of negotiations concerning Outer Mongolia; Peking, 1928).

Pye, Lucien Wilmot, *Warlord Politics: conflict and coalition in the modernization of Republican China* (New York, 1971).

'Rō-Shi kōshō ni motozuku Tō-Shi tetsudō mondai ni kansuru iken' 露支交渉ニ基ク東支鉄道問題ニ関スル意見 (Views concerning the Chinese Eastern Railway question on the basis of Sino-Soviet negotiations; Japanese Army General Staff, July 1924). Tōyō Bunkō, Tokyo.

Rupen, Robert A., *Mongols of the Twentieth Century* (Bloomington, 1964).

Schwartz, Benjamin I., *Chinese Communism and the Rise of Mao* (Cambridge, Mass., 1951).

Seki Hiroharu 関寛治, *Gendai Higashi Ajia kokusai kankyō no tanjō* 現代東アジア国際環境の誕生 (The birth of the international environment in contemporary East Asia; Tokyo, 1969).

Sheridan, James E., *Chinese Warlord: The career of Feng Yü-hsiang* (Stanford, 1966).

Sonoda Ikki 園田一亀, *Kaiketsu Chang Tso-lin* 怪傑張作霖 (Chang Tso-lin, the hero; Tokyo, 1923).

Sovetsko-Kitaiskie Otnosheniia: Sbornik dokumentov, 1917–1957, comp. I.F. Kurdiukov, V.N. Nikiforov, and A.S. Perevertailo (Moscow, 1959).

Tang, Peter S.H., *Russian and Soviet Policy in Manchuria and Outer Mongolia, 1911–1931* (Durham, N.C., 1959).

Tikhvinsky, L.S., *Sun' Iat-sen: Vneshnepoliticheskie vozzreniia i praktika* (Moscow, 1964).

—— *Sun' Iat-sen, 1866–1966: K stoletiiu so dnia rozhdeniia* (Moscow, 1966).

Ting Ming-nan, 'Soviet aid to China during the First Revolutionary War, 1925–1927', *Current Background*, No. 194 (July 24, 1952; American Consulate General, Hong Kong).

Trotsky Archives. Houghton Library, Harvard University.

Ullman, Richard H., *Anglo-Soviet Relations, 1917–1921*: Vol. 1, *Intervention and the War* (Princeton, 1961); Vol. 2, *Britain and the Russian Civil War* (Princeton, 1968).

USDS: United States, Department of State, Decimal Files.

Vilensky, V.D., *Kitai i Sovetskaia Rossiia* (Moscow, 1919).

——— 'Dal'nevostochnyi uzel', *Vestnik N.K.I.D.*, 2:20–6 (Aug. 13, 1919).

——— *Kitai: Politiko-ekonomicheskii ocherk* (Moscow, 1923).

——— *Rossiia na Dal'nem Vostoke* (Moscow, 1923).

——— *Za velikoi Kitaiskoi Stenoi* (Moscow, 1923).

——— *Sun' Iat-sen: otets Kitaiskoi revoliutsii* (Moscow, 1924).

Wai-chiao wen-tu 外交文牘 (Diplomatic documents; Peking, Ministry of Foreign Affairs, 1921).

Wang Yü-chün 王聿均, *Chung-Su wai-chiao ti hsu-mo* 中蘇外交的序幕 (The first phase of Sino-Soviet diplomacy; Taipei, 1963).

Weigh, Ken Shen, *Russo-Chinese Diplomacy, 1689–1924* (Shanghai, 1928).

White, John Albert, *The Siberian Intervention* (Princeton, 1950).

Whiting, Allen S., 'The Soviet Offer to China of 1919', *Far Eastern Quarterly*, X:345–54 (Aug. 1951).

——— *Soviet Policies in China, 1917–1924* (New York, 1954).

Yoshimura Michiō 吉村道男, *Nihon to Rōshiya* 日本とロシア. (Japan and Russia; Tokyo, 1968).

Glossary

Aoki Nobuzumi 青木宣純

Banzai Rihachirō 坂西利八郎

Chang Ching-hui 張景惠
Chang Ch'iu-pai 張秋白
Chang Hsi-jo 張奚若
Chang Huan-hsiang 張煥相
Chang I-p'eng 張一鵬
Chang Shao-tseng 張紹曾
Chang Shou-tseng 張壽增
Chang Ssu-lin 張斯麐
Chang Tso-lin 張作霖
Chang Tsu-shen 章祖申
Chang Tsung-ch'ang 張宗昌
Chang Tsung-hsiang 章宗祥
Chao Ch'üan 趙泉
Ch'en Ch'i-hsiu 陳啟修
Ch'en I 陳毅
Ch'en Lu 陳籙
Ch'en Wen-ts'e 陳問策
Cheng Ch'ien 鄭謙

Chi-Chiang ts'ou-i hui-wu ch'u 吉江籌議會務處
Chi Chin-ch'un 汲金純
Chi Ching 秬鏡
Chi-Hei chiang-fang ts'ou-pei ch'u 吉黑江防籌備處
chi-mi 羈縻
Chia-yin jih-k'an 甲寅日刊
Chiang Heng 江亨
Ch'ien Neng-hsun 錢能訓
ch'ih-hua 赤化
ch'ih-se ti-kuo chu-i 赤色帝國主義
Chin Yün-p'eng 靳雲鵬
ching-ch'a ch'üan 警察權
ching-li 經理
Chou Tzu-ch'i 周自齊
Chu Ch'ing-lan 朱慶蘭
Ch'u Ch'i-hsiang 褚其祥

Fan Ch'i-kuang 范其光
Feng Kuo-chang 馮國璋
Feng Te-lin 馮德麟
Feng Yü-hsiang 馮玉祥
Fu Chiang 傅疆
Fu-hsiang 福祥
Fujii Kōtei 藤井幸槌

Gotō Shimpei 後藤新平

Hatakeyama Kōtarō 畠山幸太郎
Hayashi Gonsuke 林權助
Hayashi Yasakichi 林彌三吉
Higashi Otohiko 東少彥
ho-pan 合辦
Ho Shou-jen 何守仁
Ho Tsung-lien 何宗蓮
Hsi-pei pien-fang chün 西北邊防軍
Hsi-pei ts'ou-pien shih 西北籌邊使

hsien-jen nei-ko 賢人內閣
Hsü Shih-ch'ang 徐世昌
Hsü Shu-cheng 徐樹錚
hsüeh-hsi yüan 學習員
hu-lu ch'üan 護路權
hua-ch'iao 華僑
hua-kung 華工
Huang Ch'eng-hsu 黃成坼
Huang Fu 黃郛
Huang Jung-liang 黃榮良
Huang Luan-ming 黃鸞鳴

Ishii Kikujirō 石井菊次郎
Isomura Toshi 磯村年

Kao Tsai-t'ien 高在田
Kawakami Toshitsune 川山俊彦
Koo, Wellington V.K., see Ku Wei-chün
Ku Wei-chün 顧維鈞
K'u-Wu-K'o-T'ang chen-wu shih 庫烏科唐鎮撫使
Kung-pu chü 工部局
kunikusaku 苦肉策
Kuo-chia chu-i 國家主義
Kuo Sung-ling 郭松齡
Kuo Tsung-hsi 郭宗熙

Li Chia-ao 李家鳌
Li Chieh 利捷
Li Ch'üan 利川
Li Hung-mo 李鴻謨
Li Shih-chung 李世中
Li Yüan 利遠
Li Yüan 李垣
Liang Shih-i 梁士貽
Lin Chien-chang 林建章
ling-shih hui-shen 領事會審

Liu Ching-jen 劉鏡人
Liu Kuan-hsiung 劉冠雄
Liu Shao-chou 劉少周
Lu Cheng-hsiang 陸徵祥
Lu Pang-tao 路邦道

Meng-chiang ching-lüeh shih 蒙疆經略使
Meng En-yüan 孟恩遠
Min-cheng pu 民政部
Motono Ichirō 本野一郎

Nan-hsiang 南翔
Nishihara Kamezō 西原亀三

O-shih wei-yüan hui 俄事委員會
O-yüeh yen-chiu hui 俄約研究會
Ōtani Kikuzō 大谷喜久藏

Pan-li chieh-shou K'u-Ch'ia shih-wu wei-yüan 辦理接收庫恰事
    務委員
Pao Kuei-ch'ing 鮑貴卿
Pao P'u 抱扑
Pi Kuei-fang 畢桂芳
Pien-fang chün 邊防軍

Saitō Suejirō 齊藤季治郎
Satō Naotake 佐藤尚武
Shao Heng-chün 邵恒濬
Sheng-fu 勝福
Shih Chao-ch'ang 施紹常
Shih Chao-chi 施肇基
shih-cheng chüan 市政權
Shun-t'ien shih-pao 順天時報
ssu-fa ch'üan 司法權
Sun Lieh-ch'en 孫烈臣
Sun Pao-ch'i 孫寶琦

Sung Hsiao-lien 宋小濂
Sung Huan-chang 宋煥章
Sze, Alfred Sao-ke, see Shih Chao-chi

Tanaka Giichi 田中義一
T'ao Hsiang-kuei 陶祥貴
T'e-chung ssu-fa kuan hsüan-jen chang-ch'eng 特種司法官選任
　章程
t'e-p'ai yüan 特派員
T'ieh-lu chiao-she chü 鐵路交涉局
t'ieh-lu hui-shen 鐵路會審
T'ien Chung-yü 田中玉
Ting Chin 丁錦
Ts'ai Ch'eng-hsün 蔡成勳
Ts'ai Yün-sheng 蔡運升
tsan-hsing pan-fa 暫行辦法
Ts'ao Ju-lin 曹汝霖
Ts'ao Jui 曹銳
Ts'ao K'un 曹錕
Ts'ao Yün-hsiang 曹雲祥
Tseng Yü-chün 曾毓雋
tu-hu shih 都護使
Tu-pan Chung-O chiao-she shih-wu kung-shu 督辦中俄交涉事
　宜公署
Tu-pan Chung-O hui-i kung-shu 督辦中俄會議公署
Tu-pan ts'an-chan shih-wu ch'u 督辦參戰事務處
Tuan Ch'i-jui 段祺瑞
Tuan Chih-kuei 段芝貴
Tung-sheng t'e-pieh ch'ü 東省特別區
Tung-sheng t'e-pieh ch'ü ching-ch'a pien-chih ta-kang 東省特別
　區警察編制大綱
Tung-sheng t'e-pieh ch'ü fa-yüan pien-chih t'iao-li 東省特別區
　法院編制條例
Tung-sheng t'e-pieh ch'ü shih-cheng kuan-li chü 東省特別區市
　政管理局
Tung Shih-en 董士恩

tung-shih hui 董事會
tzu-chih 自治

Wai-kuo tzu-i teng jen-mien chang-ch'eng 外國諮議等任免章程
Wang Chan-yüan 王占元
Wang, C.T., see Wang Cheng-t'ing
Wang Cheng-t'ing 王正廷
Wang Ching-ch'un 王景春
Wang Shih-chen 王士珍
Wang T'ing-chen 王廷楨
Wang Ts'ung-wen 王崇文
Wei Po 魏渤
wei-t'o 委託
Wu Chun-sheng 吳俊陞
Wu Chung-hsien 吳仲賢
Wu P'ei-fu 吳佩孚

Yamanashi Hanzō 山梨半造
Yang Tseng-hsin 楊增新
Yeh Kung-ch'o 葉恭綽
Yen, W.W., see Yen Hui-ch'ing
Yen Hui-ch'ing 顏惠慶
Yen Shih-ch'ing 顏世清
yu kai kung-ssu i-shou ching-li 由該公司一手經理

Index

About the Author

Sow-Theng Leong received his Ph.D. degree from Harvard University for work in modern Chinese history. It was from his doctoral dissertation that the idea for this book originated. In gathering material for the study, Dr. Leong several times visited Taiwan to consult the archives of the Chinese Foreign Ministry. For three years he was assistant professor of history at the International Christian University in Tokyo, and a part of the research for the book was carried out while he was in Japan. Most of the writing was completed during a year as a research fellow in the Department of Far Eastern History at the Australian National University.

Dr. Leong is now a lecturer in the Department of History at the University of Melbourne.

Text phototypeset in Bembo by University Composition Systems. Printed on Perkins & Squier Vellum Offset, basis 55, by Halliday Lithograph.

te